WORLD HERITAGE CONSEF

The UNESCO World Heritage Convention has become one of the most successful UN instruments for promoting cultural diplomacy and dialogue on conservation of cultural and natural heritage. This book provides an overview of the convention through an interdisciplinary approach to conservation. It shows that based on the notion of outstanding universal value and international co-operation for the protection of heritage, the convention provides a platform for sustainable development through the conservation and management of heritage of significance to humanity.

With increasing globalization of heritage, World Heritage Conservation is reviewed as an emerging interdisciplinary field of study creating new opportunities for inclusive heritage debate both locally and globally, requiring common tools and understanding. With over a thousand properties inscribed on the World Heritage List, from biologically diverse sites such as the Central Amazon Conservation Complex to the urban landscape of the metropolis of Rio de Janeiro, this book will help students, researchers and professionals in the identification, protection, conservation and presentation of World Heritage. Targeted at a diversity of disciplines, the book critically describes the strategies for implementing the convention and the processes of heritage governance for sustainable development.

Claire Cave holds a Ph.D. in zoology from University College Dublin, Ireland. She is coordinator of the World Heritage Management Programme and co-designer of the World Heritage Conservation Distance Learning Programme, in the School of Archaeology, University College Dublin.

Elene Negussie holds a Ph.D. in geography from Trinity College Dublin, Ireland. She is co-designer of the World Heritage Conservation Distance Learning Programme and former lecturer on the World Heritage Management Programme at University College Dublin, Ireland. Since 2014 she has been site manager for the Hanseatic Town of Visby, at Region Gotland, Sweden.

WORLD HERITAGE CONSERVATION

The World Heritage
Convention, Linking
Culture and Nature for
Sustainable Development

Claire Cave and Elene Negussie

Routledge
Taylor & Francis Group

earthscan
from Routledge

LONDON AND NEW YORK

First published 2017
by Routledge
2 Park Square, Milton Park, Abingdon, Oxon OX14 4RN

and by Routledge
711 Third Avenue, New York, NY 10017

Routledge is an imprint of the Taylor & Francis Group, an informa business

British Library Cataloguing-in-Publication Data
A catalogue record for this book is available from the British Library

Library of Congress Cataloging-in-Publication Data
A catalog record for this book has been requested

ISBN: 978-0-415-72854-6 (hbk)
ISBN: 978-0-415-72855-3 (pbk)
ISBN: 978-1-315-85163-1 (ebk)

Typeset in Bembo
by HWA Text and Data Management, London

Printed in Great Britain by Ashford Colour Press Ltd

CONTENTS

FIGURES

TABLES

PREFACE

Internationalism became a key principle in the twentieth century advocating cooperation amongst nations and peoples, reflected in the forming of the United Nations in the aftermath of World War II. The adoption of the Universal Declaration of Human Rights in 1948 reflected the need for internationally agreed principles to secure the rights of each person with regard to freedom, justice and peace. The World Heritage Convention of 1972, the principal focus of this book, emanates from a similar discourse of universalism and notions of protecting cultural and natural diversity.

However, multilateralism is increasingly challenged as reflected in Britain's referendum vote in 2016 in favour of leaving the European Union, and, in the following year, the US withdrawal from the United Nations Paris Accord, a global agreement on climate action to reduce greenhouse gas emissions and to adapt to a green economy. Still, the need for joint international action to conserve and manage cultural and natural resources seems to make more sense than ever, as demonstrated by the evolving theory and practice of World Heritage Conservation and more broadly the United Nations 2030 Agenda for Sustainable Development. In addition, the Anthropocene has been recognized as a crucial epoch in which climate and environmental change are intrinsically linked to human activity.

In 2002, the University College Dublin master's programme in World Heritage Management was established with the specific purpose of contributing to capacity building for World Heritage. It set out to provide education and training on the theoretical and practical basis for the conservation and management of the world's cultural and natural heritage, and has supported research aimed at tackling practical management problems at World Heritage sites and protected areas globally. In 2012, the authors of this book developed an online distance learning programme in World Heritage Conservation, also at UCD, and in response to UNESCO's launch of a World Heritage Capacity Building Strategy. It aimed to equip professionals with knowledge and skills tailored around the World Heritage Convention. The resulting research and course material form the core material of this book.

In the spirit of encouraging greater participation and understanding of best practices in heritage conservation this book is meant mainly for three kinds of readers. First, it is written for anyone who simply wants to know more about the convention. Such a reader may have heard of the convention and wants to understand exactly how it works. Second, it is meant for students at undergraduate and postgraduate levels and scholars with an interest in heritage conservation and sustainable development. Finally, this book will assist policy makers and practitioners from a broad range of disciplines in the implementation of the convention, from those involved in the nomination of World Heritage sites to those engaged in their conservation and management.

We would like to acknowledge receipt of a grant from National University of Ireland, which made it possible to include colour images, and an award from the UCD College of Social Sciences and Law Research Funding Scheme which provided for the indexing. Thanks are due to the following individuals and organizations for permission to reproduce images: Martin Harvey, Government of Ireland (Department of Arts, Heritage, Regional, Rural and Gaeltach Affairs), ICOMOS France, IUCN, Laponiatjuottjudus, UNESCO and Wikimedia Commons. In addition, thanks are due to Francesca Rausa who helped produce drawings.

We are both most grateful to the Earthscan/Routledge team, particularly Tim Hardwick, Ashley Wright and Amy Louise Johnston for patiently guiding the manuscript to completion. Furthermore, we are thankful to the UNESCO World Heritage Centre for granting observer status at World Heritage Committee meetings, which gave direct insights into the World Heritage decision process. We are particularly indebted to Marielle Richon who was the focal person for universities and Mechtild Rössler, Director of the World Heritage Centre.

Claire Cave would like to acknowledge her colleague Fergus O'Gorman who launched her into the field of heritage conservation many years ago, as well as the Heads of the UCD School of Archaeology, Gabriel Cooney and Graeme Warren, for their support during the process of writing the book. Jens Carlsson and John Finarelli are also thanked for their support. Claire is particularly indebted to Clair Grealis, Christine Brady, Elaine Duffy, Denise Harold and Jennie Moriarty for their help and companionship. Josephine Cave, Laura Cave and Sean Cave deserve special mention, and many thanks to Vjekoslav Novak who provided selfless assistance.

Elene Negussie is indebted to Andrew MacLaran who in 2005, after mentoring her doctoral and postdoctoral research in geography at Trinity College Dublin, directed her towards the UCD master's programme in World Heritage Management. This led to extensive involvement in curriculum development, teaching and research supervision in cultural heritage and historic urban landscapes. Gratitude is extended to the Irish Research Council, the Royal Irish Academy and the Heritage Council for research awards, and to Poul Holm for collaboration during a research fellowship in environmental humanities at the Trinity Long Room Hub. Finally, special thanks are due to family and friends for continuous support and encouragement throughout the book process.

INTRODUCTION TO WORLD HERITAGE CONSERVATION

The Convention concerning the Protection of the World Cultural and Natural Heritage ('World Heritage Convention') has arguably become one of the most successful instruments of the United Nations (UN) in promoting cultural diplomacy, dialogue and international cooperation on heritage conservation. Adopted in 1972 by the General Conference of the United Nations Educational, Scientific and Cultural Organization (UNESCO) at its 17th Session in Paris, its core principle is to conserve cultural and natural heritage sites, or 'properties', of outstanding universal value.[1] Sites that have been identified with such a value are considered to transcend the relevance of national boundaries and time. They belong not merely to a specific nation, but to humankind as a whole and are to be identified, protected, conserved, presented and passed on to future generations (UNESCO, 1972, article 4).

The idea of heritage universality depends on joint forces for conservation through international cooperation and solidarity. The origins of the convention can be traced to attempts in the 1960s to save threatened sites, such as the Abu Simbel temples and Venice, through the mobilization of international support. Furthermore, the convention was anchored in a mission for peace. As stated in the preamble to the Constitution of UNESCO: 'since wars begin in the minds of men, it is in the minds of men that the defences of peace must be constructed' (UNESCO, 1945). By conserving the common history of humankind in its diversity, the necessary preconditions are created for enhanced understanding and tolerance between the peoples of the world. From this perspective, it is not surprising that World Heritage sites have increasingly come under attack in nations affected by war and terrorism.

The concept of World Heritage has developed from a limited and exclusive exercise of safeguarding a small number of cultural, natural and mixed cultural/natural sites into a complex task of using them as potential platforms for integrated conservation and sustainable development. 'Potential' since the success of these noble aims depends on the will, resources and efforts of the signatories to the World Heritage Convention and a wide range of stakeholders from local to international levels. So far, 193 states parties have signed the convention and over a thousand properties have been inscribed on the World Heritage List. These range from biologically diverse sites such as the Central Amazon Conservation Complex in Brazil to the Great Wall of China. With an expanding number of prospective World Heritage properties, all of which face conservation challenges, there is a growing need for in-depth understanding of the convention, its original intent and implementation. The World Heritage process starts with the nomination of sites and continues with strategies for their conservation and communication, as well as monitoring and mitigation of threats to their intact survival.

As the title of this book suggests, 'World Heritage Conservation' has emerged as an interdisciplinary field of study and practice that draws on the broader aims of sustainable development. It provides a multifaceted lens for understanding contemporary human interaction with the environment in a globalized world in which heritage conservation is increasingly defined and regulated by international treaties. The World Heritage Convention is unique in its focus on the conservation of both cultural and natural heritage on behalf of humanity. Its linking of culture and nature has brought closer traditionally separate disciplines and sectors concerned with 'cultural heritage' and 'environmental conservation' and their respective specialized niches. This book gives an overview of the convention through an interdisciplinary approach. It critically examines strategies for implementation and processes of heritage governance for environmental sustainability in the broadest sense of the term. The integrated conservation perspective together with the practical orientation is the foremost contribution of the book, which adds to a growing body of literature concerned with the convention.

The World Heritage phenomenon

A key event that led to the emergence of the World Heritage Convention was the White House Conference in Washington held in 1965, which called for an international trust to save the cultural and natural treasures of mankind. Furthermore, campaigns to rescue the Abu Simbel temples in 1959 and Venice in 1966 from flooding due to man-made and natural causes required mobilization of resources at a scale which demonstrated the need for international cooperation. The period after World War II was characterized by calls for peace, internationalism, globalization and environmental movements. The forming of the UN in 1945 created opportunities for a global platform for debates on heritage and environmental issues through its many specialized agencies. However, international conservation has been traced to the late 19th century. Hall (2011, pp1–2) describes the period from 1870 to 1930 as a formative period 'when the protection of specific places, or sites, moved from a cause of national and imperial concern to one of international concern'. Furthermore, the preservation of the Niagara Falls in the 1870s through cooperation between Canada, Britain and the USA 'should be regarded as the first successful example of an international preservation effort'. However, international conservation came to a halt in the 1930s when global recession and a second world war led to 'national autarchy' (ibid, p25).

In *Many Voices, One Vision* Cameron and Rössler (2013) provide an insight into the thinking around the creation and early evolution of the World Heritage Convention. It assesses what the convention achieved between 1972 and 2000, put in the context of what it set out to achieve, noting that 'although the text of the Convention remains constant, its application has changed with the evolving understanding of heritage conservation theory and practice' (ibid, p244). The World Heritage concept has been developed into a comprehensive conservation ambition incorporating notions of cultural and natural diversity, human rights and sustainable development. It spans across the remits of several international conventions, instruments and programmes and has resulted in a much broader scope than envisaged at the inception.

At first the linking of culture and nature conservation under the same international treaty may have seemed like an odd fish. The three advisory bodies under the convention, the International Union for Conservation of Nature (IUCN), the International Council on Monuments and Sites (ICOMOS) and the International Centre for the Study of the Preservation and Restoration of Cultural Property (ICCROM) have traditionally worked mostly separately. However, over the years progress has been made in the integration of their work concerning World Heritage.

World Heritage may be regarded as a modern phenomenon but the idea of certain places being of exceptional value is not new. The Seven Wonders of the Ancient World was a list compiled by ancient historians from the second century BC, including significant man-made structures from the classical era. From the Hanging Gardens of Babylon to the Statue of Zeus at Olympia, only one of them, the Great Pyramid of Giza, is still standing. Furthermore, there are many accounts of early travellers who reported on the amazing structures they encountered. For example, the Portuguese missionary and explorer Francisco Álvares expressed a sense of awe in his descriptions of the rock-hewn churches of Lalibela in Ethiopia: 'I am weary of writing more about these buildings, because it seems to me that I shall not be believed if I write more' (Pankhurst, 2005, cited in Negussie, 2012).

The notion of a universal heritage has been expanded beyond the remit of the World Heritage Convention. Within UNESCO, the Memory of the World Register was established in 1992, highlighting the need to safeguard documentary heritage and significant collections around the world. Examples include the personal collection of Swedish film director Ingmar Bergman, the Book of Kells in Ireland and historic manuscripts in the National Archives of Ethiopia. Similarly, the Proclamation of Masterpieces of the Oral and Intangible Heritage of Humanity was established in 2001, later superseded by the List of Intangible Cultural Heritage. It emerged from work leading up to the UNESCO Convention for the Safeguarding of the Intangible Cultural Heritage of 2003. It concerned intangible aspects of heritage such as traditional practices, knowledge and skills that communities recognize as part of their cultural heritage (UNESCO, 2003a). While these types of heritage are often referred to as 'World Heritage', the focus of this book is on heritage as defined in the World Heritage Convention, embracing and linking culture and nature.

The global growth in tourism is increasingly associated with World Heritage. The use and promotion of World Heritage sites as key tourism destinations have highlighted the dual effects of heritage tourism, i.e. having both positive and negative impacts on conservation and sustainable development. Places such as Venice have become symbols not only of conservation victories, but also the paradoxical nature of the World Heritage designation itself, which often threatens heritage places by increasing their potential as valuable assets in the visitor economy. This has created a demand for solutions to achieve sustainable heritage tourism frameworks. Shackley (1998) explored visitor management in relation to cultural sites drawing on a range of case studies (including Kraków, Poland; Giza, Egypt; and Ninstints, Canada). Furthermore, UNESCO has published practical manuals and tools on how to manage tourism at World Heritage sites directed at site managers (e.g. Pedersen, 2002). Other scholars have dealt with tools and measures for achieving sustainable heritage tourism (Timothy & Boyd, 2003) within the broader scope of heritage studies. The contested nature of heritage has also been tackled from the point of World Heritage and heritage tourism (Harrison & Hitchcock, 2005).

The nomination of World Heritage properties is merely the beginning of the World Heritage process. Over the years there has been an increasing demand for guidance on how to manage sites. Leask and Fyall (2006) provided an integrated approach to tackling several key issues involved, particularly from a tourism perspective, ranging from stakeholder participation, visitor impact and management and marketing with case studies covering both cultural and natural perspectives. Furthermore, field-specific guidelines to management have been published, e.g. for archaeology (Cleere, 1989) and marine sites (Douvere, 2015). Since the Universal Declaration on Cultural Diversity of 2002 the significance of cultural diversity in the conservation of World Heritage sites has been emphasized (Offenhäußer et al., 2010). In terms of practical guidance, *Management Guidelines for World Cultural Heritage Sites* provided a pioneering resource for site managers at cultural sites (Feilden & Jokilehto, 1998). UNESCO later produced two reference manuals for cultural and natural sites respectively: *Managing Natural World Heritage* (UNESCO et al., 2012) and *Managing Cultural World Heritage* (UNESCO et al., 2013).

Writings have so far tended to concentrate on either cultural or natural dimensions of the convention, apart from the mixing of cultural and natural case study examples. Nevertheless, holistic perspectives of the convention and its linking of culture and nature conservation have increasingly come to the fore. Galla (2012, p4) described the convention as 'the fundamental unifying framework for natural and cultural heritage conservation' and observed shifts towards: 'a holistic ethic of conservation in bringing together people and their heritage across the binary of nature/culture divide.'

There is a two-sidedness to World Heritage. Like heritage in general, it filters through a system in which it can become manipulated and politicized to serve specific interests in ways that marginalize the ultimate goal of conservation. For example, strategies for heritage conservation have often failed at guarding against commercialization, commodification and gentrification processes that may threaten the intrinsic character of places. In the case of Venice, which is far from exclusive, the local population and services that provide for daily life have gradually been pushed out of the city to cater for the needs of tourism and a wealthy elite. Heritage sites are increasingly viewed as a commercial product and World Heritage in particular has become a commercial brand for tourism (Albert & Ringbeck, 2015). Nevertheless, the potential of the convention as being for greater purposes than the tourism business is reinforced by UNESCO's motto 'building peace in the minds of men and women' (Di Giovine, 2008). This goal has become ever more relevant since the deliberate destruction of the Buddha statues in the Bamyian Valley by the Taliban in Afghanistan in 2001, which added a new cynical reality to World Heritage and the limits of international law (Francioni & Lenzerini, 2008).

World Heritage Conservation – an interdisciplinary field of study

In its role as an international conservation instrument the World Heritage Convention has had 'undeniable influence on global practice in cultural and natural heritage conservation' (Cameron & Rössler, 2013, p221). The convention stimulated the international community to recognize the way that societies interact with nature and to understand that nature is a critical component of World Heritage. International dialogue resulted in a shift away from the conventional concept of heritage as constituting cultural monuments, groups of buildings and sites to an approach which encourages diversity and openness to new types of heritage. 'It has contributed to an extraordinary international dialogue on heritage matters, fostering a new understanding of heritage theory and practice' (ibid.).

The influence of the convention is reflected in the continued growth of the World Heritage List as well as the Tentative List of potential World Heritage properties.[2] These lists represent an incredible diversity of heritage types, including major ecosystems from around the world, geological and geomorphological features, cultural landscapes and monuments and sites dating from prehistoric to modern times. There are extensive conservation challenges associated with this growth in global heritage. Heritage properties are threatened by factors such as development pressures, unsustainable tourism, insufficient management, illegal activities, looting, war, conflict and natural disasters. Sørensen and Evans (2011) highlight the fragility of heritage sites due to a lack of connectedness with people: 'It is being recognised that the perceived meaning of heritage, its usefulness, values and functionality affect how threatened it is; without meaningful engagement, heritage is endangered' (ibid., p40). Furthermore, they highlight threats to the knowledge potential of a heritage site based on tensions between different knowledge systems, such as academic and community programmes. They emphasize the importance of recognizing 'that there are different forms of knowledge that […] contribute to society in different ways' (ibid., p41).

The rise of a global heritage has contributed to the emergence of World Heritage Conservation as an interdisciplinary field of study creating new opportunities for inclusive heritage debate and dialogue both locally and globally, requiring common tools and understanding. This is set against the backdrop of universal concern about the need for global ecological sustainability. As cited by Barry (2014, p543), 'accelerating human pressures on the Earth System are exceeding numerous local, regional, and global thresholds, with abrupt and possibly irreversible impacts upon the planet's life-support functions' (United Nations Environment Programme [UNEP], 2012). These pressures refer to global processes including climate change, biodiversity loss (terrestrial and marine), stratospheric ozone depletion, ocean acidification, global freshwater use, change in land use and chemical pollution (Rockström et al., 2009a, p472).

Brundtland et al. (2012, p11), state that the only way forward is 'to eradicate poverty and reduce inequality, make growth more sustainable and inclusive, production and consumption more sustainable, combating climate change, and respecting other planetary boundaries. This will require recognizing, understanding and acting on interconnections between the economy, society and the natural environment.' Furthermore, it places humanity at a crossroads and accentuates its moral obligations to navigate wisely into the future. As stated by former United Nations Secretary-General Ban Ki-moon, 'we are the first generation that can end poverty, the last that can end climate change' (UN, 2015a). Crucial to the understanding of these interconnections is acknowledging that culture is at the heart of all human endeavours. Culture plays a significant role in the decision making and human activities that underpin environmental, social and economic considerations (Dessein et al., 2015). Consequently, integrating culture in the sustainability debate is essential in identifying successful models of sustainable development. This approach poses a huge challenge within the spheres of science and politics as culture and sustainability are complex and contested concepts that require multidisciplinary and cross-sectoral policies as well as a whole new way of thinking (ibid.).

Investment in the protection and conservation of heritage sites is closely correlated with economic growth and has become an effective and targeted strategy in alleviating poverty in so-called developing countries. Furthermore, 'global heritage sites are important contributors to local and national identity and pride, and act as critical links to show our common history, societal development, and scientific progress' (Global Heritage Fund (GHF), 2010, p8). Similarly, an assessment by IUCN into the benefits and ecosystem services supplied by natural World Heritage properties identified positive contributions to society and the economy ranging from cultural and spiritual values, recreation and tourism, resources for building knowledge, employment and education to flood prevention, water provision and carbon storage (Osipova et al., 2014a). In generating awareness of the irreplaceable value of World Heritage and the current accelerating decline in cultural and natural diversity, international instruments such as the convention can promote appropriate long-term management and conservation strategies to ensure sustainability.

Historically, from a science point of view there has been fragmentation between the disciplines dealing with conservation of cultural and natural heritage, which have tended to operate independently and in isolation from one another. On a societal level, the sectors dealing with culture and nature conservation have likewise tended to work separately. The World Heritage Convention can provide the framework for the concepts of cultural and natural heritage to be considered as interdependent and for the application of interdisciplinary conservation and protection methods. Recognizing the intrinsic relationships between culture and nature in World Heritage Conservation allows for the transfer of this understanding into policy, which is implemented at the level of identification, conservation and management of heritage within the context of the broader quest for sustainable development. This is evident, for example, in the Connecting Practice project undertaken by ICOMOS and IUCN 'to explore, learn and create new methods of recognition and support for the interconnected character of the natural, cultural and social value of highly significant land and seascapes' (IUCN & ICOMOS, 2015, p2).

It may be argued that using World Heritage sites as a platform for interdisciplinary approaches to culture and nature conservation is a limited exercise in that it excludes the broader landscapes within which they are located (Proctor & Pincetl, 1996). However, World Heritage Conservation has the potential to provide an international platform through which conservation thinking translates into areas of heritage and environmental research, policy and practice beyond the prestige of World Heritage properties. In addition, shifts within World Heritage practice itself are reflected in the historic urban landscape approach which highlights the need for a holistic culture–nature understanding in relation to World Heritage cities (UNESCO, 2011a). Furthermore, the World Heritage Convention has the potential to encourage 'non-Western' views on heritage and its management. Particularly relevant are those approaches which do not separate culture and nature but rather treat them holistically as indivisibly interrelated aspects of the world in which people live. World Heritage can play a significant role in educational exchange and in facilitating learning through communication of best practice, knowledge and understanding of different conservation and management strategies. A major challenge is to overcome inbuilt Eurocentric biases in the implementation of the convention. This is understood with respect to the dominance of European cultural categories and distribution of World Heritage properties as well as the dominance of the European and North American world view in assessing heritage values (Albert & Ringbeck, 2015).

The growing global understanding of the interlinkages between culture and nature and the prominent role of the convention reinforce the role of World Heritage Conservation and the need for stimulating interdisciplinary approaches to sustainability. Larsen and Wijesuriya (2015, p6) maintain that 'the time has come to revisit current policies and practices and thus to respond to a major opportunity to reassert the contribution of world heritage to the effective and equitable protection of cultural and biological diversity'. Furthermore, 'the challenge is about creating a new space, new institutional practices and a new language to address interconnected natural and cultural values' (ibid., p13). Using common terms as a means of integrating knowledge is a useful starting point as noted by Harmon (2007, p389): 'When it comes to conserving the world's natural and cultural heritage, the way forward is to build on shared ethics, using common terms of reference, in a facilitated, interdisciplinary team whose participants focus on working together to achieve progress on the ground rather than arguing about whose interpretation of the world is "right".'

In the academic field, there is ongoing debate and recognition of the necessity to view cultural and natural heritage as interrelated and interdependent rather than as separate domains (Pilgrim & Pretty, 2010). However, it is a significant task to break down disciplinary divisions, particularly within the organizational and funding structures of academic institutions and journals. In meeting the challenges posed by the interdisciplinary nature of heritage, a possible first step is to use the available 'tool boxes' of other disciplines, to learn from other fields and methodologies in order to move closer to a synthesis of different approaches (Richon, 2007, p186). From this perspective, World Heritage Conservation can contribute to a gradual integration of knowledge, concerns, tools and methodologies amongst the scientific community.

The inherently interdisciplinary nature of World Heritage Conservation is reflected in the diversity of the World Heritage properties and the application of theory, research and practice required to identify, protect, conserve, present and manage heritage properties. Traditionally, cultural disciplines, or humanities, include architecture, history, archaeology, art history, sociology and anthropology while natural science disciplines include botany, zoology and geology. Human and physical geography as well as environmental sciences provide cross-disciplinary approaches to heritage conservation in the context of understanding how humankind interacts with and conceptualizes the environment. Political science, conflict resolution, law, management, economics, communication and marketing address issues of governance, public participation, legislation, evaluation and uses of heritage. Furthermore, a diversity of relevant sub-disciplines such as environmental psychology, cultural ecology and landscape ecology, provide conceptual frameworks to bring together the natural and human sciences in understanding the interrelatedness of culture and nature and how they are valued.

Linking culture and nature: towards holistic conservation

New thinking and skills are required concerning the links between cultural and natural heritage conservation for holistic approaches to conservation strategies in order to tackle global environmental change and to achieve sustainable development. The World Heritage Convention has provided a platform for doing so through engagement at the interface of culture and nature, both in a scholarly and practical sense. By understanding arguments about the role of 'culture in nature', e.g. perspectives of anthropologists concerned with protected area conservation (West & Brockington, 2006) and 'nature in culture', e.g. natural scientists engaged in cultural landscapes (Philips, 1995; 1998), the interface of culture and nature can be optimized.

The convention has assisted in development and application of shared concepts and principles such as authenticity and diversity, although marked by obvious disciplinary and practical differences. It has also supported the establishment of common strategies for conservation in which interdisciplinary thinking is fundamental. By adopting culture–nature perspectives the concepts of authenticity and diversity might be explored comparatively: both the role of cultural diversity in nature conservation and the extent to which biodiversity is significant in cultural heritage conservation. While traditionally primarily used in cultural heritage conservation, authenticity is increasingly debated in addressing natural heritage conservation with regard to the concept of naturalness (Dudley, 2011). Furthermore, with recognition of the role of humans in both culture and nature, the idea of heritage as a social construction is becoming better understood after misconceptions and antagonistic debate between the disciplines.

The linking of culture and nature in conservation thinking and practice may be seen as an exercise of re-establishing lost connections. From this perspective, the dichotomy of culture and nature is not universal; instead, it is 'a product of modern industrial thought shaped by the need to control and manage nature'. In contrast to industrialized thought the combined concept of culture and nature is a majority view in most resource-dependent communities (Pilgrim & Pretty, 2010, p1).

Modern conservation tools such as 'protected areas' may be seen as a product of Enlightenment or 'Western' thinking. As observed by Philips (1998, p21): 'An externalized view of nature conditioned thinking during the period of European exploration and domination of the world. Whether arriving in the New World, Africa, Australia or other parts of the globe, Europeans saw only "wilderness", "primitive places" and the world "in a state of nature" […]. It is thus hardly surprising that few Europeans recognized the hand of humankind in the "landscapes" which they colonized.' Such notions came to influence the conceptual basis for 'protected areas' which aimed to 'protect' nature from human influence. However, since their early formation, protected areas have become important tools for conservation as well as the source of debate and action on solving problems associated with the historical separation between culture and nature. As noted by West and Brockington (2006, p609): 'Regardless of their sufficiency or reality on the ground, protected areas are coming to form a way of thinking about the world, of viewing the world, and of acting on the world (a large and often contested part of the world), which in itself can have important effects.' The same may be argued for World Heritage sites, which may be used as a focus for achieving sustainable development.

Similarly, cultural landscapes have become important instruments in bridging culture and nature conservation. However, Philips (1998, p28) contended that cultural landscapes as a concept, while increasingly demonstrating the culture–nature link in specific locations, is somewhat misleading since 'there are cultural aspects to practically every landscape on earth, it follows that practically all landscapes are cultural landscapes'. Hence, the term 'landscape' is more appropriate from the point of avoiding misleading perceptions of 'pristine' landscapes separate from culture. This is illustrated in the case of Lapland, where the Sami people pushed for recognition of Laponia as a cultural landscape instead of a natural landscape in the work towards a Swedish World Heritage nomination.

In recent decades new sub-disciplines have emerged that acknowledge and conceptualize the relationship between human societies and nature, e.g. environmental politics (Steinberg & VanDeveer, 2012), ecological economics (Daly & Farley, 2011), environmental history (Hughes, 2016) and ecological anthropology (Moran, 2008). They discuss diversity in relation to culture and nature as fundamental to resilience of natural systems. They emphasize the feedback loop between cultural systems and the environment and the need to protect the diversity of both in order to cope with global change.

In recognizing the role of human societies in the global degradation of the marine and terrestrial environments and at the same time realizing the critical role that ecosystem services play in supporting human societies, a new epistemic approach is required that places human–nature relations at its core (Jahn et al., 2010). The relatively new concept of social-ecological systems (SESs) is consequently gaining traction in response to this need. According to Resilience Alliance (2010, p6) 'natural resources management issues are not just ecological or social issues, but have multiple integrated elements. These systems, in which cultural, political, social, economic, ecological, technological and other components interact, are referred to as social-ecological systems. SES emphasize the "humans in nature" perspective in which ecosystems are integrated with human society.' Hughes et al. (2007) provide case studies of the role that World Heritage properties can play in testing the adaptive approaches necessary to address the complex ecological, social, political and economic interlinkages in resource management. The cases of the Great Barrier Reef and the Grand Canyon National Park highlight the capacity of World Heritage sites to enable large-scale trials of possible management solutions and to disseminate the resulting experience for improved stewardship of heritage resources. In addition, the term eco-culture has been proposed as an advancement of the social–ecological system concept where 'ecocultural systems not only comprise the social institutions and distinct frameworks of a community, but also the worldviews, identity, values, distinct cultural practices and behaviours that make a community or group culturally distinct' (Pretty, 2011, p131).

An important element of SES theory is the idea of resilience. Walker et al. (2004, p2) define resilience as 'the capacity of a system to absorb disturbance and reorganize while undergoing change so as to still retain essentially the same function, structure, identity, and feedbacks'. Resilient societies may be understood as having the capacity to absorb disturbance, such as a financial crisis, political upheaval or climate change, adapt to change and continue to develop (Stockholm Resilience Centre, 2016). The resilience debate has been tackled from various viewpoints and expanded beyond the social–ecological system approach. For example, cultural resilience 'stresses the notion of the cultural memory of the community as a formative strength of collective consciousness, foundation of continuity' (Girard, 2012, p60). Furthermore, city cultural resilience has been defined as 'the internal energy, the inner force (vitality) that allows the city to react to external forces, adapt to them, and conserve its specific identity in the long run, in spite of turbulent transformation processes, and to design win–win solutions' (ibid.). Ecocultural resilience has been suggested as a holistic approach to resilience-building to address 'the interconnected complexity of human and ecological systems (Pretty, 2011, p131).

Thus, resilience is a term common to disciplines relating to both natural and cultural heritage conservation and, as discussed by Maffi (2010), ecosystems and social systems are affected in similar ways by many of the same stress factors, for example over-exploitation, development pressures, changes in land use and homogenization. The World Heritage Convention is stimulating discussion on the interconnectedness of cultural and natural resilience by promoting the role of World Heritage in strengthening resilience and reducing disaster risks. Jigyasu (2014, p9) asserts that 'heritage, both tangible and intangible, is not just a passive resource liable to be affected and damaged by disasters. Rather it has a proactive role to play in building the resilience of communities and saving lives and properties.' To this end, the UNESCO World Heritage Centre and the advisory bodies under the convention play an active role in highlighting the importance of heritage in disaster risk reduction and work to integrate it into the activities of the UN Office for Disaster Risk Reduction (UNISDR) (WHC, 2013).

With international conservation and World Heritage at the forefront, common concepts and principles such as authenticity, diversity, integrity, restoration and resilience are increasingly applied to both culture and nature conservation. These terms have similar foundations in terms of intrinsic meaning but in practice have different meaning and interpretation from the perspectives of 'culture' and 'nature'. However, a common language and terms of reference are important tools in bridging the gap between the natural and social sciences and in establishing a mechanism to integrate cultural and natural heritage conservation (Harmon, 2007). Likewise, there are common effects of globalization such as homogenization through the loss of cultural and place distinctiveness and biotic homogenization where native floral and faunal diversity of regions have been replaced by agricultural, invasive and generalist species. Recognition of the intrinsic relationships between culture and nature in World Heritage Conservation, although operating through different mechanisms and methodologies, has the potential to challenge the states parties to the convention to acknowledge heritage as something dynamic, interrelated and complex and to encourage new and holistic practices for conservation and sustainable development.

Outline

The aim of this book is to provide an overview of the World Heritage Convention and the protection and sustainable use of World Heritage sites through an interdisciplinary approach to conservation. Interdisciplinary is defined as 'of or pertaining to two or more disciplines or branches of learning' (Oxford English Dictionary, 2015) and is used to describe situations where the perspectives, methods and/or technologies of different disciplines are brought together to address a common problem or issue. The interdisciplinary approach primarily reflects the perspectives of the authors: Claire Cave is a natural scientist and zoologist with a special interest in conservation biology; Elene Negussie is a social scientist and human geographer with a special interest in urban conservation. The authors bring together their different insights and understandings to examine the cultural and natural perspectives of World Heritage Conservation. This is also the title of their jointly developed distance learning programme for professionals working with the convention.

The chapters describe the operation of the World Heritage Convention and the strategies for conservation of World Heritage in the face of the formidable challenges of this global era. Case studies from the authors' research and field experience as well as examples from the literature are used to explore the diverse issues. Chapter 1 'World Heritage and sustainable development' provides a contextual background to the convention, its role in merging cultural and natural heritage and the shift towards addressing heritage of humanity in the context of sustainable development. It also gives an introductory background to UNESCO and the UN System, and international instruments that are linked to the convention, such as other UNESCO conventions and multilateral environmental agreements (MEAs).

Chapter 2, 'Defining World Heritage', explores the concept of 'outstanding universal heritage', its defining criteria and components. The definition of World Heritage is examined together with key principles such as representation, diversity, integrity and authenticity as fundamental values in sustainable development. It is argued that World Heritage needs to be understood as a social construction often incorporating contested interpretations. World Heritage governance is then investigated in Chapter 3 'Governing World Heritage'. The wide range of actors, interests and stakeholders ranging from agencies and decision makers at the international level, to national and regional level authorities and local custodians of heritage are discussed. A central question here is whether participatory frameworks for heritage governance are effective.

The Global Strategy for a representative, balanced and credible World Heritage List is discussed in Chapter 4 'Implementing the World Heritage Convention'. World Heritage Conservation is supported by an evolving system of guidelines, principles, objectives and strategies reflecting the development of key concepts and ideas on World Heritage as a prerequisite for sustainable development. However, the way in which these are applied has implications for the credibility of the World Heritage List and the role of the convention in providing a framework for strengthening and diversifying World Heritage. There are often clashing priorities on the ground in relation to how World Heritage designation is used and this is explored in Chapter 5 'Using World Heritage'. The different uses of World Heritage sites, particularly those relating to economic gains and tourism purposes, and the competing interests of stakeholders at various levels are critically examined.

Monitoring of the state of conservation of World Heritage sites is perhaps one of the most successful outcomes of the convention. In Chapter 6 'Managing World Heritage', the designation of World Heritage sites is discussed as the mere beginning of a long-term process of management and threat mitigation for the preservation of cultural and natural sites. Furthermore, the emerging recognition of traditional management systems and the impact of external factors have brought World Heritage into the broader sustainability debate. However, the ability of the states parties to effectively resource monitoring activities and accommodate participatory management determines the level of conservation and sustainability achieved.

One of the original ideas behind the World Heritage Convention was the recognition of the need for international assistance and cooperation on heritage of outstanding universal value. Chapter 7 'Creating conservation capacities' explores how this notion has evolved into a wide range of programmes, strategies and activities for building capacities for the conservation of the heritage of humanity. However, it questions the impact of the disparity in countries' abilities to identify, protect and manage global heritage. Chapter 8 'Endangered heritage' takes a closer look at man-made and natural threats, including unsustainable activities and international conflicts, which have placed many of the world's most iconic monuments, sites and landscapes in danger. It examines mechanisms for monitoring and rescuing endangered heritage with case studies to exemplify various threats and interventions to safeguard endangered World Heritage.

The concluding chapter 'Towards a holistic approach' synthesizes the main arguments and critically evaluates both successes and failures in the application of the World Heritage Convention and its potential as a focus for sustainable development of the world's cultural and natural resources. It discusses the increasingly politicized practices and the credibility of the World Heritage process. Finally, it highlights the need for interdisciplinary approaches and collaboration to overcome divisions to sustain the heritage of humanity for future generations.

Notes

1 World Heritage 'sites' and 'properties' are used interchangeably throughout this book expressing the same meaning. The term 'property' is the formal term of the World Heritage Convention.
2 On average 22 properties are added each year, based on the number of properties inscribed each year between 2006 and 2015.

1

WORLD HERITAGE AND
SUSTAINABLE DEVELOPMENT

In the aftermath of World War II, there was increasing concern among the international community about the long-term protection of cultural and natural heritage sites and out of this growing recognition emerged the concept of a common heritage for humanity. The Convention concerning the Protection of the World Cultural and Natural Heritage, known henceforth as the World Heritage Convention, was adopted by the General Conference of UNESCO (United Nations Educational, Scientific and Cultural Organization) in 1972. As noted in the preamble to the convention, there was a general awareness that 'the cultural and natural heritage are increasingly threatened with destruction not only by the traditional causes of decay, but also by changing social and economic conditions which aggravate the situation with even more formidable phenomena of damage or destruction' (UNESCO, 1972).

Since the World Heritage Convention came into force, the rate of change of social, economic and environmental conditions globally has continued unabated. The concept of sustainable development has emerged in response to the resulting environmental concerns and it is promoted across the globe as a means to address the vastly complex environmental and societal problems in an equitable and integrated fashion for both current and future generations. As the World Heritage Convention aims to protect the world's diminishing cultural and natural resources, it is important to ask by what means the concept of sustainable development has been incorporated into the ethos of the convention and how the principles of sustainability are practised through the global network of World Heritage properties. The convention needs a coherent strategy to determine the desired goals of the sustainable development of World Heritage properties.

This chapter provides a contextual background to the World Heritage Convention and outlines the historical background and the shift towards the concept of a heritage of humanity. The role of World Heritage in the context of sustainable development is considered as well as the question of what sustainable development means in practice. Debate and definitions of sustainable development have initially rested on three dimensions: the economic, the environmental and the social. Until relatively recently 'culture' has often been overlooked as a significant component and this chapter considers its promotion as a fourth dimension. UNESCO, the United Nations (UN) System and the role of other conventions that are linked to the World Heritage Convention in conservation and sustainable development are also explored.

Evolution of the World Heritage Convention

The history of the World Heritage Convention is tied to the emergence of UNESCO following the establishment of the UN in 1945. The inter-governmental body of UNESCO was formed in the hope of perpetuating peace, through 'humanity's moral and intellectual solidarity' (UNESCO, 1945, preamble). UNESCO gained recognition as a neutral international organization that could assist in the reconstruction of education systems and culture in war-torn countries. This put it in a unique position to generate international support to rescue the Nubian monuments in Egypt in light of development plans to build the Aswan High Dam on the river Nile.

The convention emerged as a tool to unify the member states of the UN in safeguarding heritage, a unique and irreplaceable property 'to whatever people it may belong' (UNESCO, 1972, preamble). The emphasis is on the concept of heritage for all humankind and of the international community's responsibility to protect and conserve it through interdisciplinary means.

Formation of UNESCO

The United Nations was formed by 51 countries in 1945 to replace the League of Nations which had failed in its mission after World War I to 'promote international cooperation and to achieve international peace and security' (League of Nations, 1919, preamble). Soon after its formation in October 1945, the UN held a conference for the establishment of an educational and cultural organization. This organization was to secure a lasting peace based on advancing mutual understanding between peoples through education and the spread of culture and, consequently, the UN Educational Scientific and Cultural Organization was founded (UNESCO, 2012a). The preamble of the UNESCO Constitution captures this sentiment of peace and understanding by stating: 'since wars begin in the minds of men, it is in the minds of men that the defences of peace must be constructed' (UNESCO, 1945, preamble). This message is engraved in ten languages on a stone wall standing in the Square of Tolerance at the UNESCO headquarters in Paris, inaugurated in 1996 (Figure 1.1).

FIGURE 1.1 Stone wall at Tolerance Square, UNESCO headquarters in Paris (credit: Elene Negussie)

The promptness with which UNESCO was founded following the establishment of the UN was due to the prior efforts of the Conference of Allied Ministers of Education (CAME) held during World War II. CAME promoted the establishment of an international educational organization out of concern for the need to reconstruct education systems after the war. The early conception of an intellectual and educational organization necessary for the construction of a peaceful, democratic and civilized international society proved popular and the endeavour gathered momentum following ratification of the UN Charter (Mundy, 1999).

UNESCO's formation should therefore be understood in the context of post-war feelings and the shared conceptualizations of an ideal post-war world order. This collective vision had been set in motion by the Atlantic Charter of 1941. The Charter was a policy statement drafted by President of the USA, Franklin D. Roosevelt, and British Prime Minister, Winston Churchill, and agreed by the Allies, which set out 'certain common principles on which they base their hopes for a better future for the world' (Atlantic Charter, 1941, para2). The eight goals included self-determination of peoples, freer trade and 'assurance that all the men in all the lands may live out their lives in freedom from fear and want' (Atlantic Charter, 1941, para8). The Charter inspired the creation of multilateral institutions such as those agreed at the Bretton Woods Conference in 1944 (the General Agreement on Tariffs and Trade (GATT); the International Monetary

Fund (IMF); and the International Bank for Reconstruction and Development (IBRD, today the World Bank), as well as the Declaration of Human Rights, the first draft of which was considered at the first session of the UN General Assembly in 1946). Unlike earlier forms of multilateralism, the post-war agreements and charters promoted concern for issues of social policy and human well-being as well as setting goals for security, peace and establishment of a stable, liberal, world economy. Furthermore the Atlantic Charter had set an unconventional precedent as an international instrument that recognized individuals or 'all men in all lands' rather than limiting its scope to the interests of the traditional sovereign nation states (Borgwardt, 2006).

These sentiments are reflected in the UNESCO Constitution which declares that 'a peace based exclusively upon the political and economic arrangements of governments would not be a peace which could secure the unanimous, lasting and sincere support of the peoples of the world, and that the peace must therefore be founded, if it is not to fail, upon the intellectual and moral solidarity of mankind'. Furthermore, 'the wide diffusion of culture, and the education of humanity for justice and liberty and peace are indispensable to the dignity of man and constitute a sacred duty which all the nations must fulfil in a spirit of mutual assistance and concern' (UNESCO, 1945, preamble). Consequently, UNESCO's mission statement as defined in its Constitution is 'to contribute to peace and security by promoting collaboration among nations through education, science and culture in order to further universal respect for justice, for the rule of law and for the human rights and fundamental freedoms which are affirmed for the peoples of the world, without distinction of race, sex, language or religion, by the Charter of the United Nations' (UNESCO, 1945, article 1). UNESCO's mandate continues to be highly relevant as culture is increasingly at the frontline of conflict with extremist groups such as the so-called Islamic State of Iraq and the Levant (ISIL) in Iraq and Syria targeting individuals and groups on the basis of their cultural, ethnic or religious affiliation. The ongoing systematic nature and scale of attacks on culture highlight the strong connection between the cultural, humanitarian and security dimensions of conflicts.

International safeguarding campaigns

The identity of UNESCO as a neutral, multilateral agency dedicated to furthering peace and security was critical to the success of its landmark project to save the Nubian monuments of Egypt and Sudan. In 1954, the Egyptian government put together a proposal to build the Aswan High Dam on the River Nile. This was at a time of political instability in the region, following a military coup in Egypt in 1952 and the forced withdrawal of British troops from the Suez Canal in 1954. Funding from the World Bank for the construction of the dam fell through and Egyptian President Abdel Nasser accepted aid from the former Soviet Union. The situation was further complicated when President Nasser nationalized the Suez Canal, which provoked a widely condemned invasion by

Israeli and Anglo-French forces. During this time UNESCO supported the establishment of the Documentation and Study Centre for the History of Art and Civilization of Ancient Egypt in Cairo. In 1955, it funded a field expedition to document and record the Nubian monuments which would be submerged by the dam's reservoir waters. Accordingly, the Egyptian Minister for Culture recognized UNESCO as a neutral alternative to other Western political institutions and approached the Director-General for assistance in safeguarding the Nubian monuments (Hassan, 2007).

UNESCO's response was rapid and the decision to launch a worldwide appeal to protect the Nubian monuments which included the Abu Simbel temples and other archaeological treasures was adopted by the Executive Board of UNESCO at its 55th session. In 1959, UNESCO initiated a public relations and fund-raising campaign, with the support of the Egyptian and Sudanese governments, and collected $40 million from 50 countries to contribute towards the conservation of the monuments. This marked the start of a 20-year campaign to save the temples and an incredible feat of archaeological engineering as the 22 monuments and architectural complexes of the Abu Simbel and Philae temples were taken apart, moved to dry ground more than 60m above their original site, and put back together piece by piece (Figure 1.2) (Berg, 1978).

The project, coordinated by UNESCO, was regarded as an outstanding success and was remarkable both for the scale of international cooperation and for the interdisciplinary approach which was put in place to save the

FIGURE 1.2   Abu Simbel temples, Egypt (credit: Dennis Jarvis)

archaeological heritage. UNESCO established an Executive Committee to lead the international campaign which secured not only funding but equipment and technical expertise from member states. The project mobilized diplomats, fundraisers and patrons as well as experts ranging from Egyptologists and archaeologists, to architects, engineers and geologists. Part of the organizational framework included national committees which were set up in countries as far apart as Japan and Peru to further the campaign. Egypt provided relics and masterpieces of ancient Egyptian art from its state collections to be exhibited abroad to raise funds and increase publicity (UNESCO, 1962). Furthermore, Egypt offered artefacts as gifts to countries that provided support, in fact four Nubian temples were transferred abroad; Dandur to the USA, Taffa to the Netherlands, Dabod to Spain, Ellesiya to Italy, and the Kalabsha gateway to Germany (UNESCO, 2013a). Consequently, the temples have been exhibited in these countries ever since; Dendur in the Metropolitan Museum of Art in New York; Taffa in the Rijksmuseum van Oudheden in Leiden; Dabod in the Parque del Oeste in Madrid; Ellesiya in the Museo Egizio at Turin and the Kalabsha gateway in the Egyptian Museum in Berlin.

Despite the spectacular success of the international campaign to save 'the heritage of mankind', nothing could be done to protect the vernacular homes and villages of the Nubian inhabitants of the reservoir area. They were forced to relocate to areas outside their ancestral home and to government-built accommodation (Mohamed, 1980). In an effort to recognize and raise awareness of Nubian history and culture, plans were put in place by UNESCO to establish a museum in Aswan. This was accomplished in 1997, when the Nubia Museum, designed to reflect traditional Nubian architecture, was opened to serve as a focal point for Nubian culture both through its role as a community museum for the Nubian people and as an education point for visitors (UNESCO, 2013b). The museum exhibits a vast number of artefacts that were recovered during the 20-year-long campaign and also acts as a research and documentation centre. However, there was a distinct lack of local capacity to manage and develop the museum and UNESCO together with the International Council of Museums (ICOM) provided training programmes for staff.

The issues surrounding lack of capacity had been more widely revealed by the scarcity of skilled and professional expertise in Egypt to monitor and conserve the newly rescued sites following the cessation and departure of the international campaign. According to the state body responsible for managing the Abu Simbel temples, the Supreme Council of Antiquities, the site is still dependent on UNESCO to supply expertise for training in conservation and management techniques (Egyptian Supreme Council of Antiquities, 2000; Hassan, 2007). The need to develop a regional training centre to provide for long-term monitoring of the Nubian monuments persists. Conservation is thus as much about retaining traditional building skills as retaining the actual monuments. Another outcome of the international campaign was a dramatic increase in tourism. The Abu Simbel temples in particular became a hotspot destination for tourists, no doubt due to the global media coverage of their relocation, and today approximately a million tourists are thought to visit each year (Egyptian Supreme Council of Antiquities, 2000). The landmark campaign was prophetic in many ways as mass tourism, capacity building for long-term management and the impacts of development continue to be the principal concerns in conserving World Heritage today.

The rescue of the Nubian monuments was followed by several further internationally acclaimed UNESCO campaigns to protect endangered cultural heritage sites, such as the campaign to save Venice and its Lagoon in Italy following disastrous floods in 1966. Following an appeal for aid from the Italian government, UNESCO launched an international operation which brought in major contributions from public and private sources worldwide. The spirit of the campaign is ongoing and UNESCO continues to channel funding for research and preservation, not only of the historic centre of Venice, its monuments and its cultural heritage but also the entire ecosystem of its surrounding lagoon. Further projects were launched in Indonesia and Pakistan in the 1970s and the precedent of international concern for the conservation of universally appreciated heritage had been established.

Towards a heritage of humanity

In 1954, UNESCO launched its first international convention in the field of cultural property protection. The 1954 Convention for the Protection of Cultural Property in the Event of Armed Conflict, adopted at The Hague in the Netherlands, was a response to the enormous scale of the destruction of cultural heritage during World War II. States parties to the convention agreed to respect cultural property within their own territory as well as within the territory of other states parties and to avoid inflicting unnecessary damage in conflict situations (UNESCO, 1954, article 4). In 1964, UNESCO put forward a resolution for the creation of the International Council on Monuments and Sites (ICOMOS), which was adopted at the Second Congress of Architects and Specialists of Historic Buildings held in Venice. ICOMOS was founded in 1965 in Warsaw, following the adoption of the Charter on the Conservation and Restoration of Monuments and Sites (Venice Charter), which stipulated the need for international principles to guide conservation. It was formed as a non-governmental organization working towards the promotion and application of theory, methodology and scientific techniques for the conservation of cultural heritage (ICOMOS, 2012). Subsequently, in the late 1960s, the cultural sector of UNESCO together with ICOMOS began to develop a convention to protect the common cultural heritage of humanity. UNESCO's focus was on the success of its programmes to safeguard the monuments of the world. Initially it did not consider collaboration between its cultural and natural sectors; it would take external influences to promote the concept of linking cultural and natural heritage conservation under the UNESCO umbrella (Batisse & Bolla, 2005).

Emphasis on the global importance of nature conservation came from the International Union for the Conservation of Nature and Natural Resources (now IUCN), which was one of the few organizations acting internationally in the field of natural heritage at that time. IUCN was struggling to generate funds to meet the challenges of conservation and, in 1961, the World Wildlife Fund was formed. It established a base at IUCN's headquarters in Morges, Switzerland, and its primary function was to raise funds through international appeals to assist nature conservation societies worldwide. IUCN's work meanwhile was focused on protected area management and it published the first global list of national parks and reserves in the 1960s. Highlighting the international importance of protected areas, it put out a call for international collaboration on the protection of natural sites (Batisse & Bolla, 2005).

The USA played a pivotal role in establishing the link between culture and nature and the idea that the conservation of both should be placed at the same level. In 1965, at a White House Conference on International Cooperation in Washington, DC, members of a Committee on Natural Resources recommended that a 'World Heritage Trust' be created with the primary goal of stimulating international cooperative efforts to protect 'the world's superb natural and scenic areas and historic sites for the present and the future of the entire world citizenry' (Train, 2003, p36). IUCN developed an analogous proposal for its members in 1968 and combined their efforts to promote the concept with those of the White House. Soon after, in 1971, US President Richard Nixon stated in his environmental message that: 'It would be fitting by 1972 for the nations of the world to agree to the principle that there are certain areas of such unique worldwide value that they should be treated as part of the heritage of all mankind and accorded special recognition as a part of a World Heritage Trust' (Nixon, 1971). The year 1972 marked the centenary of the establishment of Yellowstone National Park in the USA, a significant event as Yellowstone was considered the first national park of modern times and played an important role in developing the concept of protected areas as a conservation tool.

1972 was also important because it was the year of the United Nations Conference on Human Environment, held in Stockholm, Sweden, in June. This was the UN's first major intergovernmental conference on international environmental issues. It led to the Declaration of the United Nations Conference on the Human Environment (UN, 1972), which proclaimed that:

'Man is both creature and moulder of his environment, which gives him physical sustenance and affords him the opportunity for intellectual, moral, social and spiritual growth. In the long and tortuous evolution of the human race on this planet a stage has been reached when, through the rapid acceleration of science and technology, man has acquired the power to transform his environment in countless ways and on an unprecedented scale. Both aspects of man's environment, the natural and the man-made, are essential to his well-being and to the enjoyment of basic human rights the right to life itself.'

Furthermore, it marked the beginning of modern political and public awareness of global environmental problems and as such was a turning point in the development of international environmental politics. IUCN, ICOMOS and UNESCO presented their different proposals for protecting the cultural and natural heritage of humanity at the UN conference in Stockholm and, subsequently, a single text was agreed upon by all parties concerned and the Convention concerning the Protection of World Cultural and Natural Heritage was adopted by the General Conference of UNESCO on 16 November 1972.

Spirit of the Convention and Operational Guidelines

The text of the World Heritage Convention is made up of 38 articles which define cultural and natural heritage and set out the duty of each state party to identify, protect, conserve and present the heritage within its territory as well as strengthen appreciation for this heritage through educational and information programmes. The convention also defines the scope of the World Heritage Committee, the World Heritage Fund and conditions for international assistance as well as matters concerning ratification and denunciation for the convention.

The first Committee Meeting adopted the Operational Guidelines for the Implementation of the World Heritage Convention, a document which set out the general principles for the implementation of the convention based around four functions: to draw up a World Heritage List, to prepare a List of World Heritage in Danger, to determine how best to use the World Heritage Fund and to assist member states in the conservation of their properties of outstanding universal value (UNESCO, 1977a). The document also provides a set of criteria which are used to identify cultural and natural heritage of outstanding universal value (see Chapter 2). The Operational Guidelines are regularly revised to reflect the decisions of the World Heritage Committee and to incorporate new knowledge and concepts in the context of heritage values and conservation. Consequently, it is a dynamic document and an essential reference in relation to interpreting and implementing the convention.

'The spirit of the convention' has become an important concept with regard to the implementation and credibility of the convention. It refers to the original intent and purpose of the convention as an international instrument drafted by the founders for the cooperative and voluntary protection of cultural and natural sites of outstanding universal value. The emphasis is on solidarity, the shared aims and collective responsibility of the international community to protect and conserve heritage for all humanity. Besides the holistic approach to nature and culture, the convention was innovative in the concept of an intergovernmental committee responsible for the international governance of cultural and natural sites. The concept of sustainability may also be considered inherent to the spirit of the convention regarding the intent to protect cultural and natural heritage from changing social and economic conditions. The spirit of the convention is often intimated in Committee meetings in an effort to remind members of this commitment to international cooperation and safeguarding of a common heritage. In 2010, it was successfully used by the then Director of the World Heritage Centre, Kishore Rao, to support an argument for a new strategy of cooperation between the advisory bodies and the states parties in preparing nominations (Rao, 2010).

The concept may be traced back to the first World Heritage Committee meeting held in Paris in 1977. The 15 state party members of the Committee, Australia, Canada, Ecuador, Egypt, France, Germany, Ghana, Iran, Iraq, Nigeria, Poland, Senegal, Tunisia, USA and former Yugoslavia, reiterated the fundamental objectives of the convention, highlighting that it was the first time the international community as a whole was called upon to assume responsibility for protecting heritage of outstanding universal value. The Director-General also referred to the 'spirit of cooperation' among the advisory organizations which included ICOMOS and IUCN and encouraged their continued collaboration into the future (UNESCO, 1977a). As the World Heritage Committee Meetings have become increasingly politicized and the pressures of development challenge the integrity of heritage sites worldwide, the concept of the spirit of the convention assists in reminding of the true character and purpose of the World Heritage Convention. It is an important benchmark to guide the long-term credibility of the convention.

Approaches to sustainable development

The landmark Brundtland definition of sustainable development was stipulated by the World Commission on Environment and Development (WCED) in 1987, in a report entitled Our Common Future. The definition articulated that sustainable development is development that 'meets the needs of the present without compromising the ability of future generations to meet their own needs' (WCED, 1987, para27). The ambiguity of the Brundtland definition allows for different cultures and sectors of society such as government, business, NGOs and civil society to interpret and apply the concept according to their priorities and goals. While this cross-sectoral support and usage may be considered a positive achievement, the lack of universal agreement on the process for realizing sustainable development and apparent widespread misuse of the term threatens the long-term accomplishment of the original objective (Waas et al., 2011). In this context, the World Heritage Convention has the opportunity to act as a 'standard-setter for best practice' by concretizing desired measures for sustainable development through the stewardship of World Heritage (UNESCO, 2015a, p2). The sustainable development perspective is generally explained by the concept of the 'three pillars' of economic development, social development and environmental protection, which should be considered as 'interdependent and mutually reinforcing' (UN, 2002, para5).

Defining sustainable development

The concept of sustainable development was first launched by the International Union for the Conservation of Nature (IUCN) in 1980 in a document entitled World Conservation Strategy: Living Resource Conservation for Sustainable Development. The strategy determined that in order for development to be sustainable it 'must take account of social and ecological factors, as well as economic ones' (IUCN, 1980, para1.3). This is underscored by the belief 'we have not inherited the earth from our parents, we have borrowed it from our children' and that ultimately conservation and development are mutually dependable and should be viewed by the international community as compatible issues (ibid., para1.5). This strategy, for the first time, considered that development was a means for achieving conservation rather than being exclusively damaging to it.

The Brundtland report maintained focus on the environment and development and explicitly stated that the two are inseparable. Brundtland specified that 'the environment does not exist in a sphere separate from human actions, ambitions, and needs […] the environment is where we all live; and development is what we all do in attempting to improve our lot within that abode' (WCED, 1987, p3). The report represented a shift in thinking regarding economic development, redefining a new era of economic growth that would be 'based on policies that sustain and expand the environmental resource base' (ibid.). Echoing the IUCN World Conservation Strategy, the report stated that many of the critical challenges to sustainability are related to inequities in development, poverty, and population growth within and between nations. However, the Brundtland report moved the discussion forward by putting greater emphasis on human development concerns and the political, economic and social obstacles to their realization.

In its definition of sustainable development, the Brundtland report brought the concept of intergenerational equity to the fore. The only limits to development were proposed to be those imposed by technology and social organization, which, it stated, could both be managed for the proposed new era of economic growth. Significantly, the purpose of sustainable development was to facilitate the eradication of poverty and to meet 'the basic needs of all' and to provide everybody with the opportunity to 'fulfil their aspirations for a better life'. 'Such equity would be aided by political systems that secure effective citizen participation in decision making and by greater democracy in international decision making' (WCED, 1987, para28). The conclusion was that such aspirations required 'changes in the domestic and international policies of every nation', thus the emphasis on a global approach to addressing the 'common' concerns was emphatic (ibid, para48).

In the intervening decades many definitions of sustainable development have emerged. For example, the Irish government, in its strategy document 'Our Sustainable Future: A framework for sustainable development for Ireland'

(Government of Ireland, 2012, p10), states that 'sustainable development is a continuous, guided process of economic, environmental and social change aimed at promoting well-being of citizens now and in the future. To realize this requires creating a sustainable and resource-efficient economy founded on a fair and just society, which respects the ecological limits and carrying capacity of the natural environment.' Most countries have now adopted national strategy documents which incorporate sustainable development into planning and policy making (Perdan, 2004).

In defining sustainable development there is some disparity in emphasis on what is to be sustained and what is to be developed as well has how the two should be linked and over what time period (Kates et al., 2005). The Brundtland definition simply refers to the 'future' and consequently definitions may range from 'sustainability for the next generation, when almost everything is sustainable, to forever, when surely nothing is' (ibid., p12). Different disciplines bring different priorities to the debate. The environmental sciences have played a significant role in highlighting the importance of sustaining the environment (or life support systems) and this emphasis has strengthened over time with research into ecosystem services and global change. Business and economics focus on economic growth and the type of capital that is available to support human well-being, including natural capital. This in turn has created a discussion around weak and strong sustainability relating to how easily natural capital (natural resources such as biodiversity, oil and minerals) may be traded or replaced with human technology. Strong sustainability acknowledges that there is certain critical natural capital, such as the ozone layer, which is vital to human existence and cannot be recreated (Hopwood et al., 2005). Social sciences explore the political process and human development through goals such as improved health, education, equity and rights. The emphasis is on good governance and just development. Environmental justice has emerged as an important concept linking social and environmental sustainability issues. It examines the availability of ecosystem services to different levels of society and which groups suffer the most from the negative impacts of environmental degradation and pollution (Elliott, 2013). The definition of sustainable development will continue to evolve as 'needs' change between generations and between cultures. Technological advances play a big role in generating change. For example, since the Brundtland report, global communication via the internet and the developments in genetic engineering have had a significant impact on discourses relating to social equity and natural processes (Redclift, 2005).

Sustainable development is currently understood in the context of a globalizing world and the debates around problems such as climate change, global economic recessions and the persistence of poverty. The mounting evidence that humanity is driving global environmental change, involving biological, chemical and geological processes, on an unprecedented scale, has led scientists to suggest that we are living in a new epoch called the Anthropocene (Crutzen & Stoermer, 2000). Consequently, some have proposed a new definition for sustainable development which states that development should meet 'the needs of the present while safeguarding Earth's life-support system, on which the welfare of current and future generations depends' (Griggs et al., 2013, p306). In the context of this book sustainable development is concerned with how to address socio-economic issues in tandem with environmental concerns.

Culture as a fourth dimension

Sustainable development is generally represented by the model of the 'three pillars' of economic, social and environmental issues. The pillar metaphor represents economic development, social equity and environmental protection as three components that need to be considered equally and in unison in order to enable an effective framework for sustainable development. In recent years, other models have been put forward including a Venn diagram and nested circles. The Venn diagram of three interlocking circles depicts sustainability at the intersection of the three circles of economic, environmental and social factors. This model highlights the small area of overlap between the three factors and demonstrates the extensive work that needs to be done to expand this area of overlap and to reconcile the need for compromise between the three factors to achieve sustainability. An alternative model of nested circles depicts the sphere of economy nested within society which is nested within the environment. This model reflects the co-dependency of all three factors and the fact that societies decide the economic models in use but are limited by the capacity of the environment to support their activities. The depiction of the nested spheres places humanity within the environment, which is lacking in the other models, and is also effective in demonstrating the need for an integrated approach across disciplines in addressing the challenge of sustainable development (Elliott, 2013; Waas et al., 2011). The use of the term 'dimensions' rather than pillars is increasingly employed to capture the complexity of the three interacting systems and the integrated approach required to understand them (UN, 2015b).

While much of the official discourse revolves around the three dimensions of sustainable development, culture is increasingly promoted as a fourth. Considering that culture incorporates the 'knowledge, practices, beliefs, worldviews and identities of societies' (Pilgrim & Pretty, 2010, p3), it should be obvious that it is integral to the sustainability debate. Culture is also significant in that it may be considered a finite resource, similar to the natural environment, and it needs to be sustained. Yet, its inclusion remains limited at both the scientific and political levels (Dessein et al., 2015). During the World Summit on Sustainable Development in Johannesburg in 2002, a roundtable discussion identified cultural diversity 'as a source of innovation, creativity and exchange' and consequently 'a key means of securing the sustainability of every form or expression of development, tangible and intangible' (UNESCO & UNEP, 2003). However, culture did not receive a mention in the Johannesburg Declaration.

The argument for culture as the fourth dimension of sustainable development has been promoted by indigenous peoples' initiatives such as the Earth Charter and organizations such as the United Cities and Local Governments (UCLG) organization. In 2010, UCLG adopted the policy statement 'Culture, Fourth Pillar of Sustainable Development' and campaigned for the 2012 UN Conference on Sustainable Development, also known as Rio+20 because it was a 20-year follow-up to the 1992 UN Conference on Environment and Development. The organization concluded that their efforts to influence Rio+20 achieved little success as there was not yet a critical mass of actors in the UN System, at the level of governments or among civil society, that were willing to campaign towards fully integrating culture into international development policies (Cullen, 2012; Hawkes, 2001).

In a significant step forward, the 2013 UN General Assembly produced a resolution that recognized culture as both an enabler and a driver of sustainable development. The resolution acknowledged that appreciation of the role of culture in providing a sense of social cohesion and identity encourages policies which are sensitive to cultural perspectives and as a result are more effective and inclusive. Critically, the resolution made direct links between culture and the three dimensions of sustainable development. Culture, through cultural heritage and cultural and creative industries, contributes to social and economic development. Also, the inherent links between cultural diversity and biodiversity supports environmental sustainability (UN General Assembly, 2013). The role of culture as fundamental enabler of sustainability was further affirmed in the UNESCO Hangzhou Declaration of 2013 (2013c).[1] In 2015, the UN launched a development agenda entitled the UN 2030 Agenda for Sustainable Development (UN, 2015b). The Agenda set out a framework of 17 Sustainable Development Goals (SDGs) to be achieved by 2030 in the pursuit of eradicating poverty and protecting the planet. However, despite the previous UN Resolution and the Hangzhou Declaration, there was little mention of culture in the 2030 Agenda (see Chapter 7). The challenge may be that the theoretical and conceptual understanding of culture within the sustainable development framework remains ambiguous and consequently it is inadequately translated into environmental and social policies (COST, 2011). Nevertheless, there is growth in recognition of culture as part of the development debate and culture is now indicated as an outcome in the majority of UN Development Assistance Framework programmes (UN System Task Team, 2012).

Policy and guidelines

Sustainable development is not mentioned within the text of the World Heritage Convention adopted in 1972. However, the convention includes the concept of intergenerational equity and supports the potential for sustainability in the commitments outlined in articles 4 and 5, which recognize that: 'States parties have a duty of ensuring the identification, protection, conservation, presentation and transmission to future generations of the cultural and natural heritage', as well as 'to adopt a general policy which aims to give the cultural and natural heritage a function in the life of the community and to integrate the protection of that heritage into comprehensive planning programmes' (UNESCO, 1972). Thus, states parties commit to incorporating national heritage conservation and policies into wider development strategies and long-term planning.

The revisions to the text of the Operational Guidelines for the Implementation of the World Heritage Convention illustrate a gradual adoption of sustainable development goals by the World Heritage Committee over the years. The first mention of sustainability entered the Operational Guidelines in 1994 with reference to the 'sustainable use' of cultural landscapes (UNESCO, 1994a, para38). In the 2015 edition the term 'sustainable use' is applied more widely to all World Heritage properties. It emphasizes the need for states parties to consider the role of sustainability in the protection and management of World Heritage through uses that are 'ecologically and culturally sustainable and which may contribute to the quality of life of communities concerned' without impacting on the values for which the properties were nominated (UNESCO, 2015b, para119). States parties are advised that their nominations of potential World Heritage properties must demonstrate how sustainable development principles are integrated into the management system (UNESCO, 2015b, para132). Similarly, states parties are advised that the advisory bodies will consider issues of sustainability in their evaluations of the properties (UNESCO, 2015b, annex 6).

In 2011, the UNESCO General Assembly of states parties to the World Heritage Convention adopted the 'Strategic Action Plan for the Implementation of the Convention, 2012–2022', which requires the Committee to continue to integrate sustainable development strategies into World Heritage policies (UNESCO, 2011b). The Strategic Action Plan set six World Heritage goals to assist in structuring the work of the convention between 2012 and 2022. For example, the third goal is that 'heritage protection and conservation considers present and future environmental, societal and economic needs'. The World Heritage Centre together with the advisory bodies have drafted an implementation plan, which identifies three main activities to ensure increased consideration of issues surrounding sustainable development. These include: 1) developing methodologies to assess the social and economic impacts of World Heritage properties on communities as well as evaluating strategies for investment in sustainable development; 2) developing clear policies on conservation and sustainable development; 3) developing tools to assist states parties in integrating heritage protection into planning processes and on effective community engagement (UNESCO, 2012b). The General Assembly has requested that the Plan is updated biennially and the outcomes reported to each General Assembly. Unfortunately, lack of funding has hampered progress to date.

In the spirit of the convention, an expert group, established by the World Heritage Centre,[2] worked voluntarily to produce a policy proposal on the integration of sustainability perspectives in World Heritage processes, which was adopted in November 2015. It advises states parties to 'recognize and promote the World Heritage properties' inherent potential to contribute to all dimensions of sustainable development and work to harness the collective benefits for society, also by ensuring that their conservation and management strategies are aligned with broader sustainable development objectives' (UNESCO, 2015a, para4).

Integration into World Heritage processes

The adoption of the 2015 policy on integrating a sustainable development perspective in the implementation of the convention was a breakthrough in advancing the application of sustainability in practice at World Heritage properties. References to sustainable development within the 2015 Operational Guidelines are more statements of intent than guidelines and do not provide sufficient practical recommendations to those involved in the protection of World Heritage properties. It is important that stakeholders can view World Heritage Conservation objectives within a larger framework of social, economic and environmental values and needs, as heritage conservation could otherwise be seen to be in conflict with achieving sustainable development. The policy document stresses that 'if the heritage sector does not fully embrace sustainable development and harness the reciprocal benefits for heritage and society, it will find itself a victim of, rather than a catalyst for, wider change' (UNESCO, 2015a, para5).

The policy proposal highlights that recognition of the interdependence of biological diversity and local cultures is an important factor in progressing any sustainability policy at World Heritage properties, particularly with its function in supporting the resilience of communities. It also affirms that all dimensions of sustainable development are equally necessary and should be applied to all categories of World Heritage properties, cultural and natural. Hence, although the convention is already instrumental in conserving biodiversity and geodiversity, environmental sustainability should be promoted more generally to all World Heritage properties. This involves the identification and inclusion of the interlinkages between biodiversity and cultural diversity in conservation and management strategies as well as protecting ecosystem services and promoting the potential of properties to reduce disaster risks.

States parties are urged to integrate a sustainability perspective by promoting 'environmental, social and cultural impact assessment tools' when undertaking planning in any sector that may impact on World Heritage properties (UNESCO, 2015a, para15). The policy provides guidelines with regard to strengthening the representation of the three dimensions of sustainable development in the management of properties. In the case of environmental sustainability, states parties can promote the use of sustainable energy sources, apply sustainable consumption and production patterns, incorporate traditional knowledge and practices in management and risk assessment, and support public awareness-raising, education and training (ibid.). In relation to social equity, World Heritage properties should be managed according to principles of gender equality, respect and equal participation of all stakeholders. The policy proposal stresses the importance of good governance and that local residents are entitled to adequate consultation and free, prior and informed consent. States parties are urged to enhance the quality of life and well-being of the people living adjacent to World Heritage properties by ensuring the availability of basic infrastructure and securing the environmental health of the property. In terms of economic development, states parties are encouraged to identify and promote opportunities for public and private investment, innovation and local entrepreneurship, quality tourism and capacity building in order to alleviate poverty and enhance sustainable livelihoods. Strategies should include economic diversification between tourism and non-tourism activities, using local resources and skills, preserving local knowledge systems, encouraging local tourism and reinvesting tourism-generated revenue into the management of the property (ibid.).

Once the policy has been integrated into the Operational Guidelines, the incorporation of sustainable development will, for the first time, be explicitly required in World Heritage Conservation. The length of time it has taken to adopt a sustainability policy reflects wider inertia on the part of states parties to pursue sustainable development in national policies. However, experience gathered in the daily implementation of the convention is generating extensive understanding of the potential of World Heritage to achieve sustainable development. The publication, *World Heritage: Benefits beyond borders*, brings together 26 case studies which provide examples of positive implementation of sustainable development principles. Examples include cross-border cooperation and community participation in the restoration of Djoudj National Bird Sanctuary in Senegal, and equitable income generation for the local population at Angkor in Cambodia (Galla, 2012).

UNESCO within the UN system

The World Heritage Convention's position within the UN system gives it a profound basis for the advancement of its sustainable development policy in relation to World Heritage sites. The debate on mainstreaming sustainable development has been slow to acknowledge the role of heritage and culture in the development process. However, the recent 2030 Agenda for Sustainable Development made a direct reference to the protection and safeguarding of the world's cultural and natural heritage (UN, 2015b). The high profile of World Heritage in the sustainability agenda has alerted the international community to the potential of the convention. This is important from the point of view of integrated policy making and planning across national, regional and international strategies. However, the greater potential of the UN and its entities are limited by the priorities and agendas of the decision makers, i.e. the member states (Askew, 2010). The success of the UN in addressing global issues is increasingly hampered by 'gridlock': the manifestation of stalled decision making and inability to cooperate effectively on issues of global concern (Hale et al., 2013). As stated by the Irish President, Michael D. Higgins: for the UN to be effective 'requires a profound and integrated rethink of international politics; it demands little less than a new paradigm of thought and action, grounded in a reconciliation between ethics, economics, ecology and cultural diversity'.[3]

The UN system

The primary role of the UN is to serve as an international forum for addressing global concerns. Its basic structure is fundamentally the same as it was when it was set up in 1945. It consists of the six principal organs of the UN: General Assembly; Security Council; Economic and Social Council; Trusteeship Council; International Court of Justice and the Secretariat. The mandate of the UN has continued to grow and evolve and over the intervening years various commissions, departments, programmes, specialized agencies and other UN Entities have emerged which report to the six principal organs.[4] The work of the UN is directed by its member states, i.e. only the governments can make decisions and these take the form of resolutions, treaties, declarations, agendas and so on. The General Assembly is the main deliberative and policy-making organ of the UN; it includes representatives of all 193 member states, each with a single vote (UN, 2014a).

UNESCO is a specialized agency under the Economic and Social Council for the UN (ECOSOC). Other specialist agencies under ECOSOC include the International Labour Organization (ILO), the Food and Agriculture Organization (FAO), the World Health Organization (WHO), the World Bank Group, the International Monetary Fund (IMF) and the World Tourism Organization (UNWTO). These form part of the UN's platform for social and economic issues. The mandate of ECOSOC is to facilitate and encourage debates, discussions and policy recommendations on the world's social, economic and environmental challenges. Non-governmental organizations (NGOs) and leaders in the business sector and academic fields as well as governmental policy makers meet regularly with ECOSOC to discuss pressing sustainable development challenges.

The governing bodies of each of the specialized agencies are made up of representatives of the member states of the UN. Therefore, a lot of the work involves intergovernmental negotiations and deliberations resulting in collective decisions that shape new international, regional and national policies and actions. Contrary to the wider public perception the implementation of these decisions and policies is usually non-binding and dependent on the willingness of the states parties. However, the greater participation of a wide variety of non-governmental and civil society organizations in UN decision-making processes has increased the role of public pressure in encouraging governments to follow up on their commitments. This enlargement of the scope for participation and advocacy reflects the ethos of the UN Charter and has been encouraged in recent years (UN-NGLS, 2007).[5] At the UN Climate Change conference (COP21) in 2015, civil society groups presented a petition advocating a strong agreement for climate change solutions signed by 6.2 million people from around the word. In his address to the conference, Secretary-General Ban Ki-moon stated that he 'counts on grassroots organizations to help keep governments accountable, so they implement what they have committed to in words' (UN, 2015c).

UNESCO

UNESCO is a specialized agency with a self-determined mission under the umbrella of ECOSOC. However, it also participates in and contributes to the work of ECOSOC and ultimately that of the UN System. Therefore, the UN 2030 Agenda and Sustainable Development Goals (SDGs) will influence the principal objectives which underpin UNESCO's strategies and activities. As identified in its Medium-Term Strategy for 2014–2021, UNESCO's overarching mandate is to foster equitable sustainable development and to promote peace and security (UNESCO, 2014a). This will be tackled through the five main programmes of work: 1) Education, 2) the Natural Sciences, 3) Social and Human Sciences, 4) Culture, and 5) Communication and Information. The World Heritage Convention is positioned within the culture programme, and the offices of the World Heritage Centre are located in the UNESCO headquarters in Paris[6] (Figure 1.3).

FIGURE 1.3   The Symbolic Globe monument on the piazza of UNESCO in Paris (credit: Elene Negussie)

The governing bodies of UNESCO are the General Conference and the Executive Board. The General Conference is made up of the representatives of the member states and it meets every two years. Observers from NGOs, intergovernmental organizations and non-member states may also attend. The role of the General Conference is to determine the policies and goals of UNESCO, to establish the work programme and to set the budget. The agreed work programmes and budget allocations together with benchmarks and expected results are published annually. The General Conference also elects the members of the Executive Board and appoints the Director-General (DG) of UNESCO.

Ms Irina Bokova, formerly the Minister of Foreign Affairs and Ambassador of Bulgaria, was the first female elected to the post of DG in 2009. Within the structure of UNESCO, the DG is charged with the responsibility of 'protecting and promoting heritage and cultural expressions' through the effective implementation of related conventions (UNESCO General Conference, 2012). It is to the DG of UNESCO that the states parties to the World Heritage Convention submit their ratification or acceptance of the convention (UNESCO, 1972, article 36) and it is the UNESCO General Conference that may make revisions to the World Heritage Convention. The role of Ms Bokova and her successors also involves highlighting the work of the five programmes of UNESCO around the world and supporting activities and events which aim to assist and contribute to the goals of UNESCO. Correspondingly, Ms Bokova has been outspoken against destructive events such as the military attacks on the World Heritage properties in Syria, Iraq and Mali.

The UNESCO mandate to build bridges towards peace and security is integral to the implementation of the World Heritage Convention. It is essential to respect and promote environmental, social, economic and cultural rights throughout the World Heritage processes. The sustainable development policy states that World Heritage properties should aim to reduce societal inequalities and tackle the structural causes of inequality including discrimination and exclusion (UNESCO, 2015a). While these aims may seem idealistic there is no doubt that the prestige of the convention and UNESCO can attract support and encourage collaborative work. The World Heritage Centre has recognized this comparative advantage and put strategies in place seeking the engagement of government authorities, NGOs and the private sector in carrying out its work (WHC, 2006). In strengthening its participation and partnerships in the UN system, the World Heritage Centre can integrate the convention with the larger development context. Successful projects have included funding by the UN Foundation, support from the UN Development Programme Global Environmental Facility (UNDP-GEF), and engagement with intergovernmental agencies whose decisions may directly affect World Heritage properties such as the International Maritime Organization and the UN Forum on Forests (ibid.). In 2009, for example, UNESCO and the United Nations Environmental

FIGURE 1.4   Ahwar marshes of Iraq (credit: David Stanley)

Programme (UNEP) launched a project for the sustainable management of the cultural and natural heritage of the Iraqi Marshlands. The marshes and their inhabitants had suffered enormous damage during the armed conflicts in Iraq in the 1990s, particularly as a result of a deliberate and disastrous draining programme employed by the state authorities. The joint UNESCO-UNEP project aimed to support the Iraqi stakeholders in developing sustainable livelihoods and to build capacity to ensure their participation in ecosystem management and conservation (Figure 1.4). The project used the World Heritage criteria for guidance in developing a management plan, and based on the subsequent groundwork the state party submitted a nomination to the UNESCO World Heritage Centre (Garstecki & Amr, 2011). The Ahwar of Southern Iraq: Refuge of Biodiversity and the Relict landscape of the Mesopotamian Cities was inscribed on the UNESCO World Heritage List in 2016 in recognition of the historical, cultural and environmental values of the area (UNESCO, 2016a).

Mainstreaming sustainability within the UN system

The steps agreed by world leaders to advance the Earth towards a more sustainable future were captured in a document entitled The Future We Want at the 2012 UN Conference on Sustainable Development (Rio+20). In the opening paragraphs, 'Our Common Vision', the UN General Assembly declares that it acknowledges 'the need to further mainstream sustainable development at all levels, integrating economic, social and environmental aspects and recognizing their interlinkages, so as to achieve sustainable development in all its dimensions' (UN General Assembly, 2012). More specifically, in paragraph 93, the General Assembly 'calls for the further mainstreaming of the three dimensions of sustainable development throughout the UN system' as well as 'the strengthening of policy coordination so as to ensure system-wide coherence in support of sustainable development' (ibid.).

The Secretary General reports annually to the General Assembly on the efforts made by the UN to mainstream sustainability in its work. By recognizing that it is essential that the potential economic, social and environmental implications of all programmes and policies are considered, regardless of their themes, the UN aims to identify synergies and avoid duplication of effort across its activities. However, this challenges the status quo of a system that was designed under a different development model and consequently will require a transformational shake-up of its approach to carrying out its activities across all its organizations (UN General Assembly, 2013). The UNESCO DG, Ms Irina Bokova, has pledged to 'take forward, step by step, the deep reform of the organization in both programmatic and structural terms, building on our achievements, to create a sharper and more efficient UNESCO' (Bokova, 2013, pIV). This is a reflection of the diminishing resources available to UNESCO as well as a need to strengthen its core operations around the dimensions of sustainable development.

The need to mainstream sustainability has led the UN to evaluate all of its endeavours, from reducing its carbon footprint and implementing a climate-neutral strategy in its operation to identifying how to integrate a holistic approach across sectoral divisions and at all levels of strategic planning and decision making. There exists an 'institutional gap between policy and practice' (Ban, 2013, para26). For example, the challenges of climate change are usually addressed from an environmental perspective (through UNEP) but the impacts of climate change also clearly affects each of the cultural, social and economic sectors. In order to employ a more holistic approach to the thematic issue of climate change across the different sectors, the UN system aims to develop multiple points of coordination to mainstream climate-change considerations. At the national level, governments also need to acknowledge the asymmetry within their departments and policies and ensure that efforts to combat climate change are developed in a cohesive way (Ban, 2013). The Secretary-General, Mr Ban Ki-moon, suggested that ultimately a broad common understanding of what it means to translate sustainable development into the work of the international community is still needed (ibid.).

The High Level Political Forum on Sustainable Development was established by the Rio+20 Conference in order to initiate a major reform in the institutional framework for sustainable development. The forum is mandated to meet annually under the auspices of ECOSOC and to report every four years to the UN General Assembly. It is envisaged that the forum will keep sustainable development high on the agendas of the world leaders and provide a platform to address sustainability issues in a holistic way, to expedite action and results and generate high-level policy guidance.

Other conventions and international instruments

With the expansion of World Heritage to include sustainable development, human rights, peace and security as well as cultural and natural diversity, the World Heritage Convention increasingly needs to be understood in the context of other international conventions and instruments. For effective policy making and sustainable conservation, the interrelated activities and goals of different designations and programmes should be communicated between responsible bodies and integrated into management and planning strategies. This is recognized in the Operational Guidelines: 'The World Heritage Committee with the support of the Secretariat will ensure appropriate coordination and information-sharing between the World Heritage Convention and other conventions, programmes and international organizations related to the conservation of cultural and natural heritage' (UNESCO, 2015b, para42).

Geoparks and Biosphere Reserves

UNESCO's natural sciences programme facilitates two protected area networks that complement the World Heritage designation. Firstly, the Biosphere Reserve network was established under the UNESCO Man & Biosphere (MAB) Programme launched in 1971 and secondly, the Global Geoparks Network (GGN), launched in 2004, is recognized under the UNESCO Global Geopark label, endorsed by the 195 Member States to UNESCO in 2015.

The motto of UNESCO Global Geoparks is 'Celebrating Earth Heritage, Sustaining Local Communities'. This is reflected in its initiative, which is to protect geological heritage while at the same time planning for the sustainable development of the people who live there, educating the public about geodiversity and supporting scientific research. To meet the requirements for designation, Global Geoparks must display geological heritage of international value, serve local economic and cultural development (particularly through tourism) and be based on strong community support and local involvement. The whole geographical setting of a park should be included in its interpretation so that the synergy between geodiversity, biodiversity and tangible and intangible cultural heritage are highlighted (UNESCO, 2016b).

As of May 2016, there are 120 Global Geoparks spread across 33 countries. In comparison, there are 16 World Heritage sites, out of a total of 1,031, that are inscribed solely for their geological or geomorphic values.[7] Therefore, the GGN offers an alternative programme for designating geological heritage sites that might not meet the requirements for World Heritage listing. Also, because of their approach to incorporating economic development and the wider landscape, Geoparks normally cover a much larger area than World Heritage properties, and so, where they do overlap, the Geopark offers a regional understanding of the geological heritage and a complementary platform for its protection, management and sustainable development. For example, thr Messel Pit Fossil Site World Heritage property is located within the larger Global Geopark Bergstrasse-Oderwald in Germany (Figure 1.5). The Messel Pit Fossil Site covers an area of 0.42 km^2 and is centred on an old shale mine which revealed a rich fossil record detailing the early stages of the evolution of mammals (UNESCO, 2015c). The Geopark takes in approximately 3,500 km^2 and exposes a diversity of geological processes which have shaped the landscape over 500 million years (Geo-Naturpark, 2015).

The MAB programme is an intergovernmental scientific programme that aims to establish a scientific basis for the improvement of the overall relationship between people and their natural environment. The Biosphere Reserves are a core element of this aim and consequently are designated based on their role in the conservation of biodiversity, in supporting sustainable economic and human development and in facilitating research, education and training in support of these efforts.

As of May 2016, there are 669 Biosphere Reserves in 117 countries, compared to 229 World Heritage properties listed for their natural heritage. The difference in numbers reflects the restrictions on human activities and stringent eligibility requirements of the World Heritage designation. In comparison, the Biosphere Reserves offer a more flexible approach, employing a zoning system that aims to promote reserves as models of land management and sustainable development. There are three interrelated zones: a buffer zone, a strictly protected core, and a transition zone which allows for human and economic development. More than 90 World Heritage sites overlap with Biosphere Reserves, indicating how

FIGURE 1.5   Messel Pit Fossil Site, Germany (credit: Werner Bayer)

different elements of the biosphere zoning system complement the values of the World Heritage designation. For example, the Ordesa y Monte Perdito National Park in Spain is the core zone of the Ordesa-Viñamala Biosphere Reserve as well as the Spanish part of the Pyrénées-Mount Perdu World Heritage site. Both the MAB programme and the Global Geoparks Network complement the World Heritage Convention in linking culture and nature. In fact, the MAB programme was the first international programme to promote the concept that people and nature are inextricably linked.

Multilateral environmental agreements

The World Heritage Convention interacts with other global multilateral environmental agreements at the level of the Secretariat and the states parties. These include treaties such as the UN Convention on the Law of the Sea (UNCLOS) (1982), the UN Convention to Combat Desertification (UNCCD) (1994) and the UN Framework Convention on Climate Change (UNFCCC) (New York, 1992). For example, in 2015, the World Heritage Committee highlighted that World Heritage properties are increasingly affected by climate change, and encouraged states parties to participate in the 21st Conference of the Parties to the UNFCCC in order to realize a universal climate agreement and galvanize global climate action (UNESCO, 2015d). The World Heritage Convention is also recognized as one of the 'big seven' biodiversity-related conventions. The six other conventions are as follows:

- International Plant Protection Convention (IPPC) (1952);
- Ramsar Convention on Wetlands of International Importance (Ramsar) (1971);
- Convention on International Trade in Endangered Species of Wild Fauna and Flora (CITES) (1973);
- Convention on Migratory Species of Wild Animals (CMS) (1979);
- Convention on Biological Diversity (CBD) (1992);
- International Treaty on Plant Genetic Resources for Food and Agriculture (2001).

In 2002, the Secretariats of the seven conventions formed the Biodiversity Liaison Group (BLG). The aim was to provide a platform for the Secretariats to explore opportunities for synergistic activities and increased coordination between conventions. The BLG platform has become an important tool in exchanging information and pooling resources within the shared goals of conservation and sustainable use. For example, the Convention on Biological Diversity (CBD) produced a ten-year strategic plan for the conservation of the world's biodiversity which is applicable not only to the biodiversity-related conventions but for the entire UN system (CBD Secretariat, 2011). The strategic plan has established targets, known as the Aichi Targets, which aim to tackle issues related to the sustainable use and safeguarding of biodiversity as well as maintaining ecosystem services and addressing biodiversity loss (ibid.). The World Heritage Convention is pivotal in assisting states parties in meeting these targets through the designation, protection and management of natural World Heritage sites. Similarly, the CBD led to the development of the Addis Ababa Principles and Guidelines for the Sustainable use of Biodiversity (AAPG) (CBD Secretariat, 2004a). As part of a joint collaboration, the BLG issued guidelines highlighting how the AAPG were relevant to each of the biodiversity-related conventions and how they could be applied as a framework for biodiversity management. The AAPG therefore, were available as a useful tool for World Heritage managers, particularly as the World Heritage Convention and its Operational Guidelines offered states parties little direction on how to manage sustainable use of natural heritage.

The implementation of multiple biodiversity-related conventions creates challenges for states parties through the burden of coordinating the associated management targets, periodic reporting and monitoring requirements. For example, the Wadden Sea World Heritage property of the Netherlands, Germany and Denmark (Figure 1.6) also includes Ramsar sites, Biosphere Reserves and the Convention on Migratory Species Wadden Sea Seal agreement. Furthermore, the site comes under the remit of EC Directives such as the EU Water Framework Directive, the Habitats Directive and the Birds Directive. The Wadden Sea ecosystem includes the coastline of the Netherlands, Germany and Denmark, and so the three countries have established a Trilateral Monitoring and Assessment programme to facilitate the monitoring and conservation of

FIGURE 1.6 Wadden Sea (credit: Michiel Jelijs)

the area as well as the reporting requirements under the different conventions and directives.

The BLG aims to harmonize the reporting process across conventions so as to reduce the burden on states and hopefully enhance the quality of information being produced, particularly in relation to monitoring, management and conservation strategies. Collaboration is important to share scientific expertise and develop effective strategies to address the major threats to biodiversity. Furthermore, it is necessary in order to deliver a coherent message to the public. In the absence of clear communication, overlapping designations are more likely to negatively impact public appreciation of the aims of the different 'labels'. However, there is a lot of work yet to be done to optimize cooperation across the multilateral environmental agreements.

Cultural heritage conventions

Since the first UNESCO convention on heritage was adopted in 1954, there has been a significant growth in international norm-setting instruments to protect cultural heritage, both in terms of number and scope. There now exists a wide range of instruments providing guidance for integrated and holistic conservation. However, the increase in international conventions brings challenges related to translating the principles into practice and national legislations. The UNESCO instruments most relevant to the World Heritage Convention are as follows:

- Convention for the Protection of Cultural Property in the Event of Armed Conflict (1954), Protocol I (1954), Protocol II (1999);
- Convention on the Means of Prohibiting and Preventing the Illicit Import, Export and Transfer of Ownership of Cultural Property (1970);
- Convention on the Protection of the Underwater Cultural Heritage (2001);
- Convention for the Safeguarding of the Intangible Cultural Heritage (2003);
- Convention on the Protection and Promotion of the Diversity of Cultural Expressions (2005).

There is much scope for increased synergies between the UNESCO conventions dedicated to the protection of cultural heritage. The need for collaboration and coordinated implementation has become urgent following the rise in incidences of cultural property destruction during armed conflict since the end of the 20th century (Van der Auwera, 2013). The 1954 Convention for the Protection of Cultural Property in the Event of Armed Conflict was the first conventional response of the international community to come to terms with acts of destruction, theft or pillaging of cultural property during armed conflict. It covers both movable and immovable cultural property, including monuments, archaeological sites, archives and museum collections. The terms of the convention aim to ensure that states parties respect each other's cultural properties in times of war. However, it also places a responsibility on states parties to take measures in times of peace to protect their cultural heritage against the effects of possible armed conflict in the future. Such measures complement activities under the World Heritage Convention to protect heritage, for example, preparing inventories and organizing appropriate bodies responsible for the safeguarding of cultural property (UNESCO, 1954). States parties may also place cultural property, including World Heritage, on the 1954 Convention's International Register of Cultural Property under Special Protection. However, the register of special protection has had limited success as evidenced by the fact that only five states parties, out of 128 that have ratified the convention, have put forward cultural property for registration.[8] In 1999, a Second Protocol was adopted, to supplement the 1954 Convention, which allowed for a List of Cultural Property Under Enhanced Protection. The new list is particularly relevant to World Heritage sites as inscribed property must be a cultural heritage of the greatest importance for humanity. The inscribed property must not be used for military purposes or to shield military sites, and the responsible state party must make a declaration confirming that it will not be used as such (UNESCO, 1999a, article 10). However, only 72 states parties have ratified the second protocol and only 12 World Heritage properties have been registered for enhanced protection. Mr Francesco Bandarin, UNESCO's Assistant Director-General for Culture, has called for wider ratification, stressing the critical importance of protecting cultural heritage in those countries in conflict or post-conflict situations (UNESCO, 2016c).

In response to widespread looting of archaeological sites and World Heritage properties in Syria during the occupation of the so-called ISIL, the DG of UNESCO, Ms Irina Bokova, has also called for ratification of the 1970 Convention on the Means of Prohibiting and Preventing the Illicit Import, Export and Transfer of Ownership of Cultural Property (AFP, 2015). The states parties to the 1970 Convention recognize that 'the illicit import, export and transfer of ownership of cultural property is one of the main causes of the impoverishment of the cultural heritage of the countries of origin of such property' and that once a cultural object is found outside its country of origin, international cooperation is necessary to protect it and support its repatriation (UNESCO, 1970, article 2). A total of 129 countries have ratified the convention but Ms Bokova urged that comprehensive ratification and widespread implementation were necessary to make the convention effective in challenging the illegal trade in cultural property in times of conflict (AFP, 2015). The 1970 convention was originally introduced to address illicit trade in cultural property in peacetime. It was a pioneer document for its time by taking a position against the uncertainties concerning the return of cultural property and providing a mechanism for restitution. However, the 1970 convention cannot be applied retroactively which means that it is not applicable to colonial and World War II claims.

Many modern conflicts are motivated by religious and cultural differences leading to deliberate destruction and persecution of cultural diversity (van der Auwera, 2013). As recognized by the UNESCO Constitution, 'preserving the independence, integrity and fruitful diversity' of cultures is important for maintaining social cohesion and supporting peace and security (UNESCO, 1945, article 1). In an effort to halt the global decline in intangible cultural heritage, the Convention for the Safeguarding of the Intangible Cultural Heritage was inaugurated in 2003. It defined intangible heritage as 'the practices, representations, expressions, knowledge, skills – as well as the instruments, objects, artefacts and cultural spaces associated therewith – that communities, groups and, in some cases, individuals recognize as part of their cultural heritage' (UNESCO, 2003a, article 2). The 2005 Convention on the Protection and Promotion of the Diversity of Cultural Expressions aims to create the conditions for cultures to flourish and to freely interact in a mutually beneficial manner in the spirit of building bridges among peoples (UNESCO, 2005a, article 1). Both of these conventions complement the World Heritage Convention in recognizing that intangible and tangible cultural (and natural) heritage are interdependent and that tangible heritage takes on its shape and significance within the larger framework of intangible heritage (Bouchenaki, 2003).

Notes

1 The Hangzhoul Declaration was the final declaration at the UNESCO International Congress 'Culture: Key to Sustainable Development' in 2013. The Declaration was entitled 'Placing Culture at the Heart of Sustainable Development Policies'.
2 The expert group met in Germany in 2014 with support from the German Government, and the Government of Vietnam contributed to a meeting in Vietnam. Ten Vietnamese site managers also contributed to the discussions, providing valuable insights on the practicalities of policy implementation at World Heritage sites (UNESCO, 2015).
3 The President of Ireland, Michael D Higgins, was speaking at the World's first Humanitarian Summit in Turkey in May 2016.
4 The UN has put together an organizational chart to explain how these different entities are interlinked which is available on its website http://www.un.org.
5 Article 8 of the UN Charter states that: 'The United Nations shall place no restrictions on the eligibility of men and women to participate in any capacity and under conditions of equality in its principal and subsidiary organs'. Article 71 states that: 'The Economic and Social Council may make suitable arrangements for consultation with non-governmental organizations which are concerned with matters within its competence. Such arrangements may be made with international organizations and, where appropriate, with national organizations after consultation with the Member of the United Nations concerned'.
6 UNESCO is the only UN organization with headquarters in Paris; New York, Geneva, Nairobi and Vienna are the four main headquarters of the UN.
7 Out of a total of 1,031 World Heritage sites in 2015, 197 were natural and 32 were mixed (cultural and natural). Of these, 75 sites were designated under criterion

(viii) which distinguishes the sites' geological heritage. Of these, 16 were designated solely under criterion (viii).

8 One reason for the low uptake may be the requirement that listed sites must be situated at 'an adequate distance from any large industrial centre' or from any 'important military objective' (UNESCO, 1954, article 8), which is difficult to fulfil considering the number of monuments located in cities and built-up areas.

2

DEFINING WORLD HERITAGE

World Heritage entails the idea that certain cultural and natural heritage sites are of outstanding universal value (OUV) and of importance to humanity as a whole and thus its protection is the duty of the international community. World Heritage is philosophically underpinned by both universalism and cultural relativism (Jokilehto, 2006). Universalism relates to the idea of universal application and relevance, suggesting that some beliefs and values are universally recognized as truths regardless of cultural context. Cultural relativism suggests that all customs and values are culture-specific. In World Heritage Conservation, this is reflected in cultural variation in management systems and the quest for a culturally representative World Heritage List.

This chapter explores the criteria, conditions and factors that determine World Heritage designation, including review of specific categories such as mixed sites, cultural landscapes, serial and transboundary sites. It also explores World Heritage as a socially constructed process, incorporating both consensus and contested interpretations of what constitutes heritage (Graham et al., 2000). Consideration of whether World Heritage is truly universal and whether value judgements are objective or subjective is essential in coming to terms with potential shortcomings in political discourse and practical application of the convention. Furthermore, understanding heritage as a human-driven process helps explain the evolving nature of heritage conceptualizations and how these are being shaped by temporal socio-historical contexts, positioned knowledge frameworks and shifting paradigms. It also suggests continued development of World Heritage concepts in the future as heritage values progress and lead to new paradigms.

Heritage values and international conservation

How heritage is valued and conserved forms part of a social construction process shaped by cultural, historical, economic, political and social factors. This has been noted particularly for cultural heritage, but also in relation to natural heritage given the evaluation systems at work in the conservation of natural environments. World Heritage Conservation doctrine rests on norm-setting instruments established mainly since the second half of the 20th century. However, heritage conservation is not a new phenomenon: 'every society has had a relationship with its past, even those which have chosen to ignore it' (Harvey, 2001, p320). While international conservation doctrine has been critiqued for its predominately Western-based philosophy, the convention, in its aim to unite all the nations of the world in the conservation of a global heritage, has broadened the horizon of heritage discourse. It has also reinforced the need for a rights-based approach to conservation given its place within the UN system.

Global heritage, a social construction

Understanding heritage as a social construction emerged primarily from the disciplines of human and social sciences and has become widely accepted in cultural heritage theory, particularly for its revealing of the power structures at work in heritage narratives. Since the 1980s, cultural geographers began to draw attention to issues relating to meaning, values and the social construction of places, stressing the relevance of people's values and ideas in the shaping of built environments, without ignoring the political-economic context within which culture exists (Anderson & Gale, 1992). Similarly, heritage evaluations and conservation activities take place within specific temporal contexts, shaped by cultural, economic, social and political factors, as demonstrated in the shifting approaches towards conservation and value judgements on what constitutes heritage over time (Negussie, 2004). Heritage values are to some extent subjective and the question of whose heritage is being conserved depends on what is officially recognized as heritage and how it is interpreted (Tunbridge, 1994). Heritage conservation is 'a contemporary product shaped from history', a cultural process in which 'heritage is a present-centred cultural practice and an instrument of cultural power' (Harvey, 2001, p336).

Nature has likewise been explored through the social-construction lens (e.g. Bird, 1987; Greider & Garkovich, 1994; Gerber, 1997; Proctor, 1998; Demeritt, 2002), notably within disciplines concerned with constructivism and critical theory (e.g. anthropology, geography, environmental history and sociology). This entails that nature is, similarly to its cultural counterpart, shaped by societal frameworks reflecting the cultural, philosophical and political values of society. Nature is therefore subject to the ideas of humans who play an active role in the framing of perceptions of nature and landscapes. The debate has been subject to both scepticism and harsh rejection. Soulé and Lease (1995, pXVI) suggested that 'social relativism can be just as destructive to nature as bulldozers and chain saws'. Snyder (1998) dismissed the idea of nature as a social construction entirely, viewing that notion as a product of European enlightenment thinking and commercial and use agendas. The critique is rooted in the need to protect the intrinsic value of biodiversity and nature conservation. However, for Proctor (1998) the divide between constructivists and anti-constructivists has been subject to misinterpretation amongst nature scholars. Similarly, Demeritt (2002, p768) emphasized the importance of understanding the complexity of the term nature and to make a 'distinction between claims about the social construction of our concepts of nature and of nature in a material and physical sense'.

Without a proper understanding of the values of nature, heritage as a social construction lacks meaning and is even destructive since, without distinction between intrinsic and extrinsic values, the loss of biodiversity could at worst be determined not to be in crisis. It lends itself better to the reasons why protected areas are designated and how they have been used to exclude people from them to protect biodiversity, which paradoxically also eliminates people's knowledge and traditional forms of protection from these (West & Brockington, 2006, p611). With recognition of the role of humans in both cultural and natural heritage conservation, the idea of heritage as a social construction has become better understood. The social construction notion is useful in understanding World Heritage conceptually since 'its essence is shaped by human values, internationally agreed criteria and selection procedures at both national and international levels' (Negussie, 2006a). This is clearly reflected in the evolution of World Heritage concepts and in models of governance. It also explains the critical observation made by Pocock (1997, p267) that the World Heritage List is 'the sum of scrutinized national heritage' which means that 'at any one time the pattern of world heritage is a reflection of the competence, complexion and activity of the states' nominating committees'. From this perspective, the validity of the claim of universality in World Heritage can be questioned.

From monuments and sites to landscape perspectives

Cultural heritage conservation has developed into a modern international movement in which organizations such as ICOMOS and UNESCO play an important norm-setting role in defining and updating conservation thought and practice.[1] Temporal shifts have occurred, from state and expert-led preservation of ancient and extraordinary monuments to concern for larger areas and the more ordinary legacies of the past. New holistic understandings of the relationships linking individual components into larger and more complex landscapes has led to a broadened perspective of cultural heritage, requiring interdisciplinary and integrative management through inclusive community-based approaches. Cultural heritage has become defined as embracing tangible moveable objects (e.g. artefacts and museum objects), immovable resources (e.g. monuments, sites, landscapes) and intangible forms of heritage (e.g. traditions and skills).

The evolution of cultural heritage conservation charters reflects a shift from modern universalism to post-modern relativism. Those of earlier periods reflected European expert-led perspectives on conservation theory based on universal principles that emanated from Western enlightenment thought, in which religion and spiritual form became separated from the scientific and rational (Wells, 2007). The Athens Charter for the Restoration of Historic Monuments was adopted at the First International Congress of Architects and Technicians of Historic Monuments in Athens in 1931. Its key principles became revived and developed in the International Charter for the Conservation and Restoration of Monuments and Sites of 1964 ('Venice Charter'), the founding document of ICOMOS. It reflected theoretical thinking that emerged during the reconstruction phase of European cities after World War II, when decisions had to be made on how to reconstruct built environments either damaged or destroyed by war. It was also a reaction against 18th century stylistic restoration, in which architects restored buildings by modifying them into their own creations of art, and later to modern movement urbanism. The Venice Charter established principles such as respect for various changes and stages of a building in restoration works, maintaining monuments in situ and preserving the setting of monuments.

The ICOMOS Charter for the Conservation of Historic Towns and Urban Areas of 1987 ('Washington Charter') addressed conservation in urban contexts. It stressed the need for integrated urban conservation and participatory planning approaches during times of recognition that the traditional values of urban living had been threatened, damaged and destroyed due to modernization processes. The historic character of a town or urban area is made up of urban patterns defined by plots and streets, relationships between buildings and green and open spaces, the formal appearance of buildings as defined by scale, size, style, construction, materials, colour and decoration, the relationship between the urban area and its surrounding setting and the different functions which an urban area has acquired over time (ICOMOS, 1987a). This broadened concern was accentuated in the Valletta Principles for Safeguarding and Managing Historic Towns, Villages and Urban Areas of 2011, which updated the Washington Charter in order to respond to new issues faced by cities, e.g. landscape values, environmental concerns and sustainable development (ICOMOS, 2011a).[2] UNESCO's Recommendation on the Historic Urban Landscape echoed many of its considerations and outlined a holistic approach to urban conservation, stressing the interrelationship between cultural and natural values (UNESCO, 2011a).

The Australia ICOMOS Charter for the Conservation of Places of Cultural Significance ('Burra Charter') established the concept of cultural significance and its associated subjectivity (Australia ICOMOS, 1999). Created by a national committee of ICOMOS it has become widely accepted and applied internationally. First adopted in 1979, and revised in 1999 and 2013, the Burra Charter moved away from an expert-led and technical approach to a more inclusive approach to conservation values considering values of non-dominant groups and the co-existence of values of different groups in determining the cultural significance of place. It established the 'Burra Charter process', a methodology commonly used in World Heritage management plans, which can be applied to all types of places of cultural significance, e.g. a monument, an archaeological site or a whole district/region.[3] The charter has been complemented with a practice note, which helps develop an understanding of how to establish both the 'cultural significance' and the 'natural significance' of a place (Australia ICOMOS, 2013a).

The Nara Document on Authenticity similarly reflected the ideas of cultural relativism through its recognition of cultural diversity, different cultural perspectives on the concept of authenticity, and different cultural relationships with natural and built environments (ICOMOS, 1994). While conservation movements in Europe became associated with material authenticity, Eastern influence has revealed the relevance of other factors such as traditional building skills and the relationship between culture and nature in building design. As observed by Chung (2005, p56): 'East Asian cultural values have placed special emphasis on and formed themselves around the organic relationship with surrounding natural settings rather than on the physical structure itself, and on the spiritual messages embodied in such structures beyond the reality of the visible material world.' With processes of globalization, modernization and commercialization having led to cultural homogeneity and loss of local distinctiveness, there has been a renewed interest in the early European search for authenticity and the need for a broadened understanding of the different attributes of authenticity.

The ICOMOS Charter on the Built Vernacular Heritage of 1999 established principles for the care and protection of vernacular buildings, i.e. traditional buildings that are locally distinctive, often coherent in style and form and the result of informally transmitted traditional knowledge in design and construction. Their conservation, which is significant in conserving cultural landscapes, depends on the conservation of form and material as well as traditional knowledge and skills forming part of the intangible heritage. This is manifested in oral traditions and expressions, performing arts, social practices, rituals and festivities, knowledge and practices concerning nature and the universe and traditional craftsmanship as stipulated in the Convention for Safeguarding of the Intangible Cultural Heritage of 2003 (UNESCO, 2003a). It stressed the synchronized relationship between tangible and intangible dimensions of heritage. This was further elaborated in the ICOMOS Quebec Declaration on the Spirit of Place, which defines 'place' as buildings, sites and landscapes, and 'spirit' as the intangible elements that bring life to places (ICOMOS, 2008a).

From wilderness to cultural landscapes

Nature conservation has been shaped by shifts from views of uninhabited wilderness areas towards holistic people-centred approaches to conserving landscapes in which cultural diversity and biodiversity are intertwined. In addition, the World

Heritage Convention has contributed to creating a 'conceptual meeting ground' for cultural landscapes and protected areas (Finke, 2013). Rashkow (2014, p818) notes that 'the global backlash against the ongoing epidemic of conservation-induced displacement based on the model of uninhabited, central government-administered wilderness parks, culminated in the 1990s. Conservation legislation around the world has since emphasized a shift toward integrating local peoples' rights and interests into the maintenance of protected areas.' However, the focus on preserving 'indigenous' human communities requires intercultural sensitivity and reflection on what this means (ibid.).

The wilderness concept emerged from the early conservation movement in the 20th century as a new school of ecology developed that raised awareness of the negative impacts of human activities on ecosystem functioning. From this perspective it was necessary to reconstitute wildlife populations to the levels that existed prior to the previous century of human involvement and to protect wild areas from industrial development to ensure their enjoyment by future generations.[4] A landmark shift in this direction was made by the introduction of legislation in the USA in 1964 to protect wilderness areas. The Wilderness Act defined wilderness as: 'an area where the earth and its community of life are untrammeled by man, where man himself is a visitor who does not remain' (US Congress, 1964, section 2c). The concept of wilderness became a powerful symbol of untouched landscapes, pristine, natural and safe from human intervention; however, the ecology of these landscapes has often been consciously shaped by people for generations, from the tundra and polar regions of Northern Europe to the outback of Australia and the savannahs of Africa.

Before the conceptualization of national parks, areas that had been set aside for their utilitarian values were associated with the aristocracy and wealthy classes in society. These were game reserves and royal hunting zones such as the Doñana National Park in Andalucia, Spain, now a World Heritage site. A famous exception to the aristocratic attitude towards national parks is Emperor Ashoka of India. He is credited with the world's first recorded nature conservation measures at state level (Singh, 1985) and his reasoning stemmed from a moral and ethical responsibility to sentient beings instilled through Buddhism. However, the earliest forms of protection of areas were those established by traditional owners of land across the globe, as reflected in contemporary understandings of cultural landscapes and sacred sites.

The modern concept of 'protected areas' applied in the conservation of natural environments is essentially a Western construct. The first modern national park was established at Yellowstone in 1872. From there the designation of national parks gradually spread to other continents. In Australia, 'The National Park' became the first national park in 1879, today known as the Royal National Park near Sydney. These early parks were established to conserve newly discovered ecosystems for future exploitation and for their utilitarian values in the face of unregulated resource extraction as a result of the Industrial Revolution. This evolved into recognition for the need to preserve biodiversity and to combat the extinction crisis. By 1960, the IUCN World Commission on Protected Areas was established for the preparation of a world list of national parks. It created the World Parks Congress as a global platform for policy makers concerning protected areas, held every 10 years. The First World Conference on National Parks was held in Seattle in 1962, followed by the Second World Conference on National Parks, held in Yellowstone in 1972 (IUCN, 2010) to mark the centenary of its foundation. Early writers and pioneers of this movement were John Muir, Gifford Pichot and Aldo Leopold.

The Third World Congress on National Parks in Bali in 1982 marked a shift from viewing protected areas as something to 'set aside' to important components of sustainable development. 'After Bali, protected areas professionals began to give higher priority to people-related aspects of protected area management such as human development, partnerships with other sectors, and working with indigenous groups and local communities' (IUCN, 2010, p6). By the Fourth World Congress on National Parks and Protected Areas in Caracas in 1992, conservation had become 'a mainstream priority' (ibid.). It preceded the Earth Summit in Rio de Janeiro in 1992, at which Agenda 21, the global plan to achieve sustainable development, and the Convention on Biological Diversity were signed. At the Fifth World Parks Congress in Durban in 2003, linkages between the core concerns of protected areas were debated, e.g. community, equity, governance, sustainable finance, capacity development and management effectiveness. A fundamental paradigm shift was noted 'that positioned conservation as part of a political process linked to human development and poverty reduction' (ibid. p7). Finally, the Sixth World Parks Congress in Sydney in 2014 stressed the role of protected areas as powerful platforms for solutions to global challenges.

Heritage diversity, a human right

The need to view heritage as a human right has been recognized in both cultural and natural heritage conservation. Conservation strategies should adopt rights-based approaches by integrating norms, standards and principles into policy, implementation and evaluation methods to ensure that rights are respected in conservation practice (Campese et al., 2009). The 1998 Stockholm Declaration of ICOMOS Marking the 50th Anniversary of the Universal Declaration of Human Rights stipulated that 'the right to cultural heritage is an integral part of human rights considering the irreplaceable nature of the tangible and intangible legacy it constitutes, and that it is threatened to in a world which is in constant transformation' (ICOMOS, 1998).[5] It outlined five specific rights that should be respected in order to ensure cultural diversity in the world:

- 'The right to have the authentic testimony of cultural heritage, respected as an expression of one's cultural identity within the human family;
- The right to better understand one's heritage and that of others;

- The right to wise and appropriate use of heritage;
- The right to participate in decisions affecting heritage and the cultural values it embodies; and
- The right to form associations for the protection and promotion of cultural heritage' (ibid.)

Cultural diversity is the recognition of a variety of cultural expressions and forms of heritage. The Universal Declaration on Cultural Diversity stipulated that 'culture takes diverse forms across time and space. This diversity is embodied in the uniqueness and plurality of the identities of the groups and societies making up humankind' (UNESCO, 2001a, article 1). Furthermore, 'heritage in all its forms must be preserved, enhanced and handed on to future generations as a record of human experience and aspirations, so as to foster creativity in all its diversity' (ibid., article 7). The declaration may be seen as a cultural equivalent to the Universal Declaration on Human Rights, adopted by the UN General Assembly in 1948 in the aftermath of World War II.

The notion of cultural diversity is clearly reflected in the ambition of the World Heritage Committee to achieve a balanced, credible and representative World Heritage List. To achieve some level of objectivity in decisions about what to conserve, systematic scientific inventories and evaluations which embrace a broad range of heritage representations is necessary at local and national levels (Negussie, 2006a). In this process it is important to recognize the contested nature of heritage. This entails that there are clashing views on what constitutes heritage and how it should be interpreted, referred to as 'heritage dissonance', which is paradoxical in that it can be both destructive and beneficial (Graham et al., 2000, p24). It can be used destructively in times of war and ethnic conflict when heritage associated with one cultural group is deliberately destroyed as in the case of the Mostar Bridge. Destroyed in 1993 during the Balkan conflicts, it was later reconstructed and reopened in 2004, and inscribed on the World Heritage List in 2005 as the Old Bridge Area of the Old City of Mostar. However, recognition of cultural diversity is a precondition for the construction of pluralist and culturally diverse societies in which everybody's heritage is recognized, celebrated and conserved.

Natural heritage conservation has likewise been influenced by a rights-based approach. The Stockholm Declaration underlined that 'Man has the fundamental right to freedom, equality and adequate conditions of life, in an environment of a quality that permits a life of dignity and well-being, and he bears a solemn responsibility to protect and improve the environment for present and future generations' (UNEP, 1972, principle 1). Furthermore, the Convention on Biological Diversity sought to ensure that any use of natural resources is equitable and ecologically sustainable. It recognized 'the close and traditional dependence of many indigenous and local communities embodying traditional lifestyles on biological resources, and the desirability of sharing equitably benefits arising from the use of traditional knowledge, innovations and practices relevant to the conservation of biological diversity and the sustainable use of its components' (UN, 1992, preamble). Furthermore, the Rio Declaration stressed the role of human rights in sustainable development (UNEP, 1992).[6]

The Millennium Ecosystem Assessment (MEA), initiated in 2001 to assess the consequences of ecosystem change, placed human well-being as the central focus for assessment, while recognizing that biodiversity and ecosystems have intrinsic values and that people make decisions concerning ecosystems based on consideration of their own well-being and that of others (MEA, 2005). The tenet of the MEA is that biodiversity benefits people through more than just its contribution to material welfare and livelihoods. Biodiversity contributes to security, resilience, social relations, health and freedom of choice and action. Good governance that respects and fulfils the requirements of international policies with regards to human rights, and encourages the participation of civil society in decision-making activities, can simultaneously support conservation and social justice. The United Nations Environmental Programme has called for an integrated approach to human rights and environmental protection. The latter 'supports human rights through securing sustainable availability of critical natural resources and ecosystem services' on which people depend (OHCHR & UNEP, 2012, p20).

Outstanding universal value

The universal claim to World Heritage relates to two UN principles: multilateralism through international cooperation and national sovereignty. The convention states that 'whilst fully respecting the sovereignty of the States on whose territory the cultural and natural heritage mentioned in articles 1 and 2 is situated [...] the States Parties to this Convention recognize that such heritage constitutes a world heritage for whose protection it is the duty of the international community as a whole to co-operate' (UNESCO, 1972, article 6[1]). OUV is essentially the cornerstone of the convention. In 2005, the World Heritage Committee defined OUV as: 'cultural and/or natural significance which is so exceptional as to transcend national boundaries and to be of common importance for present and future generations of all humanity' (UNESCO, 2015b, para49). OUV is assessed against cultural and natural criteria, measurement of authenticity and integrity and the existence of protection and management frameworks. A comparative framework is used to determine the extent to which a site represents the best example of its kind.

Cultural and natural criteria

A World Heritage nomination must meet at least one of the cultural and natural criteria (Tables 2.1 and 2.2). World Heritage properties can correspond to several criteria, either cultural or natural, or both. Initially, the criteria were outlined in two separate lists, one for cultural heritage (criteria i–vi) and one for

TABLE 2.1 Cultural criteria

Criterion	Description
i	Represent a masterpiece of human creative genius;
ii	Exhibit an important interchange of human values, over a span of time or within a cultural area of the world, on developments in architecture or technology, monumental arts, town-planning or landscape design;
iii	Bear a unique or at least exceptional testimony to a cultural tradition or to a civilization which is living or which has disappeared;
iv	Be an outstanding example of a type of building, architectural or technological ensemble or landscape which illustrates (a) significant stage(s) in human history;
v	Be an outstanding example of a traditional human settlement, land-use, or sea-use which is representative of a culture (or cultures), or human interaction with the environment, especially when it has become vulnerable under the impact of irreversible change;
vi	Be directly or tangibly associated with events or living traditions, with ideas, or with beliefs, with artistic and literary works of outstanding universal significance.

Source: UNESCO, 2015b, para77

natural heritage (criteria i–iv). However, following revisions to the Operational Guidelines in 2005, the lists were amalgamated into one set of ten criteria (i–x) (UNESCO, 2005b). The order of the natural criteria has changed in tandem with the new numbering system. Changes have also been made to the definition of criteria since first adopted by the World Heritage Committee in 1977, most notably through amendments made in 1992. The evolution and re-ordering of the criteria must be considered when reviewing World Heritage properties or comparing more recent nominations with earlier ones.

Venice and its Lagoon is an example of a cultural World Heritage property inscribed on the World Heritage List in 1987 based on each of the six cultural criteria (Figure 2.1). The city of Venice is located on the coastline in northeast Italy between the mouths of the Po and the Piave rivers. Early settlers created living conditions within the marshy shoreline by driving wooden pylons deep into the silt to build upon, and the city has grown ever since across the islands of the lagoon covering 50,000 km^2, famously becoming known as the 'floating city' and the 'city of canals'. From these humble beginnings, Venice became a major maritime power and wealthy cosmopolitan city in the Middle Ages; it was in an excellent strategic position for trade between the East and West; and later, as New World trade routes opened up, it became famous for its innovative fine art and music as well as its architectural and monumental splendour (ICOMOS, 1987b).

Venice and its Lagoon was inscribed based on criterion (i) for its 'unique artistic achievement' as a city built on 118 small islands, which 'seem to float on the waters of the lagoon, composing an unforgettable landscape whose imponderable beauty inspired Canaletto, Guardi, Turner and many other painters'. It also contains 'the highest concentrations of architectural masterpieces in the world', as proclaimed in the ICOMOS evaluation. Criterion (ii) is fulfilled through the 'influence of Venice on the development of architecture and monumental arts' and the works of painters such as Bellini and Giorgione. Under criterion (iii) Venice is considered to bear testimony to itself, as a link between the East and the West and between Islam and Christianity. Criterion (iv) is met by Venice possessing 'an incomparable series of architectural ensembles illustrating the age of its splendor'. Criterion (v) is fulfilled by Venice being 'an outstanding example of a semi-lake settlement which has become vulnerable as a result of irreversible changes' and whose coherent ecosystem, with rising and sinking water levels, is considered as important as the islands and the buildings themselves. Finally, under criterion (vi) Venice symbolizes the 'struggle of mankind against the elements' and is associated with the discoveries of Central Asia and China by Marco Polo and other Venetian merchants (ICOMOS, 1987b).

Criterion (vi) requires special attention. It relates to intangible cultural heritage and 'should preferably be used in conjunction with other criteria' (UNESCO, 2015b, para77). This restriction has effectively been in place since 1980. Of the first nine sites inscribed on the World Heritage List in 1978, two were inscribed solely under criterion (vi): L'Anse aux Meadows National Historic Site in Canada, and the Island of Gorée, Senegal. In 1979, concern was raised amongst the Committee members about the difficulty of applying criterion (vi). The original

FIGURE 2.1   Venice and its Lagoon (credit: © Elene Negussie)

wording 'be most importantly associated with ideas or beliefs, with events or with persons, of outstanding historical importance or significance' (UNESCO, 1978) lent itself to many different interpretations as well as potentially sensitive political issues related to the definition of significant historical events or famous people. Another difficulty was the probable large number of nominations that could arise and thereof the risk to the credibility of the World Heritage List.

Consequently, the application of criterion (vi) was limited and the wording was changed to: 'be *directly or tangibly* associated with events or with ideas or beliefs of outstanding *universal* significance'. Furthermore, 'the Committee considered that this criterion should justify inclusion in the List only in exceptional circumstances or in conjunction with other criteria' (UNESCO, 1980a, para18 added emphasis). Still, several properties have since been nominated solely under criterion (vi) despite the established limitations; and there have been some controversies, such as the nomination of Hiroshima Peace Memorial (Genbaku Dome), Japan, in 1996, which led to further adjustment to the wording of criterion (vi). The debate continues and the inscription of Rio de Janeiro: Carioca Landscapes between the Mountain, on the World Heritage List in 2012, also based solely on criterion (vi), has sparked further discussion on the way forward.

The Great Barrier Reef (GBR) in Australia is an example of a natural World Heritage property inscribed on the World Heritage List in 1981 based on each of the four natural criteria (Table 2.2). The GBR extends about 2,300 km off the east coast of Australia and is one of the most extensive coral reefs in the world and richest in faunal diversity. It is two million years old, dating back to major fluctuations in the sea levels caused by advancing and retreating ice in the northern latitudes during the current Quaternary period. Large numbers of

TABLE 2.2 Natural criteria

Criterion	Description
vii	Contain superlative natural phenomena or areas of exceptional natural beauty and aesthetic importance;
viii	Be outstanding examples representing major stages of earth's history, including the record of life, significant on-going geological processes in the development of landforms, or significant geomorphic or physiographic features;
ix	Be outstanding examples representing significant on-going ecological and biological processes in the evolution and development of terrestrial, fresh water, coastal and marine ecosystems and communities of plants and animals;
x	Contain the most important and significant natural habitats for in-situ conservation of biological diversity, including those containing threatened species of Outstanding Universal Value from the point of view of science or conservation.

Source: UNESCO, 2015b, para77

individual reefs, approximately 2,800, make up the GBR, and this diversity of reefs together with a complex system of water circulation have created a unique and dramatic seascape and ecosystem (Figure 2.2).

The GBR meets criterion (vii) by being of 'superlative natural beauty above and below the water, and provides some of the most spectacular scenery on earth'. It also contains superlative natural phenomena in the form of important breeding colonies of seabirds, marine turtles and green turtles, annual coral spawning, migrating whales, nesting turtles and significant spawning aggregations of many fish species. Under criterion (viii) the GBR represents 'a globally outstanding example of an ecosystem that has evolved over millennia' and which has been shaped by at least four glacial and interglacial cycles over the past 15,000 years. Furthermore, criterion (ix) is met through its 'globally significant diversity of reef and island morphologies' reflecting 'ongoing geomorphic oceanographic and environmental processes'. In terms of biological processes, 'the unique diversity of the GBR reflects the maturity of an ecosystem that has evolved over millennia'. Finally, criterion (x) applies to the GBR as 'one of the richest and most complex natural ecosystems on earth, and one of the most significant for biodiversity conservation' (WHC & IUCN, 2012).

Authenticity

Cultural sites must meet the conditions of authenticity as laid out in the Nara Document on Authenticity. Authenticity is a complex concept but essentially involves portraying the past in an accurate and truthful way. As explained in the Operational Guidelines, 'the ability to understand the value attributed to

FIGURE 2.2 Great Barrier Reef, Australia (credit: © Jeff Winslow)

the heritage depends on the degree to which information sources about this value may be understood as credible or truthful. Knowledge and understanding of these sources of information, in relation to original and subsequent characteristics of the cultural heritage, and their meaning as accumulated over time, are the requisite bases for assessing all aspects of authenticity' (UNESCO, 2015b, para80). It is important that the authenticity of a property is evaluated in the context of the criteria being proposed and that these are not presented separately as independent values.

Authenticity raises certain philosophical problems. The complexities of identifying the true and original substance of an object was famously demonstrated in the Theseus paradox put forward by Plutarch in the first century. It tells the story of the ship of Theseus that was stored and maintained as a monument by the Athenians. Over time, as the planks rotted and different parts of the ship decayed, they were replaced so that eventually the entire ship was restored. The question arises whether the renewed ship, built from new materials but still in its original form, is still the same ship. Today, it is recognized that gradual restorations over time still provide continuity for the identity of a monument (Jokilehto, 2006).

The Nara document was drafted at the Nara Conference on Authenticity in Relation to the World Heritage Convention, held in Japan in 1993. The government of Japan offered to host the meeting in response to a request by the World Heritage Committee at its 16th session. The meeting had involved extensive debate on how the test of authenticity should best be implemented. One of the principal issues arose from the fact that authenticity is interpreted differently by different cultures. The Nara conference gave particular attention to exploring the diversity of cultures and recognizing that authenticity should be considered in the context of the relevant culture (ICOMOS, 1994). The Nara document provided new definitions for the 'conditions of authenticity' that had to be met by proposed World Heritage properties. The Operational Guidelines outline the variety of attributes that may 'truthfully and credibly' express the cultural values of a property, including: form and design; materials and substance; use and function; traditions, techniques and management systems; location and setting; language, and other forms of intangible heritage; spirit and feeling; and other internal and external factors (UNESCO, 2015b, para82).

The condition of authenticity does not apply to natural World Heritage properties, although authenticity is increasingly considered in relation to the understanding of the concept of 'naturalness' (Dudley, 2011, p4). There are few if any places on earth that do not bear the traces of human influence. Consequently, it may be asked what 'natural' implies and how authenticity in nature should be defined. The Mediterranean basin, for example, is amongst the world's biodiversity hotspots, supporting 22,500 endemic vascular plant species, which is more than four times the number found in all the rest of Europe (Myers et al., 2000; CEPF, 2013). However, the Mediterranean is densely populated and has been heavily influenced by humans for at least 10,000 years. This represents the situation throughout Europe, where the majority of the landscape has been culturally modified and where the predominant landscape use is linked to agriculture and livestock rearing. The role of agricultural practices in encouraging biodiversity and species richness is evident in landscapes across the globe. For example, the Bedouin high mountain orchard gardens at the St Catherine Area World Heritage property in South Sinai, Egypt, are known to enhance biodiversity and support species richness in the heavily grazed desert environment (Dunne, 2012).

The question of what is natural is further complicated by the constantly changing nature of ecosystems. This in turn is exacerbated by the responses of ecosystems to climate change. Furthermore, biodiverse natural environments can regenerate and there is a potential of degraded landscapes to produce ecological and socio-economic benefits (Lamb & Gilmour, 2003). Consequently, the potential of ecological restoration in enhancing biodiversity is gaining traction in global environmental policy (Bullock et al., 2011). In drawing together a new definition for naturalness that recognizes elements of naturalness in both fairly pristine and substantially altered ecosystems, Dudley (2011, p155) proposed that an authentic ecosystem is: 'a resilient ecosystem with the level of biodiversity and range of ecological interactions that can be predicted as a result of the combination of historic, geographic and climatic conditions in a particular location'. Such an approach embraces change, a symptom of the global biosphere today, focusing on 'flexible durable ecosystems composed of a variety of species that might be predicted from the past ecological history and the current climatic and geographic conditions'. Whether or not elements are replaceable and the influence of history on the authenticity of a site, is reflected in the debate about the naturalness of ecosystems which resembles the Nara debate on authenticity in relation to cultural heritage. As ecosystems and the impact of humans on ecosystems are constantly changing, the question is at what point in history, location and habitat diversity an ecosystem can be said to be authentic, and to what extent formerly degraded habitats that are undergoing restoration are to be considered authentic.

Integrity

The conditions of integrity apply to all World Heritage properties, and to demonstrate integrity the critical elements of a site must be whole or intact: 'Integrity is a measure of the wholeness and intactness of the natural and/or cultural heritage and its attributes. Examining the conditions of integrity, therefore requires assessing the extent to which the property: includes all elements necessary to express its Outstanding Universal Value; is of adequate size to ensure the complete representation of the features and processes which convey the property's significance; suffers from adverse effects of development and/or neglect' (UNESCO, 2015b, para88). This implies that the property should be in a good state of conservation and that the components that contribute to its value are not negatively affected by external factors such as development or lack of maintenance or protection. Although the conditions of integrity have been applied to natural properties since 1977, it is only since 2005 that they became applied to cultural properties. It is essential that integrity is evaluated in the context of the cultural and natural criteria and that they are not presented separately as independent values.

For cultural properties, 'the physical fabric of the property and/or its significant features should be in good condition, and the impact of deterioration processes controlled. A significant proportion of the elements necessary to convey the totality of the value conveyed by the property should be included. Relationships and dynamic functions present in cultural landscapes, historic towns or other living properties essential to their distinctive character should also be maintained' (UNESCO, 2015b, para89). In the case of 'living heritage' where the inhabitants' way of life is crucial to the significance of the site, it is essential that the connection between the people and the landscape concerned is supported and conveyed adequately. For example, in the Saloum Delta in Senegal, inscribed on the World Heritage List in 2011, the integrity of the traditional practices of fishing and the exploitation of mollusc beds were demonstrated in the sustainable, traditional practices still in evidence today as well as the presence of the shell mounds and archaeological and ethnographic studies that testify to the traditional lifestyles (ICOMOS, 2011b).

For natural properties, 'bio-physical processes and landform features should be relatively intact. However, it is recognized that no area is totally pristine and that all natural areas are in a dynamic state, and to some extent involve contact with people. Human activities, including those of traditional societies and local communities, often occur in natural areas. These activities may be consistent with the Outstanding Universal Value of the area where they are ecologically sustainable' (UNESCO, 2015b, para90). For example, the integrity of properties proposed under criterion (vii), which refers to the 'superlative natural phenomena' associated with a site as well as its 'exceptional natural beauty' would be demonstrated if all the features were present that were necessary to maintain its scenic value or natural phenomena. In the case of Mosi-oa-Tunya/Victoria Falls in Zambia/Zimbabwe, the property is adequately sized and includes the adjacent catchment and upstream areas necessary to maintain the spectacular fall of water associated with criterion (vii), as well as the phenomenon of the riverine rainforest that exists within the waterfall splash zone and is dependent on the water from the spray plume.

Statement of OUV and comparative analysis

When nominated properties are inscribed on the World Heritage List, the World Heritage Committee adopts a Statement of Outstanding Universal Value (SOUV). It justifies the OUV and explains how it meets the relevant cultural and/or natural criteria, how the conditions of authenticity (for cultural properties) and integrity are fulfilled and how the requirements for protection and management have been met in order to sustain OUV over time (UNESCO, 2015b, annex 5, 3.3). OUV is the sum of all of these parts (Figure 2.3). The SOUV was introduced as a requirement in 2005. Hence, many of the earlier inscriptions on the World Heritage List do not have a formal SOUV according to this format. In 2007, the Committee introduced a procedure for states parties to submit retrospective SOUV for sites inscribed between 1978 and 2006 (UNESCO, 2007a). The statements are reviewed by the advisory bodies and subsequently adopted by the Committee. This process requires skilful consideration of the original intent of the nomination, particularly since heritage understanding may have evolved and circumstances to meet the conditions of authenticity changed. The SOUV should be based on the nomination dossier, the advisory body evaluation and the Committee decision text for inscription on the World Heritage List. The selection criteria should be carefully considered and clearly justified.

When states parties put forward World Heritage nominations, they must undertake a comparative analysis of other similar heritage sites, whether inscribed on the World Heritage List or not, and justify the exceptional character of the proposed site. The comparative analysis consists of an explanation or description of the importance of the proposed property in its national and international context (UNESCO, 2015b, para132). This was emphasized in the

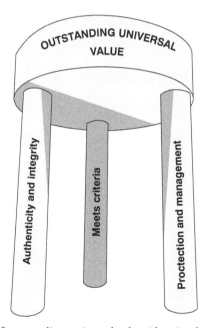

FIGURE 2.3 Pillars of outstanding universal value (drawing by Francesca Rausa)

first version of the Operational Guidelines: 'In every case, consideration must be given to the state of preservation of the property which should be evaluated relatively in comparison to the state of preservation of other property dating from the same period and of the same type and category' (UNESCO, 1978, para8). Since the adoption of the Global Strategy for a Representative, Balanced and Credible World Heritage List in 1994, further emphasis has been placed on achieving regional and thematic representation of properties on the World Heritage List (UNESCO, 2015b, annex 5, 3.2). World Heritage nominations hence need to demonstrate that they have been informed by considerations of regional and thematic representivity to fulfil the aims of cultural and natural diversity in World Heritage.

World Heritage typologies and delineation

World Heritage properties are broadly categorized into cultural and natural heritage. Introduced in 2005, mixed cultural and natural properties 'satisfy a part or the whole of the definitions of both cultural and natural heritage' (UNESCO, 2005b, para46). While the notion of 'combined works of nature and man' was enshrined in the convention text, this was not embodied until 1993 when cultural landscapes were introduced as a specific nomination category (UNESCO, 1994a). It marked a shift towards the integration of cultural and natural values in World Heritage designations. Further typologies have been introduced such as heritage canals, heritage routes and urban sites. The World Heritage Committee 'may develop additional guidelines for other types of properties in future years' (UNESCO, 2005b, annex III).

Cultural, natural and mixed heritage

The convention defines cultural heritage as monuments, groups of buildings and sites with an outstanding historical, aesthetic, scientific, ethnological or anthropological value (Table 2.3). It reflects conservation thinking at the time, using similar terminology as the ICOMOS Charter for the Conservation and Restoration of Monuments and Sites of 1964 (Venice Charter).

The Statue of Liberty exemplifies a monument. It is a neo-classical monument sculpted by French sculptor Frédéric Auguste Bartholdi in collaboration with French Engineer Gustave Eiffel, given as a gift from France to the USA in 1886 on the centenary of American independence (1876) as a symbol of liberty and alliance between France and the USA. The robed female figure bearing a torch and a tablet (*tabula ansata*) represents Libertas, the Roman goddess of freedom. It was inscribed on the World Heritage List based on criteria (i) and (vi) as 'a masterpiece of the creative spirit of man' and for its symbolic value in 'the populating of the United States, the melting pot of disparate peoples in the second half of the 19th century' (ICOMOS, 1984). There is a smaller replica of the Statue of Liberty on the Île aux Cygnes in Paris, also sculpted by Bartholdi.

TABLE 2.3   Definition of cultural heritage

Monuments	Architectural works, works of monumental sculpture and painting, elements or structures of an archaeological nature, inscriptions, cave dwellings and combinations of features, which are of Outstanding Universal Value from the point of view of history, art or science;
Groups of buildings	Groups of separate or connected buildings which, because of their architecture, their homogeneity or their place in the landscape, are of Outstanding Universal Value from the point of view of history, art or science;
Site	Works of man or the combined works of nature and of man, and areas including archaeological sites which are of Outstanding Universal Value from the historical, aesthetic, ethnological or anthropological points of view.

Source: UNESCO, 1972, article 1

Paris, Banks of the Seine is an example of groups of buildings. It includes a series of architectural masterpieces, from the Louvre and Eiffel Tower to the Cathedral of Notre-Dame, which demonstrate the evolution of Paris and its history, including the boulevards of Haussmann, which significantly influenced 19th and 20th century town planning globally. Inscribed on the World Heritage List in 1991 based on criteria (i), (ii) and (iv), it reflects the emphasis on separate or connected buildings from a historic, aesthetic and scientific point of view. The Prehistoric Sites and Decorated Caves of the Vézère Valley, located on a limestone plateau in southwestern France, demonstrate a site. Inscribed on the World Heritage List in 1979 based on criteria (ii) and (iii), it consists of 147 prehistoric sites stretching across an area of 30 km by 40 km dating from the Palaeolithic and 25 decorated caves, particularly interesting from an ethnological, anthropological and aesthetic point of view. The Lascaux cave is the most well-known with drawings dating back to 17,000 years ago. The objects and works of art including flints, faunal remains, utensils and figurative wall paintings, are testimonies to long-extinct civilizations.

Natural heritage is defined as outstanding physical, biological and geological formations, habitats of threatened species of animals and plants and natural areas of scientific, conservation or aesthetic value (Table 2.4). Purnululu National Park in Australia exemplifies outstanding physical, biological and geological formations. Located in the State of Western Australia, this landscape of nearly 240,000 ha consists of a system of cone karsts, which are unique due to interacting geological, biological, erosional and climatic phenomena. Iguazu National Park in Argentina represents a delineated area of habitats of threatened species, which is important from the point of view of science and conservation. It includes a spectacular waterfall surrounded by subtropical forest which is also a biodiversity hotspot and home to a range of threatened plant and animal

TABLE 2.4 Definition of natural heritage

Outstanding physical, biological and geological formations	Natural features consisting of physical and biological formations or groups of such formations, which are of Outstanding Universal Value from the aesthetic or scientific point of view;
Habitats of threatened species of animals and plants	Geological and physiographical formations and precisely delineated areas which constitute the habitat of threatened species of animals and plants of Outstanding Universal Value from the point of view of science or conservation;
Natural areas of scientific, conservation or aesthetic value	Natural sites or precisely delineated natural areas of Outstanding Universal Value from the point of view of science, conservation or natural beauty.

Source: UNESCO, 1972, article 2

species such as the jaguar and the ocelot. The Messel Pit Fossil Site in Germany is an example of a natural site from the points of science, conservation or natural beauty. This site is the richest in the world for understanding the living environment of the Eocene, lasting from about 57 million to 36 million years ago. It provides unique information about the early stages of the evolution of mammals with mammal fossils that are exceptionally well preserved, including fully articulated skeletons of animals of this period.

Mixed properties match the definitions of both cultural and natural heritage as defined in articles 1 and 2 of the convention (UNESCO, 2015b, para46). The Uluru-Kata Tjuta National Park, Australia, was inscribed on the World Heritage List in 1987 based on cultural criteria (v) and (vi) together with natural criteria (vii) and (viii). It thereby falls under the auspices of both ICOMOS and IUCN. The park includes features of spectacular geological formations, such as the monolith of Uluru and the rock domes of Kata Tjuta, which from a cultural point of view form part of the traditional belief system of the Anangu Aboriginal people.

Cultural landscapes

Cultural landscapes are cultural properties representing the 'combined works of nature and man' (UNESCO, 1972, article 1), falling under the advisory remit of ICOMOS. They illustrate the interaction between humankind and its natural environment in various forms, or 'the evolution of human society and settlement over time, under the influence of the physical constraints and/or opportunities presented by their natural environment and of successive social, economic and cultural forces, both external and internal' (UNESCO, 2015b, annex 3:6). They should be selected both on the basis of their OUV and of their representativity in terms of their being a clearly defined geo-cultural region and for their capacity to show essential and distinctive cultural elements of such regions. Three types of cultural landscapes have been established: clearly defined landscapes designed and created internationally by man; organically evolved landscapes; and associative landscapes. Cultural landscapes may be referred to their thematic significance although this is not specified in the guidelines, e.g. industrial, rural, urban and viticultural landscapes.

A clearly defined landscape designed and created intentionally by man 'embraces garden and parkland landscapes constructed for aesthetic reasons, which are often (but not always) associated with religious or other monumental buildings and ensembles' (UNESCO, 2015b, annex 3:10[i]). The Cultural Landscape of Sintra was inscribed on the World Heritage List in 1995 as 'a pioneering approach to Romantic landscaping which had an outstanding influence on developments elsewhere in Europe' (UNESCO, 1995a). Sintra exemplifies how the medieval aristocracy built sumptuous villas surrounded by artistically designed gardens and parks along the Serra mountains/hills (ICOMOS, 1995).

An organically evolved landscape 'results from an initial social, economic, administrative, and/or religious imperative and has developed its present form by association with and in response to its natural environment. Such landscapes reflect that process in evolution in their form and component features' (UNESCO, 2015b, annex 3·10[ii]). There are two different types of organically evolved landscape distinguishing between those where the distinctive evolutionary process has come to an end and those where it remains. Firstly, a relic (or fossil) landscape is one 'in which an evolutionary process came to an end at some time in the past, either abruptly or over a period. Its significant distinguishing features are, however, still visible in material form' (ibid.). Inscribed on the World Heritage List in 2000, the Archaeological Landscape of the First Coffee Plantations in the South-East of Cuba is an example of this category. The 19th-century plantations are situated at the foothills of the Sierra Maestra and give 'unique evidence of a pioneer form of agriculture in a difficult terrain' (ICOMOS, 2000a). The site reflects the economic, social and technological history of the Caribbean and Latin American region. Secondly, a continuing landscape is one 'which retains an active social role in contemporary society closely associated with the traditional way of life, and in which the evolutionary [cultural] process is still in progress. At the same time it exhibits significant material evidence of its evolution over time' (ibid.). This definition is exemplified in the Agricultural Landscape of Öland, Sweden, inscribed on the World Heritage List in 2000 as a unique landscape 'with abundant evidence of human settlement from prehistory continuous up to the present day' (ICOMOS, 2000b). The distinction between a relic landscape and continuing landscape is important from the point of managing change and new developments.

Finally, associative landscapes are defined 'by virtue of the powerful religious, artistic or cultural associations of the natural element rather than material cultural evidence, which may be insignificant or even absent' (UNESCO, 2015b, annex 3:10[iii]). Here, the natural landscape is the focus and how people relate and associate with this landscape spiritually, artistically and culturally. The Tongariro National Park in New Zealand became the first property to be inscribed under the cultural landscape definition in 1993. The mountains in this park, which include active and extinct volcanoes, are of cultural and religious significance for the Maori people and thus symbolize the spiritual links between a people and its environment.

Heritage canals, routes and urban sites

Heritage canals were considered as a special category in the Report of the Expert Meeting on Heritage Canals held in 1994 in Canada. Heritage canals are defined as human-engineered waterways that 'may be of Outstanding Universal Value from the point of view of history or technology, either intrinsically or as an exceptional example representative of this category of cultural property. The canal may be a monumental work, the defining feature of a linear cultural landscape, or an integral component of a complex cultural landscape' (UNESCO, 2015b, annex 3:17). The significance of heritage canals may be assessed according to four different factors: technological, economic, social and landscape.

Heritage routes are complex given their serial nature. A heritage route 'is based on the dynamics of movement and the idea of exchanges, with continuity in space and time'. Furthermore, it 'refers to a whole, where the route has a worth over and above the sum of the elements making it up and through which it gains its cultural significance'. It also 'highlights exchange and dialogue between countries or between regions' and 'is multi-dimensional, with different aspects developing and adding to its prime purpose which may be religious, commercial, administrative or otherwise' (UNESCO 2015, annex 3:24[ii]). Camino Real de Tierra Adentro, Mexico, is an example of a heritage route and a serial property consisting of 60 monuments, groups of buildings and sites (ICOMOS, 2010a). The route includes a 1,400 km part of the 2,600 km road also known as the Silver Route, which extends from Mexico City to Texas and New Mexico in the USA.

Historic towns and town centres form a distinctive World Heritage typology since 1987, referring to groups of urban buildings that fall into one of the following three classifications: uninhabited towns, inhabited historic towns, and new towns of the modern era (UNESCO, 2015b, annex 3). The World Heritage Committee met with the World Heritage Centre and the advisory bodies in Rio de Janeiro in 2013 to discuss how to mainstream the essence of the UNESCO Recommendation on the Historic Urban Landscape of 2011 into the guidelines. For example, the term 'urban site' may be considered as a more appropriate term than groups of urban buildings in the future.

'Towns no longer inhabited' refers to ancient urban sites, often archaeological in nature, consisting of 'groups of buildings noteworthy for their purity of style, for the concentrations of monuments they contain and sometimes for their important historical associations' (UNESCO, 2015b, annex 3:15[i]). Angkor in Cambodia illustrates an archaeological urban site, a town that is no longer inhabited. Inscribed on the World Heritage List in 1992, it contains the remains of different capitals of the Khmer Empire dating to between the 9th and 15th centuries.

'Inhabited historic towns', are living urban areas and recognized mainly because of their architectural interest, rather than on their past role and historical symbolic value: 'the spatial organization, structure, materials, forms and, where possible, functions of a group of buildings should essentially reflect the civilization or succession of civilizations which have prompted the nomination of the property' (ibid. 15[ii]). Examples include the Historic Centre of Rome, Italy (1980), the Old Towns of Djenné, Mali (1988), the Old and New Towns of Edinburgh, UK (1995) and the Hanseatic Town of Visby, Sweden (1995). There are four distinct types within this category: 1) towns which are typical of a specific period or culture; 2) towns that have evolved along characteristic lines; 3) historic centres that cover exactly the same area as ancient towns and are now enclosed within modern cities; and 4) sectors, areas or isolated units.

'New towns of the twentieth century' was established as a special category given the difficulty in assessing towns from more recent time periods as exemplary in a historical perspective. Consequently, preference should be given to inscription of 'small or medium-sized urban areas which are in a position to manage any potential growth' on the World Heritage List, rather than large metropolises in their entirety (ibid., 15[iii]). Brasilia was inscribed based on criteria (i) and (iv) as a landmark example in the history of town planning. It was built from scratch in 1956 as a federal capital in the centre of Brazil in 1956, led by urban planner Lucio Costa and architect Oscar Niemeyer.

Delineation of properties and buffer zones

World Heritage properties require clear boundaries. As stated in the Operational Guidelines: 'the delineation of boundaries is an essential requirement in the establishment of effective protection of nominated properties. Boundaries should be drawn to ensure the full expression of the Outstanding Universal Value and the integrity and/or authenticity of the property' (UNESCO, 2015b, para99). For cultural properties, the boundaries should reflect each of the areas and attributes that are a direct tangible expression of the OUV, as well as 'those areas which in the light of future research possibilities offer potential to contribute to and enhance such understanding' (ibid., para100). For natural properties, the boundaries 'should reflect the spatial requirements of habitats, species, processes and phenomena' that form the OUV, and, in addition, include sufficient areas 'to protect the property's heritage values from direct effect of human encroachments and impacts of resource use outside of the nominated area' (ibid., para101). Thus, the boundaries of a property must be carefully drawn up in a way that considers the values contributing to the OUV.

Properties should also be demarcated with buffer zones, intended as an additional layer of protection for the property: 'for the purposes of effective protection of the nominated property, a buffer zone is an area surrounding the nominated property which has complementary legal and/or customary restrictions placed on its use and development to give an added layer of protection to the property' (ibid., para104). Where a buffer zone is not delineated a statement must be made by the state party to explain the reason for this (ibid., paras103–106). Modifications to a buffer zone must be approved by the World Heritage Committee (ibid., para107). Increasingly recognized is the need for states parties to manage or limit major impacts also outside of buffer zones by protecting the wider setting of a World Heritage property in order to sustain its OUV (UNESCO, 2009a).

The Historic Site of Lyon stretches across a large territory of 427 ha, accounting for approximately 10 per cent of the city, surrounded by a buffer zone of 323 ha (Figure 2.4). The limits to the north, east and south reflect the fortified city up to the 19th century. To the north the site boundary follows the morphology of the old fortified city built between 1512 and 1550, which is visible through a zigzag-shaped morphological pattern in the Croix-Rousse area. To the east, the boundary follows the eastern banks of the Presqu'île (peninsula), forming the heart of Lyon between the Rhône and Saône rivers, which constitute the old defensive borders. The western boundary includes the Old Town (*Vieux Lyon*) to the west of River Saône, including the Roman sites at Fourvière Hill. The buffer zone is a more theoretical boundary aiming to provide buffer protection for the site. While there are no specific regulations for the buffer zone, from the 19th century onwards it was decided that the city would expand to the east of the historic site, which is where modern high-rise developments have been permitted and clustered.

Serial and transboundary World Heritage

The idea of a global heritage without borders is perhaps best evoked in 'serial' and 'transboundary' sites. These were first defined in 1980 initially with specific reference to cultural sites: 'States Parties may propose in a single nomination a series of cultural properties in different geographical locations' on the basis of 'historico-cultural' belonging or by their being characteristic of the same geographical zone. Furthermore, when situated in more than one nation, 'the States Parties may in agreement, jointly submit a single nomination' (UNESCO, 1980a, paras14–15). In 1988, 'natural properties' was added to the paragraphs on serial and transboundary properties (UNESCO, 1988, paras19–20). Transboundary properties may be designated either in a single geographic location, stretching across national state borders, or in multiple locations as serial properties. Due to their added conceptual, geographic and administrative complexities serial and transboundary sites require special consideration in terms of nomination, protection and management. They can potentially be used as tools for peace and cooperation, but paradoxically, transboundary sites can also illustrate political tension in regions with border disputes.

■ World Heritage property   ▨ Buffer zone

FIGURE 2.4 Delineation of the Historic Site of Lyon: World Heritage site and buffer zone

Reproduced by Francesca Rausa, based on: Ministère de l'écologie, de l'énergie, du développement durable, des transports et du logement (2011), http://whc.unesco.org/en/list/872/multiple=1&unique_number=1023

Transboundary properties

World Heritage properties that stretch across the territory of more than one state party are considered transboundary properties. The nomination of such properties depends on joint efforts and peaceful relations between states parties. Article 11.3 of the convention stipulates that 'the inclusion of a property in the World Heritage List requires the consent of the State concerned' and where border disputes exist 'the inclusion of a property situated in a territory, sovereignty or jurisdiction over which is claimed by more than one State shall in no way prejudice the rights of the parties to the dispute' (UNESCO, 1972). Transboundary properties 'should be prepared and submitted by States Parties jointly' and require joint management by states parties, preferable by the setting up of a joint management committee for coordination of management work and the formulation of a management plan. This brings an additional layer of complexity to the nomination process since it requires a high level of organization of stakeholders in more than one country (UNESCO, 2015b, para135).

While transboundary sites have increased in popularity in recent years they have featured on the World Heritage List from the beginning. The Kluane National Park/Wrangell-St. Elias National Monument (Canada–USA) was inscribed as the first transboundary World Heritage property in 1979. It was later extended to include Glacier Bay National Park and Preserve (USA) in 1992 and the Tatshenshini-Alsek Provincial Wilderness Park (Canada) in 1994. By 2000, it was re-named Kluane/Wrangell-St. Elias/Glacier Bay/Tatshenshini-Alsek. The natural property was inscribed prior to the insertion of the serial and transboundary provisions in the Operational Guidelines. By 2016, 34 transboundary properties had been designated (18 cultural, 14 natural, 2 mixed), with equal representation of cultural and natural transboundary sites.

An example of a cultural transboundary property is the Jesuit Missions of the Guaranis: San Ignacio Mini, Santa Ana, Nuestra Señora de Loreto and Santa Maria Mayor (Argentina), Ruins of Sao Miguel das Missoes (Brazil), inscribed on the World Heritage List in 1983. The remains of the Jesuit missions were inscribed based on cultural criterion (iv) as outstanding examples of a type of building and of an architectural ensemble illustrating a significant period in the history of Argentina and Brazil. The ruins of Saõ Miguel das Missões in Brazil and those of San Ignacio Miní, Santa Ana, Nuestra Señora de Loreto and Santa María la Mayor in Argentina are situated in the heart of a tropical forest and are impressive remains of five Jesuit missions, built in the land of the Guaraní people during the 17th and 18th centuries. The Brazilian part of the property was first nominated in 1982 as a single state nomination. However, the property was extended the following year, in 1983, to include the Jesuit Missions of the Guaranis in Argentina. In its evaluation, ICOMOS found that 'the inscription of the ruins of Sao Miguel on the World Heritage List is recommended within the framework of a 'global nomination' concerning the Jesuit missions of Latin America and associating the propositions of several concerned States Party[ies]' (ICOMOS, 1983). The term global nomination was used to describe the transboundary dimension and the thematic interrelationship of the missions across several countries. At the time of inscription, the World Heritage Committee endorsed this recommendation and suggested that missions located in Paraguay and Uruguay also be included for a representative illustration of the Jesuit missions of the Guaranis (UNESCO, 1984). However, Paraguay and Uruguay had not ratified the convention at the time.

The Mosi-oa-Tunya/Victoria Falls World Heritage property is an example of a natural transboundary property, inscribed on the World Heritage List in 1989 following a joint nomination by the governments of Zambia and Zimbabwe. Stretching across 68.6 km^2, the site includes the Victoria Falls (Mosi-Oa-Tunya) and is located in the Mosi-oa-Tunya National Park in Zambia and the Victoria Falls National Park in Zimbabwe (Figure 2.5). As one of the world's most spectacular waterfalls the site's OUV lies in its superlative natural formations (criterion vii) and as an outstanding example of significant on-going geological processes (criterion viii) (IUCN, 1989). At the time of inscription, the Committee 'commended the Governments of Zambia and Zimbabwe for demonstrating their commitment to co-operate in management of the site through the joint nomination' (UNESCO, 1989).

In 2006, lack of co-management was observed to be an obstacle to the site's conservation by a joint UNESCO/IUCN monitoring mission. It recommended the establishment of a Joint Ministerial Committee for effective transboundary coordination and the development of a joint integrated management plan, particularly given the various pressures associated with tourism development (WHC & IUCN, 2006). Efforts have been complicated by an ownership dispute amongst the Zimbabwean heritage management authorities. The Zimbabwe Parks and Wildlife Management Authority (ZPWMA) is the principal body in charge of the Victoria Falls National Park and Zambesi National Park. However, the National Museums and Monuments of Zimbabwe (NMMZ) agency also claims a stake in the site and particularly the designated Special Area within it, which implies national monument status. This is further complicated by the two organizations operating under different ministries and the economic interests at stake through tourism use of the site (Makuvaza, 2012).

Serial properties

Serial properties consist of a series of component parts that may be spread across geographical areas either within the territory of a state party, or across the territories of several states parties as 'serial transnational properties'. The nomination of a serial property requires special attention to the identification of OUV in that it must be demonstrated in the series as a whole as supposed to the individual parts of the site concerned. While the component parts are important, it is the way they are linked and relate to one another which determines the OUV. The links must be demonstrated in at least two of the following ways. Firstly, the component parts 'should reflect cultural, social or functional links over time' and illustrate landscape, ecological, evolutionary or habitat connectivity. Secondly, the component parts should contribute to the OUV of the property as a whole in a 'substantial, scientific, readily defined and discernible way'. Thirdly, to avoid 'excessive fragmentation of component parts' serial properties need to demonstrate 'overall manageability and coherence of the property' (UNESCO, 2015b, para137).

The number of serial nominations has grown significantly in recent years, something that has placed greater demands on the advisory bodies in their evaluation work. This requires the development of new tools and working methods, particularly considering the limited resources of the evaluation bodies. Consequently, ICOMOS developed a special evaluation format in 2009 to guide in the evaluation process with guiding questions (ICOMOS, 2011b). Serial nominations may be submitted for evaluation over several nomination cycles if the first property of the series has an OUV in its own right. The property may then be extended and added to. However, this requires planning from the states parties concerned and that the World Heritage Committee is informed (UNESCO, 2015b, para139).

FIGURE 2.5 Mosi-oa-Tunya/Victoria Falls ©UNESCO (credit: Véronique Dauge)

Struve Geodetic Arc is an example of a cultural serial transnational property. It was a successful joint nomination in 2005 by ten states parties (Belarus, Estonia, Finland, Latvia, Lithuania, Norway, Republic of Moldova, Russian Federation, Sweden and Ukraine). The property consists of a chain of survey triangulations stretching across over 2,820 km, which served as points of a survey carried out by a Baltic-German astronomer by name of Friedrich Georg Wilhelm Struve, between 1816 and 1855. It helped determine the shape and size of earth and was significant in the development of topographic mapping. The property includes 34 out of 265 of the original station points (ICOMOS, 2005).

Construct for peace and reconciliation?

Transboundary properties embody the idea of World Heritage as a symbol of international cooperation. They have the potential to act as instruments for peace and reconciliation in coherent areas divided by the borders of modern nation states. The Waterton-Glacier International Peace Park was established in 1932 as the world's first peace park and was later inscribed on the World Heritage List in 1995. Waterton Lakes and Glacier National Parks converge on the border between Canada and the USA respectively, and were designated as a single transboundary area by the Canadian parliament and the US Congress as a symbol of 'peace and goodwill between the two nations rather than as a mechanism for conflict resolution' (Tanner et al., 2007, p183). This set a precedent for a worldwide conservation movement to establish transboundary national parks, demonstrating cooperation in conservation and management based on ecological boundaries rather than political borders.

IUCN has since 1997 promoted environmental diplomacy through cross-boundary heritage sites using the 'parks for peace' concept as 'a tool to enhance regional cooperation for biodiversity conservation, conflict prevention and reconciliation, and sustainable regional development' (Sandwith et al., 2001, p1). This resembles the notion of World Heritage as a transboundary peace project. Dallen (1999, p182) explored the role of cross-boundary international parks and monuments in relation to sustainable tourism development, noting that 'political boundaries have a history of hindering collaborative planning, which has resulted in imbalances in the use, physical development, promotion, and sustainable management of shared resources'.

Closer scrutiny of protected areas and their serving as peace instruments reveal historical biases and conflicts. Protected areas is essentially a Western construct, and, historically, this designation was exclusive in promoting protection of wilderness areas with limited appreciation of the pre-existing cultures and peoples that lived within and impacted on these areas. The 'Yellowstone model' refers to the process in which the indigenous peoples of areas are excluded from protected areas that are given protection based on merits of these being valued as wilderness areas (Schelhas, 2001). In the case of the Waterton-Glacier International Peace Park, the continued integration of the Blackfoot people in the management of the park is essential for the credibility of the park as a peace project. Paradoxically, West and Brockington (2006, p613) suggest that: 'protected areas, like many development interventions, are sometimes instrumental in fuelling social conflict between groups. It is ironic that African transboundary conservation areas, which can require displacement and fuel ethnic tensions, have sought popular support as "peace parks".'

The Temple of Preah Vihear, a Cambodian property located on a steep cliff in a mountain range overlooking the Cambodian plains, has been subject to a contentious border dispute between Cambodia and Thailand (Figure 2.6). It was inscribed on the World Heritage List in 2008 as 'a unique architectural complex of a series of sanctuaries linked by a system of pavements and staircases on an 800 metre long axis' and as 'an outstanding masterpiece of Khmer architecture, in terms of plan, decoration and relationship to the spectacular landscape environment' (UNESCO, 2009b). The border, drawn up in 1907 by French cartographers following an agreement between the Siam (later Thailand) and French colonial authorities, has been disputed since the 1930s. A ruling in Cambodia's favour by the International Court of Justice in 1962 resulted in unresolved ownership of 4.6 km² of land immediately around the site, having led to continued dispute (Silverman, 2010). The border conflict was revived in 2008 at the time of the World Heritage inscription: 'Preah Vihear has become a bone of contention between Cambodia and Thailand, and the armed conflict that arose immediately after the UNESCO listing shows the political dimension such a certification may have' (Hauser-Schäublin, 2011, pp33--34).

In its evaluation ICOMOS noted the original intention for a joint nomination and that the two countries concerned had agreed for Cambodia to seek inscription first in 2008, followed by Thailand in order to include associated areas within its territory. Thai support was later withdrawn and tensions increased in early February 2011. The state-of-conservation reporting in conjunction with the

FIGURE 2.6 Temple of Preah Vihear, Cambodia ©UNESCO (credit: Chan Vitharin, source: Nao Hayashi)

35th Session of the World Heritage Committee found that: 'the tense situation along the Cambodian-Thai border led to increased tensions and confrontations between the two countries since their recent confrontation began in 2008. As reported by both sides, armed forces exchanged fire, from 4 to 7 February, causing a number of civilian and military deaths, displacement of civilian populations and physical destruction' (UNESCO, 2011c). The Committee encouraged the two states parties 'to use the *1972 Convention* as a tool to support conservation, sustainable development and dialogue' (UNESCO, 2011c). Nevertheless, the complexities surrounding the dispute are rooted in deeply embedded colonial and post-colonial histories and contested heritage discourses (see Hauser-Schäublin, 2011). It remains to be seen whether World Heritage status will deepen further the dispute or help promote dialogue and peaceful negotiations between the two states.

Notes

1 Several other international bodies play an important role in shaping conservation thought such as regional organizations (e.g. European Union) and research institutes concerned with heritage conservation (e.g. The Getty Institute).
2 The Valletta Principles were developed by CIVVIH, the International Committee on Historic Towns and Villages of ICOMOS, as a complement to the Charter for the Conservation of Historic Towns and Urban Areas (Washington Charter).
3 The Burra Charter process consists of a sequence of investigations, decisions and actions based on three basic steps. 1) understand the significance; 2) develop policy and 3) manage in accord with policy.
4 Early writers and pioneers of this movement were John Muir, a Scottish-American naturalist and Aldo Leopold, an environmentalist whose writings helped shape modern environmental ethics.
5 The Stockholm Declaration emerged from the United Nations Conference on the Human Environment held in Stockholm in 1972.
6 The Rio Declaration was adopted at the Rio Earth Summit in 1992.

3

GOVERNING WORLD HERITAGE

World Heritage governance is best understood as a process involving different stages of decision-making by a multitude of actors at various levels, some more visible and influential than others, from the nomination to the management and monitoring of sites. As a cross-disciplinary process, heritage conservation involves different steps and actions over time, i.e. heritage formation, inventorying, designation, protection, conservation and commodification (Howard, 2003). The heritage process is comparable with the duties ascribed to states parties under the World Heritage Convention, which are to ensure the identification, protection, conservation, presentation and transmission to future generations of cultural and natural heritage as defined in the convention (UNESCO, 1972, article 4).

With the expanding role of World Heritage sites as platforms for sustainable development, in which integrated conservation of culture and nature is recognized as key to achieving resilient societies, the number of stakeholders concerned has grown along with new demands for transparency and participation. This chapter presents key actors and organizations involved in governing World Heritage, seeking to determine whether participatory frameworks are successful. It demonstrates a complex web of stakeholders involved in lengthy processes shaped by power dynamics and competing interests, ranging from environmental lobbyists to natural resource extractors. In a global society in which the power of governments has been dispersed through governance regimes that rely on a multitude of international as well as local actors and policy frameworks, understanding of both opportunities and limitations in exercising influence in heritage decision-making is essential.

Actors in World Heritage decision-making

The states parties as the signatories to the World Heritage Convention are responsible for the nomination of sites and the management commitments that follow their inscription on the World Heritage List. They are formally represented by their permanent UNESCO delegations, supported by government ministries and departments or national heritage organizations. The World Heritage Committee is the primary decision-making body, assisted by the UNESCO World Heritage Centre and guided by the International Centre for the Study of the Preservation and Restoration of Cultural Property (ICCROM), International Council on Monuments and Sites (ICOMOS) and International Union for Conservation of Nature and Natural Resources (IUCN) as advisory bodies under the convention. World Heritage decision-making is crafted so as to balance the sovereignty of states parties and their obligations to the international community. Beyond these formalized bodies are several other actors, e.g. NGOs, research communities, businesses, local communities and individuals, who contribute to sustaining World Heritage on the ground. International mobilization of the interests of NGOs and indigenous peoples has further strengthened local voices. The engagement of local communities in World Heritage and sustainable development was highlighted during the 40th anniversary of the convention in 2012 and needs to be fully realized in management strategies.

States parties

The World Heritage Convention is open to all states subject to ratification, acceptance or accession. Ratification and acceptance essentially carry the same meaning.[1] Once the convention has been ratified or accepted, the country in question becomes a party to the convention, hence the term 'state party', which implies that the convention applies in full. Accession is relevant to states that are non-members of UNESCO but that may on invitation by the General Conference accede to the convention (UNESCO, 1972, articles 31–32). States parties may renounce the convention by following certain rules and procedures (article 35). Although, to date, no state party has denounced the convention, there have been extraordinary instances in which states parties have threatened to do so. In 2011, Thailand decided to denounce the convention during the 35th Session of the World Heritage Committee, due to unresolved border issues at the Temple of Preah Vihear. Located in Cambodia, the site had become damaged during border clashes between Thailand and Cambodia after its inscription on the World Heritage List in 2008. Following general elections only a few weeks later, the new Thai Government reversed the decision of the previous administration (Bangkok Post, 2011). The example demonstrates the complexity surrounding the nomination of sites where border disputes between states parties exist. A study of the dispute concluded that 'it ought to be difficult to gain inscription on the World Heritage List for a site being claimed by two countries, even without a larger boundary conflict' (Silverman, 2010, p15).

By 2016, there were 192 states parties to the convention.[2] One of the principal roles of states parties is the identification and delineation of World Heritage properties situated on their territories (UNESCO, 1972, article 3). Furthermore, states parties have an intra- and intergenerational responsibility concerning World Heritage properties as outlined in article 4: 'Each State Party to this Convention recognizes that the duty of ensuring the identification, protection, conservation, presentation and transmission to future generations of the cultural and natural heritage referred to in articles 1 and 2 and situated on its territory, belongs primarily to that State.' To fulfil these responsibilities states parties need to ensure that effective measures are taken in relation to their cultural and natural heritage, such as: adopting integrated conservation policy; maintaining appropriate services and the relevant expertise to implement conservation policy; as well as developing scientific and technical research to counteract threats that endanger heritage. States parties should also ensure that they take necessary legal, scientific, technical, administrative and financial measures to identify, protect, conserve, present and rehabilitate heritage on their territories, as well as develop national and regional training centres to support this and promote scientific research in this field (ibid., article 5).

While respect for national sovereignty is a fundamental principle of the UN, states parties undertake to help facilitate protection of World Heritage through cooperation with the international community. Article 6 outlines the principle of sovereignty and the international commitment: 'Whilst fully respecting the sovereignty of the States on whose territory the cultural and natural heritage mentioned in articles 1 and 2 is situated, and without prejudice to property right provided by national legislation, the States Parties to this Convention recognize that such heritage constitutes a world heritage for whose protection it is the duty of the international community as a whole to co-operate.' The same article obliges states parties to assist other states in their work to conserve World Heritage and not to take any deliberate measures that might damage such heritage on the territory of other states parties directly or indirectly. This spirit of cooperation for the heritage of humanity was one of the triggers of the convention and is summed up in article 7: 'For the purpose of this Convention, international protection of the world cultural and natural heritage shall be understood to mean the establishment of a system of international cooperation and assistance designed to support States Parties to the Convention in their efforts to conserve and identify that heritage.'

States parties also have duties to strengthen public awareness and respect of World Heritage through educational and information strategies and to keep the public informed of any dangers that may threaten it (article 27). When international assistance towards World Heritage properties has been received they have a special responsibility to raise awareness of issues such as threatening factors and the need for conservation, and to inform the public of the receipt of international assistance (article 28). Furthermore, they have a reporting duty to UNESCO on matters concerning legislative and administrative provisions, as well as actions relating to the convention (article 29). For instance, if a state party makes any legislative changes affecting World Heritage properties, it must inform UNESCO of this. States parties also have a financial duty through mandatory contributions towards the World Heritage Fund. This is separate from those contributions that are obliged by the UNESCO membership.

Bahamas is the most recent country to have ratified the convention in 2015. Singapore ratified the convention in 2012 after it had withdrawn its membership from UNESCO in 1985 for financial reasons due to rising membership fees, around the same time as the USA and the UK also withdrew from UNESCO citing concerns over mismanagement and corruption (*The Telegraph*, 1984). While the UK rejoined UNESCO in 1998 and the USA in 2002, Singapore did not rejoin until 2007. Unlike Singapore, the USA and the UK had both ratified the convention before withdrawing from UNESCO in 1973 and 1984. Nevertheless, since rejoining, Singapore has established a National Commission for UNESCO, which together with the ratification of the convention signalled its commitment to working with UNESCO. There are several other UNESCO members that have not yet ratified or accessed the convention, including Somalia, South Sudan, Timor-Leste and Tuvalu.

Palestine's ratification of the convention on 8 December 2011 following its admission to UNESCO on 31 October of the same year was surrounded with controversy. Its admission led countries such as the USA, Israel and Canada to suspend their membership contributions, which severely constrained the financial capacity of UNESCO. The ratification of the convention opened up the opportunity for 'cultural self-determination' of the Palestinian people, as stated by a state party representative following the inscription in 2012 of Palestine's first World Heritage property, Birthplace of Jesus: Church of the Nativity and the Pilgrimage Route, Bethlehem. However, according to an Israeli representative it 'damaged the image of the convention', since Palestine is not recognized as a nation state by the UN.[3] Thus, some perceive the inscription as a major political manoeuvre. An evolving body of literature is considering the political motives of states parties in their seeking of World Heritage designation in areas of border dispute and conflict (e.g. Gori, 2013; Silverman, 2010).

World Heritage Committee

The World Heritage Committee is the intergovernmental UN decision-making body for the implementation of the convention. It makes decisions concerning the inscription of cultural and natural properties on the World Heritage List and the List of World Heritage in Danger (LWHD), requests for international assistance and use of the World Heritage Fund. Furthermore, it sets the parameters for how the convention is to be implemented. Article 11.5 of the convention established that the Committee should define the criteria on the basis of which a property would be deemed of Outstanding Universal Value (OUV). The Committee is also responsible for the development of World Heritage policy in the form of strategic objectives and for revision of Operational Guidelines for the Implementation of the World Heritage Convention.[4]

Representation on the Committee rotates under the election by the General Assembly of States Parties. There are 21 states parties on the Committee at any one time and the elections are organized in such a way that different regions of the world are equitably represented. The following five regions have been defined by UNESCO: 1) Africa; 2) Asia and Pacific; 3) Arab States; 4) Europe and North America; and 5) Latin America and Caribbean. In 2014, the 21 states parties of the Committee were the following: Algeria, Colombia, Croatia, Finland, Germany, India, Jamaica, Japan, Kazakhstan, Republic of Korea, Lebanon, Malaysia, Peru, Philippines, Poland, Portugal, Qatar, Senegal, Serbia, Turkey and Vietnam. The representatives of the states parties serving on the Committee should be 'persons qualified in the field of cultural or natural heritage' (UNESCO, 1972, article 9.3). The delegations of the states parties are usually made up of ambassadors and permanent delegates to UNESCO together with the relevant heritage experts.

The term of office of members of the Committee is six years, but most states parties voluntarily retire from the Committee after four years as recommended in the Operational Guidelines in order to ensure equitable representation and rotation (UNESCO, 2015b, para21). The membership terms are staggered so that the entire Committee does not retire at the same time. For example, at the 19th Session of the General Assembly of States Parties in 2013, 12 states parties were outgoing from the Committee and consequently 12 seats were available to be filled by newly elected members. Any state party that had not been on the Committee for the last four years was eligible to present itself for election but, of the available seats, one is normally reserved for states parties with no property on the World Heritage List (UNESCO, 2015b, para22).

World Heritage Centre

The World Heritage Centre acts as the Secretariat to the World Heritage Committee and is responsible for managing the day-to-day administration of the convention, organizing the meetings of the Committee and General Assembly of States Parties and any World Heritage-related issues within UNESCO (Figure 3.1). The role of the Secretariat is stipulated in article 14.1 of the Convention: 'The World Heritage Committee shall be assisted by a Secretariat appointed by the Director-General of the United Nations Educational, Scientific and Cultural Organization' (UNESCO, 1972).

Established in 1992 specifically for the purpose of assuming the role of the Secretariat, the centre 'assists and collaborates with the States Parties and the Advisory Bodies' and 'works in close cooperation with other sectors and field offices of UNESCO' (UNESCO, 2015b, para27). Its establishment coincided with the 20th anniversary of the convention and was considered a vital factor for its successful implementation. Previously, the Secretariat relied on contributions from the Culture and Science sectors of UNESCO, reflecting the traditional sectoral division between the disciplines dealing with the conservation of culture and nature. Furthermore, the lack of a central body responsible for managing the convention not only exacerbated the perceived division between cultural and natural heritage but also created difficulties for the Secretariat in dealing with the increasing number of decisions made at the meetings of the World Heritage Committee concerning a steadily expanding World Heritage List.

The World Heritage Centre is responsible for updating the World Heritage List and coordinating the evaluation of the nomination files submitted by states parties. It organizes the reports on the state of conservation of World Heritage properties and the monitoring missions requested by the Committee. Furthermore, it organizes international assistance from the World Heritage Fund and works to mobilize extra funding for properties when required. It also provides assistance and advice to states parties on producing nomination files and on implementation of the strategic objectives of the convention. Moreover, it promotes and raises awareness of the convention (UNESCO, 2015b, para28), for example, through publication of freely available manuals and educational materials.

FIGURE 3.1 The World Heritage Centre, located within the building complex of UNESCO in Paris (credit: Elene Negussie)

The Director of the World Heritage Centre is appointed by the Director-General of UNESCO who oversees five sections (education, natural sciences, social and human sciences, culture, and communication and information) dedicated to each of the global regions: Africa; Asia and Pacific; Arab States; Europe and North America; and Latin America and Caribbean.[5] The centre includes a team of specialist experts involved in different projects linked to World Heritage strategies, e.g. World Heritage and Sustainable Tourism Programme, World Heritage Cities and the World Heritage Marine Programme.

Advisory bodies

ICCROM, ICOMOS and IUCN serve as the three designated advisory bodies under the World Heritage Convention. Their advisory role is enshrined in article 8.3 of the convention: 'A representative of the International Centre for the Study of the Preservation and Restoration of Cultural Property (Rome Centre), a representative of the International Council on Monuments and Sites (ICOMOS) and a representative of the International Union for Conservation of Nature and Natural Resources (IUCN), to whom may be added, at the request of States Parties to the convention meeting in general assembly during the ordinary sessions of the General Conference of the United Nations Educational, Scientific and Cultural Organization' (UNESCO, 1972).

The special role of the advisory bodies is emphasized in article 13.7, which addresses the need for the World Heritage Committee to cooperate with national organizations, NGOs, public and private bodies and individuals on implementation of the Convention. Furthermore, article 14.2 states that the Director-General of UNESCO should utilize 'to the fullest extent possible' the services of the three bodies 'in their respective areas of competence and capability' in the Committee's documentation, the agenda of its meetings and in implementation of its decisions. More specifically, the role of the advisory bodies is to:

- Provide advice on the implementation of the convention;
- Assist the Secretariat in preparing documentation for decisions to be made by the World Heritage Committee;
- Assist with development of global strategies, periodic reporting and the effective use of the World Heritage Fund;
- Monitor the state of conservation of World Heritage properties and review requests for international assistance;
- Evaluate properties nominated for inscription on the World Heritage List for presentation at Committee meetings (for ICOMOS and IUCN); and
- Provide advice at meetings of the World Heritage Committee and the Bureau (UNESCO, 2015b, paras30–37).

The advisory bodies participate in joint missions together with UNESCO in monitoring the state of conservation of properties when requested by the Committee. However, the advisory function is not exclusive to the three designated bodies, as seen above in article 8.3 of the convention and explained in the Operational Guidelines: 'The Committee may call on other international and non-governmental organizations with appropriate competence and expertise to assist in the implementation of the programmes and projects' (UNESCO, 2015b, para38).

The mission of the advisory bodies is framed by widely disparate disciplines since their focus is on cultural and natural heritage conservation respectively, fields that are themselves interdisciplinary. However, the search for holistic approaches in the achievement of conservation and sustainable development has created new opportunities for cooperation and synergies between the organizations. Nevertheless, the World Heritage remit of the advisory bodies is a major challenge with an expanding portfolio of work and in times of financial constraints. A joint report to the World Heritage Committee in 2012 stated that: 'The resources available to the *World Heritage Convention* are becoming ever more stretched and the financial issues impacting UNESCO will also have implications for the *Convention*, including new financial challenges facing the World Heritage Fund. The Advisory Bodies are providing increasing levels of their own resources to meet shortfalls in available funding for their work in implementing the *Convention*' (UNESCO, 2012c, p8).

ICCROM

ICCROM, or 'the Rome Centre', is an intergovernmental heritage organization composed of 135 member states in 2016. Established in Rome in 1959 on invitation of the Italian Government, following a decision at the 9th General Conference of UNESCO held in New Delhi in 1956, its governance and remit are outlined in the ICCROM Statutes (ICCROM, 2013). It is governed by a General Assembly consisting of delegates from its Member States, a Council with selected experts from the member states and a Secretariat with a Director-General and staff. The member states make mandatory contributions to the organization as fixed by the General Assembly. ICCROM works to promote the conservation of all types of cultural heritage globally through information, research, training, cooperation and advocacy for conservation of both immovable and moveable cultural heritage through interdisciplinary collaboration. It hosts training activities on an annual basis, runs a scholarly fellowship programme, facilitates a specialized conservation library and produces publications such as guidance manuals on heritage conservation.

Its World Heritage mandate is 'being the priority partner in training for cultural heritage, monitoring the state of conservation of World Heritage cultural properties, reviewing requests for International Assistance submitted by States Parties, and providing input and support for capacity-building activities'

(UNESCO, 2015b, para33). For example, ICCROM launched a World Heritage Global Training Strategy for Cultural Heritage in 2000, expanded in 2001 to include natural heritage in cooperation with the IUCN. In 2009, ICCROM undertook a training strategy (Africa, 2009) for heritage expertise in African countries especially.[6] In 2011, it jointly developed the World Heritage Capacity Building Strategy together with ICOMOS and IUCN, approved by the World Heritage Committee at its 35th session in Paris (UNESCO, 2012d).

ICOMOS

ICOMOS is a non-governmental cultural heritage organization founded by a group of architects in 1965, with an international Secretariat in Paris. Its work is based on the principles of the 1964 International Charter on the Conservation and Restoration of Monuments and Sites, the founding charter of ICOMOS (the Venice Charter). It works to promote the application of theory, methodology and scientific techniques in the conservation of cultural heritage. This work has resulted in specialized charters and principles on conservation, which help inform professionals and institutions of best practices in the field of cultural heritage conservation. Furthermore, scientific symposiums in connection with larger meetings are instrumental to the advancement of conservation thinking (Figure 3.2). The organization has a two-tiered structure with international level functions and a network of national committees with members from various professions and practices concerned with heritage conservation.[7]

The ICOMOS Statutes, first adopted by the Constituent Assembly in Warsaw in 1965 and amended in 1978 at the 5th General Assembly in Moscow and the 18th General Assembly in Florence in 2014, outline the organizational structure of ICOMOS. It consists of a General Assembly, Executive Committee, Advisory Council and several specialized International Scientific Committees. The latter are the specialized 'technical organs' of ICOMOS and operate within the statutes and rules of procedure of ICOMOS, but may establish their own structure and governing mechanisms.[8] They are essential to the scientific work of ICOMOS, with specializations ranging from heritage documentation and the theory and philosophy of conservation to the conservation of historic towns and villages, 20th century architecture and cultural landscapes.

The World Heritage mandate of ICOMOS is: 'evaluation of properties nominated for inscription on the World Heritage List, monitoring the state of conservation of World Heritage cultural properties, reviewing requests for International Assistance submitted by States Parties, and providing input and support for capacity-building activities' (UNESCO, 2015b, para35). The need for close cooperation with UNESCO and ICCROM was stipulated in the ICOMOS Statutes (ICOMOS, 1978). It convenes a World Heritage Panel for the evaluation of cultural and mixed cultural/natural properties nominated for inscription on the World Heritage List, including members of the Executive Committee and international experts invited for their specific field of expertise

FIGURE 3.2   17th ICOMOS General Assembly meeting held at the headquarters of UNESCO in 2011 © Adrien Lhommedieu / ICOMOS France

on an annual basis. In 2006, the Executive Committee approved a Policy for the implementation of the ICOMOS World Heritage Mandate to ensure credibility and the highest available degree of professional expertise in all its World Heritage-related work.

IUCN

IUCN was founded in 1948 as the first international environmental non-governmental organization (NGO) with headquarters in Gland, Switzerland. As stipulated in the IUCN Statutes: 'since protection and conservation of nature and natural resources are of vital importance to all nations, a responsible international organization primarily concerned with the furthering of these aims will be of value to various governments, the United Nations and its Specialized Agencies and other interested organizations' (IUCN, 2012, preamble). It is a professional global network with over 1,300 member organizations in 160 countries, including both government and non-governmental organizations.

IUCN consists of the World Conservation Congress, the Council, the National and Regional Committees and Regional Fora of Members, the Commissions and the Secretariat. Held every four years, the World Conservation Congress draws together leaders from government, the public sector, NGOs, businesses and UN agencies for discussions on how to improve management of the natural environment (Figure 3.3). It defines the policy of IUCN and makes recommendations to governments and national and international organizations. Furthermore, it provides 'a public forum for debate on how best to conserve the integrity and diversity of nature and to ensure that any use of natural resources is equitable and ecologically sustainable' (IUCN, 2012, 20[m]). The Council is the principal governing body in between the sessions of the World Conservation Congress and sets the strategic direction and policy guidance for the work of IUCN. The National and Regional Committees are formed to facilitate cooperation between members and to coordinate the work of the organization. In between the sessions of the World Conservation Congress, Regional Fora may be held to allow for members' participation in the preparation and evaluation of the work of IUCN. The Commissions bring together voluntary experts from various disciplines, which assess the state of the world's natural resources. The Secretariat is decentralized with 1,000 staff in 45 offices across the world, led by a Director-General appointed by the Council for the implementation of IUCN's policy and programme as established by the World Conservation Congress and the Council.

The role of IUCN under the World Heritage Convention is similar to that of ICOMOS, although in relation to natural properties and mixed cultural/natural properties: 'evaluation of properties nominated for inscription on the World Heritage List, monitoring the state of conservation of World Heritage natural properties, reviewing requests for International Assistance submitted by States Parties, and providing input and support for capacity-building activities' (UNESCO, 2015b, para37). IUCN has developed a World Heritage programme within the organization. In 2014, the World Heritage Outlook was launched as a tool for global assessment of natural World Heritage.

FIGURE 3.3 IUCN World Conservation Congress held in Hawaii in 2016 (credit: IUCN/Maegan Ginidi)

Other stakeholders

World Heritage Conservation requires participatory and inclusive approaches that allow for the involvement of a wide range of stakeholders, from government ministries and local authorities to NGOs and local community interest groups. The need for inclusive governance and engagement of a broad range of stakeholders is stipulated in article 13.7 of the convention. The cooperative measures have been further developed and defined in the Operational Guidelines: 'a partnership approach to nomination, management and monitoring provides a significant contribution to the protection of World Heritage properties and the implementation of the Convention' (UNESCO, 2015b, para39). Partnership approaches are thus encouraged to protect and conserve World Heritage, including 'those individuals and other stakeholders, especially local communities, governmental, non-governmental and private organizations and owners who have an interest and involvement in the conservation and management of a World Heritage property' (UNESCO, 2015b, para40).

A key question emerging from discussions of stakeholder participation is what it means in practical terms. As noted by Millar (2006, p38), 'theoretically "all the peoples of the world" are stakeholders in World Heritage. In practice, until recently, a limited number of stakeholders – governments, conservation experts and local authorities – were involved in the process. Local people, local amenity and community groups, local businesses, tour companies and visitors were largely left out of the consultation and management processes.' While there is often a gap between theory and practice, the need for local community engagement has increasingly been promoted by the World Heritage Committee. The involvement of local people has been described as 'an important cross-cutting issue throughout World Heritage management' (UNESCO, 2012e, p20). The need to enhance the role of communities in the implementation of the World Heritage Convention was adopted by the Committee as one of five strategic objectives.

Private sector stakeholders may include businesses operating at World Heritage properties, or firms involved in conservation practices and individuals such as property owners. Voluntary sector stakeholders range from local volunteers active in the management activities for a site to NGOs and local communities with a direct stake in World Heritage sites. Stakeholders from the public sector include those authorities that are responsible for heritage policy and its implementation, or in the capacity as owners of heritage sites. At local government level, the elected councillors play a key role in decisions affecting World Heritage sites, from the allocation of conservation resources to decisions concerning development proposals affecting sites. The emphasis on broad stakeholder participation is linked not merely to a rights-based approach to heritage conservation, but also to the need for shared responsibility in terms of the costs of World Heritage designation: 'the majority of the investment required will often need to come from the private sector, and in many cases from hundreds or thousands of individuals and families who need to see these sites as dynamic living places where they can raise their families with an acceptable standard of living' (Rebanks, 2009, p6).

World Heritage decision-making

The Ordinary Session of the World Heritage Committee is the principal point of World Heritage decision-making. The Bureau meets in conjunction with the Committee sessions. Furthermore, the General Assembly of States Parties to the World Heritage Convention meets during the bi-annual sessions of the General Conference of UNESCO. UN decision-making is based on the one-nation-one-vote rule and two-thirds majority voting. This principle was enshrined in the UN Charter in 1945 to reflect the sovereign equality of nations, and is applied in decisions of the UN General Assembly and the Economic and Social Council.[9] It is also reflected in the UNESCO Constitution, under which 'each Member State shall have one vote in the General Conference' subject to payment of its contributions (UNESCO, 1945, article IV.8). Similarly, each state member of the World Heritage Committee has one vote and 'decisions of the Committee shall be taken by a majority of two-thirds of its members present and voting' (UNESCO, 1972, article 13.8).

Ordinary sessions of the World Heritage Committee

The World Heritage Committee meets once a year, normally between June and July, for the Ordinary Session, when most decisions are made concerning World Heritage properties (Figure 3.4). To ensure transparency the decision texts are made available to the public on the World Heritage Centre website, and, in 2012 the ordinary session of the Committee was live streamed on the Internet for the first time.

While the agenda of the meeting has grown significantly over the years, decision-making mainly concerns the following: inscription of properties on the World Heritage List; the World Heritage Fund and allocation of financial assistance towards World Heritage properties; the state of conservation of inscribed properties; inscription or deletion of properties on the LWHD; the strategic objectives of the convention; and the implementation of the convention (UNESCO, 1972, articles 11, 13, 14, 21 and 29; UNESCO, 2015b, paras24–25). The Committee also decides on issues such as the location and time of the next annual session, for which any of its members may invite the Committee to hold its next meeting in their countries.

At each session, according to the Rules of Procedure, the World Heritage Committee is present together with representatives of the advisory bodies, the Secretariat, the observer states parties to the convention and other observers such as public or private organizations or individuals. Their observer status is granted based on their involvement in World Heritage related issues: 'The United Nations and organizations of the United Nations system, as well as, upon written request, at least 15 days prior to the date of the session of the Committee, other international governmental and non-governmental organizations, permanent observer missions to UNESCO and non profit-making institutions having activities in the fields covered by the convention, according to criteria defined by the World Heritage Committee, may be authorized by the Committee to participate in the sessions of the Committee as observers' (UNESCO, 2015e, rule 8.3).

At the meeting, the advisory bodies present their reports and respond to any questions by the Committee in its decisions. The observers, including those states parties that are not serving on the Committee for the time being, may only address the meeting with the prior consent of the Chairperson. A state party within whose territory a World Heritage property under discussion is located may not speak unless expressly invited by the Committee. This is regardless of whether the state party concerned is a Committee member or not. Previously, if the state party was invited to speak, it could not present an argument in favour of or against a particular side of the debate but could only address specific questions posed by members of the Committee. However, now, a state party 'may be invited by the Chairperson to present their views after the Advisory Bodies have presented their evaluation of the site proposed by the State, a report on the state of conservation of a property on their territory, or to support the approval of an assistance request submitted by that State' (UNESCO, 2015e, rule 22.7). This change to the rules could be seen as a double-edged sword. It gave states parties the opportunity to argue against any critique by the advisory bodes, to prepare statements countering their recommendations for reactive monitoring missions and so on. If the Committee cannot agree on a decision related to a nominated or inscribed property the decision may then be put to a vote. Voting is normally by a show of hands, but may also be conducted by secret ballot.

Observers regularly participate at the World Heritage sessions. However, in 2012, participation was more pronounced in that environmental NGOs and civil society representatives had for the first time organized an independent forum on the protection of World Heritage properties in advance of the Committee meeting. The forum sought to discuss conservation concerns around properties globally and to consider strategies to increase public participation in decision-making mechanisms at the Committee meetings. This may lead to a greater number of participants representing civil society in the future, which will enlarge the audience and potentially affect the decision-making process at Committee meetings.

The Chairperson of the Committee at the annual ordinary session is normally a representative from the state party hosting the meeting. For example, the 36th Session of the World Heritage Committee held in St Petersburg in 2012, was chaired by Eleonora Mitrofanova, the Ambassador and Permanent Delegate of the Russian Federation to UNESCO. When the Committee examined

Russian World Heritage properties or new nominations, the Chairperson had to step down temporarily from the Chair position and hand over to the Vice-Chairperson. Furthermore, during the discussions the Russian delegation could not contribute to the debate unless asked to address a specific question by another Committee member through the Chairperson. These procedures are undertaken to guard against impartiality and to ensure credibility of the relevant discussions. Two Russian sites generated extensive debate. Firstly, in the nomination of Lena Pillars Nature Park, IUCN recommended that inscription be deferred to allow the state party time for development of a management plan. However, the Committee decision was to inscribe the site on the World Heritage List. Secondly, in its state of conservation report on the Virgin Komi Forests World Heritage property, IUCN proposed its inscription on the LWHD because of threats caused by the preparation of a gold mine within the site. Concerned parties, NGOs, indigenous groups and stakeholders related to these sites were represented by various observers attending the session, including World Wildlife Fund Russia, Greenpeace Russia, Natural Heritage Protection Fund Russia and Environmental Watch on North Caucasus. Some requested permission to speak and were allocated two-minute slots to address the Committee at the discretion of the Chairperson. Nevertheless, the Committee decided against inscription on the LWHD.

FIGURE 3.4 The World Heritage Committee at its 36th Session in St Petersburg in 2012 (credit: Claire Cave)

Bureau and extraordinary sessions

Established by the World Heritage Committee, the Bureau acts to coordinate the meetings of the Committee. The seven Bureau members, the Chairperson, five Vice-Chairpersons and the Rapporteur, are elected from the delegations of different states parties serving on the World Heritage Committee at the end of each ordinary session. The members of the Bureau are eligible for immediate re-election for a second term of office. As with the election of the Committee itself, care is taken to ensure that the Bureau includes representatives from the different regions of the world and from both cultural and natural heritage backgrounds: 'In electing the Bureau, due regard shall be given to the need to ensure an equitable representation of the different regions and cultures of the world and a proper balance between the cultural and natural heritage as provided in the Convention' (UNESCO, 2015e, rule 13.3).

The Vice-Chairpersons assist the Chairperson in running the meetings. The principal role of the Rapporteur is to ensure that the Committee's decisions are accurately recorded in both English and French, the working languages of the Convention. The Rapporteur works with the Secretariat to keep track of amendments to the draft decisions submitted by Committee members and assists the Committee in the appropriate wording and language used in the decision texts.

The World Heritage Committee occasionally also meets at extraordinary sessions, arranged when at least two-thirds of the Committee members request it. Only 11 extraordinary sessions have been held since 1981, the last one in 2015. The extraordinary sessions have tended to deal with issues such as the examination of international assistance requests, amendments to the rules of procedures and on occasion the election of Bureau members. The Bureau meets during the sessions of the Committee 'as frequently as deemed necessary' (UNESCO, 2015e, rule 12.2). Furthermore, the Bureau conducts its own meetings at which representatives of the advisory bodies, observer states parties as well as other international governmental organizations and NGOs are present.

General Assembly of States Parties

The General Assembly of States Parties (GASP) has two tasks. Firstly, it determines the uniform percentage of states parties' contributions to the World Heritage Fund (UNESCO, 2015b, para17). This is enshrined in article 16.1 of the convention, which also stipulates that decisions regarding such contributions require that the majority of the states parties are present and voting. Secondly, it elects members to the World Heritage Committee (UNESCO, 2015b, paras17–18). This role is stipulated in article 8.1 of the Convention stating that the Committee should be: 'elected by States Parties to the Convention meeting in general assembly during the ordinary session of the General Conference of the United Nations Educational, Scientific and Cultural Organization.'

The GASP also adopts resolutions to do with the strategic work concerning the convention. For example, at the 20th Session of the GASP, held in Paris in 2015, it adopted the revised policy document entitled Policy for the Integration of a Sustainable Development Perspective into the Processes of the World Heritage Convention (UNESCO, 2015a). The resolution established the document as a first step in integrating sustainable development into the processes of implementing the convention and invited the World Heritage Centre and states parties 'to continue engagement through an ongoing consultation process involving all stakeholders to enrich the policy document' (UNESCO, 2015f, p8).

Governance and stakeholder participation

The need for stakeholder participation has gained increasing recognition in World Heritage governance. However, the term 'stakeholder' is often used vaguely to fulfil the requirements of democratic and inclusive approaches. Stakeholder analysis is therefore essential in each stage of the World Heritage process to identify stakeholders, legitimacy and ability to exercise influence. The convention refers indirectly to stakeholder engagement in article 5(a), which asks states parties 'to adopt a general policy which aims to give the cultural and natural heritage a function in the life of the community.' In 1996, participation was introduced in the Operational Guidelines: 'Participation of local people in the nomination process is essential to make them feel a shared responsibility with the State Party in the maintenance of the site' (UNESCO, 1996a, para14).

World Heritage governance

The term 'governance' has been widely used since the 1980s to mean 'all processes of governing, whether undertaken by a government, market, or network, whether over a family, tribe, formal or informal organization, or territory, and whether through laws, norms, power or language. Governance differs from government in that it focuses less on the state and its institutions and more on social practices and activities' (Bevir, 2013, p1). Political scientists have debated whether a shift from government to governance has occurred and questioned the validity of such a shift (Koch, 2013). The UN Commission on Global Governance promoted global governance as 'part of the evolution of human efforts to organize life on the planet', rather than global government, which could lead to 'an even less democratic world than we have – one more accommodating to power, more hospitable to hegemonic ambition, and more reinforcing of the roles of states and governments rather than the rights of people' (Commission on Global Governance, 1995, pxvi).[10] Furthermore, IUCN has defined environmental governance as 'the means by which society determines and acts on goals and priorities related to the management of natural resources. This includes the rules, both formal and informal, that govern human behavior in decision-making processes as well as the decisions themselves.

Appropriate legal frameworks on the global, regional, national and local level are a prerequisite for good environmental governance' (IUCN, 2016).

World Heritage governance may be defined as an overarching term for the process of governing the heritage of humanity according to a regime of internationally formulated and evolving rules, ethics and concepts. It involves a wide range of actors, interests and stakeholders on different scales, from organizations and decision-makers at the international level to national authorities and local heritage custodians. It mixes aspects of global governance, participatory governance, environmental governance, urban governance, and so on.

The shift in focus on local community engagement has implied a greater role of 'indigenous peoples' and traditional knowledge systems in the World Heritage process, allowing for new holistic perspectives on the conservation of culture and nature. Furthermore, the operation of the convention within the UN system has strengthened the role of indigenous peoples in governance and integrated conservation strategies. In 2000, the World Commission on Protected Areas and the Commission on Environmental and Social Policy established the Theme on Indigenous and Local Communities, Equity and Protected Areas (TILCEPA), seeking 'the full and effective recognition of the rights and responsibilities of local communities in the development and implementation of conservation policies and strategies that affect the lands, waters and other natural and cultural resources to which they relate' (IUCN, 2005a, pxx).

The 'Laponia process' demonstrated a lengthy process that led to a new joint management approach, linking traditional management practices with the modern heritage management system. The Laponian Area, in northern Sweden, was inscribed on the World Heritage List as a mixed cultural/natural site in 1996. The land of Laponia, or *Sápmi*, stretches across Norway, Sweden, Finland and part of the Russian Kola Peninsula (Figure 3.5). Divided by national borders, it is the home of the Sami people, who still use the area in a traditional way based on the seasonal movement of lifestock (reindeer). Work towards a management plan for the Laponian Area began with the nomination of the property. The official authorities in charge of heritage and environmental protection undertook work towards a management plan according to common procedure. However, the process was characterized by conflicts between actors at the regional authority and local levels. The local Sami villages formed an association, *Mijá Ednam*, defending their interests in the area and the right to manage what had been granted World Heritage status, particularly given the central place of the Sami culture in the World Heritage nomination (Laponia, 2013).

While the nomination of the Laponian Area had initially focused on the 'wilderness' qualities of the site as a natural area, UNESCO recommended that the Sami culture should form part of a future successful nomination (Jonsson, 2013). This condition gave the Sami people special international recognition of their cultural impact on Laponia as a 'cultural landscape'. In 2011, the main parties negotiated and signed an agreement for the establishment of a common management organization and management plan for the World Heritage site.

FIGURE 3.5 Laponia: Land of the Sami people (credit: Carl-Johan Utsi © Laponiatjuottjudus)

FIGURE 3.6 Jojk performance, the traditional folk song of the Sami people (credit: Laponiatjuottjudus © Laponiatjuottjudus)

The Sami people are in the majority on the board of the organization that carries responsibility for all management in the area, attempting to integrate traditional knowledge into the management work, in which the Sami elders play a key role in transmitting ancestral knowledge (Jonsson, 2013). The Laponia model demonstrates a shift from a modern heritage management model, in which the regional authorities in Sweden carry the main responsibility, towards a stronger sense of self-governance for the Sami people who have managed this landscape for generations (Figure 3.6).

Engaging stakeholders and local communities

States parties are encouraged 'to ensure the participation of a wide variety of stakeholders, including site managers, local and regional governments, local communities, non-governmental organizations (NGOs) and other interested parties and partners in the identification, nomination and protection of World Heritage properties' (UNESCO, 2015b, para12). Since the introduction of this paragraph in the Operational Guidelines in 2005, reference to stakeholder participation has been inserted throughout the guidelines (e.g. in sections on the establishment of tentative lists, the nomination process, management systems and sustainable use).[11] For example, World Heritage management plans should be framed through participation by a broad range of actors, interests and partners, from representatives of government departments, local authorities, NGOs and private bodies to local communities, including amenity groups, local businesses, residents, owners and concerned individuals, in order to be 'bottom-up' rather than 'top-down' or a combination of both. The role of local communities in the World Heritage process was stipulated as one of the five strategic objectives of the World Heritage Committee: to 'enhance the role of Communities in the implementation of the World Heritage Convention' (UNESCO, 2015b, para26).

The importance of informing and engaging stakeholders and the general public is increasingly recognized as an important and often mandatory part of environmental decision-making (Philips, 2003). The Åarhus Convention on Access to Information, Public Participation in Decision-making and Access to Justice in Environmental Matters, adopted in 1998 at the Fourth Ministerial Conference in the 'Environment for Europe' process under the United Nations Economic Commission for Europe (UNECE), held in Denmark, established rights of the public with regard to the environment. The convention required states parties to guarantee rights of access to information, public participation in decision-making and access to justice in environmental matters. It established the goal of 'protecting the right of every person of present and future generations to live in an environment adequate to health and well-being.' Open to accession by non-UNECE countries as well, it has been ratified by 46 countries (UNECE, 2013).

The way in which the terms 'stakeholder' and 'community' are defined and the extent to which these are able to exercise influence need reflection (Waterton & Smith, 2010). Key questions arising from these terms are who is a stakeholder, who may be regarded as forming part of a local community, what communities exist within a given local community and how the legitimacy and relevance of different actors should be recognized in the World Heritage process. Different cultural contexts may also determine whether stakeholders include private landowners in a Western sense of land ownership or in a communal/traditional ownership context. In Africa, relationships between local communities and administrative organizations often involve conflict since traditional conservation and management methods at heritage sites become overridden by modern legal state systems, which implies competition between traditional and modern heritage management systems for legitimacy and influence (Mumma, 2003).

The complexity of the above-mentioned terms was explored in a study of natural resource management at Lake Naivasha, a site on Kenya's Tentative List, in which both the lake environment and access to water was at stake (Billgren & Holmén, 2008). While work towards a natural resource management plan for the lake could be viewed as 'bottom-up' in its engagement of stakeholders, it involved specific challenges such as decision makers' recognition of the competing views of 'nature' amongst the different stakeholders and the limited representation of 'local community' in the process. The stakeholders included a broad range of interests, from the large-scale farmers and tourist operators to the subsistence farmers and fishermen who depended on the lake directly for their livelihoods. Nevertheless, questions of 'who should be given the mandate to manage the lake and who has the ability to do so' proved difficult to answer (ibid., p550).

Similarly, the definitional problem of community in heritage management was noted as problematic in southern Africa where colonialism led to the disenfranchisement of local communities. There, community participation has on the one hand provided opportunities for restoring lost connections between heritage sites and local people who, like indigenous peoples in Australia and North America, had been unjustly removed from their lands during colonialism and with protected area designation (Chirikure et al., 2010, p34). In the case of the Khami Ruins National Monument, a World Heritage site south-west of Bulawayo in Zimbabwe, the management and action plans drawn up in association with its inscription on the World Heritage List in 1986 mention the need to involve local communities. However, in reality this did not occur due to difficulties in defining who the local community was and whether its participation should be 'based on historical links or proximity to a heritage resource'. In contrast, in Ethiopia at World Heritage sites such as Aksum and Lalibela, local communities have stronger connections to their heritage landscapes (ibid.).

The role of stakeholders and their ability to influence depends on the existing governance context and democratic maturity of a country. Kellert et al. (2000) explored community natural resource management (CNRM) as an overall community-based approach to resource management based on variables covering economic, social and environmental objectives with case studies in

Kenya, Nepal and the USA.[12] These suggested that 'the reality often falls far short of the rhetoric and promise of CNRM. The complexity of goals, interests and organizational features of CNRM renders its implementation exceedingly difficult' (ibid., p713). Furthermore, the study suggested variation in success between different countries and continents. In relation to 'empowerment', for example, the CNRM approach had resulted in a more significant shift in power to local and indigenous peoples in the US case studies compared to in Kenya and Nepal.

In some instances, legislation does not permit stakeholders to participate in management decision-making. For example, Polet and Ling (2004) found that Vietnamese Government regulations stipulate that stakeholders other than the officially appointed management boards cannot take part in management decisions at protected heritage sites. However, inclusive conservation management methods may still be pursued within the legal framework and according to the capacities of the relevant stakeholders. For example, Vietnamese local authorities have the prerogative to engage local communities by sharing information and carrying out consultations for management planning. Thus, heritage managers have a responsibility to apply good governance according to local circumstances and aspirations of local peoples within the existing legal frameworks.

Stakeholder identification and analysis

Participatory approaches in the World Heritage process require practical tools for the identification of stakeholders and recognition of any barriers that may prevent meaningful participation. Stakeholder analysis is essential from the point of view of policy makers, site managers and professionals in charge of site management. A methodology on stakeholder analysis was included in a toolkit presented by UNESCO, Enhancing our Heritage Toolkit: Assessing Management Effectiveness of Natural World Heritage Sites. It proposed that stakeholders should be classified according to their influence on a site's values, both positively and negatively, and based on resource dependency on the site in question. This requires collection of data to identify who the relevant stakeholders are, their relationship with the site and their present level of engagement with the site concerned. It is necessary to identify all stakeholder groups relating to a World Heritage property, e.g. those who have an interest or connection with the site and those who impact on or are affected by the management of the site (UNESCO, 2008a).

A study of stakeholder collaboration at the Kokoda Track and Owen Stanley Ranges, a site on Papua New Guinea's Tentative List, used four attributes to analyse stakeholders: levels of power (a stakeholder's ability to influence), legitimacy (of the relationship), urgency (of the stakeholder's claim) and proximity (of a stakeholder to the area). By identifying stakeholder groups, these attributes were listed in a matrix in which the different attributes were analysed for the various groups (Bott et al., 2011) (Table 3.1).

TABLE 3.1 Stakeholder attribute identification analysis

Stakeholders	Attributes			
	Power	Legitimacy	Urgency	Proximity
Local authority	Medium	High	High	High
NGO	Low	High	Medium	Medium
Local community	Very high	Very high	High	High

Source: Bott et al., 2011.

World Heritage management plans show varying levels of stakeholder engagement since 'community participation is not an event but a process which evolves over time' (Chirikure et al., 2010, p41). For example, the community engagement objectives of the management plan for the Tasmanian Wilderness, a mixed cultural and natural site in Australia representing one of the last expanses of temperate rainforests in the world, have been developed since its first publication in 1992.[13] The revised version contained specific objectives on community engagement to: engage the public in planning and management 'in a meaningful way'; to 'harness community ideas and resources'; to facilitate voluntary activity in management; and to enable better understanding of community values and expectations on the part of the authorities. The plan outlined specific prescriptions in relation to advisory groups, volunteers and community groups. Furthermore, it expressed a commitment to monitoring levels and types of participation of the Tasmanian community in World Heritage-related activities, processes, projects, partnerships and events (Parks and Wildlife Service, 1999, p63).

In 2004, the first State of the Tasmanian Wilderness World Heritage Area Report was produced as a measure to assess and improve management of the area and to make it more open, informed and accountable with evidence-based assessment of management performance (Parks and Wildlife Service, 2004). This included key stakeholder assessment and critical comments and suggestions for improvements. The stakeholder assessments were gathered through targeted questionnaires directed at key stakeholder groups who were invited to assess and provide critical comments on management performance for the area during the first management plan period (1992–1999). For example, in the view of the Tasmanian Aboriginal Land Council, management of Aboriginal heritage had been poor, partly due to a lack of effective communication between the managing agency and the Aboriginal community: 'Despite the frequently stated position of involving the Aboriginal community more in management of the TWWHA, our involvement has been limited to infrequent and inappropriate projects whereby ownership of cultural knowledge has been hijacked by PWS/ Government.' The concern was raised together with the suggestion that the Aboriginal community 'should have greater access to resources and own the cultural information' and that the entire area being an Aboriginal landscape should mean involvement of the Aboriginal in all aspects of management (ibid., p205). Hence, follow-up and monitoring of stakeholder participation measures is necessary in order to achieve implementation of meaningful participation in the management of World Heritage properties.

Good governance: a precondition for sustainable development

Good governance is a prerequisite for sustainable development. This principle was built into the early action programmes on sustainable development that emerged from the Rio Declaration and Agenda 21 in 1992. It was reaffirmed at the Rio+20 Conference on Sustainable Development in 2012, which acknowledged that 'good governance and the rule of law at the national and international levels are essential for sustained, inclusive and equitable economic growth, sustainable development and the eradication of poverty and hunger' (UN, 2012, para252). However, the meaning of good governance is an empirically unexplored concept (Fukuyama, 2013). While transparency and participatory mechanisms have been built into the World Heritage system, there are varying levels of capability amongst different nation states for implementing such measures depending on political tradition, economic capacity and democratic maturity. Furthermore, tendencies towards diminished authority of the advisory bodies, increasing politicization and economics over conservation as a motivator of World Heritage nominations threaten the credibility of the convention.

Diminished authority of the advisory bodies

A shift away from reliance on the advisory bodies in the World Heritage Committee's decisions concerning nominations and registering of sites on the LWHD has been observed. In 2012, the advice of the advisory bodies was overturned in nearly half of the decisions concerning new nominations.[14] In most cases where the advice was 'not to inscribe' a property, the Committee still decided to either 'refer', 'defer' or 'inscribe' the properties concerned on the World Heritage List. Similarly, the Committee has tended to dismiss recommendations to include endangered properties on the LWHD where states parties have opposed this. This has sparked debate and discussion on the future credibility of the convention. As noted by ICOMOS following the 34th Session of the World Heritage Committee in Brasilia in 2010: 'The frequency of occurrences where the Committee's decisions diverged from the recommendations of the Advisory Bodies was noted by many observer State[s] Parties in attendance and was the subject of discussions throughout the session. For some, the cumulative weight of these decisions seemed to imply a desire on the part of the Committee for fewer rigors in demonstrating Outstanding Universal Value, as well as greater leniency concerning the protective structures that the World Heritage Operation[al] Guidelines require to be in place prior to inscription in the World Heritage List' (ICOMOS, 2010b).

This tendency was accentuated the following year at the 35th Session of the World Heritage Committee in Paris in 2011, as noted by ICOMOS President Gustavo Araoz: 'Last year in Brasilia, a trend began to emerge whereby the Committee repeatedly rejected the advice of ICOMOS, and in 44% of the cases proceeded to inscribe sites on the World Heritage List in spite of the fact that in the judgment of ICOMOS the requirements for inscription prescribed by the Operational Guidelines had not been met. Likewise, the Committee chose to ignore the joint advice of ICOMOS and the World Heritage Centre regarding the inclusion of highly threatened sites in the List of the World Heritage Sites in Danger [...] This year these trends were even more accentuated and the strategies and arguments presented by the Committee members to override the Advisory Bodies recommendations seemed to be more carefully planned and orchestrated' (Araoz, 2011).

Similarly, Tim Badman, Director of the IUCN World Heritage Programme, made the following reflection at the end of the 36th Session of the World Heritage Committee in St Petersburg in 2012: 'The Committee chose to react to concerns raised by criticising the advice they get from IUCN and our sister advisory bodies and how it is provided, rather than looking to its own performance [...] a feeling of "shoot the messenger". The effort to transfer responsibility elsewhere for the Committee's wish to not follow its own rules (the operational guidelines which we follow in the advice we give) is pretty disappointing. The fundamental fact is that if the World Heritage Committee does not follow its own written rules, the credibility of the Convention will be lost forever. Central concern lies on the choices the Committee makes when development and economic projects conflict with conservation objectives. In several high profile cases conservation was not the top priority this year' (Badman, 2012).

The advisory bodies, including ICCROM, jointly expressed their concerns in a report to the World Heritage Committee prior to the 2012 meeting: 'The Advisory Bodies note the emergence of general concerns regarding the continued trend for the Committee not to adhere to its own Operational Guidelines in some of its decisions, notably those on nominations. They consider that this trend represents a critical threat to the credibility and reputation of the *World Heritage Convention*, and, if continued, could result in decisions that are impossible to implement' (UNESCO, 2012c, p8).

Different reasons may explain the discrepancy between the advice and the decisions. The Committee has in some cases shown greater leniency towards inscription of sites in under-represented regions, which may be seen as an attempt to fulfil the aims of achieving a globally representative World Heritage List. However, this is not justified where a site does not meet the requirements of OUV. Another factor is the interest of states parties in having their sites inscribed for prestige and economic reasons. Furthermore, the credibility of the composition of the advisory bodies in the use of regional expertise has been questioned by sections within the Committee, who have called for greater transparency of the evaluators on whose assessments advice is based. Committee members representing economically disadvantaged nations also differ in their understanding of the significance and urgency of the inscription of sites. Inscription is often seen as imperative from a conservation point of view, even when considered premature from the point of whether formal management frameworks are in place or not. Moreover, they need to be more assertive in their development trajectories and therefore more prone to accepting development impacts on heritage sites. Some African nations have argued that finding harmony between conservation and infrastructural developments and mining activities are particularly complex issues in Africa, it being a comparatively underdeveloped continent.

Guarding against politicization

The increasing breach between the positions of the advisory bodies and the Committee, besides tendencies of regional alignments in decisions and lobbying activities in connection with the meetings, has led to perceptions of increased politicization of World Heritage Committee decision-making. This threatens the credibility of the World Heritage Convention.

One of the effects of politicization is that it leads to inconsistencies that impact negatively on conservation overall. In relation to the extractive industries, Turner (2012, p30) noted the risk of slackening environmental performance of the private sector: 'Those companies that have adopted a more committed stance towards natural World Heritage Sites have been influenced by their perception that these properties are selected on strictly neutral, technical grounds, and that the World Heritage Committee takes its decisions on this basis. They sometimes gain the impression that this is not fully the case, and that these decisions are less consistently based on technical criteria, and more influenced by other (sometimes apparently political) considerations, than they had expected. Furthermore, they sometimes sense that State Parties themselves are not fully scrupulous in respecting the OUV of their World Heritage properties.' Consequently, the 'no-go area' commitment of firms in protected areas, which has protected these from exploration of oil and minerals and so on, may be deemed both commercially disadvantageous and inefficient in securing conservation goals. The development of specific policy may prevent inconsistencies in decisions. In 2013, IUCN outlined its position in an advice note on mining and oil/gas projects, stating that this should not be permitted within natural World Heritage sites, or if located outside World Heritage sites should not impact on these. Furthermore, boundary changes should not be used to facilitate mining activities (IUCN, 2013a).

There are several examples where states parties have sought to modify the boundaries of properties due to exploration and development interests in an area. For example, the Virgin Komi Forests in Russia was proposed for inscription on the LWHD in 2011 following a joint World Heritage Centre/IUCN reactive monitoring mission to the site due to gold mining and boundary changes to the Yugyd Va National Park, the northern component of the property, which removed the legal protection status of part of the property.[15] The mission considered that 'mineral exploration and exploitation are not acceptable within World Heritage properties' and that 'the State Party should be urged to immediately reverse the boundary changes made to the property and to halt the gold mining project', (UNESCO, 2011d, pp52–53). The site was not placed on the in danger list, although the Committee urged the state party to follow the recommendation of IUCN at several Committee meetings.

The Committee decisions, particularly those contrary to the recommendations of the advisory bodies, are often characterized by alignment on the basis of regional affiliation and political like-mindedness. For example, northern European countries have shown a stronger commitment to abiding by the recommendations of ICOMOS, ICCROM and IUCN.[16] Furthermore, emerging economies have tended to unite on development-related issues affecting World Heritage properties. Additionally, politicization has been observed in geo-politically sensitive decisions where secret ballot was required, something that may intensify in the future. In 2012, the Birthplace of Jesus: Church of the Nativity and the Pilgrimage Route, Bethlehem, was inscribed as a Palestinian World Heritage property on an emergency basis for reasons of threats to the site posed by the political situation. While ICOMOS favoured resubmission of the property through the normal nomination process, since technical expertise confirmed that the situation could not be referred to as an emergency situation, the site was nevertheless inscribed on an emergency basis through secret ballot in which 13 of 19 valid votes were in favour.

Lobbying in connection with World Heritage Committee meetings may also jeopardize the credibility of the convention. The objectivity of decisions is at risk when states parties seek the approval of their agendas behind the scenes of the Committee decisions. States parties may gain an advantage by organizing side events at the meetings that may contribute to creating favourable outcomes of Committee decisions. Countries differ in their abilities to lobby both in terms of the size of their delegations and in their financial capacities.

World Heritage governance and sustainability

Good governance is imperative in order for World Heritage sites to be used as platforms for achieving sustainable development. Principles of good governance such as rule of law, participation, transparency, accountability and so on must be achieved at all levels.[17] The World Heritage Convention has provided opportunities for participatory approaches to gain firmer ground in heritage management, particularly through its close relationship with other UN programmes and objectives such as the protection of rights of indigenous peoples and local communities. Furthermore, transparency through international auspices of heritage sites has brought greater awareness of local conservation issues and concerns.

Nevertheless, the conflictual nature of heritage and the unequal positions of participants in the World Heritage process remain a major challenge: e.g. indigenous peoples whose traditional livelihoods may not receive the same recognition as private landowners and business people whose activities are founded within state-based frameworks, regulations and legal systems. Similarly, political difficulties can occur in determining who represents whom at the different stages of the World Heritage process. Furthermore, there is a risk that World Heritage properties will be used to suit the needs of the state party, e.g. through site boundary modification. Another challenge to good governance may be limited resources to facilitate broad inclusion, in terms of both monetary and cultural capital. It is an expensive and time-consuming process to engage an extensive range of stakeholders in participatory decision-making and planning for heritage conservation and management. It also requires adequate skill sets to negotiate consensus solutions, organize and disseminate necessary information and collect and store relevant data.

Attempts have been made to link principles of good governance in environmental conservation and heritage management. Borrini-Feyerabend et al. (2006) demonstrated ways for managers in addressing good governance in protected areas. For example, participation should be ensured through encouragement of free expression of views and fostering trust between stakeholders. Furthermore, consensus orientation can be addressed by fostering dialogue and achieving collective agreements. Also, equity is respected by ensuring fairness of opportunity for all stakeholders in the management plan process and promotion of participatory mechanisms for decision-making.

Notes

1 The term acceptance is used in addition to ratification merely to provide for differences in the constitutional procedures at the nation-state level.
2 The ratification status of states parties is updated on the World Heritage Centre website, see http://whc.unesco.org/en/statesparties/.
3 On 29 November 2012 the UN General Assembly voted to accord Palestine 'non-member observer state' status in the UN, with 138 votes in favour, 9 against and 41 abstentions.
4 The outgoing members in 2013 were: Cambodia, Estonia, Ethiopia, France, Iraq, Mali, Mexico, Russian Federation, South Africa, Switzerland, Thailand and United Arab Emirates (see UNESCO, 2013d).
5 Ms Irina Bokova has been Director-General of UNESCO since 15 November 2009 and was elected for a second term in 2013. Ms Mechtild Rössler was appointed Director of the World Heritage Centre in 2015.
6 Africa 2009 was a partnership project undertaken in cooperation with African cultural heritage organizations, UNESCO and the International Centre on Earthen Architecture (CRATerre-EAG).
7 There are 101 National Committees of ICOMOS with scope for further committee formations, particularly in Africa.
8 The Scientific Council was established under the Eger-Xi'an Principles for International [Scientific] Committees of ICOMOS in July 2008.

9   This rule has been questioned in proposals to reform the UN system since states differ significantly in population size, economic power and international contribution.

10   The Commission on Global Governance was an independent organization established in 1992 with the support of the UN Secretary-General Boutros Boutros-Gali. It produced a report 'Our Global Neighbourhood' criticized by pro-sovereign movements objecting to increased influence of the United Nations.

11   See paras 12, 40, 64, 108, 111, 117, 119 and 123 (UNESCO, 2015).

12   The CNRM approach was defined based on the following: a commitment to involve members of the local community and local institutions in the conservation/management of natural resources; attempts to devolve power from central state government to local institutions and indigenous peoples; linking the objectives of socioeconomic development and environmental conservation; legitimization of local and/or indigenous resource and property rights; integration of traditional values and knowledge in modern resource management (Billgren & Holmén, 2008).

13   The Tasmanian Wilderness stretches across over 1 million hectares and gives testimony to human occupation for over 20,000 years. It was inscribed on the World Heritage List based on seven of the ten cultural and natural criteria for defining OUV – (iii), (iv), (vi), (vii), (viii), (ix) and (x).

14   Of the 27 new nominations evaluated in 2012, only 22 were decided upon since 5 nominations were withdrawn. Of these, the Committee decision was different from the recommendations of the advisory bodies in 10 of the nominations.

15   The site covers 3.28 million ha of tundra and mountain tundra in the Urals and one of the most extensive areas of virgin boreal forest remaining in Europe. It was inscribed for its valuable evidence of the natural processes affecting biodiversity in the taiga.

16   In 2011, Committee members Australia, Estonia, Sweden and Switzerland more frequently concurred in the opinions of the Advisory Bodies concerning inscriptions on the World Heritage List and LWHD.

17   UNDP (2007) established characteristics of good governance relating to: participation, rule of law, transparency, responsiveness, consensus orientation, equity, effectiveness and efficiency, accountability and strategic vision.

4

IMPLEMENTING THE WORLD HERITAGE CONVENTION

The implementation of the World Heritage Convention is supported by an evolving system of guidelines, principles and strategies. This adaptable approach reflects the ongoing development of key concepts and ideas on World Heritage; its meanings, values, conservation, presentation and governance. The key instruments for implementing the convention are the World Heritage List, the List of World Heritage in Danger (LWHD) and the process for monitoring the state of conservation of World Heritage properties.

In identifying heritage properties of universal significance, the Committee is limited in choice to properties nominated by the states parties to the convention. Therefore, as argued by Ashworth and van der Aa (2006, p149), the World Heritage List 'largely depends on each state party's ability and willingness to nominate sites [...] Thus World Heritage inscription is a compromise reaction among national governments to national nominations and interests.' This implies that the list is heavily influenced by the priorities of national governments which would appear to contradict the very concept of the World Heritage List, i.e. a highly selective and exclusive register of heritage sites of universal importance.

However, the identification and conservation of World Heritage is changing and evolving in line with international discourse on heritage, the environment and sustainable development. In the context of the convention, it is possible to see an expansion of the concept of heritage value from one which 'tends to emphasize the material basis of heritage' (Smith, 2006, p3) to one which incorporates a more diversified and holistic approach recognizing socio-cultural processes and a more anthropological conception. This chapter takes a closer look at key policies and strategies in implementing the convention and the contribution of new approaches to the conservation of heritage of outstanding universal value (OUV) through a credible World Heritage List.

World Heritage policy

The Operational Guidelines for Implementing the World Heritage Convention (hereinafter referred to as the Operational Guidelines) are fundamental to the implementation of the convention, both as a methodological tool, and in the bringing together of principles and strategies to address key issues and concerns relating to World Heritage properties. The guidelines are guided by the strategic objectives, which are periodically reviewed by the World Heritage Committee in order to facilitate the implementation of the convention and in an attempt to ensure that new threats and challenges to World Heritage are addressed effectively (UNESCO, 2015b). The nomination of properties to the World Heritage List, although an extensive process, is not an end in itself. Conservation of World Heritage properties, once inscribed on the List, is a primary objective of the convention and, therefore, monitoring of their state of conservation is a fundamental activity. Many properties become endangered due to natural and man-made causes that may impact negatively on their conservation, sometimes to the extent that they need to be placed on the LWHD for urgent actions to be taken by the states parties.

Operational Guidelines

The first version of the Operational Guidelines was adopted at the first Session of the World Heritage Committee in 1977. It then consisted of a 16-page document which set out the general principles for the implementation of the convention based around four principal procedures: to draw up a World Heritage List, to prepare a LWHD, to determine how best to use the World Heritage Fund, and to assist member states in the conservation of their properties of OUV (UNESCO, 1977b). The Operational Guidelines has grown into a critically important document of over 160 pages, which provides extensive information, not only to the Committee and Secretariat, but to the states parties, site managers, stakeholders and other partners on how to meet the requirements of the convention.[1]

The Operational Guidelines have evolved to include new provisions to meet the aim of establishing 'an effective system of collective protection of cultural and natural heritage of outstanding universal value in accordance with modern scientific methods' (UNESCO, 1972, preamble). A recent addition to the principal procedures for the implementation of the convention is 'the mobilization of national and international support in favour of the convention', which first appeared in 2005.[2] The debate around sourcing funds and raising awareness for World Heritage had been ongoing for many years. In 1992, a critical evaluation of the implementation of the convention highlighted that at that time, the World Heritage List only represented half the world's countries. Furthermore, most of the states parties to the convention 'lack or have insufficient human and financial resources [and] that the machinery provided for the convention is sadly lacking. Even more widespread [were] situations in which there [were] very few associations to support government heritage-conservation work, and in which promotional activities are either non-existent or insignificant' (UNESCO,1992a, para5.5). This led to the development of a strategy to increase public awareness, involvement and support of the convention.[3]

The fact that the Operational Guidelines are regularly revised has resulted in significant changes to the text over the years to incorporate new knowledge and concepts in the context of heritage values and conservation. The inclusion of the cultural landscape criteria in 1992 triggered further changes to the wording of the Operational Guidelines, such as affirming for the first time that the participation of local people in the nomination process was essential, as well as recognizing, also for the first time, customary law and traditional management practices as viable strategies in the protection and management of World Heritage sites. The term sustainable was also introduced to the guidelines, in the acknowledgement that the 'protection of cultural landscapes can contribute to modern techniques of sustainable land-use and can maintain and or enhance natural values in the landscape' (UNESCO, 1995b, annex 3; Rössler, 2003/2005). These developments had wider implications in the implementation of the convention and reflected international policies and standards emerging in relation to global action on sustainable development, for example, Agenda 21 from the United Nations Conference on Environment and Development (UNCED) in 1992. This included a paradigm shift in natural heritage conservation; moving from exclusionary protected areas to involving local and indigenous peoples in the governance and management of natural resources and consequently linking biodiversity conservation to the conservation of cultural diversity (Philips, 1998; 2005). Similarly a 'human rights' perspective was emerging which recognized the rights of local people and indigenous peoples to access, manage and govern the use of biological resources as an inseparable aspect of their cultural identity and survival (Logan, 2012). The international standards in sustainability and empowerment for the protection of cultural and natural heritage are reflected in the best practice strategies and strategic objectives of the convention.

Best practices and strategic objectives

Maintaining the credibility of the World Heritage List requires strategic planning and implementation of best practices in identifying, conserving and managing such sites. World Heritage sites are recognized as the most exceptional heritage places in the world and as such should act as models for best practice conservation. Because of the large number and variety of World Heritage properties it is not possible to apply a single, universal, best practice approach to the conservation and management of every site. However, general strategic objectives, identified by the World Heritage Committee, play an important role as guiding principles that underlie the aims of the convention and act as benchmarks for its implementation.

The 2002 Budapest Declaration on World Heritage, adopted at the 26th Session of the World Heritage Committee in Budapest, reaffirmed the commitment of the Committee to the notions of universality and heritage diversity as central features of the convention and important tools for achieving sustainable development through dialogue and mutual understanding.[4] Furthermore, the Committee recognized that World Heritage was faced with increasing challenges and recommended a number of measures to address these, such as: inviting states parties to reflect a diverse range of cultural and natural heritage in their new nominations; seeking to achieve a balance between conservation, sustainability and development; highlighting the need to cooperate in the protection of heritage; promoting World Heritage through communication, education, research and training; and seeking the active involvement of local communities in identifying, protecting and managing World Heritage properties (UNESCO, 2002).

In order to achieve this, the Committee established four key objectives relating to Credibility, Conservation, Capacity-building and Communication. These objectives, together with the later addition of a fifth objective for Communities,[5] have become known as the '5 Cs', or the five strategic objectives of the convention. The '5 Cs' are described in the Operational Guidelines as follows (UNESCO, 2015b, para26):

- Strengthen the Credibility of the World Heritage List;
- Ensure the effective Conservation of World Heritage Properties;
- Promote the development of effective Capacity-building in States Parties;
- Increase public awareness, involvement and support for World Heritage through Communication;
- Enhance the role of Communities in the implementation of the World Heritage Convention.

The Budapest Declaration states that the aim of best practices and strategic objectives should be 'to ensure an appropriate and equitable balance between conservation, sustainability and development, so that World Heritage properties can be protected through appropriate activities contributing to the social and economic development and the quality of life of our communities' (UNESCO, 2002, para3c). The five Cs provide a fundamental framework for the implementation of the convention and inform best practices for the protection and sustainable management of sites. However, strategic objectives are changeable and reflect the interpretations and concerns of their time. For example, in the early years of the convention it was considered good practice to prepare World Heritage nominations at the government level without consulting local communities and other stakeholders (Rössler, 2012). The Operational Guidelines stated that in order 'to maintain the objectivity of the evaluation process and to avoid possible embarrassment to those concerned', states parties should refrain from publically indicating that a site was being considered for

World Heritage status (UNESCO, 1992b, para14). Clearly, the intention here was to avoid disappointment and blame where nominations were not successful. Fifteen years later, in 2007, the right of indigenous peoples and local people to have a meaningful role in identifying how their heritage is identified and managed in a World Heritage context became one of the objectives informing best practice in implementing the convention.

Reporting and monitoring

In order to ensure that the states parties are fulfilling their duties under the convention, the World Heritage Committee has established a system of measures for reporting and monitoring of the condition of World Heritage properties.[6] There are two main methods, namely 'periodic monitoring' and 'reactive monitoring'. Periodic reporting is implemented through regular invitations to states parties to submit a report that gives a review of the state of conservation of each property within their territories. This review follows a 'Six-year Periodic Reporting Cycle', and is implemented on a regional basis. In other words, regional strategies that run over a six-year period are established for each world region and are expressed in the Regional State of the World Heritage Report. Following the submission of periodic reports, the Committee reviews the reports at its annual session at which decisions are made concerning any actions that need to be taken. These actions may involve the inclusion of a property on the LWHD, deletion from the World Heritage List or the sending of a reactive monitoring mission to a specific site or property.

Reactive monitoring is required for properties that are facing specific threats that are serious enough to warrant consideration of deleting the property from the World Heritage List or of inscribing the property on the LWHD. The intention behind this mechanism is to offer the states parties concerned technical support in order to avoid such steps. A reactive monitoring mission is usually carried out jointly by the World Heritage Centre and representatives of the advisory bodies. The reactive monitoring reports include information on the scale of the threats and whether there have been improvements in the conservation of a property since the last report to the Committee. The reports also follow up on the implementation of previous decisions of the Committee and evaluate any damage and loss of OUV, including aspects of integrity and authenticity.

Since the introduction of the convention, the Secretariat has together with the advisory bodies reviewed thousands of reports on the state of conservation of World Heritage properties. This mechanism has resulted in 'one of the most comprehensive monitoring systems of any international convention' (UNESCO, 2012f, para5). In 2012, the Secretariat presented a report at the 36th Session of the Committee Meeting in St Petersburg, which drew the attention of the Committee to a number of recurrent issues affecting the state of conservation of properties in that year (based on examination of 144 properties). In terms of the nature of the threats, it was noted that globally:

'The main groups of threats affecting the properties are due to management issues, development projects, illegal activities (such as poaching and illegal logging), social and cultural uses of heritage (mainly, impact of tourism activities), transportation infrastructures (mainly construction of roads), biological resource use or modification (such as encroachment, cattle grazing), physical resource extraction (mostly due to mining-related activities). A significant proportion of the properties are also affected by utilities infrastructures, mostly development of dams' (UNESCO, 2012f, para2).

A comprehensive State of Conservation Information System has been established to address the growing body of data and need for systematic monitoring and recording of threats. This computerized information system consists of a database of the reports on properties examined by the Committee since 1979. It is hosted on the UNESCO World Heritage Centre website and is publicly available for all stakeholders of the convention. The Information System is an exceptional tool that allows for comprehensive analyses of the threats affecting the properties, their evolution over time, and examples of mitigation measure and effective strategies for tackling said threats (WHC, 2015a).

World Heritage List

The World Heritage List constitutes the full list of properties that have been confirmed by the World Heritage Committee as sites of OUV. The first twelve properties, eight cultural and four natural, were inscribed on the List at the second session of the Committee in 1978.[7] From these modest beginnings the List has continued to grow so that by 2016 the number had grown beyond 1,050. The List is published on the UNESCO World Heritage Centre website. The entries for each property on the List contains both a summary and long description of the property in question and includes links to relevant maps, documents, images and other details, such as year of inscription, the criteria for which it merits OUV, size of the property and so on.

Nominations to the World Heritage List are not considered unless the nominated property has already been included on the state party's tentative list (UNESCO, 2015b, para63). A tentative list is an inventory of sites that states parties consider to be of potential OUV and which they intend to nominate for World Heritage designation in the future (UNESCO, 2015b, para 62). The tentative list, together with a brief description of the properties and justification of their OUV, must be submitted to the Secretariat, which, after presenting it to the Committee, publishes the details on the World Heritage Centre website. States parties are encouraged to reexamine and resubmit their tentative list at least every ten years (UNESCO, 2015b, para65).

The inscription of sites on the World Heritage List has become such a prestigious symbol for states parties, for reasons such as tourism and raised international profile, that new inscriptions are added every year and the List is updated annually rather than every two years as originally envisaged in the convention text (UNESCO, 1972, article 2.2). There is often a sense of celebration and achievement at the Committee Meetings when a site is approved for inscription. In 2012, the delegation of Chad celebrated when the Lakes of Ounianga was inscribed as the country's first World Heritage property. Not only did the designation represent an acknowledgement of the enormous efforts that were required to prepare a nomination by a country with comparatively reduced technical and administrative capacities, but it would do much to improve the image of Chad, a country normally associated with war, conflict and strife.

List of World Heritage in Danger

Properties are considered for inscription on the LWHD when threats such as armed conflict, natural disasters and urban encroachment imperil the values and criteria for which a property was first designated. Considering the original spirit and intent of the convention, which was to ensure international mobilization for the conservation of threatened sites, the World Heritage Committee inscribe threatened properties on the LWHD to raise awareness of their plight. The list consists of properties that require major conservation actions for which assistance has been requested and allows the Committee to highlight the threats and publicize the need for major operations and aid from the international community.

A property may only be inscribed on the LWHD if it is already on the World Heritage List. The first property to be inscribed on the LWHD was the Natural and Cultural-Historical Region of Kotor, Montenegro (formerly Yugoslavia) in 1979 (Figure 4.1). This cultural property was simultaneously inscribed on the World Heritage List and the LWHD at the 3rd Session of the World Heritage Committee in response to an appeal for aid following devastating earthquakes. The earthquakes caused considerable damage to the monuments of the historic towns and settlements within the site. The property was not removed from the LWHD until 2003 following extensive restoration of the damaged buildings.

It is the states parties' responsibility to draw the Committee's attention to existing threats to properties situated within their jurisdictions, but individuals, non-governmental organizations, or other groups may also inform the Committee about potential and/or imminent dangers (UNESCO, 2015b, para172). In urgent cases such as the outbreak of war, the Committee can recommend that an affected property be placed on the LWHD without having received a formal request. Once a property has been inscribed on the LWHD, the Committee develops a series of recommendations and required actions, in consultation with the relevant state party, to ensure that the property's values are restored or that the threat will be dissipated so that the property can achieve a 'desired state of conservation' (UNESCO, 2015b, para183). On meeting the required corrective measures, the property is removed from the LWHD and consequently monitored regularly with annual reviews of its state of conservation.

FIGURE 4.1 Kotor city walls, Montenegro (credit: Guy Teague)

A property inscribed on the LWHD receives consistent attention from the Committee, the advisory bodies and the wider conservation community. The Committee considers every site on the LWHD annually and decides on one of the following actions: to maintain the property on the LWHD; to request additional measures for the conservation of the property; to delete the property from the LWHD; or consider the deletion of the property from both the LWHD and the World Heritage List (UNESCO, 2015b, para191). In some instances circumstances prevent the Committee from making informed decisions about the state of conservation of endangered properties, for example where the situation on the ground is too dangerous to monitor a site. In the 1990s, the five World Heritage properties within the Democratic Republic of the Congo were placed on the LWHD as a result of armed conflict. As of 2016, the properties have been on the LWHD for an average of 21 years. The conditions continue to be dangerous and in 2012 tragedy struck one of the sites, the Okapi Wildlife Reserve, when seven park staff were killed by armed rebels and many more were taken hostage or have disappeared.

In recent years it has become apparent that not all states parties view the inscription on the LWHD as a positive step to alleviate the threats and pressures on World Heritage sites situated within their territories. While some states parties request inscription on the LWHD in order to call for international support, others perceive it as an international criticism or disapproval of their management of the sites. Increasingly, there is a perception of the LWHD as a way of punishing states parties, rather than as an effective conservation tool to protect World Heritage as was originally intended. This shift in opinion has accompanied the increasing use of properties for the purposes of tourism and economic development. States parties resist inscription on the LWHD because of the risk of unfavourable media attention and the potential damage to the image and reputation of the site as a tourist destination.

Delisted sites

Two properties have been deleted from the World Heritage List: the Arabian Oryx Sanctuary of Oman, delisted in 2007 and Dresden Elbe Valley in Germany, delisted in 2009. The Arabian Oryx Sanctuary was inscribed as a natural site in 1994 and deleted from the World Heritage List in 2007 following plans by the government to reduce the area of the site by 90 per cent in order to allow oil exploration.

The inscription of the Arabian Oryx Sanctuary on the World Heritage List in 1994 was controversial because it went against the recommendations of the advisory body. IUCN advised that the property did not meet the conditions of integrity and the nomination should be deferred. Although the site supported species of international interest, such as the Arabian gazelle, *Gazella gazelle cora,* the houbara bustard, *Chlamydotis macqueenii,* and the last wild population of the Arabian oryx, *Oryx leucoryx,* which had been reintroduced into the area in the 1980s (Figure 4.2), the long-term viability of the natural values of the site was in serious doubt. The nominated site was not an established protected area and was a legally undefined zone without a management plan or management body in place. The vegetation in the area was deteriorating rapidly due to unregulated human exploitation and livestock damage, and the population of Arabian oryx was at that time too small to guarantee that the species would survive into the future (IUCN, 1994). Prophetically, IUCN also warned of the danger of potential oil exploration (ibid.), which would be a consistent threat while the boundaries remained undefined. The Committee decided to inscribe the site under natural criterion (iv), which in 1994 reflected the importance of the site for in-situ conservation of biological diversity and threatened species. The Committee decision was based largely on political considerations. It noted that it was satisfied with the political will of the Omani Government to implement a management regime and to define the exact boundaries of the site (UNESCO, 1994b). However, the Omani government never fulfilled its obligations. From 1995 to 2006 the World Heritage Committee made repeated requests for the state party to submit details of a management plan and defined boundaries for the site. In 2006, the state party informed an IUCN monitoring mission that the area of the property was to be reduced to 10 per cent of its former size to allow oil and gas exploration. In response to a letter from the World Heritage Centre indicating that this action was in violation of the convention and the Operational Guidelines, the state party of Oman invited the Committee to delete the property from the World Heritage List in 2007 (UNESCO, 2007b).

Dresden Elbe Valley, located in Saxony at the City of Dresden, was inscribed as an 18th and 19th centuries cultural landscape based on four cultural criteria in 2004. The valley was described as an outstanding example of land use, representing an exceptional development of a major Central European city. The art collections, architecture, gardens and landscape features of the valley were recognized for their contribution to Central European developments in the 18th and 19th centuries (UNESCO, 2004). ICOMOS classified Dresden Elbe Valley as a continuing cultural landscape in its evaluation (ICOMOS, 2004a). In other words, a landscape in which the evolutionary cultural process is still in progress. This stands in contrast to a relict landscape in which the evolutionary process has come to an end at some time in the past. A continuing cultural landscape may be viewed as one in which dynamic change should be possible.

In 2006, the World Heritage Committee inscribed Dresden Elbe Valley on the LWHD as a result of the approval, by Dresden City Council, of a proposal to build the Waldschlösschen Bridge (Figure 4.3). The construction planning had already begun following a referendum which resulted in more than a two-thirds majority vote by the citizens of Dresden in favour of the bridge (Schoch, 2014). However, the Committee considered the bridge development to irreversibly damage the values and integrity of the property based on the findings of an independent visual impact study (UNESCO, 2006a). The Committee gave the German authorities an ultimatum by stating it was inscribing the property on the LWHD, with a view to considering delisting the property from the World Heritage List if the plans were carried out (ibid.). However, instead of delisting in 2007, the Committee decided to send reactive monitoring missions in 2008. The reactive monitoring mission also concluded that the bridge would irrevocably damage the OUV of the cultural landscape (UNESCO, 2009c). The threat of delisting became very real following the deletion of the Arabian Oryx Sanctuary from the World Heritage List in 2007. However, in 2009, the state party submitted a report confirming that the bridge foundations had been completed and the development would go ahead as planned. Consequently, the Committee decided to delete the Dresden Elbe Valley from the List (ibid.).

FIGURE 4.2 The Arabian oryx (credit: Charles Sharp)

FIGURE 4.3   Waldschlösschen Bridge, Dresden (credit: Bertram Nudelbach)

Arguably, since the Dresden Elbe Valley was inscribed as a continuing cultural landscape, the valley should be seen as a cultural product shaped by dynamic change. However, in its justification for recommending delisting, ICOMOS stressed that the statement of OUV had made a clear link to the visual beauty of the landscape and its impact on landscape painting by celebrated painters as well as writers and poets (ICOMOS, 2004a). Thus, the statement of OUV became a key reference point for the Committee's decision. In this case, the visual value of the site, as manifested by the 19th century painters, constituted a key component of the OUV. Unlike Oman, which was fully aware that the decision to allow oil and gas exploration would irretrievably damage the OUV of the Arabian Oryx Sanctuary, the state party of Germany made substantial efforts to engage with the concerns of the Committee. Dresden City Council considered alternative options, such as building a tunnel or reducing the scale of the bridge, to maintain the site on the List. However, these options were ultimately considered unviable from an environmental point of view. Overall, the situation may have been avoided if, at the time of inscription, the state party had made it clear to the Committee that plans for the bridge were in place as advised in the Operational Guidelines (UNESCO, 2015b, para172).

Improving the representativity of the List

The nature of the expansion of the World Heritage List has invited considerable debate over the years. By the 20th anniversary of the convention, there were serious concerns about the imbalance between the number of cultural and natural properties listed and in the distribution of properties across the world. The introduction of the cultural landscape category encouraged a more holistic view of the interaction between people and the environment and opened up opportunities for a greater representation of cultural diversity on the List. In 1994, the Global Strategy for a Representative, Balanced and Credible World Heritage List was launched to ensure that the World Heritage List reflects the global diversity of heritage and to guide the Committee in improving the regional and conceptual representation of heritage of OUV.

Balance between cultural and natural sites

In terms of numbers, cultural properties have dominated the World Heritage List since the first inscriptions in 1978. This is despite the Committee's concern, since its first meeting in 1977, that efforts should be made to ensure that the List reflects a balance between cultural and natural properties (UNESCO, 1977b, para18). Nonetheless, by 2016, there were 802 cultural sites, 197 natural sites and 32 mixed sites. The chart below illustrates the number of properties in each category that have been inscribed since 1978 (see Figure 4.4).

In 1980, the Committee approved a series of measures in an attempt to improve the balance between cultural and natural heritage. These measures included recommendations to states parties to engage the relevant authorities from both cultural and natural sectors to develop and update their tentative lists. Similarly, the Committee stipulated that it should give priority to nominations of properties that were underrepresented and to ensure that there was a balance in the number of experts from cultural and natural fields represented on the Committee's bureau. States parties were also encouraged to promote experts in the field of cultural and natural heritage as their representatives at the Committee meetings in compliance with the convention (UNESCO, 1980b). The predominance of cultural site nominations continued nonetheless.

A critical analysis of the convention in 1992 raised the question as to whether cultural and natural heritage inscriptions should be equivalent in number, or even aim for equal numbers (Pressouyre, 1996, p20). One of the inherent difficulties in trying to achieve a balance in numbers has been the differences in size of the properties as a result of the application of the standards of integrity (ibid.). Natural properties have necessarily been large in size to meet the conditions of integrity required to conserve on-going geological processes (criterion viii), ongoing ecological and biological processes (criterion ix) and natural habitats for endangered species (criterion x). In contrast, during the early years of the convention, cultural sites often occurred at a much smaller scale, and consequently in greater numbers, as isolated monuments and groups of buildings. Lately, the size of cultural properties has increased in line with new understandings of cultural landscapes, historic urban landscapes and cultural routes. However, the size of natural properties also continues to increase as international concern grows over the loss of resilience of fragmented ecosystems.

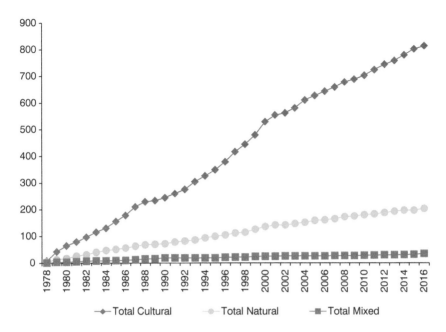

FIGURE 4.4 Number of cultural, natural and mixed sites on the World Heritage List 1978–2016 (credit: Claire Cave)

Different approaches to identifying cultural and natural properties have also contributed to the numerical difference in inscriptions. In 1976, IUCN indicated that it would be possible to define major categories that should be represented on the List and prepared a draft list for natural properties. ICOMOS, instead, considered that 'it was not possible to define and list, *a priori*, the major categories or types of monuments and sites of great importance' (UNESCO 1976, paraII.7). The List has been influenced therefore by the different value judgements or different classification systems used in the different disciplines dealing with cultural and natural values. The scientific and systematic approach, which characterizes the study of the natural sciences, determines the identification of properties that represent outstanding examples of different categories of natural heritage, such as biogeographical regions, biodiversity priorities or events in the history of evolution. IUCN has published guidelines identifying potential candidate sites based on analysis of conservation priorities in the marine and terrestrial environments (Abdulla et al., 2013; Bertzky et al., 2013). In contrast, according to ICOMOS, 'cultural heritage is not predisposed to clear classification systems. One of the main reasons for this is the need to take account of qualities, which are subjective, and of the value that society may give to those qualities' (ICOMOS, 2004b, p3).

Cultural landscapes as a holistic approach

In 1992, the World Heritage Convention became the first international legal instrument to protect cultural landscapes and to recognize landscapes as an interface between cultural diversity and biodiversity. Up to then, the distinction between cultural and natural was creating difficulties in recognizing and identifying potential World Heritage sites. The separation of people from nature and the lack of recognition of lived-in working landscapes were exclusionary and made it difficult to realize sustainable solutions to heritage conservation (Philips, 2005). It was hoped that this broadening of the interpretation of what constituted heritage would make the convention more accessible to a wider diversity of cultures.

A truly integrated approach to recognizing landscapes within the World Heritage criteria has been made difficult by article 2 of the convention. Article 2, which defines natural heritage, does not allow for cultural attributes. The definition is limited to biological or physical factors, important for their values to science, conservation or natural beauty and not for their influence on or integration into society. Article 1, which defines cultural sites, allows sites to include natural attributes through the 'combined works of nature and man' and 'their place in the landscape' (UNESCO, 1972). Consequently, landscapes were incorporated as a cultural category under article 1. This has implications with regard to the definition of cultural landscapes in the Operational Guidelines. The definition emphasizes humanized landscapes that have arisen as a result of interactions with the environment. There is less emphasis on biodiversity richness and ecosystem processes that may have come about as a result of human influences. The definition refers to the 'evolution of human society and settlements over time, under the influence of the physical constraints and/or opportunities provided by the natural environment' (UNESCO, 2015b, annex 3). It asserts that protection of cultural landscapes can 'maintain or enhance natural values in the landscape' and support 'biological diversity in many regions of the world' (ibid.). Nevertheless, a cultural landscape can only be inscribed on the World Heritage List based on its cultural characteristics. It could be argued, therefore, that the current approach does not embrace the truly integrated concept of landscapes as embodiments of cultural and natural interactions. This anomaly has been addressed by the use of mixed sites. In the case of the Ecosystem and Relict Cultural Landscape of Lopé-Okanda in Gabon, inscribed on the List as a mixed site in 2007, IUCN recognized that the diversity of habitats is the result of both natural processes and the long-term influence of humans. The interrelationship between humans and biodiversity richness is highlighted under natural criterion (ix) (IUCN, 2007).

The introduction of the cultural landscape category reflects a trend towards a more holistic view of the environment and recognition of the interaction between people and the land. It expands the understanding of cultural heritage beyond a definition of specific monuments, buildings and sites. For Traditional

Owners of the Uluru-Kata Tjuta National Park in Australia and the Maori of Tongariro National Park in New Zealand, the whole landscape has significance and the distinction between natural places and cultural places has little meaning. These sites were originally inscribed as natural sites because the convention had not been equipped to recognize living landscapes. According to Philips (1998, p28), landscapes 'were usually too modified to be acceptable as "natural" sites, and too "natural" to be accepted as cultural sites'. However, the arrival of the cultural landscape concept made a significant contribution to the recognition of intangible values and to the heritage of indigenous peoples. In the case of Tongariro, its re-nomination in 1993 acknowledged the 'fundamental role of the natural landscape, through oral tradition, in defining and confirming the cultural identity of the Maori people' (Lennon, 2006, p457).

The Global Strategy

The World Heritage Committee faced challenges from the earliest inscriptions in achieving equitable regional and cultural representation on the World Heritage List. In 1994, the following gaps and imbalances were identified in relation to cultural heritage sites: European sites were over-represented, as were historic towns and religious buildings compared to other types of property. Sites associated with Christianity outnumbered those associated with other religions and beliefs. Prehistory and the 20th century were under represented and vernacular architecture and all living cultures figured very little on the List (UNESCO, 1994c, para2). One of the critical issues was that 'from its inception the List had been based on an almost exclusively "monumental" concept of cultural heritage' (ibid.). World Heritage needed to acknowledge the significant developments that had been made in scientific and societal understanding of the complex and multidimensional notions of cultural heritage present in cultures across the globe. To enhance the List, designations would have to move towards an anthropological and thematic approach that would 'be receptive to the many and varied cultural manifestations of outstanding universal value through which cultures expressed themselves' (ibid.). The debate about the representation of cultural diversity 'led to one of the major achievements of the World Heritage Convention, namely the intellectual theorization of the heritage field through research of definitions and comparative frameworks' (Cameron & Rössler, 2013, p73).

An imbalance also existed with regard to the regional representation of natural sites in the early years of the convention. The majority of inscribed natural properties occurred within Africa and Europe and North America, while some of the most biodiverse regions of the world were under-represented. To encourage nominations, IUCN regularly produced inventories and guidelines regarding natural sites that it considered of potential World Heritage quality. However, IUCN emphasized that OUV rather than representativity of the earth's ecosystems is the priority for natural World Heritage and, as biodiversity is not evenly distributed or restricted by political boundaries, a geographical balance in the number of natural World Heritage sites is ultimately not achievable. Rather, the coverage of globally significant biodiversity and geodiversity values is important (Bertzky et al., 2013; Magin & Chape, 2004; IUCN, 1982; 2004).

The Global Strategy for a Representative, Balanced and Credible World Heritage List was adopted by the World Heritage Committee in 1994 in order to address the imbalances. The strategy aimed to ensure that the List reflected the global diversity of heritage and to guide the Committee in improving the regional and conceptual representation of heritage of OUV. The mechanisms to achieve this include encouraging countries to become states parties to the convention and promoting efforts to prepare tentative lists and nominations of properties from under-represented categories and regions. In 1996, a group of experts, commissioned by the Committee, recommended that the World Heritage List should be restricted to a minimum number of sites, stating that the critical issue was to fill the gaps in the List while not losing its manageability and credibility through an unreasonable number of inscriptions. Concern had also been expressed that there was an urgent need to focus on the problems of management and protection of existing properties especially those listed as in danger. Failure to conserve the OUV of existing sites would undermine the credibility of the convention (UNESCO, 1996b, para4). The Committee has resisted any calls for a restriction to the number of inscriptions to the List. However, many of the recommendations of the 1996 expert meeting have since been employed. These include the development of a single set of criteria and a common approach to evaluating the integrity of both cultural and natural sites in an effort to bring about a more coherent approach to linking culture and nature.

In 2004, ICOMOS produced a report, known as 'Filling the Gaps', which analysed the cultural properties on the World Heritage List and tentative lists in terms of three frameworks: typological, chronological-regional and thematic. The results highlighted gaps in the List associated with certain types or categories of properties and recommended an applied methodology for identifying and assessing heritage resources at regional levels. The report also concluded that gaps persisted because of the lack of capacity among states parties, including knowledge, resources or formal structures, to successfully nominate properties (ICOMOS, 2004b).

To sum up, the Global Strategy initiated a broad sweep of changes to the implementation of the convention and an unprecedented increase in research to investigate the concept of heritage. The strategy continues to be a critical element of the implementation of the convention and a progress report is presented at each annual Committee meeting. Current work involves efforts to define a global conservation strategy in recognition that conservation is the highest priority of the convention. The conservation strategy aims to include training, capacity building and management to address pressing conservation challenges. Also, it is recommended that priority should be given to international assistance for the conservation and management of existing properties and to make full use of the mechanism of placing sites on the LWHD (UNESCO, 2015g).

Shaping the World Heritage List

The first step in the nomination of properties to the World Heritage List is the creation of a tentative list. Consequently, tentative lists play a critical role in the identification of World Heritage; they are the means by which outstanding universal heritage is elucidated and new interpretations of heritage categories take form. As a result of the Global Strategy for a Representative, Balanced and Credible World Heritage List, the development of tentative lists is supported by regional meetings and comparative and thematic studies organized by the World Heritage Centre and the advisory bodies. Thematic studies are carried out by the advisory bodies to try and identify possible gaps in the representativity of natural and cultural heritage on the List. Once the tentative list is finalized, the states parties prioritize the properties for nomination. Each state party may make up to two nominations per year provided that at least one is a natural property or a cultural landscape. This restriction reflects the aims of the Global Strategy to balance the List and to reduce the number of nominations from states parties with large numbers of inscriptions such as Italy (51), China (50), Spain (45), France (42) and Germany (41).[8]

Tentative list process

The tentative list acts as an indicator for the future content of the World Heritage List. The tentative list enables the Secretariat and the advisory bodies to observe the direction that World Heritage Conservation is taking and allows for analyses to complement the Global Strategy. These analyses include trends in heritage conceptualization and themes at national, regional and biogeographic levels. Because of the significant role that tentative lists play in influencing the imbalances of the List, it is important that those states parties without such inventories prioritize their development and that existing Lists are updated regularly to reflect priorities of conservation and the current thinking on cultural qualities and values (ICOMOS, 2004b). In 2016, out of 193 states parties to the convention, 182 had submitted a tentative list bringing the total number of candidate World Heritage sites to 1,693.

Regional meetings, organized by the Secretariat, the advisory bodies and other relevant stakeholders, for the development and harmonization of tentative lists are becoming increasingly popular and effective. These meetings or workshops encourage states parties to assess their tentative lists in the context of gaps in the World Heritage List and themes that are common to neighbouring countries within a region. This can improve cooperation amongst states parties and encourage collaboration in identifying shared heritage and support in developing nominations for those countries with less capacity. For example, the Secretariat and ICOMOS have been assisting the states parties in Central Asia in identifying new types of property based on the theme of the Silk Road. States parties include the countries of Kazakhstan, Kyrgyzstan, Tajikistan, Turkmenistan and Uzbekistan, among which the average number of inscribed properties in 2016 was three. This process has spurred a series of cooperative meetings and exchange of ideas between the countries, each of which has submitted revised tentative lists adding up to a total of 52 potential properties. The project continues to grow with participation from countries such as Afghanistan, Iran, Italy, Japan and Mongolia. In 2014, the first major success was realized with the inscription of a 5,000 km section of the Silk Road network, the Chang'an-Tianshan Corridor; a serial transboundary route through China, Kazakhstan and Kyrgyzstan (Figure 4.5).

One of the most decisive elements for a state party in developing a tentative list is community involvement. Local support at this early stage of the nomination process is important in dictating the future success of the conservation of heritage properties. The Operational Guidelines remind states parties 'to ensure the participation of a wide variety of stakeholders, including site managers, local and regional governments, local communities, non-governmental organizations (NGOs) and other interested parties and partners in the identification, nomination and protection of World Heritage properties' (UNESCO, 2015b, para12). However, there are many challenges to achieving this objective. Firstly, the states parties represent a diverse range of governance structures, policies and national legislations. Secondly, by the very nature of the convention, governments are responsible for submitting the official documents related to prospective and nominated properties. Consequently, there is a tendency to focus on that which the government experts or dominant socio-political group(s) consider significant in heritage terms rather than consult with local or minority communities (Logan, 2012). Similarly, there is a tendency to identify a wider significance for a property and to broaden the definition of the heritage values to satisfy the international audience rather than give significant recognition to the local values (Witcomb, 2012).

FIGURE 4.5 Tian Shan Mountains of Silk Road, Kyrgyzstan (credit: Thomas Depenbusch)

Thematic and comparative studies

A number of thematic programmes and initiatives have been adopted by the World Heritage Committee with a view to identifying, conserving and managing under-represented types of properties.[9] In addition, to aid in the evaluation of proposed World Heritage properties, ICOMOS and IUCN have been requested to carry out thematic studies. The studies highlight the potential OUV of particular categories of heritage and outline issues relating to the integrity and management of these areas.

IUCN has completed thematic studies on the following: forest protected areas; wetland and marine protected areas; mountain protected areas; volcanoes, caves and karst landscapes; fossil sites; and desert landscapes. The desert landscape study, for example, concluded that there are 'large gaps in the coverage of desert landscapes and geomorphological features in existing World Heritage properties' (Goudie & Seely, 2011, p25). It identified nine potential sites located in Australia, Chad, China, Pakistan, the United Arab Emirates (UAE) and the USA. In 2015, China already had 48 inscribed sites and Australia 19, but UAE and Chad had only one inscribed property each, and neither of their tentative lists included the suggested desert landscapes. Similarly, Pakistan and the USA were fairly well represented on the World Heritage List (6 and 23 inscribed properties respectively), but only the USA had submitted a site for nomination in the last 15 years. The desert landscape study has clearly identified a natural heritage category that had not been recognized or pursued by the states parties. This may reflect the view that these biomes are among the least biodiverse and as such have not been traditionally viewed as important targets for conservation. A study produced by IUCN in 2004 found that less biodiverse habitats such as cold winter deserts and tundra were not represented amongst World Heritage sites (Magin & Chape, 2004).

In the years immediately after the launch of the Global Strategy, ICOMOS completed thematic studies linked to specific types of cultural heritage such as fossil hominid sites, railways, heritage canals and heritage bridges. More recently, ICOMOS has completed thematic studies on silk roads; early human expansion and innovation in the Pacific; astronomy and archaeoastronomy; and cultural landscapes. These themes link back to the programmes and activities adopted by the Committee within the framework of the Global Strategy, such as astronomy and World Heritage; cultural landscapes; and human evolution: adaptations, dispersals and social developments (HEADS). The HEADS theme aims to identify those sites that are outstanding 'demonstrations of traces of the earliest interaction between humankind and the land, early cultural behaviour and creative expressions' (UNESCO, 2014b, para61). It also aims to preserve these vulnerable and ancient properties from progressive deterioration. Rock art is a significant sub-theme within this activity and ICOMOS has completed five thematic studies on rock art based on different regions of the world. The thematic studies highlight the fact that this art form represents one of the basic expressions of human culture over millennia, but also that it faces many serious threats and is extremely vulnerable to destruction (Clottes, 2011). In a vast region such as Central Asia, assessing the rock art sites is challenging, particularly to determine the state of conservation of properties that may contain more than a thousand individual images. The standard of documentation and archives vary from country to country which makes it difficult to understand the significance of different rock art sites and make comparative analyses. The shortage of resources and the lack of enforcement of protective legislation are also recurrent problems. However, the thematic studies provide significant baseline information regarding the types of rock art and their geo-cultural context which will assist in developing nominations as well as recommending strategies to highlight the historic and cultural importance of this heritage and to support much-needed documentation and research (Clottes, 2011).

Preparing nomination files

The nomination process is complex and relies on substantial documentation, which may be one of the key reasons why some countries are not represented on the World Heritage List. As indicated by the growth in size and complexity of the Operational Guidelines, successful nominations increasingly depend on the abilities of the states parties to the convention to draw on well-documented heritage resources informed by principles of diversity and representation. A 'lack of technical capacity to promote nominations, lack of adequate assessments of heritage properties, or lack of an appropriate legal or management framework, which either individually or collectively hinders the development of nominations, or the development of successful nominations' are key factors contributing to lack of representativity from some regions (ICOMOS, 2004b, p94). There are 28 states parties without any properties inscribed on the List and 38 with just one in 2016.[10]

The nomination process begins with the submission of a nomination file. The file should include all necessary information to describe the property and justify its inclusion on the List in accordance with the Operational Guidelines. The nomination files are detailed and expansive documents, often numbering several hundred pages. The justification for inscription, a critical element of the nomination file, includes a comparative analysis as well as a statement of OUV and a statement of integrity and/or authenticity. The comparative analysis can be an unexpectedly difficult task to complete. Here the states parties must compare the property to other similar properties that occur within and beyond the territories of the states parties regardless of whether they are already on the List or not. This often requires specialist expertise that can relate the individual qualities of the nominated property to other sites with similar characteristics and identify the singular features that distinguish the nominated property. The thematic and comparative studies produced by the advisory bodies can play an important role in developing this section of the nomination file.

In the early days of the convention, the nomination files were short and brief, often limited to the name of the property and a brief description followed by contact details for the states parties. In many cases the files did not include a statement of OUV or detailed maps or photographs. In response to the Global Strategy, the World Heritage Committee has asked states parties to retrospectively submit statements of OUV for their inscribed properties.

Typically, more economically developed countries are better equipped to submit comprehensive and successful nomination files. The nomination file for the Prehistoric Pile dwellings around the Alps World Heritage property, a serial site including the six countries of Austria, France, Germany, Italy, Slovenia and Switzerland, was an impressive demonstration of organization, available resources, expertise and cross country coordination. The site is an unusual and complex property consisting of 111 individual archaeological locations of the remains of stilt houses dated from the Neolithic and Bronze Ages which required specific documentation and comprehensive academic support for the justification for inscription. This nomination file was commended by ICOMOS for its presentation, content and accurate inclusion of the information necessary to address the issues and requirements for a successful inscription.

The nomination process follows a strict timetable to ensure that the Secretariat and the advisory bodies have sufficient time to appraise and assess the large number, and increasingly complex, nomination files that are submitted annually. This timetable or nomination cycle takes approximately one and a half years between submission of the nomination file to the Secretariat and the decision of the World Heritage Committee.[11] The states parties are encouraged to make contact with the Secretariat at an early stage in the nomination process to receive guidance and assistance on the preparation of the nomination files. Otherwise, if omissions in documentation or information are identified later on and a file is considered incomplete and rejected, the proposal is delayed for at least a year.

Towards a credible World Heritage List?

The Global Strategy for a Representative, Balanced and Credible World Heritage List has achieved the overarching goals to increase the number of states parties to the convention and the diversification of inscribed properties. By the end of 2016 there were 193 states parties to the convention, compared to 139 in 1994, and over 84 per cent of states parties had at least one property inscribed on the List. Progressively, inscriptions have come to include cultural heritage identified in the ICOMOS 'Filling the Gaps' report, such as prehistoric heritage and rock art, industrial heritage, 20th century properties, cultural routes, cultural landscapes and vernacular architecture, all previously under-represented categories. However, this has not restricted the continued numerical dominance of European cultural properties since European states parties have also been successfully nominating sites in those categories, e.g. the Prehistoric Pile

Dwellings around the Alps and the Decorated Cave of Pont d'Arc, Ardèche, both in France; the Major Mining Sites of Wallonia, Belgium; the Berlin Modernism Housing Estates, Germany; the Vineyard landscape of Piedmont: Langhe-Roero and Monferrato, Italy; and the Decorated Farmhouses of Hälsingland, Sweden.

There has been significant progress in identifying and inscribing much of the world's outstanding terrestrial natural heritage. IUCN has indicated that the majority of the world's biomes contain World Heritage properties (Magin & Chape, 2004). IUCN also stresses that 'not all biomes and habitats contain areas of OUV, even if they otherwise have high conservation values'. Overall it is the role of the world's protected area network at both national and international levels to ensure representativity of the Earth's major biomes and ecosystems (ibid., p111). However, identification of protected areas is often subject to national priorities and political negotiation. Representativity may be a secondary consideration where a protected area designation conflicts with potential resource extraction or development. As a result, protected areas and hence World Heritage designations, tend to be concentrated on land that is otherwise too remote or unproductive to be important economically (Margules & Pressey, 2000).

A recent IUCN report adopted a novel species irreplaceability analysis to identify existing protected areas of global conservation priority that had the potential for World Heritage nomination (Bertzky et al., 2013). This approach was considered highly relevant because the concept of irreplaceability and uniqueness relate strongly to OUV.[12] As more data becomes available, irreplaceability can be applied to identify further conservation priorities such as endangered ecosystems on the IUCN Red List of Threatened Ecosystems (ibid.). In contrast an analysis of the marine environment has found that a large majority of the world's marine biogeographic provinces and geological features do not contain World Heritage properties. States parties are encouraged to increase their efforts, with the support of IUCN and marine scientists, to identify and nominate marine sites of potential OUV (Abdulla et al., 2013).

A significant challenge to the implementation of the Global Strategy is lack of funding. Since the USA withdrew payment of its fees,[13] UNESCO has undergone severe financial constraints and the World Heritage Centre and the advisory bodies are restricted in their ability to implement some of the programmes and initiatives associated with the Global Strategy (UNESCO, 2015g). One such initiative, the Upstream Process, has been affected. The Upstream Process aims to find options for improving and assisting states parties undertaking the arduous task of nominating a property.

Overall the Global Strategy has made enormous strides in improving the credibility of the World Heritage List. It is critical, however, to maintain focus on the state of conservation of the sites after they are inscribed and to ensure that inscription does not become an end in itself. The external auditor to UNESCO recommended that inscriptions on the World Heritage in Danger List should be applied more readily where states parties have failed to adapt appropriate protection and management measures. Similarly, properties that have irremediably lost their

OUV should be deleted from the List (UNESCO, 2011e). Furthermore, the annual evaluation of the progress of the Global Strategy lacks indicators to monitor results and reviews the representation and distribution of heritage sites according to geopolitical boundaries. This type of interpretation makes it difficult to determine the results of the Global Strategy according to the notions of credibility, representativity and balance in an objective manner (ibid.). Appropriate indicators could emphasize the representation of properties according scientific criteria, such as biogeographical provinces with regard to natural properties, and spatio-temporal grids by type of heritage, epoch and civilization for cultural properties.

Towards a regional approach

A regional approach is increasingly being brought to the implementation of the World Heritage Convention. International discussions around sustainable development and climate change have shifted perspectives from one of local conservation to a realization that transnational collaboration is required to address challenges that transcend the legal and geographic reach of national borders. A regional approach has been extended to the process of periodic reporting. This provides a mechanism for regional cooperation and exchange of information and experiences among states parties concerning World Heritage. Furthermore, there is increasing recognition that individual properties and sites are not isolated islands of conserved heritage, but part of larger environmental systems with cultural and natural linkages over a widespread area. World Heritage properties have the potential to contribute to the large-scale planning required to address issues of connectivity and to improve the capacity of fragmented landscapes to provide the ecosystem services upon which we rely.

Regional periodic reporting and cooperation

Periodic reporting became an official monitoring tool for the World Heritage system in 1998 when the procedures were incorporated into the Operational Guidelines. This followed years of debate about protecting state sovereignty while at the same time recognizing the need for the World Heritage Committee to receive information on the state of conservation of World Heritage sites (Cameron & Rossler, 2013). The Operational Guidelines state that 'States Parties are requested to submit reports to the UNESCO General Conference through the World Heritage Committee on the legislative and administrative provisions they have adopted and other actions which they have taken for the application of the *Convention*' (UNESCO, 2015b, para199). The requirements of the periodic reports include an overview of the general obligations of the state party to the convention as well as the state of conservation of World Heritage properties within their territories. The general obligations include adopting policies which give heritage a function in the life of the community; providing services to protect, conserve and present heritage; developing scientific and technical studies and research to prevent and mitigate threats; fostering centres for training; ensuring appropriate legal, administrative and financial measures are in place; and helping other states parties (UNESCO, 1972, articles 5–6).

The World Heritage Committee has established a six-year periodic reporting cycle based on a regional approach. The regional approach encourages states parties to work together to meet their obligations under the convention and provides a platform for sharing knowledge and experience on how to deal with issues specific to a particular region. The periodic reports have been published in the World Heritage Centre Paper Series (e.g. Periodic Report Africa, 2003; Periodic Report and Regional programmes Arab States, 2004; Periodic Report Latin America & the Caribbean, 2004; Understanding World Heritage in Asia and the Pacific Region, second cycle 2010–2012; Understanding World Heritage in Europe and North America, second cycle 2012–2015). The reports describe the numerous national, regional and international meetings and workshops which were organized by the states parties to encourage active participation in implementing the convention. In the Asia-Pacific region, for example, a significant challenge was to collect baseline data in order to begin to identify and evaluate threats, legislation and management issues. The regional periodic reporting exercise has allowed for the establishment of regional databases for and by states parties to enable effective networking and assessment of trends and strategies in heritage conservation. The meetings are supported by the World Heritage Fund and other extra-budgetary funds. For example, the Government of Japan granted funds under the UNESCO Japan-Funds-in-Trust programme to support Asian states parties.

The dissemination of information and identification of common challenges and difficulties in terms of conservation policies, practices and promotional activities is critical to identifying solutions and monitoring progress in states parties' effectiveness in implementing the convention. In the Arab region, the reporting exercise demonstrated that efforts to integrate heritage in national management and development policies were at an embryonic stage. Institutional frameworks in the Arab region were strongly centralized which meant that heritage services were largely unequipped to meet the needs for the preservation of heritage because of a lack of integration into the wider economic and social frameworks. Reports recognized that while all the Arab states parties had undertaken scientific and technical studies on heritage within their countries, the majority were carried out by foreign consultants. In response, the World Heritage Committee organized national review meetings to address the problems identified by individual states parties as well as regional thematic expert meetings and capacity building workshops to advise on the identification of underrepresented heritage (World Heritage Centre, 2004).

Facilitating connectivity in conservation

World Heritage has the potential to be one of the most important mechanisms in supporting the rapidly developing connectivity approach to nature and biodiversity conservation. This approach recognizes that conservation strategies need to ensure connectivity between ecosystems and the wider land and seascapes to conserve biological diversity. Fragmented ecosystems do not have the capacity to support biological processes such as species migration and climate change adaptation, and lack of connectivity between ecosystems contributes significantly to the loss of wildlife populations (Worboys et al., 2010).

The Papallacta Declaration of 2006, developed by connectivity conservation management experts at an IUCN WCPA workshop in Ecuador, summed up the connectivity conservation concept as: 'The maintenance and restoration of ecosystem integrity requires landscape-scale conservation. This can be achieved through systems of core protected areas that are functionally linked and buffered in ways that maintain ecosystem processes and allow species to survive and move, thus ensuring that populations are viable and that ecosystems and people are able to adapt to land transformation and climate change. We call this proactive, holistic and long-term approach connectivity conservation' (Worboys, 2008, p2). An important premise of connectivity conservation is that humans are considered an integral component of ecosystems and their involvement and contribution is critical to the success of these strategies.

Given that connectivity would play a critical role in assuring the long-term OUV of World Heritage properties, there is enormous scope for the World Heritage Committee, advisory bodies and states parties to consider a more active role in supporting connectivity conservation. Relevant actions could take the form of expansion of existing World Heritage sites, strategic designation of transboundary and serial sites and integration of World Heritage properties into regional planning for conservation areas. World Heritage properties are already playing an important, if *ad hoc*, role in connectivity conservation. The extension of the Cape Floral Region Protected Areas serial property (Figure 4.6) was 'designed to facilitate functional connectivity and mitigate for the effects of global climate change and other anthropogenic influences' (UNESCO, 2015h). Similarly, the extension to Mount Kenya National Park/Natural Forest included a corridor which facilitates wildlife movement and acts as a buffer against climate change impacts. The Committee commended the state party its efforts to enhance ecological connectivity and encouraged Kenya to explore further opportunities to create connectivity within the larger ecosystem complex (UNESCO, 2013e). Ecological connectivity is now regularly referred to in Committee decisions since the Committee first mentioned it in 2007.

The potential of regional harmonization of tentative lists for conservation connectivity is evident in the example of the European Alps. A World Heritage Working Group was established under the mandate of the Alpine Convention to appraise the possibility of transboundary and serial transnational World Heritage sites across the Alps. The Alpine Convention of 1995 is an international treaty between the Alpine Countries (Austria, France, Germany, Italy, Liechtenstein, Monaco, Slovenia and Switzerland), for the sustainable development and protection of the Alps. Its mandate includes the development of common strategies to ensure the connectivity between natural habitats in the Alpine region and to mitigate the environmental transformation brought about by climate change (Alpine Working Group, 2014).

World Heritage sites are only one link in the chain of possible connectivity conservation areas. Linkages between World Heritage sites and other protected areas and designations must be explored as part of collaborative efforts with other conventions and regional planning. This is particularly important in the case of large-scale operations, such as the Mesoamerican Biological Corridor (MBC). The MBC includes 526 protected areas interlinked across the seven Central American countries. The World Heritage Convention and the Man and Biosphere programme together provide a fundamental protected area framework in the region, with seven natural World Heritage properties and 26 Biosphere Reserves (Muller & Patry, 2011). There is opportunity to promote the importance of linkages between the designations and to encourage further dialogue among the states parties in order to develop a robust common agenda to ensure the viability of the MBC.

Joining frontiers through serial sites

The success of regional planning for World Heritage across borders is evident in the growth of serial transboundary nominations. However, these types of nominations require extensive coordination between states parties to identify the potential OUV and to work together to develop common goals for conservation and sustainable development. The enormous scale of this undertaking has been

FIGURE 4.6 Cederberg daisies in the Cape Floral Region, South Africa (credit: Jon Wade)

encapsulated in the efforts to realize the phased, serial transnational site of the Frontiers of the Roman Empire. This is an ambitious project which aims to produce a multinational World Heritage property incorporating countries in Europe, Asia and Africa (Breeze & Jilek, 2008).

The Roman Empire, at its greatest extent in the 2nd century AD, stretched over 5,000 km from the Atlantic coast of Scotland, through Europe to the Black Sea, and from there to the Red Sea and across North Africa to the Atlantic coast of Morocco. The remains of the frontier, known as the 'Roman Limes', consist of vestiges of built walls, ditches, forts, fortresses, watchtowers, the limes road and civilian settlements (UNESCO, 2008b). The World Heritage property exists as a transnational site between Germany and the UK. The German components include two sections of the Roman Limes which cover a length of 550 km from the north-west of the country to the Danube in the south-east (Figure 4.7). In the UK, the frontier is represented by Hadrian's Wall (118 km) in England, and the Antonine Wall (60 km) in Scotland.

Interest in developing a single, international World Heritage site based on the theme of the Roman Frontier grew following the extension of the original UK property to include the German component. Ultimately, it was realized that there was potential to expand the property to include the entire 5,000 km length of the border line. This would require advanced strategies to develop transnational cooperation and to ensure a harmonized approach to the nomination and

FIGURE 4.7   Main gate of Saalburg Roman Fort, Germany: part of the Roman Limes (credit: Carole Raddato)

management of the sites. Initial financial support came from the European Union's Culture 2000 programme which facilitated data collection and a public awareness campaign involving Austria, Germany, Hungary, Poland, Romania, Slovakia, Slovenia, Spain and the UK (Breeze & Jilek, 2008).

Next, Hungary and Slovakia initiated plans to expand the Danube component of the World Heritage property. The experience of Hungary and Slovakia would then be used to inform the remaining countries in the Danube Limes theme. This included the entire 2,800 km Danube river frontier running through eight individual countries: Germany, Austria, Slovakia, Hungary, Croatia, Serbia, Romania and Bulgaria. The Roman Limes in Hungary and Slovakia alone consists of over 200 individual sites representing a complex system of frontier installations along the Danube River for a distance of 420 km. Furthermore, unlike the inscribed properties in Germany and the UK, these sites were located in densely populated areas. To identify those elements of the Limes that would meet the requirements of OUV and also be manageable was an extremely ambitious task. The project was supported by the Central Europe Programme and co-financed by the European Union Regional Development Fund to the amount of almost two million Euros. The principal aims of the project were to create a scientific concept to define the Danube River Limes and to identify the requirements for their protection as well as develop proper management structures and demonstrate best practice in the nomination process and management planning. The management challenges, lessons learned and solutions identified by the project were published in 2011 (Dyczek et al., 2011). Concurrently, Germany and the Netherlands have initiated collaborative work to submit a further extension to the property consisting of the Roman garrisoned river frontier along the river Rhine (RWTH-Aachen University, 2015).

The value of transnational nominations lies in the necessity to promote scientific, artistic, educational, cultural, political and commercial links across states parties. The Frontiers of the Roman Empire project has had many positive outcomes. It has created networks of archaeologists and cultural resource managers across Europe and established twinning partnerships between museums and schools along the frontiers. It has also improved public awareness and understanding through websites, exhibitions and different forms of media. Finally, it has substantially improved documentation and understanding of the archaeological sites and generated guidelines for the protection, management, presentation and interpretation of the Roman military sites. The foundations have been set to develop conditions for truly open international cooperation and the project continues to grow (Breeze & Jilek, 2008).

Marine programmes and seascapes

Marine ecosystems are under-represented on the World Heritage List. The identification of marine World Heritage properties, to be meaningful from an ecosystem perspective, requires a regional approach and collaboration between neighbouring countries. This is because marine ecosystems, due to the three-dimensional and fluid nature of the marine environment, are highly complex and occur over wider spatial scales with relatively indistinct boundaries compared to terrestrial ecosystems. It is anticipated that connectivity and serial sites will play a significant role in future nominations, particularly from the point of view of biodiversity conservation where the high mobility of both juveniles and adults of marine species will necessitate access to larger areas to maintain ecological processes (Abdulla et al., 2013). Furthermore, the available data sets on global marine biodiversity are quite incomplete, and an expert-driven approach can be used regionally to greater effect to understand marine ecosystem functioning at appropriate scales (ibid.).

There is growing recognition of the need to apply the landscape or seascape concept to the marine properties to recognize the intimate links between people and the marine ecosystems. The seascape is understood to mean the coastal landscape and adjoining areas of open water and their interrelationship, including views from land to sea, from sea to land and along the coastline (Hill et al., 2001). For example, the rich cultural heritage associated with the seascapes of Ireland include the traditional values placed on the sea as a recreational resource and livelihood source; the wealth of archaeological sites and underwater cultural heritage; and intangible heritage in the form of myths, legends, literature and poetry. Also important are associations with historic events such as the arrival of the Vikings and the establishment of the port cities of Dublin and Waterford and poignant events in the departure of the 'famine ships' and periods of mass emigration.

The coast and related seascape is a finite resource under almost continual pressure for development to meet commercial, residential, transport and industrial needs as well as the growth of alternative energy developments and wind turbines. Consequently, proper conservation, management and sustainable development of the coasts and the adjoining seas should be prioritized, not least because there is a substantial tourism industry dependent upon high quality coastlines and seascapes, as well as coastal communities that are in turn heavily dependent on the income generated by the tourist industry (Hill et al., 2001).

The World Heritage marine programme is addressing some of these issues. It launched the Pacific World Heritage Action Plan in 2009 which aims to work with all the countries of the Pacific in their efforts to protect the cultural and biological diversity of the region. The World Heritage Centre is also working with Conservation International on the Eastern Tropical Pacific Seascape Project as well as other international instruments such as the UN International Maritime Organization. The Papahānaumokuākea World Heritage property on the Hawaiian islands was inscribed in 2010 as a mixed site. It is one of the largest marine protected areas in the world and it is recognized for the richness and diversity of the species and marine habitats as well as its value to the living traditions of the Hawaiians as a cultural landscape and unique seascape (UNESCO, 2010a).

However, the challenges ahead in implementing the World Heritage Convention include the true integration of cultural and natural values of the oceanscapes and seascapes and identification of their role in addressing the specific ecological, cultural and socio-economic problem(s) of a particular area. There is also a growing movement among the conservation community to protect the marine environment in the ocean area beyond the national jurisdictions of the exclusive economic zones.[14] The international waters or 'high seas', which are beyond any country's jurisdiction, accounts for approximately 64 per cent of the marine environment, but these lack regulations or enforcement to implement integrated sustainable management and conservation efforts. This will raise challenges for the convention with regard to the issues surrounding the legal and political intricacies of protecting international waters (Obura et al., 2012).

Notes

1 The 2015 version of the Operational Guidelines contains more than 90 pages of annexed information which, for example, provide guidelines on the inscription of specific types of properties as well as the format for nomination of properties and the International Assistance request form.
2 The 2015 version identifies the four principal procedures for the implementation of the convention as: The inscription of properties on the World Heritage List and the LWHD; The protection and conservation of World Heritage properties; The granting of International Assistance under the World Heritage Fund; and The mobilization of national and international support in favour of the convention.
3 At the time of the 30th Anniversary in 2002, the Secretariat established the World Heritage Partnerships for Conservation Initiative (PACT) to help raise awareness, mobilize funds and implement activities with private sector companies in order to meet the ever-growing challenges and costs involved in sustaining the OUV of World Heritage properties.
4 The Budapest Declaration on World Heritage was adopted in 2002 in association with the UN Year for Cultural Heritage and the 30th Anniversary of the World Heritage Convention.
5 The 5th C – for 'Communities' – was added in 2007 at the 31st Session of the World Heritage Committee in Christchurch, New Zealand.
6 It was decided at the 16th Session of the World Heritage Committee in Phuket, Thailand in 1994 to include a section on systematic monitoring in the Operational Guidelines.
7 The first sites inscribed were: L'Anse aux Meadows National Historic Park (Canada); Nahanni National Park (Canada); Galápagos Islands (Ecuador); City of Quito (Ecuador); Simien National Park (Ethiopia); Rock-Hewn Churches, Lalibela (Ethiopia); Aachen Cathedral (Federal Republic of Germany); Historic Centre of Kraków (Poland); Wieliczka Salt Mine (Poland); Island of Gorée (Senegal); Mesa Verde National Park (USA); and Yellowstone National Park (USA).
8 These inscriptions date from 2016.
9 There are 21 programmes and activities identified by the UNESCO World Heritage Centre, ranging from thematic studies to conservation challenges to small island developing states and world heritage volunteers. Further information is available at: whc.unesco.org/en/activities.
10 The small number of properties does not reflect the length of time since the state party ratified the convention. Of the 38 states parties that have a single property on the List the majority ratified the convention over 20 years ago.

11 The deadline for submission of the complete nomination file is 1 February and, if the nomination is accepted by the Secretariat, the file will be processed and evaluated by the advisory bodies in time for the Committee Meeting the year after it was submitted. This timetable also applies to the submission of retroactive statements of OUV.

12 The irreplaceable areas were identified using the IUCN / UNEP-WCMC World Database on Protected Areas and the IUCN Red List of Threatened Species. It also included Alliance for Zero Extinction sites (AZEs). AZEs are defined as the last known places where highly threatened species survive. They hold ≥95 per cent of the global population of Critically Endangered or Endangered animal or plant species.

13 USA withdrew payment of its dues following the decision to make Palestine a member of UNESCO in 2011. Consequently the USA lost its UNESCO voting rights due to the arrears.

14 The exclusive economic zone is the zone where coastal nations have jurisdiction over natural resources. It extends no more than 200 nautical miles from the coastal baseline.

5

USING WORLD HERITAGE

The World Heritage Convention stipulated the need for states parties to adopt policy 'which aims to give the cultural and natural heritage a function in the life of the community and to integrate the protection of that heritage into comprehensive planning programmes' (UNESCO, 1972, article 5a). The ways in which heritage monuments, sites and landscapes are used have implications for conservation and sustainable development. Incompatible uses, loss of functional diversity and overuse of World Heritage sites can potentially damage or even destroy the essence of their value. This may occur due to lack of management, neglect of conservation principles, and exploitation for short-term economic gains.

World Heritage designation may either support or alter the sustainability path of heritage sites depending on how uses are managed. While conservation is the principal aim of the convention, national governments have increasingly sought designation to stimulate tourism in the pursuit of economic development. However, these sites are also milieus where people sustain their living, which can lead to conflicting interests and concerns. This chapter explores different uses of World Heritage sites. Issues examined include how sustainable use is defined, the two-sided impact of tourism on sites, use of World Heritage status and communication, overuse and the role of local communities in maintaining living heritage and place identity.

Heritage uses

A distinction can be made between intrinsic and extrinsic values of both culture and nature to understand the tension that exists between different heritage uses. Intrinsic value refers to something that has a worth in itself, while extrinsic value, or utilitarian value, means that something has been attached with value. Heritage has increasingly been referred to as 'economic', 'cultural' and 'natural' capital. The use of heritage as capital implies that it is ascribed with extrinsic values. While the utilitarian value of heritage sites is important to their conservation, this may also impact negatively on their intrinsic value. The way in which heritage is used is linked to shifting societal priorities, perceptions and paradigms that need to be understood for the long-term conservation of World Heritage sites.

Intrinsic and extrinsic values

'Intrinsic value' was cited in the 1983 version of the Operational Guidelines, stating the following: 'Where the intrinsic qualities of a property nominated are threatened by action of man and yet meet the criteria set out in paragraphs 20 to 25, an action plan outlining the corrective measures required should be submitted with the nomination file' (UNESCO, 1983, para19). This paragraph has been left more or less intact in later versions of the guidelines (UNESCO, 2015b, para116).

Stephenson (2008, p130) developed a cultural values model for an integrated approach to landscape assessment in which culturally valued natural attributes were included. In this model, based on forms, relationships and practices, the latter included both human practices and natural processes 'in order to reflect that human practices and the processes of nature are a continuum of dynamic action rather than conceptually separate' (ibid., p134). Asking whether material culture identified as heritage could be said to have an intrinsic value, a static and universal value, or whether heritage value should be seen as extrinsic and socially constructed, Mason (2002, p8) found that 'the answer seems to lie somewhere in between: value is formed in the nexus between ideas and things'. Furthermore, Mason noted that the intrinsic-value argument in cultural heritage conservation is comparable with the intrinsic argument in environmental conservation, in which nature is considered as intrinsically valuable. Thus, a key question is whether the intrinsic–extrinsic value argument is valid in both cultural and natural heritage conservation, and what implications such an understanding has for the use of World Heritage sites. This raises dilemmas in the use of the World Heritage Convention for conservation in its own right versus for purposes such as for increasing socio-economic benefits and tourism.

John Ruskin, an English art critic of the Victorian era, firmly believed in the intrinsic value of art. Associated with the Western modern conservation movement and architectural theory that emerged in the 19th century, he critiqued political economy perspectives for failing to recognize the inherent or intrinsic qualities of art. Since then, the duality in the value of cultural objects has been noted within several disciplines of the humanities and social sciences. From the perspective of cultural economics, Throsby (2011, p281) noted that 'it takes the form of a straightforward distinction between the economic value and the cultural value of cultural goods and services'. Here, 'the economic value of a cultural commodity is that assessed by the means of economic analysis', while cultural value 'is assumed to be multifaceted, unstable, and lacking a common unit of account', including values such as aesthetic, spiritual and historical values (ibid., pp281–282). In his comparison of Ruskin's theories with modern economics of art and culture, Throsby concluded that: 'Whether one nowadays describes the duality of value attaching to art as being intrinsic versus instrumental, aesthetic versus utilitarian, or cultural versus economic, the origins can be found in Ruskin's pointed contrast between what he calls the "true" value of art and its exchange value in the market place' (ibid., p291).

Similarly, ecosystem analysts have traditionally distinguished between intrinsic and extrinsic values of biodiversity, or use values and non-use values (Gaston & Spicer, 2004). The intrinsic or inherent value of biodiversity refers to the right of species to exist independently of any extrinsic or utilitarian values that these may have to humans. This philosophical concept is enshrined in the preamble to the Convention on Biological Diversity. It stated that the contracting parties are: '*Conscious* of the intrinsic value of biological diversity and of the ecological, genetic, social, economic, scientific, educational, cultural, recreational and aesthetic values of biological diversity and its components' (UN, 1992).

In ecosystem analysis, extrinsic, or utilitarian values can be divided into three categories. Firstly, direct use values of goods include production of food, sources of effective medicines, bio-control of unwanted and harmful species such as disease vectors and agricultural pests, source of industrial materials, timber, fibres, dyes and ecotourism. Secondly, indirect use values represent the values that are derived from the many services that ecosystems provide such as atmospheric regulation, climatic regulation, nutrient cycling, pollination and soil formation. Use values reflect a utilitarian approach to the way that natural heritage is valued. Some of the more abstract extrinsic values in nature are frequently misidentified as intrinsic values: for example, aesthetic value, which refers to the pleasure that the beauty of biodiversity provides to humans. Thirdly, non-use values include option values (potential future value as goods and services), existence value (value of knowing something exists) and bequest value (value of knowing that something will be there for future generations) (Maclaurin & Sterelny, 2008).

The categories used here are not rigid: different authors and organizations use slightly different ways to categorize extrinsic values reflecting the diversity of interpretations of different value types. For example, option or potential value is often included as a use value since option value is based on the future use that biodiversity might have; others consider it as a non-use value since it is, by nature, an abstract concept and the potential use that something might have is undetermined. Increasingly, there are direct attempts to measure the true economic value that society gains from the use of natural resources (Jeffries, 2006). However, critically, indirect uses also relate to the cultural services provided by ecosystems, such aesthetic, recreational, spiritual and educational benefits. The Economics of Ecosystems and Biodiversity (TEEB) is a global initiative launched by the European Commission in 2010 to make the values of nature visible and 'to mainstream the values of biodiversity and ecosystem services into decision-making at all levels' (TEEB, 2016).

The significance of people's ideas of identity and belief systems in valuing nature has been emphasized in socio-cultural approaches. There is a myriad of distinct cultural traditions and knowledge for relating to the natural world, and different elements of biodiversity and geodiversity are important to different cultures. For example, in Australia, aboriginal communities have considered places to have intrinsic value but not necessarily the individual animals and plants that occur therein. Frequently, indigenous and traditional communities incorporate the natural landscape into their cultural identity and outlook, and thus culture is not considered separately to nature but as forming part of a totality (Posey, 2000).

Heritage as capital

Heritage is often described as a form of capital that can be utilized for specific purposes given its utilitarian potential. Heritage duality suggests that there is a tension in the use of heritage as a cultural versus economic resource (Graham et al., 2000). The use of heritage as an economic resource implies that heritage can be used for economic gains and that 'a growing commercial heritage industry is commodifying pasts into heritage products and experiences for sale as part of a modern consumption of entertainment' (ibid., p1). This is particularly evident in the case of heritage tourism, which often becomes associated with generating economic revenue. This can potentially damage the heritage resource itself and its right to exist undisturbed, i.e. if its having an intrinsic value is accepted, and its uses by local communities whether as a cultural, social or natural resource.

The view of heritage as economic capital has been subject to criticism. Throsby (2002, p101) suggested that conservationists have accused economists of 'adopting a narrow economizing attitude to heritage decisions, turning attention away from the essential cultural values of heritage toward a more market-driven approach'. The critique lies in the justification of conservation mainly for the purpose of creating economic opportunities of income, employment and tourist revenue, rather than motives being anchored in the recognition of the intrinsic value of heritage. This argument is significant in that it reveals a tension between the intrinsic and extrinsic values of heritage and in unsustainable utilization through exploitation. However, for Throsby 'an economist's approach to heritage is in fact more sophisticated than one simply focusing on financial revenues and costs', although at the same time, 'the criticism does have validity in highlighting the problems raised by the economic necessity of reducing all values to material terms' (ibid.).

Nature has similarly been conceptualized as natural capital through several perspectives. For example, natural capital has been defined as 'the natural resources and the ecological systems that provide vital life-support services, in particular to all economic activities' (Hawken et al. cited in Antrop, 2006, p191). Furthermore, a distinction has been made between strong and weak sustainability: 'Strong sustainability is maintaining the ecological capital intact. Weak sustainability refers to the principle of maintaining a combination of economic activity and environmental quality' (Hediger cited in Antrop, 2006, p191). Monetary evaluation of nature has been put forward to ensure that environmental concerns are taken seriously in government decision-making and in business. Nunes and van den Bergh (2001, p218) explored economic valuation of biodiversity and methods of calculating monetary values to changes in biodiversity, noting that 'most studies lack a uniform, clear perspective on biodiversity as a distinct concept from biological resources'. However, they concluded that monetary valuation of changes of biodiversity can be useful if certain conditions are fulfilled: 'that a clear life diversity level is chosen, that a concrete biodiversity change scenario is formulated, that a multidisciplinary approach seeking the identification of direct and indirect effects of the biodiversity change on human welfare is used, and, very importantly, that the change is well defined and not too large' (ibid.). Shifts towards understanding the pivotal place of heritage conservation in socio-economic development has been recognized in development strategies as well as in national efforts to turn around economic downturns through enabling the conservation sector for wider societal benefits (Gustafsson, 2009; Mackin & Davidson, 2012). The use of heritage as capital may be positive as long as the intrinsic qualities of cultural as well as natural heritage are recognized.

Shifting societal priorities

Heritage uses may shift over time as a result of temporal societal contexts, shaped by political, economic, social and cultural factors, which could ultimately determine the conservation of OUV and how World Heritage sites are managed and used. For example, neo-liberal shifts and privatization of publicly owned heritage properties affect heritage management through increased ownership mobility (Negussie, 2006b) which may in turn affect heritage uses. The functional diversity and social balance of historic towns can be affected negatively by property speculation and profit-driven uses. The heritage sector is particularly vulnerable during times of economic recession when properties may be affected by budgetary cutbacks in relation to conservation and management.

Heritage runs the risk of becoming exploited when utilized as economic assets. For example, financial crisis in Greece caused by the 'Great Recession' led the authorities to turn to heritage sites for income generation, which attracted media attention: 'In a move bound to leave many Greeks and scholars aghast, Greece's culture ministry said […] it will open up some of the debt-stricken country's most-cherished archaeological sites to advertising firms and other ventures. The ministry says the move is a common-sense way of helping "facilitate" access to the country's ancient Greek ruins, and money generated would fund the upkeep and monitoring of sites. The first site to be opened would be the Acropolis' (AFP, 2012). The Acropolis, in Athens, was inscribed on the World Heritage List in 1987 based on five of the six cultural criteria as 'universal symbols of the classical spirit and civilization and form the greatest architectural and artistic complex bequeathed by Greek Antiquity to the world' (UNESCO, 2014c). While the management system for the property was deemed sufficient according to the state of conservation periodic reporting mechanism, visitor and tourism pressure was identified as one of the threats to the site, together with environmental pressure and natural disasters. Visitor statistics from 2004 estimated over a million visitors to the site based on ticket counts (UNESCO, 2006b). Further commercialization may thus be questioned, not only in terms of the impact of commercial use on wear and tear of the monument, but also on the intangible values of the site.

Motivations for World Heritage designation

The pursuit of World Heritage designation has become linked to motivations for using the label for socio-economic development. In 2008, the Lake District World Heritage Project commissioned a study to investigate economic and social gains made from designation with the view to identifying best practices of using the World Heritage brand for socio-economic gain. This was motivated by the economic cost of attaining World Heritage status, which had led to debate in the UK about costs versus benefits of achieving designation. The study found that the impacts 'are rarely accidental or unintended – they are overwhelmingly the result of coordinated and well thought through efforts to achieve targeted change' (Rebanks, 2009, p1). Where significant impacts have been achieved there has been a clear understanding of how World Heritage status can be used to generate change. Thus, World Heritage is 'what you make of it'. Furthermore, 'where the status has been used to full effect it has brought partners together, leveraged additional funding, led to new development and enhanced educational benefits, improved conservation and even led to regeneration in some locations' (ibid., p1).

The study distinguished between four types of World Heritage site based on the perceptions that management and stakeholders hold of World Heritage status, and concluded that there is a strong link between the perceptions and the socio-economic impact:

- Celebration Designation: World Heritage status is viewed as a celebration or reward for already preserved heritage;
- Heritage SOS Designation: World Heritage designation was achieved as an emergency alert for outstanding heritage at risk;
- Marketing/Quality Logo/Brand: World Heritage is seen as a quality brand and marketing tool;

- Place Making Catalyst: World Heritage status is used as a powerful engine for economic development in which heritage is used as a tool to develop new place identities and place-changing programmes of actions.

With focus on the two latter categories the study found that when designation is sought for marketing or branding purpose this is done mainly to gain tourism impacts. Only places that use designation as a place-making catalyst use it to achieve wider socio-economic impacts and fundamental community change. The consultative and reflective nomination process was highlighted as essential, since 'those sites that go through a detailed process of consultation and strategy development looking at what WHS status will mean for their communities and economy tend to be the sites that go onto to deliver these impacts' (ibid., p35).

Sustainable use of World Heritage

Specific reference to sustainable use in World Heritage policy is a relatively recent development. However, the use of heritage sites is a central concern within both cultural and natural heritage conservation and is reflected in various conservation charters and principles. Inappropriate uses are those that impact negatively on cultural and natural significances, and, in the case of World Heritage sites they may have an adverse effect on the OUV. However, sustainable use may be more difficult to determine when confronted with new proposed uses. While some uses are considered appropriate, overuse may still be harmful and use limits should therefore be established according to the capacity of the site.

Policy and principles

Sustainable use was incorporated into the Operational Guidelines in 2005 and has since been further developed into the following: 'World Heritage properties may support a variety of ongoing and proposed uses that are ecologically and culturally sustainable and which may contribute to the quality of life of communities concerned. The State Party and its partners must ensure that such sustainable use or any other change does not impact adversely on the Outstanding Universal Value of the property' (UNESCO, 2015b, para119). Furthermore, 'use and function' is one of the attributes of authenticity as established in the Nara Document on Authenticity and central in the assessment of OUV for cultural properties (ICOMOS, 1994). The original use of a cultural site should be considered in its conservation for truthful presentation of the past. However, the survival of built heritage often requires adaptive reuse, which may in some cases provide a more sustainable solution to conservation than attempting to maintain the original use as societies change.

ICOMOS principles on conservation constitute important benchmarks against the evaluation of sustainable use for cultural properties. The 'Venice Charter' stated that: 'The conservation of monuments is always facilitated by making use of them for some socially useful purpose. Such use is therefore desirable but it must not change the lay-out or decoration of the building. It is within these limits only that modifications demanded by a change of function should be envisaged and may be permitted' (ICOMOS, 1964, article 5). The 'Washington Charter' stressed that the various functions that have been acquired in towns and urban areas over time contribute to their historic character (ICOMOS, 1987b, article 2e) and that 'new functions and activities should be compatible with the character of the historic town or urban area' (article 8). The 'Valletta Principles' elaborated further on this: 'The introduction of new activities must not compromise the survival of traditional activities or anything that supports the daily life of the local inhabitants [...] Before introducing a new activity, it is necessary to consider the number of users involved, the length of utilization, compatibility with other existing activities and the impact on traditional local practices. Such new functions must also satisfy the need for sustainable development, in line with the concept of the historic town as a unique and irreplaceable ecosystem' (ICOMOS, 2011b, 4b).

The Charter on the Built Vernacular Heritage stated that 'adaptation and reuse of vernacular structures should be carried out in a manner which will respect the integrity of the structure, its character and form while being compatible with acceptable standards of living' (ICOMOS, 1999b, guideline 5). Furthermore, ICOMOS and the International Committee for the Conservation of the Industrial Heritage (TICCIH) have jointly drafted guidelines on the conservation of industrial heritage structures, sites and landscapes recognized that the heritage value 'may be greatly jeopardized or reduced if machinery or other significant components are removed, or if subsidiary elements which form part of a whole site are destroyed' (ICOMOS & TICCIH, 2011, II.9). At the same time it acknowledged that 'appropriate original or alternative and adaptive use is the most frequent way and often the most sustainable way of ensuring the conservation of industrial heritage sites or structures' (ibid., III.10).

In response to the need for an international approach to the sustainable use of natural resources, the World Conservation Congress adopted the IUCN Policy Statement on Sustainable Use of Wild Living Resources in 2000. It recognized that 'both consumptive and non-consumptive use of biological diversity are fundamental to the economies, cultures, and well-being of all nations and peoples' and that 'use, if sustainable, can serve human needs on an ongoing basis while contributing to the conservation of biological diversity' (IUCN, 2000, paras2–3). Furthermore, it recognized that in many cases the sustainable use of wild living resources is affected by a combination of factors including biological, social, cultural and economic. The statement promoted sustainable use of wild living resources as an important conservation tool since it brings socio-economic benefits for people to conserve them. However, this requires minimization of biological diversity loss and an adaptive management approach based on a sustainable use regime. The adaptive approach incorporates a system of monitoring, evaluation and continuous review and updating of management plans which should successfully reflect the varied and changeable use strategies employed by people in changing circumstances. Adaptive management, by its nature, also encourages a flexible and innovative approach to addressing management issues, where somewhat experimental interventions can be employed to solve problems where there is not a lot if information available (Lockwood, 2006). Further guidance has been developed on sustainable use of natural resource such as the Addis Ababa Principles and Guidelines for the Sustainable Use of Biodiversity. It provided a framework for governments to develop and implement policies on sustainable use to promote conservation of biodiversity through a series of interrelated practical principles and operational guidelines (CBD Secretariat, 2004a).

Identifying sustainable uses

World Heritage sites will be successful where these facilitate useful purposes in accordance with good conservation practice. Appropriate uses are unique to individual sites and need to be identified through participatory management processes. In the nomination of the Fagus Factory in Alfeld, Germany, authenticity was easily demonstrated by the fact that the factory was still in operation and producing shoes true to its original function. Any reconstruction work and rebuilding that had taken place over the years was shown to have followed the original plans and drawings in consultation with an expert panel. In line with the changing practices in shoe production and the modernization of energy supply, the changing functions of the different buildings have not impacted on their architecture or original structure. They have all been preserved and adapted for new purposes sympathetic to their form and design. In contrast, an industrial plant nomination put forward by Mexico in 2011, the Fundidora Monterrey Blast Furnaces, a steel factory, was rejected since authenticity had been compromised partly due to extensive modifications but also due to the introduction of new functions such as the creation of a leisure park. The site had been transformed to the extent that it no longer gave testimony to the industrial past for which it was nominated. A third example, the Zollverein Coal Mine Industrial Complex in Essen, Germany, demonstrates that adaptive reuse of industrial sites may be achieved without disturbing the OUV of the site. The complex was transformed into a cultural centre with art studios, etc., much of its original features still intact.

In relation to natural World Heritage properties, sustainable use is often linked to the sustainable use of natural resources and recreation. Increasingly, the local communities in protected World Heritage areas are recognized as fundamental parts of the ecosystems and need to play an active role in the management of the natural resources. In particular, people surviving on subsistence livelihoods rely heavily on natural products harvested from their surrounding environment including medicinal plants, food (e.g. wild animal and plant products), fodder and wood for fuel (Ilukol & Cave, 2012). Balancing conservation with human use of the site is therefore essential. With regard to recreation, use by visitors and the associated tourism industry is one of the most ubiquitous management issues for World Heritage sites. Communication and collaboration between site managers and the people that harvest the resources are critically important processes in identifying appropriate uses. The stakeholders must find a way to protect biodiversity and ecosystem processes and at the same time avoid negative impacts on human livelihoods.

Mount Kenya National Park/Natural Forest was discussed at the World Heritage Committee meeting in 2013 as a result of the proposal to expand its borders to include the Lewa Wildlife Conservancy (LWC). The Conservancy consists of private and community-owned lands managed by a non-profit organization seeking to protect endangered species and habitats and to initiate and support community development programmes (LWC, 2013). In Kenya, the implementation of policies and legislation enabling local communities to benefit from wildlife use is one the furthest developed in East Africa (Jones et al., 2005a). The Kenya Wildlife Service (KWS), a state corporation, has promoted the formation of wildlife conservancies amongst owners of large tracts of land, especially amongst local communities, as a long-term strategy to increase range for biodiversity conservation and management in the country. This is an important strategy since approximately 60–70 per cent of wildlife is found outside of state-run protected areas. The most common form of tenure arrangement for privately conserved areas in Kenya is the 'group ranch'. These ranches are regulated by the Land (Group Representatives) Act of 1968 and are defined as: demarcated area[s] of rangeland to which a group of pastoralists, who graze their individual owned herds on it, have official land rights (Jones et al., 2005a, p69).

Formed in 1995 as a non-profit organization, the Lewa Wildlife Conservancy (LWC) evolved from a cattle ranch, where the private owners had set aside some land for a rhino sanctuary in 1983. Over time, the wild rhino numbers recovered within the refuge and the landowners decided to dedicate the entire ranch to conservation. Today, LWC provides an interesting combination of individual and community conservation efforts as it has expanded to an area greater than 162 square kilometres (40,000 acres) and includes land owned by the conservancy, by communities and other private landowners and national forest (Ngare Ndare Forest Reserve). In 2013, it was incorporated into the Mount Kenya National Park/Natural Forest World Heritage site with the full support of IUCN. The motivation for landowners to allocate land for wildlife and wild habitats is partly in response to declines in wildlife numbers, and partly due to economic opportunities through wildlife-based tourism and other resource uses. The IUCN evaluation report found that LWC had developed an amicable relationship with neighbouring communities and ensures that they receive benefits from the protected area. These include cooperative programmes such as providing support to several local schools; provision of job opportunities and employment; provision of health care; support of potable and irrigation water;

forestry and women micro-credit schemes; controlled dry season livestock grazing inside LWC by local communities; and community based ecotourism (IUCN, 2013b).

The innovative strategy of the management of the area is also evident in the work to address conflict between people and elephants. LWC is located in an area of high population growth, which has resulted in increased encounters between people and wildlife as well as extensive land-use change and infrastructural development. These changes to the landscape have blocked the elephants' traditional migratory routes and created major problems where elephants disturb private farms and cause extensive damage to crops. LWC reached an agreement with landowners to enable the construction of an elephant movement corridor, which included an underpass under a busy motorway. This experimental approach has proven to be highly successful with monitoring systems recording a high number of elephants moving through the underpass. An electric fence prevents the elephants straying from the route, and the corridor scheme has been credited with solving the elephant–human conflict that plagued the area for many years. This is turn has encouraged good levels of trust and a harmonious relationship between LWC and its neighbours (IUCN, 2013b; LWC, 2011).

Measuring sustainability

Measuring sustainable use of heritage sites is complex and tools still need to be developed to assess sustainability and tolerance for change. It is necessary to consider the various impacts of different uses on World Heritage sites and to execute plans that help identify which uses should be considered appropriate from the perspectives of their conservation. When determining the sustainability of different uses, different aspects of sustainable development must be considered holistically from the perspectives of cultural, economic, environmental and social impacts.

ICOMOS issued special guidelines for the assessment of development impact on the OUV of cultural sites. The Heritage Impact Assessment (HIA) tool was developed in response to the failure of environmental impact assessment (EIA) to properly address conservation of OUV at cultural World Heritage sites since its application is limited in relation to understanding cultural values. As stated in the guidelines: 'EIA frequently disaggregates all the possible cultural heritage attributes and assesses impact on them separately, through discrete receptors such as protected buildings, archaeological sites, and specified view-points with their view cones, without applying the lens of OUV to the overall ensemble of attributes' (ICOMOS, 2011c, p1). The guidelines should be used for guidance alongside the statutory EIA process in order to fully address the needs of cultural properties. In this process, managers and decision-makers should place heritage attributes at the centre of planning and 'consider whether the heritage conservation needs should be given greater weight than competing uses and development' (ibid., p4). While spatial planning involves the weighing of many different interests and concerns, unless both cultural and natural heritage attributes are valued fully, both conservation and sustainable development is at risk. From this perspective, HIA provides a useful tool in the assessment of new proposed developments for overall estimation of their impacts on the OUV of a World Heritage site. This concerns the development of large infrastructural projects as well as land-use change. World Heritage sites are vulnerable to both new infrastructures, particularly those relating to tourism which may have unintended consequences such as overuse and adverse impact on the OUV, as well as changed, use policy (ICOMOS, 2011c, p5).

The IUCN Sustainable Use and Livelihoods Specialist Group (SUSG) developed an analytical framework 'to promote a better understanding of the factors that affect sustainability of the use of living natural resources' (IUCN SUSG, 2001, p4). The factors are considered from a multidisciplinary approach to include biological, ecological, social, economic, political, cultural and historical perspectives. Firstly, there are factors related to usable living natural resources, which concerns the natural environment that is used by human societies. Secondly, there are factors related to the user population, i.e. the people who directly use or harvest living natural resources or are closely linked to the chain of users. Thirdly, external factors such as institutional, cultural and political conditions that allow for the establishment of sustainable use principles, e.g. the extent to which democratic and inclusive participatory processes are in operation. Fourthly, economic factors affect sustainable use, i.e. the economic valuation assigned by the decision-makers and users of natural resources. The Framework also takes into account the fact that the four factors identified above may in turn be affected by other external factors such as poverty, foreign debt, natural disasters and social political and economic conflicts. There is little that the management body of a World Heritage property or other protected area can do to control these external elements, but their influence and impact on sustainable use are important considerations (IUCN SUSG, 2001).

The IUCN Analytic Framework for Sustainable Use also identified adaptive management as an effective process in encouraging sustainable use. Adaptive management encourages monitoring and effectiveness evaluations, which in turn result in a continuous cycle of reviewing and revising of management plans and activities based on the outcomes of both experimental and systematic interventions. To this end the Framework includes a series of sustainable use criteria and indicators which can be adapted to different circumstances to enable managers to quantify and qualify behaviour as it relates to the sustainable use of living natural resources (ibid.).

In 2006, IUCN presented a position paper on 'Indicators of Sustainable Use of Biological Diversity (Agenda Item 23)' at a conference of the parties to the Convention on Biological Diversity. It proposed three sub-targets with proposed indicators. For example, ecological footprint was proposed as an indicator to reduce unsustainable consumption of biological resources (Table 5.1).

TABLE 5.1 Indicators of sustainable use of biological diversity

Sub-targets	Proposed indicators
4.1. Biodiversity-based products derived from sources that are sustainably managed, and production areas managed consistent with the conservation of biodiversity	Area of forest, agricultural and aquacultural ecosystems under sustainable management. Proportion of products derived from sustainable sources
4.2 Unsustainable consumption, of biological resources, or that impact upon biodiversity, reduced	Ecological footprint and related concepts
4.3 No species of wild flora or fauna endangered by international trade	Change in status of threatened species

Source: IUCN (2006).

Tourism: opportunity and threat

Tourism has grown significantly since the 1970s and by 2014 it accounted for 9 per cent of the global GDP. A forecast by the World Tourism Organization predicts that international tourist arrivals will reach 1.8 billion by 2030 (UNWTO, 2015). However, the visitor economy is vulnerable to crises such as conflict and environmental disaster. In Japan, the combination of earthquake, tsunami, nuclear disaster and a strong currency resulted in the number of foreign visitors dropping by 24.4 per cent in 2011 compared to the previous year (Demetriou, 2012). The dual impact of the visitor economy on the conservation of World Heritage sites has created a demand for guidance on how to achieve sustainable tourism. It is important to recognize that while heritage tourism generates economic revenue, some of this needs to be channelled back to the heritage resource and its conservation.

Cultural tourism

Sustainable visitor frameworks are essential for World Heritage sites since cultural tourism may both compromise and contribute to heritage conservation. Tourism may create a culture of commodification that exploits heritage to the extent that its intrinsic value becomes eroded and threatens authenticity through overuse and distorted representations of the past. On the other hand, it can enhance opportunities to experience heritage and stimulate local economies. Tourism impacts on heritage 'are caused mainly by development and visitors' (Pedersen, 2002, p30). The excessive building of hotels and other visitor infrastructure can undermine the integrity of places and too many visitors can threaten the balance of daily life of local communities.

The evolution of international tourism organizations goes back to the First Constitutive Assembly of the International Union of Official Travel

Organizations (IUOTO) held in Hague in 1947. In 1963, it initiated the United Nations Conference on Tourism and International Travel in Rome, at which recommendations were adopted on definitions such as 'visitor' and 'tourist' together with a general resolution on tourism development. In 1970, the World Tourism Organization (UNWTO) was formed, and, by 1976 the organization became a specialized UN agency of the United Nations Development Programme providing a global forum for tourism policy. In 1999, it established the 'Global Code of Ethics for Tourism' with principles relating to economic, social, cultural and environmental components of travel and tourism (UNWTO, 1999).

The ICOMOS Charter on Cultural Tourism was established in 1976 in response to the recognition that the fast growth in the tourism sector would bring consequences for the cultural heritage. It was later revised by the ICOMOS Scientific Committee on Cultural Tourism and named the International Cultural Tourism Charter in 1999. Its ethos is that access to heritage is a human right that implies duty and respect: 'A primary objective for managing heritage is to communicate its significance and need for its conservation to its host community and to visitors. Reasonable and well-managed physical, intellectual and/or emotive access to heritage and cultural development is both a right and a privilege. It brings with it a duty of respect for the heritage values, interests and equity of the present-day host community, indigenous custodians or owners of historic property and for the landscapes and cultures from which that heritage evolved' (ICOMOS, 1999a).

The charter recognized tourism as an economic factor if properly managed and that dynamic interaction between tourism and cultural heritage must be achieved through a positive approach to conservation. The main objectives of the charter are to encourage: 1) access to heritage for both the host community and visitors; 2) the tourism industry to promote and manage tourism in ways that respect and enhance the heritage and living cultures of host communities; 3) dialogue between conservation interests and the tourism industry about the importance and fragile nature of heritage places, collections and living cultures; 4) formulation of plans, policies and measurable goals and strategies for their presentation, interpretation and conservation. While the charter stresses the need for the involvement of host communities, it lacks ethical rules in areas of visitor behaviour, e.g. in relation to religion and cultural traditions. Furthermore, while it noted that tourism generates flows of capital, the question remains whether any of this capital flows back to the heritage resources directly, indirectly or at all.

There has been a lack of debate on how to achieve sustainable development in relation to cultural tourism. This partly stems from assumptions such as that 'tourism generates cultural harmony', as enshrined in the World Tourism Organisation mission statement and goal of fostering international peace and understanding. This idea derives from romantic and elitist traditions of travel in the 18th and 19th centuries. However, there is little evidence of this. Instead, cultural conflicts have developed around tourism due to a range of unequal relationships between the tourist and the host, powerful developers and operators of the international tourism industry and host country, and amongst different sectors of the host community. Any efforts to promote sustainable cultural tourism therefore depend on collaboration with local communities, recognition of the value of cultural diversity, and a forum that facilitates local community participation in decisions affecting the future of their culture heritage (Robinson, 1999).

Ecotourism

Ecotourism was defined by the World Conservation Union as 'environmentally responsible travel and visitation to natural areas, in order to enjoy and appreciate nature (and any accompanying cultural features, both past and present), that promote conservation, have low visitor impact, and provide for beneficially active socioeconomic involvement of local people' (IUCN, 1997).[1] Similarly, the International Ecotourism Society, founded in 1990, defined ecotourism as 'responsible travel to natural areas that conserves the environment, sustains the well-being of the local people, and involves interpretation and education' (TIES, 2016). 'Eco-destinations' are places that seek to attract visitors 'who look for experiences that provide a sense of closeness to the natural attractions and local communities that first brought them to a destination' (Epler-Wood, 2002). Ecotourism thus depends on protection of resources, community-based conservation strategies and responsible actions on the part of visitors and the tourism industry. A resolution adopted by the UN General Assembly in 2014 recognized that 'sustainable tourism, including ecotourism, creates significant opportunities for the conservation, protection and sustainable use of biodiversity and of natural areas by encouraging indigenous peoples and local communities in host countries and tourists alike to preserve and respect the natural and cultural heritage' (UN, 2014b).

The Galápagos, spread across 19 islands in the Pacific Ocean on Ecuadorian territories, have been described as one of the world's primary ecotourism destinations. The Galápagos Islands were inscribed on the World Heritage List in 1978 under each of the four natural criteria as significant concentrations of rare or endangered plants and animals, and which inspired Charles Darwin's theory of evolution by natural selection after his visit to the islands in 1835 (Figure 5.1). Epler (2007, p8) observed that 'if one looks solely at the direct impact of visitors on visitor sites in Galápagos, one would be hard pressed to find other areas where the objectives of ecotourism have been so successfully achieved'. A visitor management system has been developed by the Galápagos National Park Services (GNPS), including vessel fees, entrance fees and private donations to raise funds for the park (ibid.). However, in spite of the great success in building a strong tourism economy, there have been negative impacts too. With improved access, in-migration and the introduction of a residential community from Ecuador relying on imported goods and resources, and the significant increase in hotels with homogenization of tourist facilities, has

FIGURE 5.1 Galápagos Islands, Ecuador: view of Bartolomé Island (credit: Claire Cave)

transformed the islands from a small community of adventurous eco-tourists into a massive tourism hotspot. In 2007, the site was inscribed on the List of World Heritage in Danger, partly as a result of ineffective governance, a growing problem of invasive species and unsustainable growth in tourism.

Sustainable tourism frameworks

The UNESCO World Heritage and Sustainable Tourism programme aims to create an international framework for cooperative and coordinated achievement of shared and sustainable outcomes related to tourism at World Heritage properties. A toolkit for sustainable tourism has been developed to help site managers identify sustainable solutions to World Heritage tourism (UNESCO, 2017). It consists of a series of guides with practical steps, e.g. gaining understanding of tourism at a given destination, developing a strategy for progressive change, developing effective governance and engaging local communities and businesses. Furthermore, attempts have been made to establish management frameworks that ensure sustainable heritage tourism based on principles of authenticity, interpretation, access and inter- and intra-generational equity (Timothy & Boyd, 2003; Pedersen, 2002).

While authenticity is associated with presenting the past in an accurate and truthful way, 'staged authenticity' implies that 'front regions, or the locations where tourists come into contact with local environments and peoples, become decorated and superficially presented to resemble places, peoples and practices of back regions to which visitors have limited access. Backstage in this context means the authentic and true, while front stage is the staged, or inauthentic, front, which tourists see and experience' (MacCannell, 1973; 1976; cited in Timothy & Boyd, 2003, p240). Commercialization of heritage for the tourism industry runs the risk of distorting the authentic presentation of heritage. As with false and fabricated presentation of cultural practices, monuments and sites, the containment of wild animals for tourism purposes results in staged authenticity of nature.

Interpretation is about learning about the past. The convention stressed the duty of states parties not only to protect and conserve World Heritage sites but also to present and communicate their value (UNESCO, 1972, article 4). Interpretation involves explaining the past in various ways, such as through detailed on-site literature, displays, guided tours, audio and visual materials and interpretative centres. It is 'a process of communicating or explaining to visitors the significance of the place they are visiting' (Timothy & Boyd, 2003, p195). However, too much interpretation can interfere with the visitor's personal experiences and perceptions of a site. The use of interpretative visitor centres at World Heritage sites is both an opportunity for presenting their significance and a form of interference with the visitor's own experience. Nevertheless, visitor centres have the potential to act as important platforms for communication about World Heritage without being intrusive not only in relation to the values of specific sites but also in communicating the meaning of World Heritage and UNESCO's ultimate goal of peace building. In Norway, national authorities have explored the concept of 'World Heritage centres' to highlight the role of World Heritage sites as important focal points for local communities. In Regensburg, a visitor centre was developed for the Old Town of Regensburg with Stadtamhof in the Bavarian region of Germany following inscription on the World Heritage List in 2006. It was developed in a historic landmark building, a former salt barn dating to the 17th century strategically located at the stone bridge and the Danube River. In addition to presenting the site to visitors in an understandable and interactive way, it was built to function 'as a helpful tool in managing the city's tangible and intangible heritage, functioning as a public place for debate and a meeting point for the exchange of knowledge and information by professionals and experts' (URBACT, 2010, p6) (Figure 5.2).

Access relates to the level of intrusion and contact with the heritage resource that is considered acceptable. Questions to consider are to what extent access should be granted to heritage places and how privacy of the host cultures/ communities should be respected and protected. Zoning can be used to restrict access to those sites that are most sensitive and to direct visitors to other sites that can cope better with this. The Lascaux Cave in the Dordogne region of France is an example where access needed to be severely restricted for conservation reasons. Located in the Vézère valley, the Lascaux Cave was discovered in 1940 and has been considered of great importance for the history of prehistoric art depicting hunting scenes of remarkable detail and colour quality. A combination of factors such as breathing, lighting and changes in air circulations created

FIGURE 5.2 Visitor centre in Regensburg, Germany (credit: Elene Negussie)

problems to the extent that the caves had to be closed in 1963. Access to the original decorated cave was restricted and instead a replica of the decorated cave was created for visitors to see (Timothy & Boyd, 2003).

Equity relates to intra- and intergenerational access for everyone to heritage places. Equal access is not always possible for all heritage sites, e.g. for the elderly and people with physical challenges to sites in isolated areas and on difficult terrain, although it should be considered as much as possible. Furthermore, equity depends on the recognition of cultural diversity which is not always respected, and which means that heritage places often reflect a distorted representation of the past, particularly when emphasis is placed on one particular aspect of history at the expense of other relevant stories (Timothy & Boyd, 2003). In addition, those who can afford to visit places are still a minority of the world's population.

Issues relating to sustainable heritage tourism need to be adequately addressed in the World Heritage management plan, ranging from entry charges, local business development, impacts of various visitor types, damage to resources from overcrowding, information and interpretation, additional services and accessibility. Management methods need to focus on use, zoning and participation. Since overuse is often a problem for many sites, visitor numbers sometimes need to be controlled and regulated. Zoning with restricted access to the most sensitive parts of the site may be necessary and directing visitors to other sites. Participation methods empower visitors to respect heritage sites and to take responsibility in the management process, as well as local communities whose input in planning and management is essential (ibid.). Visitor flows may also be directed to protect and limit impact of large amounts of visitors on the daily life of local communities.

Following inscription of the ancient city of Petra on the World Heritage List in 1985, tourism grew significantly, from 100,000 in the late 1980s to 400,000 six years later (Ayad, 1999). This affected the daily life of the local community and the Bedouins who had lived in the ruins of Petra up until 1985. Following a Jordanian appeal to the international community, UNESCO sent a mission of experts in 1992, which led to the establishment of a management plan for the site. The plan included measures to conserve and restore the monuments, infrastructural improvements, environmental protection, local community issues and the setting up of the Petra Regional Planning Council. The Council consisted of representatives of government departments, local government and local communities with financial support from the site revenue. Unauthorized building activities by the Bedouins were considered a threat to the site. They had previously lived in and used the area for farming and grazing before being relocated in a village at the outskirts of the archaeological park, but increasingly made their living from tourism, renting houses and selling of souvenirs. With rising land value, the local families who felt marginalized and cramped in their new village were forced to add storeys to their houses that became visible from the site and were considered problematic (Ayad, 1999). This raises questions of how to balance site protection, tourism and the needs of local communities.

Venice is another example and has been described as 'a very good case of unsustainable tourism' (Russo, 1999 p43). Mass tourism has pushed local community services such as schools and hospitals out of the city. By 1999, the city population had declined to 68,000, a third of what it was in 1951 and has continued to decline ever since. The city as a living entity has consequently been threatened. Venice has suffered from the problem of 'day trippers', accounting for over 7 million annually. The local authorities used a negative publicity campaign with images of dead pigeons and garbage taken by photographer Oliviero Toscani. In response, a cultural tourism system was created with an information technology infrastructure set up to allow visitors access to details about sites and events in order to make advance bookings. The multi-service 'Venice Card' was introduced giving purchasers of the card the right to skip queues, etc. The aim was to attract high spenders and the 'serious cultural tourists'. However, it is necessary not only to manage tourism but also to diversify the economy (Russo, 1999). Tourism pressure in Venice has continued to grow beyond sustainable capacities in recent years, not least due to excessive numbers of large cruise ships entering the lagoon. In 2016, the World Heritage Committee warned it would consider placing Venice and its Lagoon on the List of World Heritage in Danger unless the state party had achieved substantial progress by 2017 (UNESCO, 2016d).

Carrying capacity

Carrying capacity has been used to set limits of acceptable change in relation to physical, ecological, social, economic and political impacts of tourism on cultural and natural environments (Mowforth & Munt, 2009). The idea is that there is a limit for the number of visitors that a heritage place can handle before it becomes degraded in relation to both physical resources and other dimensions such as the visitor's own experience and the social impacts on local communities. While the concept was initially developed in the context of natural environments and wildlife management, it was later applied to cultural sites. Scholars have identified different aspects that need to be considered in order to minimize the negative impacts of tourism on heritage places by using tools and techniques to set limits that ensure sustainable heritage tourism.

Carrying capacity 'addresses the question of how many people can be permitted into an area without risking degrading the site and the visitors' experience of it' (Pedersen, 2002, p56). Furthermore, it has been defined as 'a threshold or limit (number of people) that when crossed will begin to result in negative effects in terms of both the physical environment (ecological capacity) and visitor experiences (social capacity)' (Timothy & Boyd, 2003, p157). The physical environment concerns both cultural and natural resources. Ecological capacity relates to 'the degree to which an ecosystem is able to tolerate human interference while maintaining sustainable functioning', although 'wide variations in ecosystem resistance and resilience make ecological carrying capacity difficult to predict' (Pedersen, 2002, p56).

Social capacity is concerned with psychological and socio-cultural factors, or 'the limit beyond which the number of people in an available space would cause a decline in the quality of the recreational experience and the users' satisfaction' (Pedersen, 2002, p56). As noted by Orbasli (2000, p164) in relation to historic towns: 'while a narrow medieval street may have the physical capacity to accommodate a given number of persons, the valued image and context of a medieval quarter are lost once it is overcrowded. Acceptance of capacity, however, is all too often left to "saturation", at which point there is overcrowding and a place starts losing its attractiveness.' For example, the effect of large crowds of visitors in front of the famous Trevi Fountain in Rome at Palazzo Poli, may arguably detract from the quality experience of the place at least for some (Figure 5.3). However, social capacity also relates to the needs of the local communities who inhabit the area used for tourism and the extent to which they can sustain their lifestyles undisturbed. Shifts in services to cater for an increasing number of visitors may gradually erode the service structure for local communities.

Calculating carrying capacities is a complex task and requires collection of extensive research data and the selection of indicators and standards. Specific evaluation studies may be executed under the World Heritage management plan in order to assess carrying capacity. In the case of the Dorset and East

FIGURE 5.3 Fontana di Trevi, Rome (credit: Elene Negussie)

Devon Coast World, a natural site located in England, carrying capacity was in a study calculated at different levels: the economy of the Purbeck district, local community perceptions of tourism and the number of visitors and tourist infrastructure.[2] The study noted that 'there is no single measure for carrying capacity and because the Purbeck section of the Jurassic Coast is inextricably linked with its hinterland, where there is a large resident population, and diverse economy some of which is directly linked to the coast (e.g. tourism, fishing, farming, extraction), the specific World Heritage Site designated area cannot be viewed in isolation' (The Market Research Group, 2007, p9). Thus, the World Heritage designated part of the Jurassic Coast must be considered within a larger geographic and economic context.

Living heritage and sustainable development

Living heritage suggests that monuments, sites and landscapes are closely associated with the people who use and sustain them. ICOMOS recognized the interdependency of the tangible and intangible dimensions of heritage places in the Québec Declaration on the Preservation of the Spirit of Place (ICOMOS, 2008a).[3] Sacred sites, for example, are places endowed with spiritual meaning and significance. Urban sites are particularly complex to manage since they are 'living organisms, often densely populated, with deteriorating infrastructures and enormous developmental pressures' (ICOMOS 1993, p22). Mistakes of separating humans from monuments or areas have often been made in the interest of conservation. Historic towns have been preserved materially at the expense of functional diversity, resulting in loss of their vitality. Living heritage is also about maintaining bio-diversity, and undisturbed animal and species habitats and the people who use protected areas and landscapes to sustain their livelihoods.

Sacred sites: respecting values

Sacred sites require special attention to the traditional practices and management systems that exist to preserve them. Interpretation and visitor management are particularly important here, with rules to ensure respectful behaviour of visitors (e.g. restricted access, prohibition of photography, taking off shoes before entry). The Rock-Hewn Churches of Lalibela is a sacred site and a religious heritage, still in ecclesiastical use for practitioners of the Ethiopian Orthodox Church (Figure 5.4). The artistic achievement of the 11 monolithic churches carved out of rock give exceptional testimony to medieval and post-medieval civilization in Ethiopia. The churches are attributed to King Lalibela who set out to construct a 'New Jerusalem' in the 12th century after Christian pilgrimages to the Holy Land had been halted by Muslim conquests. The site is amongst the most significant places of pilgrimage for believers of the Ethiopian Orthodox Church, with the Ethiopian Christmas (*Genna*) and the Epiphany (*Timkut*) attracting large numbers of people each year (Negussie, 2012). The rock-hewn character of Lalibela has lent itself to comparisons with Petra in Jordan. However, the retained living character of Lalibela makes it remarkably different to Petra. A key management concern is how to manage tourism in a way that respects the spiritual value of the site. Another concern is how to cater for the vast amount of pilgrims visiting the site at the religious festivals. With processes of modernization and tourism uses the site is changing. The Church has noted that the spiritual value is being threatened due to shifts towards a more materialistic and foreign-influenced type of culture (Assefa-Wondimu, 2007). With growing emphasis on tourism, economic development and modernization, this suggests the potential for adverse impact on the traditional values of the site in the future.

In addition to major world religions, sacred sites also cover the spiritual beliefs of indigenous peoples and traditional forms of spirituality linked to a place or a landscape. The term 'sacred natural site' is used as a sub-group to sacred sites defined as 'areas of land or water having special spiritual significance to people and communities' (Oviedo & Jeanrenaud, 2006; cited in Wild & McLeod, 2008, p7). There is a close link between sacred sites and conservation of biodiversity. It is therefore essential to understand the traditional practices that have safeguarded these sites over generations and to integrate such knowledge in management practices. Sacred natural sites are often cared for through collective custodianship (Wild & McLeod, 2008). This can result in a conflict between the management of indigenous peoples associated with sacred sites and the

FIGURE 5.4 Worship at the Rock-Hewn Churches, Lalibela (credit: Elene Negussie)

governments who have imposed relatively recent forms of management regimes on protected areas. Therefore, 'identifying and interacting with custodians of sacred natural sites often requires great sensitivity, respect and trust building, sometimes in historically difficult, politically charged and very tense situations' (ibid., p7).

The UN Declaration on the Rights of Indigenous Peoples established rights in relation to sacred sites, recognizing the need for respect for indigenous knowledge, cultures and traditional practices that contribute to sustainable development and proper management of the environment (UN, 2008). Article 12.1 stated: 'Indigenous peoples have the right to manifest, practice, develop and teach their spiritual and religious traditions, customs and ceremonies; the right to maintain, protect, and have access in privacy to their religious and cultural sites; the right to the use and control of their ceremonial objects; and the right to the repatriation of their human remains'. Uluru-Kata Tjuta in Australia is an example of a sacred landscape (Figure 5.5). It was inscribed on the World Heritage List in 1987 as a mixed cultural/natural site and associative cultural landscape, defined by virtue of the powerful religious, artistic or cultural associations of the natural element rather than material cultural evidence, which may be insignificant or even absent' (UNESCO, 2012g, annex 3 10:iii). The traditional owners or custodians of the site are the Anangu Aboriginal people, for whom the Uluru, or Ayers Rock, is sacred. The rock gives evidence of the end of 'dreamtime', a period in the Anangu creation story. Visitor panels explain the sacred value of the site, asking visitors not to climb on the rock. Still, this has often been ignored.

The Yellowstone National Park in the USA became a national park in 1872, a biosphere reserve in 1976 and inscribed on the World Heritage List in 1978. Situated mainly in the State of Wyoming and also in the States of Montana and Idaho, it is famous for its geothermal features and the world's largest concentration of geysers. It was inscribed as a natural World Heritage site based on all of the natural criteria. As a sacred landscape Yellowstone is also of cultural significance and its landscape has been inhabited by the American Indians for thousands of years. Having been more or less removed from the area prior to its designation as a national park, their hunting rights and occupancy rights had gradually eroded by the late 1800s. The 'Yellowstone model' gave a name to a process in which indigenous peoples have been excluded from protected areas that are protected as 'wilderness areas'. This process has been challenged

FIGURE 5.5   Uluru Kata-Tjuta: a sacred landscape (credit: Claire Cave)

and 'blamed for harming local people, providing benefits to developed country interests at the expense of local people, high costs of park protection, and ineffective biodiversity conservation' (Schelhas, 2001, p300).

Historic urban landscapes

In 2011, UNESCO adopted the Recommendation on the Historic Urban Landscape (HUL) in response to the need for a holistic approach to urban conservation and recognition by the World Heritage Committee that decisions concerning urban sites require a special approach due to the dynamic nature of cities.[4] Urban sites had increasingly been considered for inclusion on the List of World Heritage in Danger. For example, Bordeaux, Port of the Moon achieved World Heritage status in 2007 and only a year later UNESCO sent a reactive monitoring mission to the city mainly as a result of a proposed bridge (*Bacalan-Bastide*) across River Garonne. The authorities in Bordeaux managed to convince UNESCO that a new bridge was fully compatible with the city's relationship with the river, and the OUV and the bridge contributed to the debate that led to the HUL recommendation (Negussie, 2015a). The recommendation also reflected a concern for the unprecedented pace of urbanization leading to social and spatial fragmentation and deterioration of the quality of urban environments due to excessive building density, standardized and monotonous buildings, loss of public space and amenities, inadequate infrastructure, social isolation and increasing risk of climate-related disasters (UNESCO, 2011a, para2).

The historic urban landscape is defined as 'the result of a historic layering of cultural and natural values and attributes, extending beyond the notion of "historic centre" or "ensemble" to include the broader urban context and its geographical setting' (UNESCO, 2011a, para8). This includes 'the site's topography, geomorphology, hydrology and natural features; its built environment, both historic and contemporary; its infrastructures above and below ground; its open spaces and gardens, its land use patterns and spatial organization; perceptions and visual relationships; as well as all other elements of the urban structure. It also includes social and cultural practices and values, economic processes and the intangible dimensions of heritage as related to diversity and identity' (ibid., para9). The recommendation has opened up new opportunities for proper weighing of heritage values holistically in the planning process. If matched with resolute and targeted implementation 'new development will bring added value to the historic urban landscape instead of profiting from existing values, which leads to loss of important values, including economic' (Negussie & Westerlund-Bjurström, 2014).

The recommendation established the HUL approach as an operational framework for managing change in cities through 'a landscape approach for identifying, conserving and managing historic areas within their broader urban contexts, by considering the interrelationships of their physical forms, their spatial organization and connection, their natural features and settings, and

FIGURE 5.6 The water mirror (*Le miroir d'eau*) at Place de la Bourse, Bordeaux (credit: Elene Negussie)

their social, cultural and economic values' (UNESCO, 2011a, para5). It is a way to 'define operational principles able to ensure urban conservation models that respect the values, traditions and environments of different cultural contexts, as well as to help redefine urban heritage as the centre of the spatial development process' (Banderin & van Oers, 2012, pXVII). The HUL approach promotes heritage-led development, which is about understanding conservation and development as intertwined instead of in opposition. A second example from Bordeaux illustrates how heritage can be used as a resource in urban renewal. The 'water mirror' fountain (*Le miroir d'eau*) at Place de la Bourse, previously used as a car park, formed part of a wider strategy to upgrade the urban waterfront (Figure 5.6). It resulted in better public use of the waterfront, and, from an aesthetic point of view, it accentuated the historic low-rise skyline through creating a mirror effect (Negussie, 2015a).

Humans in ecosystems

Shiretoko, Japan, is an example of a natural World Heritage property where the management of the site involved work towards a broader ecosystem-based management scheme. In this process, the fisheries sector came to play an important role by being integrated into the overall marine management plan for the World Heritage area. The 'Shiretoko approach' stands in sharp contrast to the Yellowstone model in which traditional human use of the landscape was eliminated. The fisheries sector and the local fishers were recognized as important stakeholders in the World Heritage management system and were considered part of the ecosystem. The need for balancing conservation with human use of the site was seen as essential. The Shiretoko region is one of the most productive fisheries in Japan and the fisheries sector one of the most important industries in the regional economy. The local fishers at the site were initially opposed to World Heritage listing due to fear that consequent environmental regulation would limit their traditional use of the site. But prior to the nomination of the property in 2005, the state party assured the local stakeholders that both the conservation of the ecosystem and the fisheries activities would be safeguarded. This highlights the need for balancing conservation and considering human use of the site as a natural component of the eco-system (Makino et al., 2009).

The outstanding universal value of Shiretoko lies in its extraordinary marine and terrestrial ecosystems as well as their productivity, and in its diversity of species and significance as a habitat for threatened species (Figure 5.7). The OUV derives particularly from the interrelationship between the terrestrial and the marine ecosystems (IUCN, 2005b). IUCN raised a number of concerns in its review of the nomination and management plan, including: the level of protection of the marine component; the level of fishing within the property; the potential impacts of aquaculture (or aquafarming); and the need for stricter controls of fishing. IUCN considered the legal and management planning aspects for the property to be satisfactory, noting that the latter consisted of

FIGURE 5.7 Gulf of Utoro, Shiretoko (credit: Pakku, CC BY 3.0)

several management plans for the different components of the site. However, it noted that 'the management plan may need to be revised in the future, particularly in relation to the need to address anticipated tourism pressures and to ensure the effective protection and management of marine resources within the nominated property' (IUCN, 2005b, p28).

In response, Japan took measures for a system of coordinated management between the different sectors and ministries concerned, including the fisheries. The alignment of the organizations concerned and their interrelationships 'have helped to ensure participation, to exchange information and opinions, and to build consensus between the wide-ranging interests of multiple users of the ecosystem services, supporting the legitimacy of the management plans and rules' (Makino et al., 2009, p209). This approach of 'co-ordinated consensus-building' is what is meant by the Shiretoko approach, a system in which 'the local fishers are an integral component of the ecosystem, rather than unwanted extras to be eliminated from the "original ecosystem". Moreover, local fishers are not something to be managed or controlled, but are expected to play an indispensable part of ecosystem-based management' (ibid., p213). Consequently, the local fishers' role has expanded in the context of management planning and is a good example of the opportunities to recognize viable economic activities and stakeholder participation in the context of World Heritage management plans.

Notes

1 The definition drew on that coined by Mexican Architect Héctor Ceballos-Lascuráin in 1993.
2 The Dorset and East Devon Coast contains important fossil sites and coastal geomorphologic features giving evidence of 185 million years of earth's history.
3 Paragraph 1 stated that 'the spirit of place is made up of tangible (sites, buildings, landscapes, routes, objects) as well as intangible elements (memories, narratives, written documents, festivals, commemorations, rituals, traditional knowledge, values, textures, colors, odors, etc.)'.
4 An international conference on the impact of contemporary development on urban landscapes led to the 2005 Vienna Memorandum on World Heritage and Contemporary Architecture: Managing the Historic Urban Landscape, which became the basis for recommendation UNESCO recommendation.

6

MANAGING WORLD HERITAGE

The management of World Heritage sites has grown into a holistic approach of managing outstanding universal value within a broader value-based context including the values of sustainable development. World Heritage sites are increasingly understood in the context of linkages to their surrounding environment, both in terms of their physical setting and their potential to contribute to the environmental, social and economic sustainability of the wider area (UNESCO et al., 2012). Placing sites in the context of their value to society and local culture provides for a mutually beneficial relationship between the sites and its surrounding communities which an emphasis on outstanding universal value (OUV) alone may not. However, it is a significant management challenge to maintain the values of sites while accommodating change and addressing external pressures from global phenomena such as urbanization, rising social and economic inequalities and environmental degradation (UNESCO et al., 2013). Consequently, modern approaches to management are increasingly about 'managing change' and integrating sites with wider regional and national planning. Management is no longer the sole preserve of the heritage sector; it has become a complex process requiring cross-sectoral engagement and a flexible and adaptable approach to variable conditions.

In line with the strategic objectives of the World Heritage Committee, sites should be managed through participatory approaches. Managing World Heritage sustainably should involve collaborating with stakeholders in decision-making throughout the management process. Recognition of local knowledge, pre-existing governance systems and the wide range of values associated with a place should facilitate long-term management and conservation of OUV. This chapter takes a look at the factors and practices that assist in securing an effective and sustainable management approach.

Management planning

The broadening of the understanding of the concept of heritage in recent years has resulted in an increase in the diversity of the types of landscapes, linear features and structures that are recognized as World Heritage properties. This is complemented by the increased importance given to how heritage places relate to their surroundings and wider social and economic values. As a result, management planning has become a progressively more challenging and complex process; from identifying the physical boundaries as well as the layers of social, cultural and environmental factors important for conservation of the place, to managing communication and decision-making across different jurisdictions and administrative systems in the case of transboundary serial sites.

Obligations under the convention

The inclusion of a management plan or documentation of the management system in the World Heritage nomination file has been mandatory since 2005 (UNESCO, 2015b, para132).[1] However, the Operational Guidelines recognize that a management plan may not be fully in place at the time of a property's inscription, and in such cases the relevant state party needs to indicate a timeframe and the resources available for the establishment of a plan and to provide documentation 'which will guide the management of the site until the management plan or system is finalized fully in place' (UNESCO, 2015b, para115). There are several properties inscribed in the early phase of the convention which, 35 or more years later, do not have a formal management plan finalized. The first management plan for the Island of Gorée, Senegal, inscribed on the World Heritage List in 1978, was submitted to the Committee in 2016.

The management plan or 'management system' for a World Heritage property should demonstrate how the OUV of the property is to be preserved, in terms of legislative protection as well as on a more practical level (UNESCO, 2015b, para97). The management plan may be considered as the guidance document which is developed within, and provides an overview of, the management system. The management system refers to the decision-making process concerning the overall protection of the site. It includes the legal and planning frameworks and the relevant authorities, stakeholders and organizational bodies that contribute to the conservation of the site. Management systems exist in many different formats, including traditional and informal undocumented systems. The type of management system employed is influenced by various factors such as the complexity of the property, the resources available and the regional and national governance systems (UNESCO et al., 2012; 2013).

The plan should identify a realistic vision for the medium to long-term future of the property and strike a balance between issues such as conservation, access, local community interests and sustainable economic use (UNESCO,

2015b, para112). World Heritage properties may support a variety of ongoing and proposed uses with the proviso that they are ecologically and culturally sustainable and do not impact adversely on the OUV (UNESCO, 2015b, para119). The management plan should also outline how the OUV is to be preserved through participatory means (UNESCO, 2015b, para108). Stakeholder participation is of particular importance, in both establishing and implementing the plan. However, in practice it is often the case that stakeholder participation, particularly at a grass roots level, is limited. There are many reasons for this such as the structure of the management system, power imbalance between stakeholders, lack of available resources, and different cultural perspectives. For example, managers at a site in Georgia found that stakeholders from the local community lacked the capacity to engage with the management process. The community was not organized and had little knowledge of how to participate in the decision-making process (Lisitzin, 2012). In response, the World Heritage Centre proposed the development of a regional capacity-building strategy to address similar issues across Central, Eastern and South Eastern Europe (ibid.).

States parties are also required to put in place legislative measures at all levels ranging from federal and national to regional and local and to make sure that these measures are implemented in the protection of World Heritage properties. This implies there must be national legislative instruments that can afford protection to monuments, sites, landscapes, national parks, nature reserves, etc., and authorities and institutions capable of implementing these (UNESCO, 2015b, para97). The legislative framework and institutional structure for protecting cultural and natural heritage varies between countries. For example, in some countries provisions have been introduced which protect World Heritage properties specifically (e.g. Australia, Hungary), whereas in most countries legal protection instruments are those already existing which protect national monuments and national parks.

Values-based participatory planning

The emergence of participatory planning reflects the growing perception 'of heritage as a shared property of communities and a factor in ensuring the sustainability of those communities' (UNESCO et al., 2013, p17). The participation of a broad range of stakeholders and interests in identifying the values associated with a heritage place, beyond those identified by 'experts' which often justify inscription, should potentially allow for management planning which is sympathetic to the role of the heritage property in the life of the local communities. As recognized by Johnston (1992, p4), 'pragmatically, many of us also acknowledge that where we have succeeded in protecting places, it is very often because the value of the place to a particular community has meant powerful community action to support protection of the place'.

Angkor, Cambodia was inscribed on the World Heritage List in 1992 for its architectural, archaeological and artistic significance as testament to a past civilization which has disappeared (UNESCO, 1992c),[2] yet the local population see Angkor as an ongoing, integral part of their culture (Mackay & Sullivan, 2008).[3] For years, the official conservation and management focus was directed at the monuments of the relic 'archaeological site' (Figure 6.1). The values associated with the contemporary inhabitants' local knowledge and their continuing cultural and religious connections to the Angkor temples and Khmer civilization were not incorporated into policy-making and priorities for management. The people living within the site and in the surrounding areas were excluded from the decision-making (Miura, 2011; Mackay & Sullivan, 2008). Furthermore, Angkor faced serious problems in terms of reconciling conservation and development. In 2007, the number of visiting international tourists reached 2 million, but approximately half of the population in the surrounding area of Siem Reap were living below the poverty line on less than 50 cents a day (Miura, 2011, p25).

The Cambodian Authority for the Preservation and Safeguarding of Angkor and Surrounding Areas (APSARA) launched the 'Living with Heritage' project in 2005 to promote sustainable development and to consider the social, economic and environmental issues that threaten Angkor and impact on the growing number of people who live and work within its boundaries.[4] The project took a consultative approach, engaging stakeholders at all levels, in order to identify all the cultural values associated with the place as well as the means to manage these values. According to Mackay and Sullivan (2008, p3), this holistic approach has contributed to a new understanding of Angkor: 'What has been interpreted in the past as a "site" or the "remains of a lost civilization" is now understood as a

FIGURE 6.1   Monument at Angkor, Cambodia (credit: Claire Cave)

complex and different place: not just one site, but a great many interrelated sites, together comprising a layered cultural landscape of World Heritage significance; not the ruins of a former society, but the hub of a still thriving culture and religion.'

Beyond boundaries

To be effective in conserving heritage of outstanding universal value, World Heritage properties must have adequate boundaries and be managed in the context of the broader landscape and/or seascape. The convention requires states parties are asked to 'to integrate the protection of [World] heritage into comprehensive planning programmes' (UNESCO, 1972, article 5a). The emphasis on heritage conservation being integral to planning is crucial in reconciling conservation strategies with local and regional planning and ensuring that equal weight is applied to the values associated with the heritage property and to those identified in the planning and development process.

Delineation of the boundary has a significant impact on how activities within and adjacent to a World Heritage property are regulated and on the long-term maintenance of a site's integrity. The successful implementation of planning regulations and restrictions associated with different types of land use within the World Heritage property and buffer zone are dependent on agreement with the responsible authorities and stakeholders. Consequently, it is important that the extent of the boundaries is clearly understood, not only from an administrative and regulatory point of view but from a local perspective. Disagreements between local residents and official boundary designations or lack of awareness of the extent of any restrictions on particular activities may cause conflict and be the source of threats to the integrity of properties. The Monastic City of Clonmacnoise and its Cultural Landscape, a site included on Ireland's Tentative List, illustrates this case well. The proposed nomination was thrown into disarray following protests by local residents who felt they had not been consulted about the extent of the boundaries and buffer zone and feared the impact of potential planning restrictions on their livelihoods. At Angkor, it was found that the official, mapped boundaries were meaningless to local people and poorly implemented because of lack of coherence between the straight lines on the map and the local land-use patterns and landscape features (Gillespie, 2013). Gillespie (ibid., p290) recommended that spatial regulations and boundaries need to 'take account of localized, normative accounts of landscape regulation' particularly where the Western approach to mapping is not well understood.

World Heritage sites have the potential to contribute substantially to broader conservation and development agendas beyond their boundaries. In the case of the Blaenavon Industrial Landscape World Heritage property in Wales (Figure 6.2), UK, the World Heritage nomination was used as a catalyst to boost social, economic and environmental activities for the benefit of the surrounding communities. Blaenavon is a relict iron making and coal mining landscape (UNESCO, 2014d). Inscribed on the World Heritage List in 2000,

FIGURE 6.2   Blaenavon Industrial Landscape World Heritage property in Wales (credit: Loco Steve)

the site is managed by the Blaenavon World Heritage Site Partnership (BWHSP) which brings together a group of public-sector bodies and organizations which set out a vision to 'protect the cultural landscape, increase cultural tourism, provide education opportunities and change perceptions of the area to assist economic regeneration' (Blaenavon World Heritage Site Partnership, 2011, pIV). Once a seriously depressed post-industrial community, the BWHSP has successfully raised investment of over £35 million in heritage-led regeneration programmes to improve the cultural and natural environment. The success of these projects in the upgrading, promotion and presentation of the landscape, natural environment and historic town has in turn encouraged public pride in the heritage site and brought a halt to the population decline of the past 90 years. Effective coordination and strategic planning between local and regional groups and stakeholders have provided the town and its landscape an option for a sustainable future (Thomas, 2012). Crucial to the success of the management planning was the establishment of management objectives based on a strategic long-term view (30 years) and medium-term objectives (5 years) which considered the dynamic, living perspective of the landscape.

Joint management: serial and transboundary sites

Serial and transboundary properties require particular coordination of management since they contain separate components which may be located far from each other and fall under different jurisdictions and administrative systems. Clear communication and decision-making together with alignment of policies between the relevant authorities are essential. The Operational Guidelines recommend the establishment of joint management committees for transboundary properties (UNESCO, 2015b, para135) and, for serial nominations, 'a management system or mechanisms for ensuring the coordinated management of the separate components' (UNESCO, 2015b, para114). Serial nominations may be phased over several nomination cycles, thus adding another layer of complexity. The addition of a serial component to an inscribed site involves extensive planning and coordination in terms of extending the management responsibilities, resources and the participation of new stakeholders. At a minimum, the management system should be structured so that there is effective communication and coordination across all management activities to ensure:

- activities are harmonized and consequently contribute effectively to a shared set of objectives regarding the preservation of OUV;
- identification of and response to threats to the property;
- realization of ongoing obligations to the World Heritage Convention such as periodic reporting, monitoring and state of conservation reports (Engels et al., 2009, p10).

Further interpretation of the Operational Guidelines indicates that the management system should be composed of different levels of management, from local to national, all feeding cumulatively into an overarching management body with decision-making power. This system can become highly complex where there is a large number of component parts and states parties. Even more so where the property is representative of a diversity of criteria, particularly mixed sites, and thus involves interaction among different institutions, organizations and specialists related to the conservation of different elements of natural and cultural criteria.

The Prehistoric Pile Dwellings around the Alps World Heritage site was inscribed on the World Heritage List in 2011. It is a serial, transboundary site located across six countries (Austria, France, Germany, Italy, Slovenia and Switzerland) which consists of 111 small individual sites. These sites consist of the remains of pre-historic stilt houses built from around 5,000 to 500 BC. There is a common management system in place which integrates all hierarchies within the relevant authorities and across all states parties. Local communities associated with the 111 sites are included and the different national systems of conservation, management and planning are linked into an international management system through an established International Coordination Group. The states parties collaborated over a period of five years to put the management framework and nomination document in place. This included agreeing on common visions and aims for the site which are translated into concrete projects on regional, national and local levels in a regularly adapted action plan. The level of collaboration and coordination is impressive (ICOMOS, 2011f).

The difficulty of coordinating the management of a serial transboundary property can be complicated by the different capacities of the states parties involved. In the case of the Prehistoric Pile Dwellings of the Alps, it appears that Austria has limited resources to support monitoring and management, including funding of archaeologists and other specialist staff. Also, impact assessments for development of archaeological sites is not obligatory in Switzerland and the construction of jetties and mooring of private leisure boats is exempt from planning control. While this is not a significant problem at the moment it may become problematic in the future as the remains of the pre-historic pile dwellings are concentrated underwater around the edges of lakes, rivers and wetlands.

Evaluation and monitoring

In order to be successful, the management plan needs to be a flexible and operational instrument that integrates programmes to monitor the state of conservation of the site and to evaluate the effectiveness of management actions. According to the advisory bodies, monitoring is one of three processes, the other two being planning and implementation, which together create a continuous cycle of activities, strategies and feedback which enable the management system to function (UNESCO et al., 2013). The plan may consist of a series of short-, medium- and long-term actions that address a wide range of issues, such as sustainable use and benefit-sharing. These are then managed in the context of the vulnerabilities of the property to change and external pressures, as well as the impacts of the management actions and interventions (UNESCO, 2015, para111).

State of conservation

A system of monitoring is required to determine whether a management plan is achieving its objectives, of which conservation of OUV is a priority for World Heritage properties. Monitoring, involving regular surveys and observations, enables managers to assess the occurrence of negative or positive changes at a site and should be one of the principal activities in managing a property (UNESCO et al., 2012). The Operational Guidelines stipulate that 'a regular review of the general state of conservation of properties, and thus their Outstanding Universal Value, shall be done within a framework of monitoring processes for World Heritage properties' (UNESCO, 2015b, para96). There are two types of monitoring. Firstly, reactive monitoring related to reporting on properties that are under threat. Secondly, periodic reporting, which involves six-yearly state party reports to the Committee (see Chapter 4). For the periodic report, states parties are required to provide an assessment of the maintenance of the OUV and the measurements applied.

In the context of World Heritage management plans, UNESCO et al. (2013, p81) describe monitoring as 'collecting and analysing data to check that the management system is operating effectively and delivering the right results, and to identify remedial measures in the event of shortcomings or new opportunities'. The usefulness of this data is not limited to conservation strategies; effective monitoring can assist managers in dealing with issues at the wider political level also. With the data to demonstrate accurately the effects of time, surrounding conditions and human action and inaction on natural and cultural heritage, managers are in a better place to advocate for increased support and to demonstrate how and if a property is making a difference to wider society (Stanley-Price, 2004). Similarly, monitoring can inform the participatory planning process. It is often the case that there is not enough data to determine whether participatory planning outcomes have been successful in maintaining the integrity of the protected area and satisfying the needs of the participants. Monitoring has become a significant issue at World Heritage Committee meetings. The number of decisions relating to monitoring increased to an average of 103 per year between 2006 and 2016, compared to 27 per year in the preceding decade.

Critical to the success of monitoring is the development of targets and indicators which can be used to assess the status of a site's attributes. This is emphasized in the Operational Guidelines where states parties are asked to list 'the key indicators that have been chosen as the measure of the state of conservation of the whole property' in the nomination document (UNESCO, 2015b, annex 5.6a). To be effective, indicators should be cost effective and not require specialist equipment and expertise so the data can be collected, analyzed and reported regularly. Used appropriately, indicators will reflect changes that have direct implications for management on a relevant timescale (UNESCO et al., 2012, p73). Indicators may be linked to 'management triggers' whereby a threshold is set for a particular monitoring indicator and if that threshold is crossed it alerts managers to the need to consider alternative management strategies (UNESCO et al., 2012, p74). At Angkor, for example, a recommendation is in place to monitor the underground water level near monuments (HMFSC, 2013). Declining levels in ground water, due to urbanization and climate change, threaten the stability of the monuments. Setting thresholds for significant changes in ground water levels could provide early warning of a potentially hazardous situation and trigger an appropriate management response.

Adaptive management

Adaptive management emerged from the ecological sciences in recognition of the complexity and variability of ecosystem processes and functions. The uncertainty associated with the management of natural resources generated a need for an approach that incorporated experimentation and learning by doing, rather than a fixed, prescriptive response (Holling, 1978; Walters,

1986). The adaptive management approach incorporates monitoring into a system of evaluation and revision which allows for continuous updating of the management plans in line with changing circumstances and an expanding knowledge base. IUCN, the UNESCO Man and Biosphere programme and the major biodiversity-related conventions, such as the Ramsar Convention, the Convention on Conservation of Migratory Species (CMS), the Convention on International Trade in Endangered Species (CITES) and the Convention on Biological Diversity (CBD) all advocate adaptive management. Ecosystems are dynamic and change naturally as well as in response to socio-economic conditions. The changes are often unpredictable, inconsistent and surprising and require a management approach that is flexible and adaptive. The aim of the adaptive approach is to generate new knowledge and reduce uncertainties, thereby allowing managers to anticipate and cater for change (CBD Secretariat, 2004b). The generation of new knowledge requires research and feedback into an integrated learning process which leads to updated management practices to ensure that management decisions are based on best available science.

Willingness to learn through experience is at the core of the adaptive management approach. According to Spoelder et al. (2015, p390) this is achieved through three key methods. The first is 'testing assumptions': being prepared to methodically try alternative interventions to achieve the desired goal. The second is 'adaptation': utilizing the data collected through systematic monitoring to inform management effectiveness. The third is 'learning': documenting the entire process to inform decision-making and relevant participants. The result of the process of adapting to continuous change is a dynamic and evolving management plan. Management plans are often expensive and detailed documents based on a definitive plan for the site over a certain time period, for example 5–10 years, and, arguably, do not address continuously changing environments, political and socio-economic conditions and external factors such as climate change. Nor do they keep up with the growth in knowledge and expertise. Adaptive management requires an understanding that the management plan will never be complete, that what is required is continuously updated management actions and a 'continuous, iterative and developmental process' (Alexander, 2010, p24).

Adaptive management is applicable to both cultural and natural sites. The Operational Guidelines promote adaptive management for all World Heritage sites through a 'cycle of planning, implementation, monitoring, evaluation and feedback' (UNESCO, 2015b, para111b). The Australia ICOMOS Burra Charter has also advanced the concepts of monitoring and updating within the management process for cultural heritage. The Burra Charter process firstly involves understanding the significance of a place, then developing policy and a management plan, and finally monitoring management actions and policy as well as reviewing cultural significance to ensure continuing appropriateness and effectiveness (Australia ICOMOS, 2013b). UNESCO and the advisory bodies have produced guidelines which enshrine the concept of adaptive management for both cultural and natural World Heritage (UNESCO et al., 2012; 2013). Although the guidelines for managing cultural heritage do not refer specifically to adaptive management, they encapsulate the processes of monitoring, responding to change and continuously reviewing and improving management processes and strategies.

The adaptive management approach adopted for the Great Barrier Reef World Heritage site has received international acclaim (Day, 2008; Douvere & Badman, 2012). A multiple-use zoning system has been developed for the site based on the results of a series of seascape-scale experiments to examine the impact of fishing and to gather data on risks associated with ecosystem change and external factors (Hughes et al., 2007). : The zoning system maps out areas for activities such as tourism, fishing, boating, diving and research, allocating a gradation of uses from exclusive 'undisturbed' zones to 'general use' zones. It represents integrated research and unprecedented consultation, negotiation and cooperation at federal, state and local levels. The stakeholder engagement and political and financial support required to take an experimental approach and to test innovative methods are some of the main challenges that face managers in adaptive management.

Management effectiveness

The promotion of improved management effectiveness of World Heritage properties has become a priority of the advisory bodies and the Secretariat. Increased reporting on the state of conservation of properties has effectively highlighted the range of management challenges and pressures affecting the long-term preservation of World Heritage, not least of which is the inadequacy of management plans for 85 per cent of properties (UNESCO, 2013f). Evaluation of management effectiveness has emerged as a tool for site managers to assess the management process and its success in protecting the OUV of a property. Monitoring and adaptive management are key methods in validating the effectiveness of management actions. However, evaluating management effectiveness is an assessment of how well properties are being managed as a whole, from identifying values and objectives, planning and allocation of resources to measuring success of actions, outputs and achievements (Hockings et al., 2008). Evaluation enables managers to plan effectively, identify new and potential threats, secure equipment, assign staff and other resources to good effect and recognize beneficial activities and potential opportunities. According to Hockings et al. (2006a, p636), there are four main purposes for management effectiveness evaluation:

- Promoting better protected area management, including a more reflective and adaptive approach;
- Guiding resource allocation, priority-setting and project planning;
- Providing accountability and transparency;
- Increasing community awareness, involvement and support.

The methodologies used to assess management effectiveness were first developed for natural protected areas in response to growing concern over the number of so-called 'paper parks' or designated areas that lacked sound management and were considered to exist in name only (Stolton & Dudley, 1999). There was also an urgent need for data to answer questions regarding the success of protected areas in conserving biodiversity and other natural and cultural heritage resources and to understand the impact of protected areas on wider issues such as social justice and sustainable development (Hockings & Philips, 1999). Following the Fourth World Parks Congress in 1992, an international task force was established under the IUCN and the World Commission on Protected Areas (WCPA), which developed a framework for an evaluation system that could be adapted to any management structure (Hockings et al., 2006b).

A toolkit for assessing management effectiveness for natural World Heritage sites emerged from the WCPA framework as part of a project run by IUCN and UNESCO and funded by the UN Foundation (Hockings et al., 2008). The toolkit, known as the 'Enhancing our Heritage Toolkit' (EoH), is made up of 12 tools for assessing the different components of World Heritage site management effectiveness (Table 6.1). The tools consist of 12 questionnaires accompanied by scorecards and data sheets and can be grouped according to different stages of the management process. The first four tools are related to understanding a site and its current status, which involve identifying a site's value, management objectives, the threats to conservation, the relationship with stakeholders and impact of national legislation. The next four tools are linked to assessing the existing management plan and processes. These include evaluating the management plan, the boundaries and size of a site, management needs such as staff, funds and equipment, and management practices in place. The last four tools focus on identifying the achievements, which include appraising the implementation of the plan, the outputs, the status of the values of the site and finally a summary of the overall findings and a list of priority actions for the next management cycle. The toolkit is designed to be flexible and to fit in with, rather than duplicate, existing monitoring and periodic reporting systems.

Although primarily designed for natural site managers, the EoH toolkit offers a useful template for developing management effectiveness strategies for cultural sites. The UNESCO guidelines for managing cultural heritage advise cultural managers to consult EoH toolkit (UNESCO et al., 2013), and the World Heritage Committee recommends that the EoH toolkit be developed and refined for application to all properties under the World Heritage Strategy for Capacity Building (UNESCO, 2011f). There are some challenges associated with applying the toolkit to cultural sites, such as determining indicators appropriate to the individual property. However, the majority of tools can be applied with minimal amendment. Some of the tools have been employed successfully in assessing management effectiveness at cultural sites (EX.PO AUS, 2015).

TABLE 6.1 The 12 tools of the Enhancing our Heritage toolkit for evaluating management effectiveness of World Heritage sites

Tool 1: Identifying Site Values and Management Objectives
Identifies and lists major site values and associated management objectives. Together these help decide what should be monitored and analyzed during the assessment.

Tool 2: Identifying Threats
Helps managers to organize and report changes in the type and level of threat to a site and to manage responses.

Tool 3: Relationships with Stakeholders
Identifies stakeholders and their relationship with the site.

Tool 4: Review of National Context
Helps understand how national and international policies, legislation and government actions affect the site.

Tool 5: Assessment of Management Planning
Assesses the adequacy of the main planning document used to guide management of the site.

Tool 6: Design Assessment
Assesses the design of the site and examines how its size, location and boundaries affect managers' capacity to maintain site values.

Tool 7: Assessment of Management Needs and Inputs
Evaluates current staff compared to staff needs and current budget compared to an ideal budget allocation.

Tool 8: Assessment of Management Processes
Identifies best practices and desired standards for management processes and rates performance against these standards.

Tool 9: Assessment of Management Plan Implementation
Shows progress in implementing the management plan (or other main planning document), both generally and for individual components.

Tool 10: Work/Site Output Indicators
Assesses the achievement of annual work programme targets and other output indicators.

Tool 11: Assessing the Outcomes of Management
Answers the most important question: whether the site is accomplishing what it was set up to do in terms of maintaining ecological integrity, wildlife, cultural values and landscapes, etc.

Tool 12: Review of Management Effectiveness Assessment Results
Summarizes the results and helps to prioritize management actions in response.

Source: Hockings et al. (2008, p12).

Funding

Effective management is limited by the resources and capacity available to implement the World Heritage management plan. The importance of financial stability for World Heritage properties is recognized in the text of the convention, in the Operational Guidelines and in the procedures for periodic reporting. Articles 4 and 5 of the convention affirm that each state party shall 'do all it can […] to the utmost of its own resources […] to take the appropriate legal, scientific, technical, administrative and financial measures necessary' for the conservation and management of its heritage (UNESCO, 1972). The Operational Guidelines assert that states parties have the responsibility to 'consider and encourage the establishment of national, public and private foundations or associations to facilitate donations for the protection of World Heritage' (UNESCO, 2015b, para15.k). The periodic reporting process requires that states parties 'provide an assessment of the human and financial resources that are available and required for the management of the property, as well as an assessment of the training needs for its staff' (UNESCO, 2015, annex 7.II.4). Inadequate allocation of resources during economic recession or due to unpredictable fluctuations in the economies of some countries is often a threat to conservation priorities at World Heritage sites. However, there are a number of other factors that interrupt and influence financial stability over and above available funding, such as government policies, staff capacity, management structures as well as community support or lack of it. To deal with changes in resources and funding priorities, it is important to have management tools in place for the administration of funds, to incorporate budgeting considerations within the management plan and to identify capacity-building requirements in the area of financial and business planning.

The ability to secure sufficient, stable, long-term financial resources is a critical element of management planning at local, national and global levels. The Fifth World Parks Congress and the CBD have called on governments, inter-governmental organizations, NGOs and the private sector to provide additional financial support for protected areas, including World Heritage properties. Proposed actions include national-level studies of the socio-economic values of protected areas and development of national resource mobilization strategies or finance plans to implement the biodiversity-related conventions (IUCN, 2003a; UNEP, 2014).[5] The following have been identified as government policies and other institutional obstacles that intentionally and unintentionally restrict the flow of funding to protected areas (IUCN, 2003a, rec7):

- Insufficient priority allocated to the conservation of natural and cultural values against other competing budget programmes;
- Revenues from tourist income and environmental services provided by protected areas not being earmarked for protected area management;
- Inappropriate management structures that fail to channel funding to protected area management;
- Lack of mechanisms to encourage donor organizations to participate in supporting protected areas; and
- Limited use of business planning at both a protected area systems level as well as for specific protected areas.

Management capacity increasingly requires skills associated with networking and attracting resources and support for management plans. Priorities for site managers include identifying mechanisms to increase, diversify and stabilize the financial flows to the heritage site as well as applying cost-effective management approaches and monitoring methods. Good communication strategies with relevant government officials is recommended (Müller et al., 2015) as well as using the World Heritage brand to encourage NGO, trust and donor funding (UNESCO et al., 2012).

Traditional management systems

The pre-existence of an indigenous heritage management system and traditional conservation practices need to be considered in the management plan. Many local communities and indigenous peoples use traditional conservation practices and accumulated local experience to protect and effectively manage monuments and landscapes sustainably. However, traditional knowledge is not always recognized or integrated with 'modern' heritage management systems, despite international recognition of the right of people to maintain, control and protect their cultural heritage (UN, 2015d, para16). In distinguishing between 'local communities' and 'indigenous peoples', the UN advises that indigenous peoples self-identify as indigenous and that they retain social, cultural, economic and political characteristics that are distinct from those of the dominant societies in which they live. Indigenous peoples have historical continuity with the pre-colonial and/or pre-settler societies that occupied their territories (UN, undated). However, community is not defined in international law. It may be understood broadly as 'a group of people living in the same place or having a particular characteristic in common' (Oxford English Dictionary, 2016). The addition of 'local' is used to emphasize the association between a community and a particular location. A common interest in the management of a heritage site would denote a shared characteristic.

However, it should be noted that community is a complex term and within what may be regarded as a a uniform community there are often several groupings with conflicting interests.

The role of traditional systems

Traditional or indigenous management systems and practices are often linked to the management of sacred sites and sites of cultural significance, where rules and taboos may exist to reduce negative human impacts and misuse of resources. It is necessary to consider the role and opportunities of such traditional management practices in the World Heritage management plan process and to understand the significance from a sustainable development point of view. The Operational Guidelines support the incorporation of 'traditional practices' in the management plan: '[...] management systems may vary according to different cultural perspectives, the resources available and other factors. They may incorporate traditional practices, existing urban or regional planning instruments, and other planning control mechanisms, both formal and informal' (UNESCO, 2015b, para110).

The significance of traditional or indigenous knowledge in heritage conservation has been highlighted in several other conventions. The CBD recognized the need to 'respect, preserve and maintain knowledge, innovations and practices of indigenous and local communities embodying traditional lifestyles relevant for the conservation and sustainable use of biological diversity' (UN, 1992, para8.j). Similarly, the UNESCO Convention on the Protection and Promotion of the Diversity of Cultural Expressions (UNESCO, 2005a, preamble) recognized 'the importance of traditional knowledge as a source of intangible and material wealth, and in particular the knowledge systems of indigenous peoples, and its positive contribution to sustainable development, as well as the need for its adequate protection and promotion.'

The Fifth World Parks Congress Durban Accord recognized the successes of indigenous and local communities in conserving biodiversity and 'their efforts to make protected areas places of natural, cultural and spiritual convergence' (IUCN 2003b). It is important that sustainable, customary practices of indigenous and local communities are recognized and incorporated into management systems. However, the belief that all indigenous peoples live harmoniously with nature is a naive generalization. Furthermore, rapid social changes are impacting on many traditional practices that in the past promoted sustainable resource use (McClanahan, 2004; Wilshusen et al., 2002). Ultimately, successful management requires a commitment from all participants towards a long-term vision for heritage conservation and sustainable development, regardless of ethnicity, history or cultural background (McClanahan, 2004).

The Sacred Mijikenda Kaya Forests of Kenya were inscribed on the World Heritage List in 2008 under cultural criteria (iii), (v) and (vi) and represent the last remnants of the once extensive, coastal lowland forest of East Africa. The preservation of the forest fragments is due to the traditions of the Mijikenda people, the majority of whom have now moved away from the area. Discontinued as places of habitation, the kaya forests acquired a new role as communal ceremonial areas and burial grounds. These forest fragments and rich biodiversity are protected in a landscape otherwise transformed by intensive agriculture and rapidly growing coastal development. More recently, attitudes to the kayas have changed again with a growing disregard for traditional values among the younger generations of Mijikenda. This decline in knowledge and respect for traditions reflects economic, social and cultural changes in the society (ICOMOS, 2008b).

The World Heritage designation has established international recognition of the value of the Mijikenda culture in protecting the local biodiversity and will support the conservation of the sacred forests and help protect against more powerful economic and business interests. In its evaluation of the property,

ICOMOS considered that 'the exceptional value of the kayas is linked not to their uniqueness as sacred spaces, or necessarily to the fact that they were formerly habitation sites, but for the profound impact their sacrality has had on protecting pockets of "natural" coastal forests, through their association with cultural identity. The impact of the sacred spaces and the benefits they deliver is now far wider than within the local communities' (ICOMOS, 2008b, p7).

Indigenous knowledge and modernity

The international community largely accepts that 'traditional and local knowledge systems […] can make, and historically have made, a valuable contribution to science and technology' (UNESCO, 1999b, para26). However, a significant challenge lies in the means by which indigenous knowledge and management practices may be integrated into wider conservation strategies and sustainable use of natural and cultural resources. The use of the term 'traditional' in describing knowledge systems often reflects a perceived binary divide between Western science, understood as the dominant or modern knowledge system, and indigenous knowledge, seen as a residual and static knowledge system of the past (Briggs, 2005). This view has been challenged by Green (2010, p120): 'The preference to view indigenous peoples' knowledge systems – or tribal or local peoples' knowledge systems – as "traditional" reveals a dominant and colonial inclination. What knowledge system is not traditional, we might ask ourselves? What we think of as the Western knowledge system (or conventional science) is far from neutral, and is equally embedded in a long history and developed within a specific cultural context.'

Scientists and the wider society alike should generate inclusive approaches to heritage conservation and recognize the value and diversity of knowledge systems beyond that of Western science. The UNESCO Framework for Action on Science and the use of Scientific Knowledge calls on governments and NGOs to support activities and to formulate national policies that enable the wider application of traditional forms of learning and knowledge. It also advocates the promotion of better understanding of traditional knowledge systems and fostering cooperation between holders of traditional knowledge and scientists to create interlinkages of mutual benefit (UNESCO, 1999c). The framework highlights the fact that not only do indigenous knowledge systems 'harbour information as yet unknown to modern science, but they are also expressions of other ways of living in the world, other relationships between society and nature, and other approaches to the acquisition and construction of knowledge'. The knowledge systems should be nurtured particularly because of their vulnerability to globalization and the dominance of a single view of the natural world as promulgated by science (UNESCO, 1999d, para35).

Traditional knowledge is characterized by its transmission, often orally, from generation to generation. The oral transfer of knowledge may be considered a strongpoint in enabling the knowledge system to evolve and adapt within a changing cultural and environmental context (Pretty, 2008). However, the lack of understanding of indigenous knowledge systems by mainstream society and the exclusion of indigenous knowledge from long-term planning and conservation strategies make a strong case for its documentation (Ens et al., 2015). The challenge is to ensure that intellectual property rights are respected and that the knowledge is transferred in such a way that it is not de-contextualized and that indigenous peoples remain at the forefront of its dissemination. Efforts to share indigenous knowledge and practices have been recently enhanced by the establishment of the World Indigenous Network, which officially became part of the United Nations Development Programme in 2013 (World Indigenous Network, 2014).

While there are substantial difficulties in achieving recognition of alternative knowledge systems in mainstream biodiversity conservation, in other areas of heritage conservation the loss of traditional skills is readily recognized as a threat. For example, English Heritage found that the traditional building skills of craftspeople such as bricklayers, carpenters, flint-knappers, lime-plasterers, stonemasons, are crucial to the repair and care of historic buildings but are themselves threatened intangible assets in need of conservation (English Heritage, 2005, p3). Similarly, ancient techniques such as rammed earth construction are essential to the conservation of earthen architecture and archaeological sites. Traditional building materials are also increasingly valued for their sustainability and energy efficiency compared to materials associated with modern building techniques.

Co-management systems

Relationships between traditional-based management systems and state administrative organizations often involve conflict where traditional heritage practices are overridden by the modern state legal systems. However, the shift towards more holistic and sustainable approaches to heritage management has encouraged participation by local communities resulting in new forms of 'co-management' or 'joint management' where indigenous custodianship is a key element. An IUCN publication on implementing collaborative management strategies defines co-management as 'a situation in which two or more social actors negotiate, define and guarantee amongst themselves a fair sharing of the management functions, entitlements and responsibilities for a given territory, area or set of natural resources' (Borrini-Feyerabend et al., 2007, p1).[6]

The Great Barrier Reef (GBR) in Australia provides an example of the difficulties that may be encountered at World Heritage sites during the process of forming co-management between traditional owners, wider society and state authorities. The attempts at co-management revealed a clash between cultures as well as paradigms of co-management versus protected area management (Nursey-Bray & Rist, 2009). The Girringun people as traditional owners advocated their right to participate in and benefit from management. Proposed involvement included funding and training Girringun rangers, maintaining ongoing access to and traditional use of the area, such as hunting dugongs and turtles, and creating exclusive use zones where cultural activities could take place without disturbance. These proposals were rejected by the wider community who were immediately concerned about the conservation of such iconic species as dugongs and turtles and fearful of the impact of exclusion zones on tourism. The backlash from the media and public objections forced the authorities to back away from the proposals. The management priorities, which were focused on the conservation of World Heritage values through the application of Western science principles, were in conflict with the cultural rationale of the proposals of the Girringun people (ibid.).

The initial co-management attempt revealed a disconnect between the ideals of co-management and the actual practice of implementing co-management in terms of power-sharing, recognizing both traditional and contemporary management regimes and the competing priorities of economic, cultural and environmental concerns. Interestingly, the discussion that emerged was about the rights of third party users such as international tourists and fishers and their right to reap economic reward from the GBR. The perceived empowerment or equity of power sharing with the Girringun traditional owners was seen as a threat by the wider public (Nursey-Bray & Rist, 2009).

The Girringun people continued to work towards developing a co-management approach and were eventually successful in the development of a traditional use of marine resources agreement (TUMRA). The TUMRA is a legal instrument that identifies how a traditional owner group will manage their use of marine resources within their clan estate. This approach enabled both cultural perspectives to be recognized. For the Marine Park Authority it helped facilitate biodiversity objectives, as the Girringun members agreed not to hunt dugongs, and ensure the sustainable harvest of marine resources using culturally appropriate methods. For the Girringun people, although they have not asserted their right to harvest protected species, this agreement is recognized by law and provides for ongoing funding and governance support for the maintenance of what they consider their 'sea country'. Since the first TUMRA in 2005, six further TUMRA have been established between the management body and other traditional owner groups along the GBR Reef (GBRMPA, 2015).

Tenure and legislation

Traditional tenurial rights of communities have become the exception in today's world where the majority of land ownership is the preserve of private individuals, corporations or public authorities (Borrini-Feyerabend et al., 2006). Although, the history of appropriation of community land rights can be dated back to medieval times (ibid.), colonization and colonialism have played a significant role in marginalizing the relevance of customary land rights in many countries. As a result, the customary rules and laws that communities apply in managing cultural and natural heritage often lack statutory recognition or sanctioning power. However, in some cases indigenous peoples and/or local communities are fully recognized as the legitimate authority in charge of state-designated protected areas or have legal title to land and water resources (ibid.).

In the nomination of The Dolomites, a serial World Heritage property, cooperative organizations or mountain communities were recognized as collective landholders that manage the cultural landscape through traditional regulations (Government of Italy, 2008). The property was inscribed on the World Heritage List in 2009 under natural criteria (vii) and (viii) and is located in the northern Italian Alps (Figure 6.3). One local institution, the Regole d'Ampezzo (literally, 'Rules of the Ampezzo Valley'), represents the community-based governance system within one of the component parks, i.e. the Natural Park of the Ampezzo Dolomites. The Regole d'Ampezzo is the result of a federation of 11 villages that, for a thousand years, has been responsible for a large territory of forests and pastures under common property. The Regole owns close to 59 per cent of the park, while the remainder belongs to the state. Within the park, the Regole manages both its own land and state property. Outside the park, the Regole owns more than 80 per cent of the territory of the municipality of Cortina (Lorenzi & Borrini-Feyerabend, 2009). The Italian government recognized this system of collective property in the National Law on Mountains Areas of 1952. The law allowed family communes in mountain territories to continue being governed and administered according to their respective statutes and customary rules. The management aims and goals of the Regole have evolved over time to meet the changing demands of the lifestyles of the local communities. However,

FIGURE 6.3 Funes Valley, The Dolomites, Italy (credit: Navin Rajagopalan)

the overall aim to sustainably provide for the livelihoods of the local community has not changed. Consequently, timber extraction and the careful management of tourist activities allow the Regole to earn a sizeable income, all of which is reinvested in the conservation of the territory and the protected area (ibid.).

Indigenous peoples have successfully campaigned and fought for legal title to their lands in several countries. In Australia, the Aboriginal Affairs Planning Authority Act 1972 established the Aboriginal Lands Trust (ALT), a body charged with acquiring and holding land, to use and manage it for the benefit of Aboriginal people in accordance with their wishes. The participation of the traditional owners in the management of Kakadu National Park World Heritage property is supported by this legislative framework. The ALT leases the land to the Director of National Parks, and the conditions of the lease agreements support the traditional use of the park by the traditional owners as well as an Aboriginal majority on the management board.

In contrast, states authorities in other countries continue to deny traditional tenurial rights of communities. In Kenya and Ethiopia, for example, the ability of pastoralist communities to sustain their traditional management and grazing regimes has been severely undermined by changes in landownership, resulting in conflict with state conservation agencies and foreign and domestic investors in agricultural and infrastructural development (Jones et al., 2005b; Cotula et al., 2009). Lack of recognition and/or restoration of customary entitlements to land and natural resources severely hamper attempts to achieve sustainable development and social equity (Borrini-Feyerabend et al., 2006; Jones et al., 2005b).

Managing external factors

The World Heritage management plan should consider the potential external factors that may affect the property concerned, now and in the future, and how these may be dealt with. The World Heritage Centre has noted a number of recurrent trends in the types of threats that are increasingly affecting World Heritage properties and many of these threats are developments and activities that are prompted by factors beyond the local context of the sites (UNESCO, 2012f). For example, infrastructural developments and resource extraction forming part of regional and national strategies may conflict with the objectives of the management plan. Therefore, it is necessary to consider how best to utilize the management plan as an opportunity to mitigate threats and to maximize opportunities for conservation-led development.

Development projects

Development projects have been identified as one of the main threats affecting the OUV of World Heritage properties (UNESCO, 2012f). 'Development projects' is a broad term which may include transportation and other infrastructural projects as well as utilities construction and property development. Such projects can have an impact on the OUV and yet be located at a distance from the site concerned or in a different country. A development project that has generated extensive discussion amongst the World Heritage Committee was the building of a hydroelectric dam in Ethiopia (GIBE III). Concern was expressed that the dam would impact negatively on the hydrological regime of the Lake Turkana National Parks in Kenya, the world's largest desert lake. The dam was also expected to threaten the Lower Omo Valley World Heritage site in Ethiopia, renowned for the discovery of many archaeological treasures and hominid fossils, including the bone fragments of the *Australopithecus* fossil known as Lucy. It was feared that irrigation schemes, enabled by the dam as part of the Omo-Kuraz Sugar project, would threaten the fossil outcrops through sugarcane plantations and associated infrastructure including roadways, pipelines, sugar mills and large-scale settlement for workers (Monteil & Kinahan, 2015).

Urban sites are particularly prone to development projects that may threaten the OUV and change the character and setting of the sites concerned. This is due to their dynamic and expanding nature as dense living areas undergoing constant change. In Seville, the building of the César Pelli-designed Torre Cajasol caused much controversy in relation to the Cathedral, Alcázar and Archivo de Indias World Heritage property. Located in the vicinity of the historic Triana district on the left bank of the Guadalquivir River, the 178 m tall tower crossed the traditional height restriction which was two-thirds of the Giralda bell tower, which forms part of the Seville Cathedral (Figure 6.4). It has been described as the new 'protagonist' on the Sevillian skyline (Negussie & Fernández-Salinas,

FIGURE 6.4 View of the Torre Cajasol from the Giralda tower of Seville Cathedral (credit: Claire Cave)

2013). Furthermore, Liverpool – Maritime Mercantile City was placed on the List of World Heritage in Danger (LWHD) in 2012 due to plans for a large-scale development project, estimated at £5.5 billion, to be implemented over a 30-year period. The development site includes part of the inscribed property as well as its buffer zone. A UNESCO-ICOMOS reactive monitoring report concluded the development would irreversibly damage the property due to 'a serious deterioration of its architectural and town-planning coherence, a serious loss of historical authenticity, and an important loss of cultural significance' (UNESCO, 2012h, p183). The World Heritage Committee has recognized that decisions concerning World Heritage cities require a special conservation approach and understanding due to their dynamic nature. In 2011, UNESCO adopted the Recommendation on the Historic Urban Landscape stipulating a holistic approach to understanding urban conservation and managing change in urban environments (see Chapter 5) (UNESCO, 2011a).

The main difficulty in considering external factors is identifying how the management plan can envisage and mitigate for development projects that may negatively affect the OUV of a property. In the case of Liverpool, a 2015 UNESCO/ICOMOS mission welcomed the development of awareness programmes for stakeholders, promoting wider understanding and appreciation of the World Heritage site (Barbato & Turner, 2015). This, together with the participatory approach of all stakeholders in the management of the property, built trust and partnership between the management body, the developers and concerned NGOs which is crucial in reaching agreement on the measures to be taken to remove the property from the LWHD. Further recommendations include integrating public–private investment potential into the management plan to realize heritage-led regeneration and conservation projects and good practice in line with the Historic Urban Landscape approach as promoted by UNESCO (ibid.).

Resource extraction

Resource extraction includes a wide range of activities from logging and irrigation to the physical removal of fossil fuels, metals, minerals and aggregates from the earth by mining, quarrying and dredging. Extractive industries pose many dangers to World Heritage sites and in fact mining has been identified as a recurrent threat that has had a major impact on sites (UNESCO, 2007c).[7] Approximately 20–25% of the reactive monitoring reports produced by the World Heritage Centre and IUCN each year for the World Heritage Committee identify significant issues arising from mining activities (ibid.). Mining and other extractive industries are usually located outside the boundaries of World Heritage properties. However, mining together with associated exploration and prospecting activities generate wider knock-on effects due to associated infrastructural development such as the development of roads, power lines, pipelines and accommodation. Further negative impacts may be incurred by human immigration linked to job seeking or the opportunities afforded by improved infrastructure. Mining activities may also have a direct impact through subsidence, pollution of soil and water resources as well as noise and visual intrusion. Such external factors need to be taken into consideration in the management plan (Table 6.2).

Lack of communication between stakeholders, including the government ministries responsible for extractive industries and those responsible for World Heritage properties, can cause serious problems for successful World Heritage management. Difficulties arise in particular when there is a lack of understanding of the implications of World Heritage designation. The management plan should develop strategies to ensure that the appropriate conservation measures are fully understood among stakeholders and that the buffer zones are fully integrated into the broader planning frameworks. At Mapungubwe Cultural Landscape in South Africa (Figure 6.5), for example, a coal mining permit was issued by the Department of Minerals and Energy to an Australian company, Coal of Africa Ltd (CoAL), to mine in an area about 7 km from the World Heritage boundaries. This permit was awarded despite protests from the Department of Environmental Affairs (DEA) responsible for the site.

All proposals for mineral and oil/gas exploration that may impact on World Heritage properties should be subjected to rigorous impact assessments and

TABLE 6.2 Issues and threats associated with mining and mineral extraction

Component	Description
Infrastructure development	Infrastructure development is often associated with clearing of vegetation, noise and dust pollution, and waste production
Surface and groundwater use	Increase in the use of surface and groundwater resources due to mineral abstraction often results in reduction of river flows, depletion of groundwater resources, and pollution of water resources
Air quality pollution	Air pollution associated with mineral abstraction includes dust pollution and air emissions associated with industrial processes
Noise and vibrations	Increase in noise and vibrations, as a result of blasting, heavy machinery, impact on the social well-being and sense of place of an area
Impact on visual / sense of place	Impacts on visual / sense of place include visual change to landscape, introduction of new structures into the landscape, and introduction of new landforms and vegetation patterns
Socio-economic impacts	Socio-economic impacts are often associated with the influx of people into an area resulting in cultural changes, land use and resource use changes, and social changes

Source: Transboundary Consulting Africa, 2012, p65.

FIGURE 6.5 Mapungubwe Cultural Landscape, South Africa (credit: South African Tourism)

appraisal before consent and licenses are granted (IUCN, 2013a). In the case of the Mapungubwe Cultural Landscape, CoAL fenced off archaeological sites that occurred in the mining area in line with the Heritage Impact Assessment (HIA) produced by the DEA. However, the HIA had not recognized that the value of the archaeological sites lay in their setting which, according to the reactive monitoring mission, is now gone for ever as the enclosed conservation areas are surrounded by a vast industrial terrain that has entirely reshaped the local, historic landscape (Eloundou & Avango, 2012).

The failings of the HIA relate back to the DEA's lack of appreciation of the Statement of OUV for the property. This meant that there was no attempt to identify and list the attributes that convey OUV and then to consider how coal mining might impact on those attributes. Instead, archaeological sites within the mining area were considered individually and in isolation from the Mapungubwe Cultural Landscape. This was further exacerbated by the management plan which consisted of a series of plans for individual cultural sites and did not attempt to set out an umbrella strategy and vision for the landscape as a whole (Eloundou & Avango, 2012). In fact, at the time of inscription, ICOMOS had recommended that nomination be deferred in order to allow the state party to develop a comprehensive and appropriate management plan.

Illegal activities

Illegal activities take many forms, from resource use by individuals that is deemed illegal in certain circumstances, such as grazing domestic animals and collecting firewood, to large-scale problems of illegal construction or looting associated with war and conflict. In areas with poor governance and ineffective management structures individual activities can coalesce to widespread problems such as the level of poaching and trade in bush meat that affects the Niokolo Koba National Park in Senegal, which was placed on the LWHD. Similarly, managers may have to deal with different scales of illegal activities from localized offences such as selling stolen souvenirs to international activities such as the trade in endangered species coordinated by highly organized criminal groups.

Kathmandu Valley, a serial site in Nepal, was placed on the LWHD in 2003 due to the threat of uncontrolled and illegal developments, which were considered to impact negatively on the OUV of this urban landscape (Figure 6.6). It was removed from the LWHD in 2007 following the state party's submission of an integrated management system for the site. The management system included guiding conservation principles for each of the seven monument components, together with revised building by-laws and new monitoring measures. It also clearly defined the property boundaries and buffer zones. In 2011, a reactive monitoring mission highlighted the difficulty of coordinating site management across such a complex

FIGURE 6.6 Bhaktapur temple in the urban setting of Kathmandu Valley, Nepal (credit: Cheryl Marland)

urban site which includes a multiplicity of governing authorities, agencies and community groups associated with each of the seven monument zones. It also noted that the country is still in the early stages of political transition, moving from a 'hierarchically organized top down monarchical system to one which gives more authority and responsibility to the local level' (Jing & Nanda, 2011, p25). The mission commended the work of the state party in its efforts to preserve the integrity and authenticity of the site and urged it to take effective steps to enhance coordination through existing institutional frameworks and to develop site-specific management guidelines for each of the seven component parts. Effective implementation of the management plan would also involve awareness raising, capacity building and transparency in the decision-making process to prevent any misunderstandings or mistrust between stakeholders, communities and the general public.

The scale of poaching at World Heritage properties is a growing problem and is seriously aggravated by the international market for trade in endangered species or due to the chaos which accompanies civil unrest and conflict. The Manas Wildlife Sanctuary in India, for example, was placed on the LWHD in 1992 after the rhino population was wiped out during a decade-long insurgency. Fortunately, as stability has returned to the area, the site has become part of a reintroduction plan under the Indian Rhino Vision 2020 programme which aims to increase the wild population of rhinos in Assam to at least 3,000 by the year 2020 (International Rhino Foundation, 2013).

Policy recommendations and management suggestions for dealing with illegal poaching and the bushmeat trade have been produced by IUCN and the Convention on Biological Diversity bushmeat liaison group (Randolph & Stiles, 2011; UNEP, 2011). Public participation is advocated as a significant factor in successfully tackling the problem. It is important that the management strategy includes the views of the local communities regarding the role of bushmeat in their diets and cultures as well as the impacts of its unsustainable use on their livelihoods. Furthermore, it is suggested that communities should be empowered by promoting their rights to land and resource use. This together with incorporating traditional knowledge and customary laws in management planning will lead to improved management through the communities' sense of ownership and accountability (Randolph & Stiles, 2011; UNEP, 2011). Agreements should also be established with other stakeholders such as the private sector and extractive industries to ensure that their work practices support sustainable wildlife management policies and discourage their employees from engaging in poaching activities.

Notes

1 A standardized format for the nomination files which 'encouraged' the submission of management plans was adopted by the Committee at its 20th session in December 1996 (UNESCO, 1997).
2 Criterion (iii) in the 1992 edition of the Operational Guidelines stated 'bear a unique or at least exceptional testimony to a civilisation which has disappeared'.

3   At the time of the nomination, Cambodia was under the administration of a United Nations peacekeeping operation, the United Nations Transitional Authority in Cambodia (UNTAC), from 1992 to 1993. Given the situation, the World Heritage Committee decided to waive some conditions required under the Operational Guidelines for inscription and, on the basis of criteria (i), (ii), (iii) and (iv), inscribed the Angkor site simultaneously on the World Heritage List and on the List of World Heritage in Danger (UNESCO, 1992c).

4   Under the auspices of ASPARA, the 'Living with Heritage project' was run in association with the University of Sydney, the Ecole Française d'Extrême-Orient (EFE) and UNESCO from 2005 to 2009 (Mackay & Sullivan, 2008).

5   The states parties to the CBD agreed to a global strategic plan in 2010 comprising 20 'Aichi Targets'. Of these, Target 20 calls for countries to assess the financial resource needs and mobilize financial resources for effectively implementing the Strategic Plan. The CBD also produced guidelines entitled: Transforming Biodiversity Finance: A quick guide for assessing and mobilizing financial resources to achieve the Aichi Targets and to implement National Biodiversity Strategies and Action Plans.

6   The 2003 World Parks Congress defined co-managed protected areas (CMPAs) as protected areas where management authority, responsibility and accountability are shared among two or more stakeholders, including government bodies and agencies at various levels, indigenous and local communities, NGOs and private operators, or even among different state governments as in the case of transboundary protected areas.

7   Mining has been mentioned in 176 World Heritage Committee decisions made between 2010 and 2015 inclusive, which is approximately 12 per cent of a total of 1,457 decisions, http://whc.unesco.org/en/decisions/.

7

CREATING CONSERVATION CAPACITIES

World Heritage Conservation requires capacities within countries and organizations in order to respond to complex conservation and management issues on the ground. While responsibility for implementing the World Heritage Convention rests mainly with the states parties, international assistance is sometimes necessary. The World Heritage Fund was established to facilitate financial support towards the saving of cultural and natural sites of outstanding universal value (OUV). Other funds with a similar purpose had been formed prior to the convention. The World Wildlife Fund was established in 1961 having played a significant role in nature conservation. Similarly, the World Monuments Fund was created in 1965 as a private non-profit organization with the main objective of assisting in the safeguarding of endangered cultural heritage.

   This chapter explores how the original idea behind the convention, that of mobilizing international cooperation and financial assistance for the conservation of a common heritage of humanity, has evolved into a wide range of programmes, strategies and activities for the development of capacities in heritage conservation. A critical factor is the disparities between the states parties in their ability to identify, protect and manage global heritage. However, attempts to address this imbalance raise questions about relationships between 'developed' and 'developing' countries in relation to conservation approaches, priorities and practices.

Capacity building for World Heritage

Capacity building is increasingly promoted in the strategic work concerning the World Heritage Convention. It is an important factor in World Heritage Conservation given the global scope, broadened ambition and the complexities involved in implementing the convention. However, it is useful to keep a critical lens on capacity building as a concept and to address questions such as inclusiveness and to what extent implementation is effective. The advisory bodies have jointly developed a World Heritage Capacity Building Strategy to assist states parties in their duties under the convention concerning research and training. The educational, private and non-profit sectors also play a vital role in developing conservation capacities.

International solidarity

The World Heritage Convention is founded on the principle of international solidarity. It unites the international community in a common mission of working across borders for the conservation of culture and nature. Its place within the UN-system has opened up avenues for linking heritage with human rights, sustainability and international development, thus linking it to other UN agencies and programmes. Having gained a foothold in World Heritage Conservation it is worth noting that capacity building has been subject to varying interpretations. The United Nations Development Programme (UNDP) uses the term capacity development instead of capacity building. As explained in a practice note, 'capacity development commonly refers to the process of creating and building capacities and their (subsequent) use, management and retention. This process is driven from the inside and starts from existing national capacity assets. Capacity building commonly refers to a process that supports only the initial stages of building or creating capacities and alludes to an assumption that there are no existing capacities to start from. It is therefore less comprehensive than capacity development' (UNDP, 2008, p5). While capacity building is continuously referred to in World Heritage policy, the distinction is an important consideration in international projects concerning World Heritage sites, particularly when it comes to assessing the extent to which existing national resources are integrated and built upon in conservation strategies.

The above distinction is worth consideration given the role of the UNDP in international development, the lessons learnt from aid strategies and the need for equal partnership approaches. For example, in the case of the 2004 tsunami in Asia, the UN system's evaluation of the international response found that it 'had often sidelined existing national and local capacities and had in some cases even depleted them. This reflects the broader challenges of aid dynamics. Each side of the development "partnership" brings its own ideological and political preconceptions to the table. And, although stated objectives are often more or less shared, they are based on misperceptions, vested interests and power differences that hamper a balanced relationship. National ownership is grounded in priorities that are nationally determined, with leadership on national strategies, development decisions and choices' (UNDP, 2008, p4). The UNDP defines capacity development as 'the process through which individuals, organizations and societies obtain, strengthen and maintain the capabilities to set and achieve their own development objectives over time'. Furthermore, 'it uses this existing base of capacities as its starting point and then supports national efforts to enhance and retain them. This is a process of transformation from the inside, based on nationally determined priorities, policies and desired results. It encompasses areas where new capacities have to be introduced and hence, the building of new capacity is also supported' (ibid., p4).

Capacities in heritage conservation within the states parties to the convention can be strengthened in several ways. For example, the enabling of countries with scarce economic resources to participate in World Heritage Committee meetings is a way of ensuring broad participation in the aims of the convention. The development of knowledge and skills of site managers and other professionals engaged in the conservation and management of World Heritage sites similarly supports the aims of the convention. In addition, the allocation of resources for major conservation projects is an important means of enhancing capacities, not least in post-disaster recovery where sites have been critically impacted by man-made or natural disasters.

Capacity building strategy

The Budapest Declaration on World Heritage of 2002 stipulated the World Heritage Committee's commitment to effective capacity building within states parties for the implementation of the convention. The Committee is to 'promote the development of effective Capacity-building measures, including assistance for preparing the nomination of properties to the World Heritage List, for the understanding and implementation of the World Heritage Convention and related instruments' (UNESCO, 2002, para4c). Before that, the Committee adopted a Global Training Strategy for World Cultural and Natural Heritage in 2001 at its 25th session in Helsinki. This was based on the recognition that a single Global Training Strategy is needed 'integrating concern for cultural and natural heritage' (UNESCO, 2001b, p1). ICCROM had previously been responsible for a training strategy for cultural heritage exclusively. The new approach contributed to strengthened collaboration between the advisory bodies and the creation of new synergies between culture and nature. The strategy aimed 'to strengthen conservation of cultural and natural heritage worldwide by increasing the capacity of those responsible for, and involved with, the management and conservation of World Heritage sites' (ibid.).

In response to this, ICCROM and IUCN worked together over several years to establish a Capacity Building Strategy in collaboration with ICOMOS, the World Heritage Centre and other partners. In 2011, the joint work was presented as the World Heritage Capacity Building Strategy (WHCBS) and was approved by the World Heritage Committee at its meeting in Paris in the same year. The strategy proposed two paradigm shifts: firstly, 'to step beyond conventional training to embrace a capacity building approach'; and secondly, 'the change from treating natural and cultural heritage actors separately to the realization that capacity building actions can be strengthened by creating joint opportunities' (UNESCO, 2011g, pp3-4). It recognized that since 'one of the key elements of the World Heritage Convention is that it brings within one normative instrument, concern for the protection of both the cultural and natural heritage [...] an effective World Heritage Capacity Building Strategy must ensure that strong joint networks are created for cultural and natural heritage professionals' (ibid., p4).

The following definition of capacity building was adopted in the strategy based on the UNDP Capacity Development Practice Note from 2006: 'If capacity is "the ability of individuals, organizations and societies to perform functions, solve problems, and set and achieve objectives in a sustainable manner", then capacity building for the effective management of World Heritage properties will: strengthen the knowledge, abilities, skills and behavior of people with direct responsibilities for heritage conservation and management; improve institutional structures and processes through empowering decision-makers and policy-makers; and introduce a more dynamic relationship between heritage and its context and, in turn, greater reciprocal benefits by a more inclusive approach, such that missions and goals are met in a sustainable way' (ibid., pp3–4).

The strategy set different goals and actions organized around the '5 Cs' – the strategic goals of the World Heritage Committee concerning credibility, conservation, capacity-building, communication and communities – with the identification of potential implementation partners. Furthermore, it listed providers of capacity building, such as states parties, advisory bodies, the World Heritage Centre, university programmes and regional training partners. It presented a range of programmes and sought 'not only to improve the state of conservation and management of World Heritage properties, but also to collect the lessons learnt within the World Heritage system' (UNESCO, 2012d, p1). It also contained a capacity building initiative promoting the combination of cultural and natural heritage approaches as innovative and key to improving the implementation of the convention through a format of regional workshops and close cooperation with universities. In addition, the strategy involved the development of initiatives by so-called 'category 2 centres'.

Recognition of the need for capacity building was incorporated into responses to the Global Strategy for a Representative, Balanced and Credible World Heritage List. For example, in its study to address the Global Strategy, ICOMOS highlighted that lack of knowledge and resources was one of the principal reasons for gaps in representation of sites on the list. As stated in the report, 'limited capacity, lack of human resources and lack of training for the preparation of tentative lists and nomination dossiers are evident in certain regions. Special priority should therefore be given to capacity building' (ICOMOS, 2006, p92).

At the 40th Session of the World Heritage Committee in Istanbul, a World Heritage Leadership Programme was presented as a joint initiative by the governments of Norway and Switzerland. It focuses specifically 'on the inter-linkages between cultural and natural heritage in regard to site management, community engagement, resilience, and impact assessment, and will work to promote leadership networks and learning sites which will serve as good practice examples throughout the World Heritage system' (UNESCO, 2016f, p1).

Education and training

In 2013, UNESCO's General Conference adopted an integrated comprehensive strategy and guidelines for the creation and renewal of category 2 centres under the auspices of UNESCO. These are independent training and research organizations that are supported by UNESCO through formal arrangements for assisting in the implementation of its strategic programme objectives, and formally approved by the General Conference. However, their funding comes directly from the member states where they are located (UNESCO, 2013g).

To date, nine institutes and centres have been granted status as World Heritage category 2 centres (Table 7.1), of which eight are in operation (the Nordic World Heritage Fund has ceased to exist).[1] The centres either have a regional scope or work within a specific domain. The need for regional frameworks was recognized in the first Global Training Strategy in 2001, which stated that 'regional components were to be designed to meet the specific needs and cultural contexts of a given region and its heritage' (UNESCO, 2001b, p4). For example, Africa 2009 provided a training strategy for heritage expertise in African countries, undertaken by ICCROM in cooperation with African

TABLE 7.1 World Heritage Category 2 Centres

Category 2 Centres	Country	Year
Nordic World Heritage Foundation (NWHF)	Norway	2003
African World Heritage Fund (AWHF)	South Africa	2007
World Heritage Institute for Training and Research in Asia and the Pacific (WHITR-AP)	China	2007
Arab Regional Centre for World Heritage (ARC-WH)	Bahrain	2009
Regional World Heritage Institute in Zacatecas	Mexico	2009
Regional Heritage Management Training Centre 'Lucio Costa'	Brazil	2009
International Centre for Rock Art and the World Heritage Convention	Spain	2011
International Research Centre on the Economics of Culture and World Heritage Studies	Italy	2011
Centre on World Natural Heritage Management and Training for Asia and the Pacific Region	India	2014

Source: UNESCO (2016e).

cultural heritage organizations, UNESCO and the International Centre on Earthen Architecture (CRATerre-EAG). The regional approach is imperative to achieve 'people-centered change' (UNESCO, 2011g, p4) and, hence, there is a need to diversify capacity building centres within large regions like Africa, building from within the continent rather than the opposite.

Relatively few universities have been recognized as category 2 centres so far. However, as agents of critical thinking and independent research, universities play an important role as capacity developers in relation to World Heritage. Specialized programmes in the field of World Heritage Conservation have been created such as the Master's of Science in World Heritage Management and the online diploma in World Heritage Conservation at University College Dublin in Ireland and the Masters in World Heritage Studies at the Brandenburg University of Technology in Cottbus, Germany.

The UNITWIN-UNESCO Chairs Programme promotes knowledge sharing through university networking. It was established as 'a way to advance research, training and programme development in all of UNESCO's fields of competence by building university networks and encouraging inter-university cooperation through the transfer of knowledge across borders' (UNESCO, 2009d, p3). A UNESCO Chair 'may be developed within a university department by reinforcing an existing teaching/research programme in a particular field within the domains of competence of UNESCO, and giving it an international dimension' (ibid.). For example, the UNESCO Chair in Heritage Studies is positioned in the University of Technology in Cottbus.

As a mandatory tool for all World Heritage sites, the management plan process is an opportunity for linking research with practice and developing a research strategy for informed decisions concerning World Heritage Conservation. Synergies may be developed between the management organizations for World Heritage sites and research institutions for the integration of management planning and research strategies. Research to promote conservation and sustainable development at World Heritage sites may include a broad range of issues relating to state of conservation, site presentation, visitor management and environmental considerations. For example, the management plan research strategy may 'identify current state-of-research and include objectives for a long-term research agenda'. Furthermore, it is necessary to consider 'how research should be co-ordinated, how cooperation may be achieved with and between research institutions and how research projects can be integrated with the objectives of the management plan'. The research strategy requires alignment of research with the needs of the site management plan, including that carried out by academic institutions, consultancy firms and state agencies (Negussie, 2015b, p61).

In Ireland, the Brú na Bóinne World Heritage Site Research Framework was framed to achieve a best-practice approach to creating a research strategy within a World Heritage context. The Brú na Bóinne – Archaeological Ensemble of the Bend of the Boyne was inscribed on the World Heritage List in 1993 as

FIGURE 7.1 Brú na Bóinne – Archaeological Ensemble of the Bend of the Boyne, Ireland (credit: © National Monuments Service, Dep. of Arts, Heritage, Regional, Rural and Gaeltacht Affairs)

Europe's largest and most important concentration of prehistoric megalithic art, including the prehistoric sites of Brú na Bóinne, Newgrange, Knowth and Dowth (Figure 7.1). The framing of the research strategy was developed in three phases. The first phase involved identification of the state of knowledge. In the second phase, specialist position papers were presented to determine research gaps and to formulate key research questions. Thirdly, a research framework was formulated with a list of research priorities (The Heritage Council, 2009).

States parties

States parties have a central role in developing capacities for World Heritage Conservation. They have a duty to make mandatory contributions to the World Heritage Fund (see below). In addition, they are encouraged to establish national public and private foundations to support funding towards the protection of World Heritage properties (UNESCO, 1972, article 17). Furthermore, they are expected to support international fund-raising campaigns organized for the World Heritage Fund (ibid., article 18).

National governments and agencies have also supported conservation as part of development assistance and strategies for poverty alleviation and re-construction in post-conflict societies. For example, the Swedish International Development Agency worked in partnership with heritage organizations to help preserve the Stone Town of Zanzibar, Tanzania, where it supported work towards a participation-based management plan. Similarly, the German Federal Nature Conservation Agency has supported the preparation of nomination dossiers for natural World Heritage sites in the Russian Federation. Furthermore, special trust funds have been established through UNESCO when national governments have provided funds for specific projects with defined goals and objectives. For example, the Flemish Funds-in-Trust (FIT) was created, following a World Heritage Committee decision in 2000, for a project financed by Flemish authorities to develop management capacity for sites in the Arab region. Other examples include the France–UNESCO Cooperation Agreement, the Japanese FIT, the Netherlands FIT and the Spanish FIT (UNESCO, 2012k).

Bi-lateral support is often mentioned during reviews of individual sites during the state-of-conservation reporting at World Heritage Committee meetings. There is a fine balance to be struck between the principle of solidarity and the prestige of funding conservation projects for raising the profile of states parties in World Heritage governance. For example, a question arises if the leading donors stand a better chance at exercising influence within the World Heritage system.

NGOs and the private sector

NGOs and the private sector play an important role in developing capacities for World Heritage sites. In Sweden, Cultural Heritage without Borders was established in 1995 as an independent NGO working in the spirit of the Hague Convention by preserving cultural heritage endangered by war, natural disasters, neglect, poverty or political and social conflict. Its board members are appointed by the Swedish National Heritage Board, the Swedish branches of ICOMOS and ICOM, and the Swedish Association of Architects. It was established in response to the destruction of cultural monuments as a result of war on the Balkans in the 1990s and the critical need for assistance in their protection and conservation. Its work was realized within the framework of emergency aid provided by the Swedish International Development Agency (CHwB, 2016).

The Frankfurt Zoological Society is an international conservation organization that has been dedicated to the preservation of wildlands and biological diversity 'in the last remaining wilderness areas on the planet' (FZS, 2016). Initially concerned with establishing a zoo in Frankfurt, it became increasingly involved in international conservation in the 1960s following the establishment of a memorial fund, later a trust fund, in honour of Michael Grzimek, son of its director Bernard Grzimek, who died in a tragic plane accident in East Africa during fieldwork and documentary footage of animals in their natural habitat. While initially focusing on nature conservation in East Africa its involvement spread to other regions. By 2001, it had supported some 70 conservation projects in 25 countries with an annual budget of EUR 4 million (FZS, 2016).

A publication entitled The Business Planning for Natural World Heritage Sites – A Toolkit was developed for site managers to strengthen business planning capacities of non-profit organizations in charge of managing natural World Heritage sites. It emerged from a partnership project of UNESCO and the Shell foundation and was 'developed in the field with the participation of World Heritage site managers and Shell International staff with knowledge in the area of business planning' (UNESCO, 2008c, p2). The project sought to source business advice from the private sector and achieve mutual exchange between business and conservation knowledge: 'As an independent charity with a focus on business-based approaches to tackling development challenges – as well as close links to a "big" business, the Shell Foundation was ideally placed to pilot such a skills-sharing initiative' (ibid., p4).

The role of the private sector in World Heritage Conservation was highlighted at the World Heritage Committee meetings in Doha (2015) and Bonn (2016) through the organization of special panel discussions. Companies such as Google, Panasonic and Seabourn Cruise Line have partnered with UNESCO to support the aims of the convention. For example, Google's World Wonder project has enabled accesses to World Heritage sites through digital technologies and virtual navigation at sites. Panasonic has worked with the World Heritage Centre to raise awareness of and to educate young people about the importance of cultural heritage and environmental conservation. Seabourn has partnered with UNESCO to promote quality experiences of World Heritage sites and the provision of optional excursions that help raise revenue towards the World Heritage Fund through small donations (UNESCO, 2016h).

World Heritage Fund

The World Heritage Fund (WHF) was created as a special mechanism for assisting states parties to the convention in their work to safeguard World Heritage properties. As stated in article 15.1: 'A Fund for the Protection of the World Cultural and Natural Heritage of Outstanding Universal Value, called "the World Heritage Fund", is hereby established' (UNESCO, 1972). The WHF has become an important vehicle for states parties to seek support for both emergency assistance, e.g. in the case of properties on the List of World Heritage in Danger (LWHD), and preparatory assistance, such as when preparing World Heritage nominations. There is a specific procedure through which states parties can make requests for such assistance with defined priorities and restricted levels of support.

Policy and operation

The World Heritage Fund was established as a trust fund 'in conformity with the provisions of the Financial Regulations of the United Nations Educational, Scientific and Cultural Organization' (UNESCO, 1972, article 15.2). It provides support of approximately US$4 million annually for states parties who have requested international assistance for activities related to the conservation of

World Heritage properties located within their territories. The fund is financed by mandatory and voluntary contributions from the states parties. However, contributions to the fund can also be donations through gifts or bequests by other states, UNESCO, other UN organizations and public or private bodies or individuals. The compulsory contributions are made bi-annually. The amount is decided upon by the General Assembly of States Parties to the World Heritage Convention and as a general rule they must not exceed 1 per cent of the contribution made to the regular budget of UNESCO (article 16:1). In 2015, the total mandatory contributions amounted to US$1,967,862, while the voluntary contributions equalled US$1,296,891 (UNESCO, 2012j).

States parties may request international assistance for properties inscribed on the World Heritage List or to support the identification and protection of cultural and natural heritage that may be considered for inclusion on the list in the future (UNESCO, 2015, para233). The Operational Guidelines set out the procedure and format for all states parties to apply for international assistance as stipulated in the convention.[2] To apply for international assistance other than emergency assistance, states parties must first ensure that they are not in arrears with regard to their contributions to the World Heritage Fund (UNESCO, 2015b, para237). This decision was made in 1989, at the 13th Session of the World Heritage Committee in Paris, in response to the on-going delays in the payment of obligatory and voluntary contributions by the states parties (UNESCO, 1989). Prior to that, the only penalty for states parties in arrears with their payments was that they were not eligible for elections to the Committee in that year as stipulated in the convention (UNESCO, 1972, article 16[5]).

The states parties are advised to contact the World Heritage Centre and the relevant advisory bodies before completing the application in order to receive advice and to ensure that the request will match the priorities of the World Heritage Committee. The applicants are also given the opportunity to review examples of the documentation of successful applications. This is essential since the Committee has been critiqued with regard to transparency around decision-making associated with how the World Heritage Fund and incoming donations are allocated. The fact that the Committee has complete control over who gets funding makes it 'very easy for the Committee to effectively "prefer" some projects over others for ideological, political, or pecuniary reasons' (Keough, 2011, p600).

Different types of assistance

There are three types of assistance available under the World Heritage Fund: emergency assistance; conservation and management assistance; and preparatory assistance (UNESCO, 2015b, para235). Emergency assistance is directed at properties that face 'ascertained' or 'potential threats' and which have recently undergone acute deterioration due to sudden disasters, natural or manmade, such as earthquakes, war and conflict, or where disasters are imminent and threatening. It does not address deterioration that has occurred over a long period of time. The emphasis is rather on sudden and impending threats on a scale that a given state party cannot deal with alone. The state party can apply for assistance up to and over a cost of US$75,000 at any time over the World Heritage Committee calendar year. The applications are submitted to the Secretariat. Requests for US$5,000 or less can be dealt with directly by the Director of the World Heritage Centre. Requests between US$5,000 and US$75,000 can be authorized by the chairperson of the World Heritage Committee. However, requests for larger amounts require approval by the World Heritage Committee.

Preparatory assistance refers to funds that are made available to states parties that are preparing for the nomination of cultural and natural heritage properties for inscription on the World Heritage List. Similarly to emergency assistance, requests for US$5,000 or less can be dealt with directly by the Director of the World Heritage Centre, while requests beyond this amount up to US$30,000 needs to be authorized by the chairperson of the World Heritage Committee (UNESCO, 2015b, para241). States parties can request funding in order to set up or revise their tentative lists at a national or regional level, and to carry out research, prepare nomination files and to provide training and technical support for World Heritage properties. Priority is given to those states parties that are addressing gaps in the list and/or heritage categories identified by thematic studies carried out by the advisory bodies according to the Global Strategy for a Representative, Balanced and Credible World Heritage List.

Conservation and management assistance is intended to support research, training and promotion of World Heritage. For example, states parties can request support for scientific research and training for their staff in areas relating to identification, monitoring, conservation, management and presentation of World Heritage sites (UNESCO, 2015, para241). States parties can also request funds to support national, regional and international meetings for policy-makers, staff, stakeholders and management teams to exchange experiences in the conservation and management of sites, as well as raise awareness and encourage participation and involvement in the implementation of the convention. Also eligible for funding are meetings that aim to promote the convention in a wider context and to assist in the development of educational and promotional material that informs the wider public of the work of the convention. Of particular interest are the role of younger people and activities that promote their understanding and involvement in heritage protection. Unlike preparatory assistance, the available budget is not restricted to US$30,000, and for estimated costs over this amount the state party must submit their requests by 31 October for approval by the World Heritage Committee (UNESCO, 2015, para241).

At the 34th Session in Brasilia in 2010, international assistance for the amount of US$100,000 was approved by the World Heritage Committee to protect the Rainforests of the Atsinanana in Madagascar. The site was simultaneously inscribed on the LWHD because of threats to the OUV such as illegal logging and illegal resource exploitation. The Rainforests of the Atsinanana were inscribed on the World Heritage List in 2007 as a serial site for their critical importance in maintaining 'on-going ecological processes necessary for the survival of Madagascar's unique biodiversity' which includes all lemur families (UNESCO, 2007d). In the year of inscription, only 8.5 per cent of the total original forests remained in eastern Madagascar due to deforestation. In 2009, the Committee expressed its concern over the reports of continued illegal logging and called upon all states parties to the convention to be aware of and prevent any importation of illegal timber originating from Madagascar. It requested the state party to compile a detailed report outlining the state of conservation of the property and the impacts of illegal logging and hunting of endangered species.

The request for international assistance was submitted under conservation and management assistance and was reviewed in light of the fact that Madagascar had recently paid its arrears to the World Heritage Fund and that previous Committee decisions highlighted concern for the integrity of the forests. Funding was required to carry out a mapping survey of the illegal activities, to collate an inventory of the threats and to catalogue the deforested areas and remaining woods, as well as complete an impact assessment. It was agreed that a third of the money would be allocated to these activities and that a monitoring mission would be organized to assist in the development of an emergency plan. The remaining funds would then be allocated to implement the emergency plan. The World Heritage Committee recommended that the funding support should be channelled through 'reliable and recognized organizations selected by the World Heritage Centre in communication with relevant authorities' (UNESCO, 2010b, p285). In 2011, a reactive monitoring mission visited Madagascar and reported that illegal logging had halted in one of the major components of the serial site but continued in other areas. The Committee welcomed the news but urged the state party to enforce the ban on illegal logging in all areas and to implement the corrective measures suggested by the advisory body to reach the 'desired state of conservation' of the property. At the 36th Session of the Committee in 2012, it was decided to maintain the property on the LWHD and every year since.

Evaluation and support

Reviewing requests for international assistance is one of the principal roles of the advisory bodies. All requests above US$5,000 are evaluated by ICOMOS and ICCROM in the case of cultural properties, IUCN for natural heritage properties, and all three advisory bodies for mixed properties. The evaluation team consists of a panel including representatives from the relevant regional desk within the World Heritage Centre, the chairperson or a vice-chairperson of the World Heritage Committee, and representatives of the advisory bodies. Following review of the applications by the panel, a recommendation is submitted to the chairperson or the Committee, depending on the amount of funding requested for decision. The panel may also return applications to the state party for substantial revision.

The advisory bodies and review panel assess the requests for international assistance according to the following priorities (UNESCO, 2015b, paras236-239):

- Properties inscribed on the LWHD;
- States parties up to date in the payment of their compulsory or voluntary contributions to the World Heritage Fund (in requests for emergency assistance this is not a consideration);
- Priorities identified in the Regional Periodic Report programmes, World Heritage Committee decisions and the strategic objectives;
- The likelihood that the assistance will encourage and promote contributions from other sources.

A balance should be maintained 'in the allocation of resources between cultural and natural heritage and between Conservation and Management and Preparatory Assistance' (UNESCO, 2015, para240). The balance is decided on a regular basis by the Committee and currently the balance reflects a decision made at the 31st Committee Meeting in Christchurch New Zealand where 65 per cent of the total international assistance budget is set aside for cultural properties and 35 per cent for natural properties (UNESCO, 2007e). The Operational Guidelines provide an overview of the criteria applied by evaluators in assessing requests for international assistance (UNESCO, 2015b, annex 9).

The World Heritage Committee regularly encourages states parties to apply for international assistance. For example, at its 36th session in 2012 the Committee encouraged Libya to 'consider submitting an International Assistance request for the implementation of priority measures and for the development of a multi-faceted conservation and management strategy' for the Rock-Art Sites of Tadrart Acacus (UNESCO, 2012i, p101). The site was inscribed on the World Heritage List in 1985 based on criterion (iii) for its importance of thousands of cave paintings, dating from 12,000 BC to AD 100, and their representation of the different ways of life of the inhabitants that succeeded one another in this mountainous region of the Sahara. In April 2009, ten rock-art sites were vandalized with spray paint. The state party submitted a report in 2010 that summarized the significant damage that had occurred to some of the most well-known rock-art paintings in the region. A joint UNESCO/ICOMOS reactive monitoring mission took place in 2011. Consequently, a comprehensive assessment was established and detailed methodologies for conservation and restoration were defined, including a five-year action plan. However, the state party had not submitted any reports in the two years prior to the reactive monitoring mission and it was understood that the political conditions prevented the implementation of protective measures to address the damage caused by vandalism. By 2016, an International Expert Meeting on the Safeguarding of Libyan Cultural Heritage raised a concern that the site had become a crossing point by refugees seeking to gain access to northern Africa, making it further vulnerable due to an unusually large human presence (UNESCO, 2016g).

Major operations

Funding priority is given to international assistance for properties inscribed on the LWHD, i.e. properties for which major operations and international assistance are necessary for their conservation (UNESCO, 1972, article 11.4). Manovo Grounda St Floris National Park in the Central African Republic (CAR) was inscribed on the World Heritage List in 1988. It is the largest savannah park in West and Central Africa and includes important examples of dry forest, an ecosystem that is critically endangered throughout its natural range. The park was inscribed for its savannah ecosystem and diversity of habitat types critical for protecting threatened biodiversity (criteria ix and x), including iconic species such as black rhinoceros (*Diceros bicornis*), leopard (*Panthera pardus*), cheetah (*Acinonyx jubatus*) and elephant (*Loxodonta africans*) (IUCN, 1988).

At the time of inscription of the site, IUCN recommended that the nomination be deferred as no management plan was in place and professional poaching of large animals was a significant threat to the integrity of the park (Figure 7.2). Despite adequate legislation to protect the area on paper, there were few resources or funds to manage the park on the ground. There were five guards and one vehicle responsible for patrolling an area of 1,740,000 hectares. Civil wars in the neighbouring countries of Chad and Sudan had brought many weapons and hunters into the area and illegal poachers were using automatic weapons to kill elephants, giraffes, buffalos, etc. The Government had made an official agreement with a private company, Société Manova S.A., to take over

FIGURE 7.2   Poached elephant with tusks removed, Central African Republic (credit: © Martin Harvey, source: http://www.wildimagesonline.com)

management of the park and IUCN recommended that inscription should await further clarification of the role of the private company and efforts to restore the park's integrity. The property was still inscribed to encourage the Central African Republic to protect the site. Furthermore, a 10-year project financed by the EEC/FED European Economic Community/Fonds European du Developpement at a cost of US$ 27 million was planned to support sustainable development of the park.

In the following years, IUCN and World Heritage Committee members (including Canada and the US) continued to voice their concern over the lack of progress to protect the integrity of the site. Consequently, in 1997, the property was inscribed on the LWHD. A major operation was considered necessary at this stage. Heavily armed poachers arriving from Chad and Sudan had created an emergency situation where populations of large mammals were decimated. Professional poachers set up a network of camel trains to transport bushmeat and poached animal skins, rhino horns and elephant tusks out of the national park. The EU-funded development project was largely ineffective and had been interrupted on several occasions by the activities of the armed poachers.

In 2000, the UNESCO Director-General made an appeal to the permanent delegations of all countries neighbouring the Central African Republic to provide assistance in mitigating cross-border poaching and to actively combat poachers. In 2001, the state party submitted a periodic report on the state of conservation of the property. A joint IUCN/UNESCO mission was then approved to visit the property and to start work with the state party to prepare a fundraising plan for the implementation of urgent rehabilitation measures. A list of actions to address the urgent needs for the conservation of the site was developed for implementation over a 24-month period. As part of the recommendations, the state party made a successful emergency assistance request from the World Heritage Fund for the amount of US$150,000. In 2004, the Committee invited the state party to cooperate with the World Heritage Centre, IUCN, the Conservation et Utilisation rationelle des Ecosystèmes Forestiers d'Afrique Centrale (ECOFAC) programme, and other conservation agencies and donors to mobilize the necessary resources to sustain and further develop the activities foreseen under the revised Emergency Rehabilitation Plan. Further emergency assistance was awarded from the World Heritage Fund to the amount of US$50,000.

By 2009, the state party had not submitted an updated report on the state of conservation of the site and a recent joint mission by IUCN/Secretariat had indicated that the property was in imminent danger of losing OUV. The Director-General of UNESCO agreed to convene a meeting with the authorities of the three countries to try to move dialogue, and the 'reinforced monitoring mechanism' was applied for a further year to monitor the state of conservation of the property. By 2012, the World Heritage Committee reiterated 'its extreme concern with regard to the probable disappearance of almost all the flagship species of large mammals in the property due to poaching and the impact of transhumance cattle, which could bring to question the Outstanding Universal Value for which the property was inscribed' (UNESCO, 2012l). The Committee awarded a further US$30,000 in emergency assistance based on the potential, albeit a 'fragile one', for regeneration of some of the decimated populations of wildlife. Essentially, the OUV of the property has been lost. Despite the fact that the state party has not successfully implemented any of the recommendations of the Committee since its inscription on the World Heritage List in 1988 and the LWHD in 1997, the Committee seems determined to retain the property on the LWHD so that the corrective measures of the emergency plan are implemented and the feasibility of regenerating the OUV of the property is organized.

Other international assistance

The support available from the World Heritage Fund is limited and the conservation of World Heritage properties often requires other forms of national and international assistance. The World Wildlife Fund and the World Monuments Fund were both created as independent heritage funds in the 1960s prior to the establishment of the World Heritage Convention. Since then, several other funds with a similar purpose have been established, such as the Global Heritage Fund and the African World Heritage Fund.

World Wildlife Fund

The World Wildlife Fund (WWF) was established in 1961 at the headquarters of IUCN in Morges, Switzerland, as a non-profit organization in response to funding shortages of organizations such as IUCN and The Conservation Foundation in their work on nature conservation. The 'Morges Manifesto', the founding document of the WWF, was signed by leading conservationists who declared that money was needed to support people and organizations who were struggling to save the world's wildlife: 'There will be an international Trust, registered as a charity in Switzerland under a distinguished group of trustees [...] This Trust will administer funds raised on a world-wide basis by national appeals in different countries, and by a high-level supporting Club of leading citizens of many countries' (WWF, 1961). The WWF is governed by an executive team, a board of directors, honorary directors and a national council acting as an advisory group to the board. Since its establishment, it has become one of the world's largest independent conservation organizations, drawing support from 5 million people in over 100 countries. Its mission has developed from localized efforts of conserving single species and individual habitats to a broader scope of preserving bio-diversity and working towards sustainable development globally. As stated in its strategic plan for conservation, the WWF's mission is 'to stop the degradation of the planet's natural environment and to build a future in which humans live in harmony with nature, by: conserving the world's biological diversity; ensuring that the use of renewable natural resources is sustainable; promoting the reduction of pollution and wasteful consumption' (WWF, 2008, p14).

In its first decade, the WWF raised more than US$5.6 million through fundraising appeals, distributed as grants to support 356 conservation projects across the world (WWF, 2011a). Amongst its early grant support recipients was the Charles Darwin Foundation for the Galápagos Islands; the WWF still funds projects in the Galápagos Islands and has helped Ecuador in the establishment of the Galápagos National Park. Similarly, in 1969, it assisted Spain in purchasing part of the Guadalquivir Delta marshes and the establishment of the Coto Doñana National Park (ibid.). Both of these sites later became designated as World Heritage sites: the Galápagos Islands in 1978 and the Doñana National Park in 1994 (Figure 7.3). In 2011, the WWF channelled over US$200 million towards saving species and plants around the world, accounting for 85 per cent of its donations, a record figure that coincided with its 50th year anniversary (WWF, 2011b).

World Monuments Fund

The World Monuments Fund (WMF), initially named the International Fund for Monuments, was established in 1965 as a private non-profit organization working to assist in the safeguarding of endangered cultural heritage (WMF, 2005). In the words of its former Chairman Mr Charles M. Grace, it was formed by a group of individuals who 'recognized the need, long expressed by UNESCO, for an organization to assist in the costs of preserving monuments in those countries which lack the financial means of doing so alone' (IFM, 1967).

FIGURE 7.3 Doñana National Park, Spain (credit: Claire Cave)

Based in New York City, it is governed by a board of trustees. It has a staff at senior, administrative and programme levels and affiliations in Britain, France, India, Italy, Peru, Portugal and Spain. It works through advocacy, education, training, capacity building and disaster recovery (WMF, 2015). The WMF has supported projects in more than 90 countries in all regions of the world.

The Rock-Hewn Churches of Lalibela became one of the first restoration projects to receive sponsorship from the WMF. The project, a joint effort between the national authorities of Ethiopia and Italy, involved assistance by a team of Italian conservators who undertook documentation and stabilization efforts. The project also involved the removing of a bituminous coating to the external surface of the rock churches which was preventing the natural breathing of the rock and thereby causing deterioration (IFM, 1967). Other early projects supported by the fund were disaster recovery in Venice following the 1966 floods, and preservation on the Easter Island in Chile (WMF, 2015). The WMF grew significantly in the 1980s and, by 1996, it had introduced the World Monuments Watch which every second year draws international attention to cultural heritage that has become endangered in order to raise global awareness of this (WMF, 2015). The fund depends on philanthropy and private donations. Under the 'Robert W. Wilson Challenge to Conserve Our Heritage', first initiated in 1998 and later extended, the WMF received a donation of US$100 million on the condition that it would match the funding equally. It levered twice that amount in foreign investments for more than 200 sites in 52 countries (ibid.).

Other funds

Founded in California in 2002, the Global Heritage Fund (GHF) is a non-profit organization committed to the safeguarding of endangered cultural heritage sites in 'developing countries' specifically. By 2015, it had supported work at 30 sites in 19 countries (GHF, 2015). The fund is governed by a board of trustees, an honorary board of trustees, a senior advisory board and a diplomatic council. The latter consists of former US ambassadors and diplomatic officials with the view of bringing together and drawing on their experience and knowledge on specific countries (GHF, 2012). The fund has developed an integrated conservation and development methodology ('preservation-by-design-model') to help guide heritage projects, drawing on planning and increased site protection, conservation science, community development and partnerships. It also operates a fellowship programme with grants supporting scholars and professionals in fields of cultural heritage conservation to help fulfil its mission (GHF, 2012).

The African World Heritage Fund (AWHF) was established in 2006 as an inter-governmental organization, initiated by the African members states of UNESCO with the view to supporting conservation and protection of cultural and natural sites of OUV in Africa. It provides support for identification of potential World Heritage sites, conservation and management of heritage sites and rehabilitation of sites placed on the LWHD. It also offers training of heritage officials and site managers as ongoing capacity building and works to engage communities in decisions concerning their heritage and ensuring that they benefit from this. The AWHF has a board of trustees with representatives from the region and patrons that act as goodwill ambassadors for the fund. It also has a Secretariat with a small number of staff. The fund is hosted by South Africa and located in Midrand where it is registered as a trust at the Development Bank of Southern Africa. The AWHF operates two grants programmes: firstly, nomination grants to help improve World Heritage nomination files; and, secondly, conservation grants for projects to improve the state of conservation of World Heritage properties in Africa (AWHF, 2016). Contributions to the fund have come from both African and non-African countries such as Spain, China and Norway (UNESCO, 2009e).

The Rapid Response Facility was established as an emergency programme for small grants of up to US$30,000 to help protect natural World Heritage properties rapidly in times of crisis. For example, it awarded US$30,000 to the Frankfurt Zoological Society for work at the Garamba National Park, Democratic Republic of Congo, including the rehabilitation of the Ishango ranger training camp in Virunga National Park for the enhancement of anti-poaching capacity. Operated by UNESCO's World Heritage Centre, Foundation Franz Weber and Fauna & Flora International, it seeks to ensure effective responses to conservation emergencies by mobilizing funds quickly and to provide bridge and catalyst funding to help secure long-term funding solutions (RRF, 2016).

World Heritage in international development

The potential of World Heritage sites as catalysts for development became increasingly evident with the linking of heritage conservation and strategies for international development. Heritage has been recognized as an important development factor and a focus for capacity-building efforts and strategies to reduce poverty, reflected in the objectives of the World Bank, UN agencies and national governments (Negussie, 2012). National trust funds have been established by governments within donor and lending agencies incorporating culture as a tool for development. For example, the UNDP/Spain Millennium Development Goals Achievement Fund, established in 2007 for transfer of 528 million euros towards the UN Millennium Development Goals (MDGs) over a period of four years, highlighted the promotion of cultural resources. Hence the MDGs became important in incorporating heritage projects as part of international development without these having explicitly spelled out culture and heritage conservation as a vehicle for development. Nevertheless, the more recent UN Sustainable Development Goals (SDGs) have provided a step forward in this regard.

From MDGs to SDGs

The MDGs were established in the UN Millennium Declaration, adopted by the United Nations at the Millennium Summit in 2000 at its headquarters in New York. The MDGs set targets for eliminating extreme poverty by 2015 by addressing: 1) extreme hunger and poverty; 2) achieving universal primary education; 3) promoting gender equality; 4) reducing child mortality; 5) improving maternal health; 6) combating diseases; 7) ensuring environmental sustainability; and 8) developing a global partnership for development (UN, 2000). The goals manifested basic human rights, that each person on the planet has a right to health, education, shelter and security. As stated in the Declaration: 'We will spare no effort to promote democracy and strengthen the rule of law, as well as respect for all internationally recognized human rights and fundamental freedoms, including the right to development' (ibid., article 24).

Goal 7 of the MDGs highlighted the need to ensure environmental sustainability. A link was identified between bio-diversity, protected areas and socio-economic development since protected areas tend to attract ecotourism enterprises: 'Their chances of success are stronger if they can be associated with officially protected areas and are quite possibly weaker where they offer experiences within the same but unprotected landscape' (West & Brockington, 2006, p610). The MDGs promoted environmental sustainability with targets to reverse the loss of environmental sources, to improve access to water and sanitation and to improve the lives of slum dwellers. Nevertheless, the Millennium Declaration failed to recognize the imperative of conserving cultural resources and the potential use of heritage as a driver for sustainable development. The associated roadmap document concentrated on the conservation of soil, water, forests and biodiversity (UN, 2001).

Over a decade later and after a series of events highlighting the role of culture in sustainable development, the UN General Assembly adopted the Resolution on Culture and Sustainable Development in December 2013.[3] The resolution requested 'the President of the General Assembly to hold a one-day special thematic debate at the highest political level possible [...] to give due consideration to the role of culture and sustainable development in the elaboration of the post-2015 development agenda' (UN, 2013). Furthermore, it recalled a previous resolution entitled Keeping the Promise: United to Achieve the Millennium Development Goals, which had emphasized the importance of culture for development. It also noted the Hangzhou Declaration on Placing Culture at the Heart of Sustainable Development Policies, adopted at an international congress organized by UNESCO in China in 2013. The declaration emphasized 'the important contribution of culture to the three dimensions of sustainable development and to the achievement of national development objectives and the internationally agreed development goals' (ibid., para7).

The 2030 Development Agenda for Sustainable Development was adopted in September 2015 at the UN Summit for the adoption of the post-2015 development agenda by the 70th Session of the UN General Assembly. It established 17 SDGs and 169 associated targets to 'stimulate action over the next 15 years in areas of critical importance for humanity and the planet' (UN, 2015b). The new agenda has been considered by UNESCO as a significant step forward in that the international development agenda for the first time refers to culture within the framework of the SDGs and its associated focus areas, i.e. education, sustainable cities, food security, the environment, economic growth, sustainable consumption and production patterns, peaceful and inclusive societies (Figure 7.4).

The agenda declared a commitment to achieving what the MDGs had failed to achieve and to eradicate poverty in all its forms within a 15-year period. Furthermore, it took a stronger stance on sustainable development globally: 'We envisage a world in which every country enjoys sustained, inclusive and sustainable economic growth and decent work for all. A world in which consumption and production patterns and use of all natural resources – from air to land, from rivers, lakes and aquifers to oceans and seas – are sustainable [...] One in which humanity lives in harmony with nature and in which wildlife and other living species are protected' (article 9). Furthermore, it stressed diversity: 'We acknowledge the natural and cultural diversity of the world and recognize that all cultures and civilizations can contribute to, and are crucial enablers of, sustainable development' (article 36). In line with the Hangzhou Declaration, culture was integrated with the three dimensions of sustainable development and mentioned directly and indirectly in four goals (Table 7.2).

Goal 11 makes the most explicit reference to culture in the context of cities and urban development. In response to this, in 2016, UNESCO presented a Global Report on Culture for Sustainable Urban Development at the UN

FIGURE 7.4 United Nations sustainable development goals (credit: United Nations)

TABLE 7.2   Integration of culture with the sustainable development goals

Goal 4	Ensure inclusive and equitable quality education and promote lifelong learning opportunities for all	Ensure that all learners acquire the knowledge and skills needed to promote sustainable development, including [...] appreciation of cultural diversity and of culture's contribution to sustainable development (Target 4.7)
Goal 8	Promote sustained, inclusive and sustainable economic growth, full and productive employment and decent work for all	By 2030, devise and implement policies to promote sustainable tourism that creates jobs and promotes local culture and products (Target 8.9)
Goal 11	Make cities and human settlements inclusive, safe, resilient and sustainable	Strengthen efforts to protect and safeguard the world's cultural and natural heritage (Target 11.4)
Goal 12	Ensure sustainable consumption and production patterns	Develop and implement tools to monitor sustainable development impacts for sustainable tourism that creates jobs and promotes local culture and products (Target 12.b)

Source: UN, 2015b.

Conference on Housing and Sustainable Development (Habitat III) held in Quito, Ecuador, in the same year. The report called for reflection on what it means to manage change in cities using culture as driver for development, and provided guidelines 'to support decision-makers at national and local levels, experts and other stakeholders involved in urban development policies and strategies' (UNESCO, 2016g, p17). While Goal 11 refers to both cultural and natural heritage in cities, environmental sustainability is still given a more distinctive role in the SDGs as in the MDGs with two goals focusing on life below water and life on land (Table 7.3). Other goals address the role of nature and a healthy environment by addressing poverty, climate change, food and water security and reducing the risk of disasters. Arguably, had culture been given a more explicit role as the fourth pillar of sustainable development it may have gained a stronger role in the SDGs.

Heritage as tool for development

Ethiopia is a useful example to illustrate the important role of World Heritage in socio-economic development and how sites may be used as an opportunity for realizing development ambitions. Although it has been considered one of the poorest countries in the world in economic terms, the country has a wealth of heritage resources ranging from medieval castles, churches, monasteries,

TABLE 7.3 Environmental objectives in the sustainable development goals

Goal 14	Conserve and sustainably use the oceans, seas and marine resources for sustainable development.	By 2020, sustainably manage and protect marine and costal ecosystems to avoid significant adverse impacts, including by strengthening their resilience, and take action for their restoration in order to achieve healthy and productive oceans. (Target 14.2)
Goal 15	Protect, restore and promote sustainable use of terrestrial ecosystems, sustainably manage forests, combat desertification, and halt and reverse land degradation and halt biodiversity loss.	By 2020, ensure the conservation, restoration and sustainable use of terrestrial and inland freshwater ecosystems and their services, in particular forests, wetlands, mountains and drylands, in line with obligations under international agreements. (Target 15.1)

Source: UN, 2015b

archaeological sites, historic towns, traditional cultures and festivals, to fascinating landscape features that have the potential to increase the visitor economy and socio-economic development. According to the World Tourism Organization, the country has been underperforming in the tourism market given the international significance of its heritage resources, which include nine World Heritage sites (Negussie & Assefa-Wondimu, 2012). The Ethiopian Government recognized the link between tourism and poverty reduction, which has become one of the focal sectors in planning for accelerated and sustained development to end poverty.

Several international and bilateral heritage projects have been implemented with varying levels of success. In 2002, the World Bank granted a loan for a cultural heritage project to enable the Ethiopian Government in its efforts to achieve cultural heritage conservation through site planning, conservation of historic buildings and sites (e.g. the medieval castles of Gondar), the development of heritage inventories and preservation of crafts-based activities in order to maximize the tourism potential. Furthermore, UNESCO has promoted international campaigns to safeguard the principal monuments and sites of Ethiopia, in partnership with the Ethiopian Government, including implementation of the reinstallation of the famous Aksum obelisk and a shelters project to protect the Rock-Hewn Churches, Lalibela.[4]

The Rock-Hewn Churches in Lalibela include 11 monolithic churches dating from the late 12th century and were amongst the first 12 sites to be inscribed on the World Heritage List in 1978 (Figure 7.5). The site was nominated based on the first three of the six criteria defining cultural properties under the World

FIGURE 7.5 Rock-Hewn Churches, Lalibela: Bet Giorgis (House of St. George) (credit: Elene Negussie)

Heritage Convention. Figure 7.6 shows a landscape view of Lalibela. To the left is one of the three groups of rock-hewn churches covered by temporary shelters that were sponsored through an EU-funded project in order to protect the churches from rainfall and erosion. In the far centre of the picture on the hilltop is a cluster of hotel developments and a new cultural centre that also formed part of the EU-funded shelters project. The hillsides are covered by a string of thatched traditional houses and other types of dwellings. With increased economic development there is need for careful urban planning that considers the traditional layout of the town that surrounds the churches, the vernacular houses, as well as protection of landscape views, particularly with the expansion of new hotels that have increasingly been built along the edges of the hills.

With growing focus on using World Heritage sites for the generation of economic development through tourism, the need for sound site management has become urgent. In spite of the early inscription on the World Heritage List, a site management plan was not realized until 2013. The pressing need to establish a management plan for the Rock-Hewn Churches of Lalibela led to a series of partnership projects and workshops led by the Ethiopian Authority for

FIGURE 7.6 Landscape view of Lalibela (credit: Elene Negussie)

Research on Conservation of Cultural Heritages (ARCCH), the state body in charge of national heritage and World Heritage sites, supported by international agencies and bi-lateral collaborations, including support from the Norwegian Government. The workshops facilitated stakeholder participation and the integration of a broad range of issues into the management plan process. The first workshop was held in 2009 entitled 'Establishing a Management Plan Process for the World Heritage Site of Lalibela'. It was facilitated through a partnership between the World Heritage Management Programme at University College Dublin and ARCCH, jointly funded by the Ministry of Culture and Tourism in Ethiopia and the Department of Environment, Heritage and Local Government in Ireland.[5] This initiative was small compared to larger international projects, but its foremost contribution was its focus on capacity development as an inside-driven process that builds on existing national capacity assets and educational exchange, as discussed above. The project formed part of a series of additional workshops implemented by UNESCO which stressed the need to ensure sustainable development at Lalibela by tackling issues such as heritage protection, restoration, tourism infrastructural developments, water shortages, community needs and poverty-reduction through diversification of the economy (Negussie, 2012).

The workshops proposed that the management plan should consist of different framework plans. A sustainable heritage framework was needed to cover conservation actions relating to the rock-hewn churches, the historic traditional houses on the site, movable objects, policies to safeguard intangible heritage and the landscape setting. A sustainable tourism and visitor framework was required to control visitor flows, traffic and congestion, finding new methods of financing heritage and ensuring high quality authentic experiences. An environmental framework plan was deemed necessary to come to terms with environmental degradation, waste management, water policy and carbon emissions. A local community framework plan would ensure local participation in decisions concerning the World Heritage site and in the benefits of tourism (Negussie, 2012, pp80–81). This was reflected in the first formal management plan for the Rock-Hewn Churches of Lalibela that was adopted in 2013. The plan was structured around management and protection, resource conservation, tourism management and community engagement (ARCCH, 2013).

Opportunities and challenges

Heritage provides opportunities for cultural and socio-economic development and needs to be treated as a finite, valuable and delicate resource. While heritage has increasingly become promoted as a vehicle for international development, it is necessary to recognize the potential conflict between the uses of heritage as cultural, social, economic and natural capital. A key challenge to overcome is the risk of over-commercialization, exploitation of resources beyond sustainable limits and uneven economic development. The management plan process can potentially create a platform for sustainable development through its purpose of providing a long-term vision for the protection, conservation and communication of World Heritage sites. It needs to consider and balance the various interests involved to ensure holistic conservation based on local community engagement.

However, in the context of international development, internationally funded heritage projects are often marked by uneven relationships affecting governance regimes and long-term continuity. For example, a situation may develop in which international consultancy firms dominate conservation projects at the expense of national companies. World Heritage status is conducive to mobilizing funding and expertise, but international projects are not necessarily led by the national organizations where capacities need to be developed. For example, World Bank heritage projects tend to be won by an international pool of consultants, which raises questions in relation to building lasting impacts and real capacity development amongst national and local heritage custodians. Disillusion may occur when international projects fail to deliver long-term impacts and opportunities for national and local stakeholders. A key problem in capacity building is lack of communication between the different organizations involved. Overlap may arise where different bi-lateral projects intersect.

From this perspective, actions in line with the UNDP-promoted term 'capacity development' rather than 'capacity building' and the creation of strong regional platforms are a step forward. The integration of indigenous knowledge in heritage management is likewise important. National and local custodians need to be empowered through genuine partnership approaches to heritage conservation in international development. There is a need for wise use of international assistance through a people-centred approach based on good World Heritage governance.

Notes

1 The International Centre on Space Technologies for Natural and Cultural Heritage in China was established as a category 2 centre in 2011 with the Sector of Natural Sciences, although its work is also linked to World Heritage.
2 The International Assistance Request form is available in annex 8 of the Operational Guidelines. The form should be completed in English or French, the working languages of the Convention.
3 The 1st UN Resolution on Culture and Development was adopted in 2010. Since then four versions have been passed by the UN General Assembly.
4 The Aksum obelisk, or stelae, erected during the 4th century AD, was removed from Ethiopia in 1937 and brought to Italy as war booty by the Fascist regime. Following a UN agreement in 1947 and long-drawn-out bi-lateral negotiations it was returned to Ethiopia in 2005 and became a flagship repatriation project supported by UNESCO.
5 The collaboration emerged from research for a Masters thesis in World Heritage Management (see Assefa-Wondimu, 2007).

8

ENDANGERED HERITAGE

The World Heritage Convention is perhaps more relevant today than ever before in terms of the urgent need to protect endangered heritage. The convention draws attention to the changing social and economic conditions which, through 'formidable phenomena of damage or destruction' (UNESCO, 1972, preamble), threaten the state of conservation of the world's heritage. Today it is recognized that healthy social and economic conditions are dependent on resilient, functioning ecocultural systems supported by an integrated approach to cultural and natural heritage conservation. The convention's focus on international cooperation to address the challenges to conservation remains unchanged if not more urgent. However, the question is whether the will or desire is present amongst the international community to use it as a leverage to help secure sustainability.

World Heritage sites are threatened not only by the traditional problems of neglect and development but also by new factors such as terrorism and natural hazards which are increasingly understood to be exacerbated by human-induced environmental change. The evidence of humanity's impact on the planet is overwhelming including the emergence of climate change, the global mass extinction of species and the transformation of land cover by deforestation and urbanization (Ceballos et al., 2015; MEA, 2005). The Anthropocene has been described as the latest geological epoch in which human activities play a major role in altering the ecological and geological systems (Crutzen & Stoermer, 2000).[1] This chapter explores human-induced threats to World Heritage. The increasingly global nature of the threats requires a coordinated and cooperative international response. However, such a response is hampered by politics and lack of resources. Nevertheless, the convention has the potential to play a significant role in reducing disaster risks and contributing to the resilience of societies and the safeguarding of cultural and natural resources.

Threats to World Heritage

A wide range of threats and pressures affect World Heritage sites, from unsustainable use, conflict and climate change to ineffective management and urban and infrastructure development. These threats are often interrelated, increasing the vulnerability of World Heritage sites. For example, the damage induced by increased incidents of extreme weather due to climate change may be amplified by inadequate land use planning and development. Tourism and infrastructural development in coastal zones, for instance, often impair the capacity of ecosystems such as mangroves, wetlands and sand dunes to absorb storm surges and floodwaters, subsequently leaving inland areas more exposed to weather events. Furthermore, in areas troubled by conflict and unstable governments, regulations are less likely to be enforced, enabling activities such as demolition, construction and unmonitored resource use at heritage sites.

Invasive species and biological resource use

Invasive species and biological resource use, including commercial hunting, fishing and logging are among the most serious threats facing natural World Heritage sites (Osipova et al., 2014b). Analysis by the World Heritage Centre indicates that these threats are on the increase and negatively affect natural sites in all regions of the world (Veillon, 2014). The severity of the threats reflects global trends. Invasive alien species and overexploitation of biological resources are two of the five principal pressures directly driving global biodiversity loss. The other three drivers are habitat change, pollution and climate change (CBD Secretariat, 2010).

Invasive alien species are plants, animals, pathogens and other organisms introduced by humans into places out of their natural range of distribution. They become established and disperse, impacting negatively on the local ecosystem and species through competition, predation or transmission of diseases. They can also impact on agriculture, forestry and fisheries at great socio-economic, health and ecological cost (IUCN, 2008; CBD Secretariat, 2009). They are considered a leading cause of animal extinctions (Clavero & García-Berthou, 2005) and a significant threat to the ecosystem processes that are fundamental to human well-being (Pejchar & Mooney, 2009). Global trade and travel as well as the multiple pressures already generating ecosystem change facilitate and exacerbate the problem of invasive species. One of those pressures is biological resource use, the consumptive use and harvesting of wild biological resources for trade, recreation or subsistence. Activities may include trapping and hunting wild animals for the pet trade, for trophies or for meat; logging and harvesting wood for timber or fuel; and fishing and harvesting aquatic resources such as coral and turtle eggs (Salafsky et al., 2008). Factors that influence the unsustainable use of biological resources include poor governance, ineffective policies and human population growth, which generate increased demand for resources (Djoghlaf & Dodds, 2011). These factors are compounded by ineffective management of properties.

Invasive alien species and overfishing have been constant threats to the integrity of the Galápagos Islands in Ecuador since the site was inscribed on the World Heritage List in 1978. The danger posed by invasive alien species contributed to the site's placement on the List of World Heritage in Danger (LWHD) in 2007 (UNESCO, 2007f). The extension of the site to include the surrounding Marine Reserve was deferred for 15 years due to illegal fishing and exploitation of the sea cucumber. The drivers that have influenced the scale of these threats to the Galápagos ecosystems include economic and human population growth and socio-political factors affecting policies and management of the site (Watkins & Cruz, 2007). Economic growth has resulted from the steady increase in tourism to the archipelago since its designation as a national park in 1959. Furthermore, sea cucumber fishing boomed in the Galápagos following the collapse of the industry in Asia in the 1980s. The expanding tourism and fishing industries encouraged people to travel to the islands in search of work and the resulting growth in population facilitated an increase in the deliberate introduction of alien species (cats, dogs, goats, pigs, cattle, ornamental plants and crops) as well as accidental introductions via the increased boat and airplane traffic (rats, invertebrates, plants, fungi and disease-causing organisms). Approximately 1,329 introduced species have been recorded in the terrestrial ecosystems, a small proportion of which have become invasive and pose a direct threat to native and endemic species. Sixteen per cent of native vertebrates and 27 per cent of endemic plant species are considered endangered or critically endangered (Galápagos Conservancy, 2015). Poor planning and lack of resources have limited the capacity to address the issues of illegal immigration, introduced species and illegal fishing (WHC & IUCN, 2007).

Climate change

World Heritage properties across all regions of the world are impacted by climate change. This is evident from the increasing number of state of conservation reports to the World Heritage Committee highlighting climate change impacts year-on-year (Veillon, 2014). IUCN has identified climate change as the most serious potential threat to natural World Heritage sites (Osipova et al., 2014b). Recognition of the impact of climate change on cultural heritage conservation has been relatively slow (Petzet, 2008). However, the increase in frequency of extreme weather events and their direct impact on cultural properties have stimulated the international community to recognize the need for an integrated approach to tackling climate change (UNESCO, 2006c). For example, areas that have seen a rise in seasonal temperatures and in the numbers of lightning storms as well as extended periods of drought face an escalating risk of wildfires, which are potentially devastating for both people and heritage. In 2007, the Archaeological Site of Olympia was threatened by wildfires which had engulfed the Greek countryside following a summer of severe drought and heatwaves. Similarly, wildfires across the Mediterranean in 2012 threatened various World

Heritage sites including Teide National Park and Doñana National Park in Spain, Mount Athos in Greece and Laurisilva of Madeira in Portugal (UNESCO, 2012m). Similarly, wildfires in Australia threatened the Australia Convict Sites in Tasmania in 2012 and damaged large areas of the Tasmanian Wilderness in 2016.

In addition to increased frequency in extreme weather events, climate change is leading to higher ocean temperatures, ocean acidification, changes in ocean circulation, melting of glaciers and sea level rise, all of which pose a threat to marine ecosystems and biodiversity (IPCC, 2001). This is particularly worrying for coral reefs, which are already under stress from factors such as pollution, overfishing, sedimentation and physical damage from boats and other recreational activities (West & Salm, 2003). The additional threats generated by climate change will further weaken the resilience of the reef systems. In parts of the Great Barrier Reef, a combination of increased incidents of cyclones, outbreaks of the predatory crown-of-thorns starfish and mass bleaching caused by warmer temperatures has resulted in significant declines in coral cover (GRBMPA, 2014; Collette, 2007).[2,3] Ocean acidification further reduces the ecosystem's resilience by affecting the ability of the corals to build calcareous exoskeletons and thus impacting on their growth and survival.[4] The intensity and duration of the stressors as well as the relatively short periods between disturbances is compromising the ability of the ecosystem to recover (GRBMPA, 2014). This is a sobering finding considering that coral reefs are one of the most productive ecosystems in the world. Their health directly contributes to fishing industries, tourism, coastal protection as well as their cultural value to coastal communities.

The multiple and direct environmental impacts of climate change pose considerable challenges for the conservation of heritage sites. Archaeological sites and historic buildings which were designed for a specific local climate and place are particularly sensitive to changing conditions (Howard, 2013). They face increased rates of deterioration due to their new exposure to a multitude of changing parameters including temperature, atmospheric moisture, sea level, wind and biological pests. In Norway, for example, three coastal sites, Vegaøyan – The Vega Archipelago, a cultural landscape, Bryggen, a historic town, and the Rock Art of Alta will be exposed to rising sea levels, increases in precipitation, more frequent storms, warmer temperatures and greater humidity. All of which induce greater risk of flooding, direct damage by winds, coastal erosion, waterlogging, weathering, fungus and rot (ICOMOS Norway, 2008). Climate change may also impact on social and cultural aspects such as the ability of the people of the Vega Archipelago to continue their traditional way of managing the landscape and harvesting the down of the eider duck (*Somateria mollissima*).

A significant threat to terrestrial biodiversity and cultural landscapes is the response of species to changing climates such as shifting ranges and changes in the timing of biological cycles. In response to warmer temperatures, plant and animal ranges are shifting poleward and upward in elevation. This is particularly problematic for mountainous species which may face reduced geographic ranges as they move upslope. For example, the mountain tundra and alpine ecosystems in the Golden Mountains of Altai in Russia are expected to decline and become fragmented as they are encroached by the upward shifting treeline and subalpine shrubs. Shifting habitats, together with predicted unfavourable winter conditions, are likely to also threaten the region's iconic snow leopard (*Uncia uncia*) and its ungulate prey, the argali wild sheep (*Ovis ammon*). The melting glaciers will increase the risk of floods in the short-term and in the long-term reduce the water discharge to river flows and ultimately the area's total amount of available freshwater (Yashina, 2009; Colette, 2007). The changes in hydrological cycle and temperatures will also endanger the archaeological sites of the Altai, most notably the frozen tombs of the Scythian civilization, which have remained frozen and conserved in their original state since the first millennium BC (Han, 2008).

War and conflict

The damage caused by war and armed conflicts to cultural and natural heritage, both directly and indirectly, is devastating and enduring (Labadi, 2007). A well-known example is the Iraq War where, following the US-led invasion in 2003, the entire infrastructure of the country's cultural heritage was badly affected, e.g. archaeological sites, historic buildings, museums, cultural institutions, libraries, archives, technology and intangible heritage. The well-publicized looting of the National Museum of Iraq in Baghdad in April 2003 resulted in the loss of thousands of works of art and artefacts of immense value to humanity (Paroff, 2004). It was 12 years later that the museum re-opened with approximately one-third of the stolen objects recovered (BBC, 2015).

The ongoing conflicts in Yemen, Iraq and Syria unambiguously demonstrate the destructive impact of war on heritage. Syrian and Iraqi cultural and natural sites have been impacted in multiple ways, such as direct shelling during battles, collateral damage from gunfire, damage by the movement of tanks and heavy vehicles, destruction by bulldozers creating defensive works, as well as looting and vandalism resulting from the breakdown in security (Cunliffe, 2014). In complete disregard of the 1954 Convention for the Protection of Cultural Property in the Event of Armed Conflict, which Syria has ratified, the armed groups fighting in Syria have occupied important cultural sites and institutions such as medieval fortifications, archaeological mounds, museums and city centres for their strategic advantage (Ali, 2013). In fact, all World Heritage sites in Syria have suffered as a result and have consequently been inscribed on the LWHD, including the Ancient City of Aleppo, Ancient City of Bosra, Ancient City of Damascus, Crac des Chevaliers and Qal'at Salah El-Din and Site of Palmyra. At the meeting of the World Heritage Committee in 2015 in Bonn, the Committee made a statement deploring the conflict situation in Syria, Iraq, Libya and Yemen and urged all parties to fulfil their obligations under international law to safeguard heritage sites and to withdraw from World Heritage properties being used for military purposes (UNESCO, 2015i).

Natural sites are also targeted for their strategic advantage by combatants during conflict. In Syria,[5] the oases of Palmyra and forests in the region of Latakia have been deliberately destroyed to remove their potential tactical advantage for opposition groups (Ali, 2013). During Iraq's eight-year war with Iran (1980–1988), the Mesopotamia marshlands on the Iraq–Iran border were severely impacted by extensive defensive works and military infrastructure which contributed to a significant reduction in the area of marshland. Later, following an uprising in Iraq in 1991, Saddam Hussein's government set out to deliberately drain the marshes in order to punish opposition groups that had retreated to the wetlands. By 2002, less than 10 per cent of the marshes remained and the indigenous Marsh Arabs or Ma'adan were displaced and their traditional livelihoods devastated (Partow, 2008). The impact on the environment was severe. The marshes formed an ecologically important wetland system in an arid environment and provided globally important stopover points and wintering grounds for migrating birds. Environmental damage also occurs through contamination from heavy metals and toxic substances in used weaponry, from military debris and demolition waste and from destruction of chemical facilities and industrial sites. Deliberate bombing of oil tankers and oil wells during the Iraq–Iran war generated extensive damage; oil spills wreaked havoc on the marine environment and burning oil wells polluted the atmosphere with vast clouds of black smoke (ibid.). The air pollution persisted for some time and caused significant damage to cultural and natural heritage in adjoining countries (Vatandoust & Zargar, 2003).

The indirect impacts of conflict and war on cultural and natural heritage include the environmental consequences of displaced populations, collapse of governance and security, lack of information and monitoring, and loss of funding for heritage management and protection. The United Nations Office for the Coordination of Humanitarian Affairs (UNOCHA) estimated that 4.8 million Syrians have been forced to leave the country and 6.5 million are internally displaced (UNOCHA, 2016). This has resulted in the world's largest displacement crisis. One of the most severe consequences in an arid region such as the Middle East is unsustainable groundwater extraction to supply the freshwater requirements of the growing refugee camps. Excessive pumping of water from aquifers to support Palestinian refugees in Jordan led to the destruction of the Azraq Ramsar site wetland in the 1990s (MacKenzie, 2013). At one point the wetlands were reduced to 0.04 per cent of their original area and hence their ecological value was virtually destroyed. Furthermore, unstable government, absent authorities and lack of oversight make sites vulnerable to looting and unregulated development. In Historic Cairo, placed on the World Heritage List in 1979, destruction of historic buildings to allow for unauthorized high rise buildings occurred during the Egyptian political crisis of 2011–2014 (Mayer, 2014). Similarly, in Libya, significant sections of the Archaeological Site of Cyrene have been bulldozed by neighbouring farmers in order to sell land to developers (Sharpe, 2014). A war economy can also result in a funding crisis and failure of institutions such as the banking system. All five sites in the Democratic Republic of the Congo were placed on the List of the World Heritage in Danger following the commencement of conflict in the 1990s. The Congolese Institute for Nature Conservation (ICCN) and the park staff of the five natural sites have struggled to protect the parks from encroachment, poaching and extraction of natural resources because of lack of finances, transport or equipment. The park rangers have taken incredible risks to patrol the sites and were rarely paid during the years of conflict. Furthermore, efforts to provide salaries for park staff by international donors, including UNESCO, were hampered by the country's dysfunctional banking system (Mirindi, 2004).

Deliberate destruction

As discussed above, both cultural and natural heritage are frequently and deliberately destroyed during armed conflict for the purposes of tactical advantage or economic gain. However, heritage may also be the object of vandalism and ethnic violence and be deliberately targeted for ideological and iconoclastic reasons. During the wars in former Yugoslavia in the 1990s, ethnic conflicts exacerbated the negative impact of warfare on cultural heritage due to deliberate destruction. Museums, libraries, religious buildings and archaeological sites were destroyed because of reciprocal destruction between the different ethnical groups. Famously, Mostar Bridge, a 16th century Ottoman bridge located in the historic town of Mostar in Bosnia and Herzegovina, was destroyed in 1993 during the conflict. It was later rebuilt under the leadership of an international scientific committee established by UNESCO (Figure 8.1). Its reconstruction has been seen as 'a symbol of reconciliation, international cooperation and of the coexistence of diverse cultural, ethnic and religious communities' (UNESCO, 2014e). However, it remains a symbolic gesture as the different ethnic groups living in Mostar remain strictly divided (Walasek, 2016). Natural sites may also be affected by armed groups deliberately targeting iconic species. This was demonstrated by the execution of endangered mountain gorillas in Virunga National Park in the Democratic Republic of the Congo in 2007. A habituated gorilla group were deliberately murdered as a warning to park rangers investigating illegal activities in the park (Stirton, 2010). The killing of the gorillas was a form of vandalism, intentionally targeting a species of international importance as a means to threaten the authorities in order to ensure the continuation of the perpetrators' illegal activities within the conflict zone.

The destruction in 2001 of the Buddhas in the Bamiyan Valley by the Taliban regime in Afghanistan has become symbolic of global terrorism and highlights the fragility of World Heritage (Harrison, 2010, p188). The demolition of the statues was not directly linked to a military goal, but formed part of a wider strategy of the Taliban to destroy all pre-Islamic statues in the country. The Taliban were unmoved by appeals from the UNESCO Director-General and representatives of other Islamic countries to protect a cultural heritage they did

FIGURE 8.1 Old Bridge Area of the Old City of Mostar (credit: Alistair Young)

not recognize (Francioni & Lenzerini, 2003; Harrison, 2010). The two Buddha statues, 38 metres and 55 metres in height, carved into sandstone cliff faces between the 3rd and 5th centuries AD, were destroyed by the use of landmines and dynamite (Figure 8.2). The Taliban's actions may be considered as an act of defiance against the international community, which refused to recognize the Taliban government (Francioni & Lenzerini, 2003, p620). There is some suggestion that the Taliban were also protesting at the international focus on the statues rather than the humanitarian crisis in Afghanistan, which had been exacerbated by years of war, drought and sanctions imposed by the UN Security Council because of alleged associations with al-Qaeda (Harrison, 2010). Despite the fact that the Buddhas were not inscribed on the World Heritage List at the time of their destruction, the media coverage portrayed global outrage at the loss of the Bamiyan Buddhas as part of the heritage of humanity. The statues together with their associated cave temples in the Bamiyan Valley formed part of the most significant cultural treasures of Afghanistan. The demolition was a decisive moment in global politics as the Taliban's actions demonstrated their rejection of

FIGURE 8.2 Niche which once held a Buddha statue in Bamiyan Valley, Afghanistan (credit: unknown [DVIDSHUB])

international law and served to delegitimize their regime. In October 2001, the US-led coalition invaded Afghanistan with the aim of overthrowing the Taliban government and dismantling al-Qaeda. The loss of the Buddhas prompted the 2003 UNESCO Declaration concerning the Intentional Destruction of Cultural Heritage, which declared that the international community 'recognizes the importance of the protection of cultural heritage and reaffirms its commitment to fight against its intentional destruction in any form so that such cultural heritage may be transmitted to the succeeding generations' (UNESCO, 2003b, article 1). In the same year the Cultural Landscape and Archaeological Remains of the Bamiyan Valley was simultaneously inscribed on the World Heritage List and the LWHD. The site was inscribed under five cultural criteria including criterion (vi) which acknowledges that the site has suffered due to its symbolic value and is now testimony to the 'tragic destruction by the Taliban, which shook the whole world' (UNESCO, 2014f).[6]

As a symbol of the common heritage of humanity, World Heritage has increasingly come under attack by militant groups who do not share those values and feel marginalized by the international community (Harrison, 2010; Gamboni, 2001). In 2012, a militia group in Mali, named Anser Dine, deliberately damaged sacred tombs at the Timbuktu World Heritage site. Timbuktu, described as 'an intellectual and spiritual capital and a centre for the propagation of Islam throughout Africa in the 15th and 16th centuries' (UNESCO, 2014g), included three great mosques and 16 mausoleums of earthen architecture. The Anser Dine followed the same puritanical approach to Islam as the Taliban and set about destroying shrines they considered idolatrous including the mausoleums of Timbuktu. The so-called Islamic State of Iraq and Syria (ISIS) has also targeted heritage sites with religious associations for destruction as emblems of heresy to its ideology. In 2015, ISIS demolished the archaeological site of Nimrud in Iraq and, after publicly executing Khalid al-Asaad, Palmyra's retired chief of antiquities, set explosives to destroy Palmyra's Temple of Baalshamin and the Temple of Baal in Syria.[7] The dramatic video footage of the demolition of World Heritage produced by ISIS garnered huge media attention and served as a propaganda tool for its cause on social media. The combination of the symbolic value of World Heritage and the global reach of social media creates immediate publicity and maximum impact for the extremists. This poses a significant threat to cultural heritage and exposes a new vulnerability of World Heritage sites. It also asks difficult questions regarding the appropriate way for UNESCO to respond to ensure that terrorists do not receive the attention that they seek.

Development and extractive industries

Threats associated with building and development projects are among the most frequently reported threats to World Heritage properties (Veillon, 2014). Analysis of the state of conservation reports between 1979 and 2013 revealed that almost half of the properties concerned had been affected negatively as a result of building and development. Cultural properties were significantly more likely to be affected than natural and mixed properties where the factors included housing, commercial development, tourist accommodation and interpretation facilities. However, transportation infrastructure and services infrastructure (e.g. dams, pipelines, power lines, renewable energy facilities) tend to threaten proportionally more natural properties (ibid.). According to IUCN, road construction and construction of new dams together with mining and oil and gas projects are the most serious potential threats to natural heritage after climate change (Osipova et al., 2014b).

Damage to cultural and natural heritage takes place on a daily basis in many countries as part of the normal building and planning processes. In some cases appreciation for the significance of a place has not been fully developed and even where heritage protection legislation exists it is not always implemented. This may occur due to pressure for profit, particularly in urban areas where the land value is high. Development that impacts negatively on cultural heritage could be as extreme as demolition or may consist of out-of-scale developments altering views and vistas in a historic setting. It may also be in the form of redevelopment that leads to gentrification processes with loss of people and place identity. A major problem of urban sprawl is the break in the relationship between city and rural environments and the threat to cultural and ecological heritage through loss of natural landscape, loss of open spaces and landscape aesthetics and increased congestion and pollution

(Vaz et al., 2012). The old town of Antigua Guatemala was threatened by urban development, which stemmed from, inter alia, pressure from tourism, inadequate legislation, poor planning and lack of monitoring. The absence of regulation resulted in reconstruction and modification of historic buildings as well as new building developments which were unsympathetic to the original architecture and thereby affected continuity and authenticity (Savio, 2004). The growth in property prices encouraged Antiguans to sell their family homes and businesses and consequently led to gentrification processes which in turn threatened the intangible linkages between the inhabitants and their town and the overall spirit of place. Furthermore, unregulated urban development was insensitive to the natural setting of the volcanic mountain environment and surrounding forests, rivers and coffee farms (ibid.). The need for integrated urban development has become a recurrent discussion topic within the World Heritage Committee.

Threats related to mining and oil and gas exploration are becoming more frequent. Although extractive industries are impacting World Heritage sites across the world, African sites are particularly affected (Veillon, 2014). An examination of 33 natural World Heritage sites and 66 sites on the tentative list in sub-Saharan Africa revealed that 27 per cent and 23 per cent of sites respectively overlapped with oil and gas concessions (Osti et al., 2011). All concessions which overlap with World Heritage sites were granted after inscription on the World Heritage List. Durán et al. (2013) predict that metal mining activities will increasingly become a threat to protected areas as demand grows and extractive methods improve. Protected natural areas tend to be established in remote, higher altitude and inaccessible locations which are where metal deposits also tend to occur. Political resolve will be crucial to withstanding pressure for boundary modifications and granting of mining licences in designated natural areas (ibid.). Mount Nimba Nature Reserve, a transboundary site between Côte d'Ivoire and Guinea, was placed on the LWHD in 1992 following a proposal by the Guinean government to modify the boundaries on the Guinean side to allow iron-ore mining. The property has remained on the LWHD for 24 years as the World Heritage Committee attempts to determine the extent of the mining threat. The Committee has repeatedly requested the Guinean government to complete a comprehensive environmental and social impact study on the impacts of any potential mining projects adjacent to the site. In 2008, it was revealed that Côte d'Ivoire had not disclosed to the Committee that it also planned mining exploration in its part of the property.

International cooperation: key to success

Threats to World Heritage are often global and linked to external factors beyond the boundaries of the sites. The high levels of exploitation and conflict are testing the capacity of the World Heritage Convention to offer effective collective assistance. The steadily increasing number of World Heritage sites is putting strain on the system, and both states parties and the World Heritage

Committee are restricted in their actions by limited resources and the global and sometimes violent nature of the threats. The LWHD is an effective tool for encouraging international cooperation where states parties look for assistance. However, there is growing recognition of the need to coordinate conservation efforts across multiple sectors, including government and non-governmental groups and agencies, at both a national and international levels, to ensure the long-term protection of World Heritage.

World Heritage in danger

The LWHD may be seen as a measure that reflects the original intent of the convention to mobilize support from the international community towards conservation. By inscribing a property on the LWHD, the World Heritage Committee has the immediate capacity to assign financial aid from the World Heritage Fund to the endangered property. The inscription also alerts the international community that support and aid is needed to restore the site's attributes. A property may be inscribed on the LWHD in the case of either 'ascertained danger' or 'potential danger' (UNESCO, 2015b, para179). Ascertained danger refers to the circumstances where it has been proven that the danger is imminent and it is apparent that a property will lose some or all of the characteristics for which it was inscribed. Potential danger means that a property is threatened by some circumstance such as lack of conservation policy or a planned development which could have a damaging and adverse but unpredictable effect on a property's outstanding universal value. Thus, ascertained danger is more critical in terms of immediacy and level of endangerment.

In 2004, following a major earthquake, Bam and its Cultural Landscape was simultaneously inscribed on the World Heritage List and the LWHD. The desert settlement, located in the south east of Iran and built of earthen architecture between the 4th and 6th centuries BC, was a commercial centre on the Silk Road. The earthquake caused extensive damage and resulted in the collapse of the Bam Citadel, Arg-e Bam, an important symbol of the ancient city (Figure 8.3). The devastation was not limited to the citadel and it has been estimated that about 26,000 people died in the adjacent contemporary urban area during the earthquake. An international workshop for the Recovery of Bam's Cultural Heritage was set up in 2004, organized by the Iranian Cultural Heritage Organization, UNESCO and ICOMOS. The workshop set the foundations for eventually inscribing the site on the World Heritage List and the LWHD, which enabled Iran to apply for emergency assistance from the World Heritage Fund. The inscriptions also maintained international focus on the implementation of a master plan for the sustainable reconstruction of Bam City leading to its removal from the LWHD in 2013 (UNESCO, 2016i).

States parties are obliged to inform the World Heritage Secretariat if and when a site is under threat or facing changed circumstances that will impact on its conservation. They are entitled to request that a site is placed on the LWHD

FIGURE 8.3   Bam Citadel, Iran (credit: Charlie Phillips)

in order to call for international assistance where appropriate. For example, the Honduran Government called for the Río Plátano Biosphere Reserve, a biodiversity-rich area of tropical rainforest, to be placed on the LWHD on two separate occasions since its inscription in 1982. The area was traditionally occupied by indigenous peoples; however, it was placed on the LWHD due to extensive illegal encroachment by external agricultural settlers. The slash-and-burn tactics of the encroaching farmers caused widespread deforestation as well as conflict with the indigenous peoples. The rate of incursion of illegal settlers was exacerbated by ineffective management due to an inadequate budget and insufficient personnel and equipment. An IUCN mission to the property in 1995 produced recommendations for the long-term protection of the forest. These measures were based on developing a participatory management plan, establishing and demarcating the boundaries, translocating the illegal occupiers and communicating and raising awareness of the values and benefits of the forest. In the intervening 20 years the Government of Honduras has been largely successful in applying the recommendations with support from the World Heritage Fund, national and international NGOs and bilateral assistance such as funds provided by the Federal Republic of Germany. The site remains on the LWHD due to ongoing security concerns within Honduras and the lack of national resources to support continuous management.

Assistance in times of conflict

In spite of the role of the LWHD in highlighting the plight of an endangered site and prioritizing assistance for its safeguarding, the World Heritage Committee is limited in its capacity to act in any meaningful way against the threat of armed conflict. In the case of Timbuktu, the state party of Mali appealed to the Committee, at its 36th Session in 2012 in St Petersburg, to place the property on the LWHD (Figure 8.4). As mentioned previously, the property had been seized by the Anser Dine, an element of Tuareg militias that had captured the northern half of Mali earlier in the year. The Minister for Culture for Mali, Ms Diallo Fadima Toure, asked the Committee to 'please hear the cry from Mali hearts' (personal observation, 1 July 2012). She appealed to the international community and exhorted the UN 'to take concrete steps to stop crimes against cultural heritage, not only of my people, but of all people of the world' (ibid.). A debate among the Committee members ensued, but it soon became obvious that there were few, if any, options available to the Committee to provide a tangible means of safeguarding the site. As stated by the Chair of the Committee, Ambassador Mitrofanova, they could not send a mission to a conflict zone, UNESCO did not have a mandate to intervene directly and she questioned whether UN peace-keeping forces could play a role in protecting the site. Ultimately she had to concede that 'all we [the Committee] have are papers and pens, you're dealing with barbarians and criminals and we only have paper and pens' (personal observation, 2 July 2012). Having placed the site on the LWHD, the Committee called for an emergency fund and wrote a declaration condemning the destruction of the World Heritage properties of Mali. In 2014, funds were allocated to begin works on restoring the site after the Anser Dine were defeated in 2013, though not before they had destroyed approximately 4,000 ancient Timbuktu manuscripts (Bowcott, 2016).

FIGURE 8.4 Mosque at Timbuktu, Mali (credit: Emilio Labrador)

The plight of Timbuktu and the Committee's initial frustrations over its inability to act led to a wider discussion on how the convention and UNESCO should link to other conventions and international instruments to address such situations. In November 2012, Mali acceded to the Second Protocol to the Hague Convention of 1954 for the Protection of Cultural Property in the Event of Armed Conflict. This additional protocol enables states parties to submit requests for 'enhanced protection' of cultural sites (UNESCO, 1999a, article 10). In 2013, the UN Security Council included, for the first time, a mandate to protect cultural heritage as an integral part of a UN peacekeeping mission. It established the UN Multidimensional Integrated Stabilization Mission in Mali (MINUSMA) and charged it to assist 'in protecting from attack the cultural and historical sites in Mali' as well as to support the national authorities 'to bring to justice those responsible for war crimes and crimes against humanity in Mali' (UN Security Council, 2013, para16). In a landmark case in 2016, the International Criminal Court charged Ahmad al-Faqi al Mahdi, a member of the Anser Dine, with demolishing ancient mausoleums in Timbuktu as part of the Court's first war crimes trial dedicated entirely to the destruction of cultural heritage. He was sentenced to nine years in prison in what UNESCO hoped was a step towards combatting deliberate attacks on culture as weapons of war by extremist groups (UN, 2016).

Politics and national interests

International cooperation can manifest in a manner contrary to the original intent of the World Heritage Convention. States parties may lobby Committee members so that decisions regarding nominations and inscriptions on the LWHD are influenced by political alliances rather than conservation priorities. The Fortifications on the Caribbean Side of Panama: Portobelo-San Lorenzo was placed on the LWHD in 2012. The fortifications consist of 17th and 18th century military architecture built by the Spanish Crown to protect its trade interests in the Americas (UNESCO, 2012n). The property was threatened by new infrastructural development and neglect leading to significant decay. The ICOMOS recommendation of inscription on the LWHD was unanimously endorsed by the Committee and agreed by the state party. In the same year, a second property, the Archaeological Site of Panamá Viejo and Historic District of Panamá, was also recommended for placement on the LWHD for similar reasons. In this case, Panama strongly resisted the recommendation. Despite the deterioration of the historic town and the state party's non-compliance with previous recommendations, the Committee was divided with regard to whether it should place the site on the LWHD or not.

ICOMOS had previously expressed concern regarding the lack of a management plan, a legislative framework, housing policy and an adequate buffer zone for the historic town (UNESCO, 2008d). Following reactive monitoring missions as well as letters of complaint from civil society, NGOs and international heritage experts, it became apparent that the state party was also implementing an infrastructural project known as 'Cinta Costera'. This included a proposed coastal landfill and a four-lane viaduct encircling the peninsula on which the historic town of Panama was located. ICOMOS and the World Heritage Centre advised that this construction would have direct visual, acoustic, environmental and physical impacts on the historic centre (UNESCO, 2012o, p206). However, the Committee consistently overturned the advisory body's recommendation and the site was not placed on the LWHD. It was apparent that the state party resisted inscription on the LWHD because of the economic gain associated with the World Heritage designation. In a letter to the Secretariat it stated 'the historic and environmental values of the historic district are an opportunity for investors; the economic values of the buildings increase regardless of the state of conservation' (UNESCO, 2008d, p219). This was evident in the increasing gentrification of the historic town (UNESCO, 2010c, p195). In contrast to the archaeological fortifications of Portobelo-San Lorenzo which were placed on the LWHD, the Historic Centre of Panama contained real estate with potential for generating income (Figure 8.5).

The support of Panama's stance against inscription on the LWHD can be understood in the context of political alliances and lobbying (Meskell, 2014). The construction company, Oderbrecht, which won the tender for the multi-million dollar development of the viaduct, was Brazilian (UNESCO, 2012o) and during its membership of the Committee,[8] Brazil backed Panama's resistance to listing the site on the LWHD. Brazil is also part of the so-called BRICS geopolitical alliance which includes Russia, India, China and South Africa. All members of the BRICS alliance supported Panama during their time on the Committee (personal observation, UNESCO 2012; 2011a; 2009). In an unprecedented

FIGURE 8.5 Viaduct encircling Historic District of Panamá (credit: Bernal Saborio)

move, Panama also paid for Committee delegations to visit Panama City in an effort to make its case for non-inscription on the LWHD (UNESCO, 2013h). Meskell (2015) argues that the World Heritage designation has become a valuable commodity that states parties use as a bargaining tool in reciprocal negotiations inside and outside the World Heritage Convention. For example, Qatar with no obvious regional ties to Panama voiced support for Panama at the 36th session (personal observation, 2012) and signed a bilateral investment treaty with Panama in 2010 (SICE, 2015; Meskell, 2015). The occurrence of politically motivated interests driving Committee decisions is a serious challenge to the credibility of the World Heritage process and to the conservation of sites of OUV. Unless states parties realign their priorities to heritage conservation, the very label for which they strive will lose its meaning and value.

Illegal trade and trafficking

Illegal wildlife trade has become a global, multi-billion dollar industry, estimated to be worth US$7–23 billion annually (Nellemann et al., 2014). Consumer demand for exotic pets, animal skins, ornaments, traditional medicine and food is driving illegal trade in plants, live animals and animal parts. Rare and protected species fetch enormous prices on the black market. The economic return together with minimal prosecution rates make wildlife trafficking one of the most low-risk and profitable criminal activities worldwide (Rosen & Smith, 2010; Nellemann et al., 2014). Tens of thousands of species across a wide range of plant and animal taxa, including amphibians, birds, fish, mammals and reptiles, are directly affected. Illegal logging is estimated to be worth 10–30% of the total timber trade globally (Nellemann et al., 2014). In Africa, market demands are also driving the expansion of unregulated charcoal production and bushmeat hunting (Wilkie & Carpenter, 1999; Nellemann et al., 2014). The impact of unchecked and/or illegal trade in natural resources on protected areas, including World Heritage sites, is devastating. Illegal hunting is the most serious current threat to natural World Heritage sites in Africa, affecting 23 out of 37 natural sites (Osipova et al., 2014b). It is also one of the main threats to natural sites in Asia, along with logging and tourism impacts (ibid.). In fact, poaching and bushmeat hunting pose the most immediate threats to the survival of tropical vertebrates (Brashares et al., 2004; Nellemann et al., 2014).

The very nature of the trade in wild animals and plants across borders between countries requires international cooperation for successful regulation and prosecution of criminal organizations. Selous Game Reserve in Tanzania was placed on the LWHD in 2014 due to the devastating scale of poaching. Elephant and black rhinoceros numbers have dropped by nearly 90 per cent since the site was inscribed in 1982. The elephant population declined from 70,000 in 2005 to 13,000 in 2013. These alarming figures reflect the insatiable consumer demand for elephant ivory and rhino horn. Stretching across an area of 50,000km², the Selous Game Reserve was once home to globally important populations of African elephant and black rhino. Now, the reduction in their numbers is a conservation crisis. IUCN and the World Heritage Centre were alerted to the scale of the problem in Selous by the Monitoring of Illegal Killing of Elephants (MIKE) project implemented by the Convention on International Trade in Endangered Species of Wild Fauna and Flora (CITES) (UNESCO, 2013i). Following the resulting inscription of Selous on the LWHD, the Selous Elephant Emergency Project (SEEP) was launched and attracted multilateral, bilateral, NGO and private sector funding which enabled immediate anti-poaching work by the park rangers who were severely understaffed and under-resourced. In order to tackle wildlife crimes, a multi-agency task force was established by the government, and regional conferences were held to strengthen trans-border collaboration in combating the trade (UNESCO, 2015j).[9] Tanzania and China also initiated discussions on means to address the illegal movement of ivory between the two countries (UNESCO, 2016j). While this level of international cooperation is a welcome step in the right direction, more states parties need to get involved. For example, CITES has identified Thailand and China as the principal destination countries for ivory which has been illegally sourced in Tanzania, Kenya and Uganda and smuggled through Malaysia, Vietnam and the Philippines. Labelling this group of countries as the 'the gang of eight' for their role at the heart of the illegal ivory trade, the CITES Conference of Parties has urged the relevant state parties to take a more pro-active approach to halting the ivory trafficking crisis and the organized crime that it funds (Kideghesho, 2016; Carrington, 2013).

Similarly, international cooperation is also a key to success in tackling illicit trade in cultural goods. While theft and trafficking of cultural property has existed for centuries, wide-scale looting of cultural sites in conflict zones in the Middle East has gained international attention on the severity of the problem in recent decades. The extent of illegal trade in art and antiquities is difficult to measure (Campbell, 2013) but there is no doubt that it is a growing sector of criminality (UN Secretariat, 2015). Cultural objects illegally excavated from archaeological sites and stolen from spaces such as museums and places of worship are being sold in considerable volumes through legitimate auction houses and via the internet (UN Secretariat, 2010; Manacorda & Chappell, 2011). Furthermore, the illicit trade has been increasingly linked to organized crime including terrorist groups (INTERPOL, 2016).

World Heritage sites, as bastions of cultural and natural heritage and targets of looting and poaching, have an important role to play in disrupting international trafficking. The global scale of the illicit trade means that the individual actions of states parties alone are not sufficient to tackle the problem. The World Heritage Convention has become progressively more involved in coordinated international responses, drawing on several conventions and international organizations such as INTERPOL and the World Customs Organization (WCO), other UN agencies such as the UN Office on Drugs and Crime (UNODC) and specialized bodies such as the World Wildlife Fund and the International Council of Museums.

Risk preparedness

Cultural and natural heritage have always been threatened by the consequences of earthquakes, tsunami, landslides, hurricanes and fires. Climate change is increasingly being identified as a principal component of the rise in disastrous events affecting heritage sites. However, climate change is just one factor amongst many that have the capacity to exacerbate the exposure of heritage places to natural and man-made hazards. Social and political as well as environmental and economic factors can combine to intensify the damaging impact of hazards on World Heritage properties. Consequently, long-term planning and prevention in the form of heritage risk preparedness is being promoted by both national and international organizations in order to help reduce the risks to heritage collections and sites. This has been picked up in the Operational Guidelines which advise states parties to consider risk preparedness as an important factor in site management (UNESCO, 2015b, para118).

Addressing risks

The rise in the number of cultural and natural properties affected by disastrous events is reflected in the increase in World Heritage Committee decisions on the issue of risk preparedness. The earliest decisions, recorded in 1995, related to an ICOMOS application for funding to support the preparation of guidelines for risk preparedness for World Heritage sites. The project was realized with the publication in 1998 of a management manual on risk preparedness for cultural World Heritage (Stovel, 1998). The manual covered the risks of fire, earthquakes, flooding, armed conflict and other hazards such as tsunami, avalanches, storms and hazards of human origin. It highlighted an 'attitudinal shift' among conservation professionals in recognizing that addressing the risk of destruction by a single disaster is an equally, if not more, urgent priority than tackling the deterioration of a site through wear and tear (Stovel, 1998, p2). Furthermore, the need for a preventative approach through a disaster risk-planning framework was recognized rather than the traditional approach of conservation through restoration and rehabilitation post-disaster. The manual referred to the devastating events of the 1990s, such as the earthquakes in Kobe, Japan, in 1995 and in Assisi, Italy, in 1997, as well as the Gulf War in 1991 and the civil war in former Yugoslavia, to emphasize the potentially enormous scale of risks (ibid.). The Committee made its first recommendations with regard to risk-preparedness for World Heritage properties in 1998. Hurricane Mitch had swept over Central America causing serious flooding in Nicaragua, Honduras and El Salvador and prompting ICOMOS to stress the need to incorporate risk preparedness schemes in World Heritage planning (UNESCO, 1998). Similarly, Hurricane George caused severe damage to the Colonial City of Santo Domingo in the Dominican Republic, some of which could have been avoided with appropriate preventative measures. Since then, the number of Committee decisions recommending risk preparedness has steadily grown, reaching an average of ten decisions per session between 2012 and 2016.

The Secretariat and the advisory bodies produced a Strategy for Reducing Risks from Disasters at World Heritage properties, which was adopted by the Committee in 2007. The strategy aims to provide guidance on how to integrate disaster risk reduction into strategic planning for World Heritage sites as well as to integrate heritage concerns into national disaster reduction policies, thereby strengthening 'the protection of World Heritage and contributing to sustainable development' (UNESCO, 2007g, p2). The Committee described the strategy as corresponding to the spirit of article 5 of the World Heritage Convention, namely that all necessary measures should be taken to ensure the protection, conservation and presentation of the cultural and natural heritage (UNESCO, 2007g). Following amendments to the Operational Guidelines in 2004, states parties are recommended 'to include risk preparedness as an element in their World Heritage site management plans and training strategies' (UNESCO, 2015b, para118). Furthermore, states parties should address risk preparedness as part of the initial nomination process, as well as in the format for periodic reporting where factors affecting the property are dealt with as part of the state of conservation procedure. By 2010, an updated resource manual entitled Managing Disaster Risks for World Heritage dealing with risk preparedness for both natural and cultural sites was published jointly by UNESCO and the advisory bodies (UNESCO et al., 2010). Furthermore, ICOMOS has established an International Committee on Risk Preparedness (ICORP) specializing in disaster risk reduction for cultural heritage places. Similarly, IUCN has been working on raising awareness of nature-based disaster reduction under its thematic programme on Ecosystem Management (IUCN, 2013c) from which lessons can be drawn in World Heritage management planning.[10]

Identifying hazards

According to the UN Office for Disaster Risk Reduction (UNISDR) 'there is no such thing as a natural disaster, only natural hazards' (UNISDR, 2014). A disaster is the loss of life, material damage and collapse of social, economic, environmental and cultural functions that result from a natural or man-made hazard. Critically, the extent of the disaster depends on the ability of the affected community to cope using its own resources (ibid.). Therefore, assessing disaster risk requires identification and understanding of both hazards and vulnerabilities. In a World Heritage context this understanding is extended to include impacts on World Heritage values (UNESCO et al., 2010, p8). Disasters have the tendency to impact negatively on the values ascribed to World Heritage properties, which are closely attached to the functioning and collective memory of societies and communities. Thus, the hazard is the external source of a disaster and 'vulnerability is the susceptibility or exposure of a property to the hazard' (ibid.).

The identification of hazards forms part of the 'before' stage of disaster risk-planning framework, which includes risk assessment, prevention and mitigation measures for specific hazards. As suggested by Spennemann (2005, p94), 'no disaster plan will be effective [...] if the possibility of a disaster has not been considered'. The identification of both hazards and vulnerability requires the gathering of data and information concerning the relevant heritage site and its environmental circumstances (UNESCO et al., 2010). The information required is a mixture of historical and contemporary data relating to the vulnerability and exposure of the property concerned and its wider environmental and geographical context. Useful data may be retrieved from sources ranging from international organizations such as the UN and the World Bank to local level organizations such as municipal authorities. At the international level the World Bank Group has undertaken a programme of disaster risk management and global risk analysis, including identifying natural disaster hotspots, with a view to increasing access to information and supporting countries in the assessment of hazards and disaster risk (Dilley et al., 2005). The Global Facility for Disaster Reduction and Recovery (GFDRR) was established in 2006 with the primary goal to help developing countries reduce their vulnerability to natural hazards and to adapt to climate change and to mainstream disaster risk reduction and climate change adaptation into development strategies (GFDRR, 2014).

Given the varied nature of the information that needs to be gathered, inter-sectoral and interdisciplinary collaboration are required in order to produce viable risk maps and strategies for protecting and mitigating threats to heritage sites. The development of a flood-preparedness strategy for heritage properties, for example, requires information that can help establish the likelihood of flooding hazards, such as hydrological, meteorological and geological information. The relevant data informs those responsible for flood control and water management and should be integrated with planning efforts by emergency response and heritage conservation (Stovel, 1998; Howard, 2013). The availability of spatial, temporal and cross-sectoral information for World Heritage properties will vary significantly for different sites and between different countries. In some countries, where advanced heritage management strategies exist, special heritage risk maps may have been developed and coordination achieved between organizations with different specializations (UNESCO et al., 2010).

The World Heritage management plan should consider risk preparedness for at least the most common types of hazard. The 2011–16 Management Plan for the Old and New Towns of Edinburgh property, for example, states that: 'while Edinburgh is not generally afflicted by natural disasters in the way that other World Heritage Sites are, it is not immune to the effects of climate change, fire and flood risk and, like any other thriving city, the pressures of development' (Edinburgh World Heritage et al., 2011, p64). The plan included two objectives to address risk preparedness, one concerning climate change and one for the establishment of a Risk Register. The risks highlighted relate to fire safety, inadequate resourcing, flood prevention, unsustainable development pressure and climate change. Putting policies in place to asses and manage these risks may be considered as a first step towards a risk management strategy.

Assessing risk factors

Once possible hazards and vulnerabilities have been identified, heritage disaster risk assessment involves analysis of the factors that may cause disaster risk. This includes modelling potential disaster scenarios in which imagined situations are evaluated using predictions and assumptions based on estimations and available knowledge. It is necessary first to identify natural and human-induced factors putting a heritage property at risk (UNESCO et al., 2010). This includes both primary and secondary hazards, which are usually interrelated as demonstrated by the situation at the Rock-Hewn Churches, Lalibela, in Ethiopia. The exposure to weathering, in particular rainfall and humidity, over the past 800 years has resulted in the decay and degradation of the soft volcanic rock from which the churches are carved. Heavy rainfall, therefore, may be seen as a primary hazard due to factors including inadequate drainage and maintenance of the site (Delmonaco et al., 2010). The existence of biological phenomena such as vegetation has caused further deterioration of the rock and is identifiable as a secondary hazard. The colonization by plant roots has exacerbated cracks and inherent faults in the stone and increased water permeation, consequently reducing the shear strength of the rock walls of the churches (ibid.). Therefore, biological colonization is contributing to increased vulnerability of the property, vulnerability factors that need to be understood as part of risk assessment. Similarly, but on a more dramatic scale, an earthquake is recognized as a primary hazard resulting in a disaster, while a subsequent hazard, such as the fires that occurred following the Kobe earthquake in Japan in 1995, are regarded as a secondary hazard (UNESCO et al., 2010). Earthquakes can cause damage to cultural properties both directly and indirectly. A building may, for example, be damaged through partial or total collapse, through structural cracks, building instability and reduced resistance to future shocks. A building's supply lines (e.g. water, sewerage and electricity) may also be damaged, leading to risk of secondary damage caused by fire or water, or in the case of Kobe, inability to contain subsequent fires because of damaged water mains (Stovel, 1998).

The identification of vulnerability factors or those processes that together with the primary hazards might cause disaster risk to a property is important. Staying with the example of earthquakes, a building that is already in a bad structural condition may be more exposed to risk than a structurally sound building and is therefore physically more vulnerable (UNESCO et al., 2010). In earthquake-prone zones, a preparedness strategy may include the development of earthquake resistance of certain buildings (Stovel, 1998). Analysis of cause–effect relationships is also necessary and involves analysis of the relationship between primary hazards and the underlying hazards that increase a property's vulnerability and hence exposing it to disaster risk (UNESCO at al., 2010).

Factors contributing to a property's vulnerability may include physical, social, economic, institutional and attitudinal factors. The potential impact on heritage values should also be analyzed and estimated. Once this has been achieved a response plan may be developed, which amongst other things will include adequate documentation on the heritage values of the properties and a prioritization of actions based on the probability of the occurrence of risk factors as well as their level of risk. In the case of the toxic spill of the mines of Aznalcóllar north of Doñana National Park in 1998, for example, the government, regional authorities and World Heritage managers were unprepared for the impact of the accident on the natural values of the park as well as the effects on tourism, fishery and agricultural industries. The lack of risk assessment and an emergency plan for the mine, as well as the lack of institutional cooperation, adequate legislation and public communication resulted in an initially slow and damaging response to the ecological disaster which cost millions of euros and had a detrimental impact on the local economy (Bartolomé & Vega, 2002).

Reducing disaster risks

Disaster risk reduction (DRR) as defined by UNISDR is 'the systematic development and application of policies, strategies and practices to minimize vulnerabilities, hazards and the unfolding of disaster impacts throughout a society, in the broad context of sustainable development' (UNISDR, 2004, p3). The UNESCO Strategy for Reducing Risks from Disasters at World Heritage Properties seeks 'to build a culture of disaster prevention at World Heritage properties' and 'to reduce underlying risk factors at World Heritage properties' (UNESCO, 2007g, p3). Reducing disaster risks for sites therefore requires planning for resilience and creating capacities in order to implement mitigation of hazards across multiple sectors. Unfortunately, with regard to the 2015 earthquake in Nepal, the state party's efforts to develop a Disaster Risk Management Plan for Kathmandu Valley, as requested by the World Heritage Committee in 2013, were tragically late. All seven historic monument ensembles which make up the Kathmandu Valley serial site were severely damaged. While government bodies and NGOs had implemented initiatives to raise awareness for earthquake disaster risk management, Kathmandu Valley was exposed to increased earthquake disaster risk due to a history of 'uncontrolled and unplanned development, inadequate building code, lack of earthquake safety considerations, and lack of awareness among the general public as well as authorities' (Dixit et al., 2013, p633). The Nepal earthquake also highlighted the importance of ensuring that DRR is implemented on different levels, from individual and community levels to regional, country and international levels. In Nepal, there had been some progress in integrating DRR into policy and legislation at the national level (Dixit et al., 2013; UNISDR, 2015). However, there had been little progress in DRR actions at the local level, which would have had a significant effect on the impacts of the 2015 earthquake (UNISDR, 2015).

Understanding the values that need to be safeguarded in post-disaster recovery work is a critical element of disaster risk reduction for heritage sites. In addition to the naturally caused destruction, preservation is challenged when there is a lack of knowledge about heritage values that can be restored in the aftermath of a disaster. In the case of the mining disaster which occurred near to Doñana National park in 1998, the impact of the recovery projects on the natural environment was critical to the sustainability and long-term success of the rehabilitation process. The regional government of Andalusia initiated the Guadiamar Green Corridor project as a plan of action to restore the Guadiamar River and its ecosystems which had been heavily polluted by the toxic spill. However, beyond the restoration of the functionality of the damaged aquatic and terrestrial ecosystems, the project recognized the value of reinstating natural processes which had declined over time in the wider landscape. The project aimed to enable the long-term resilience of the entire Guadiamar basin through the restoration of its function as an ecological corridor between the Sierra Morena ranges to the north and the Doñana wetlands in the south. The conservation and restoration activities were integrated with policies of sustainable development and activities to improve the quality of life of the local residents. The project was multi-disciplinary, involved extensive public participation, integrated management of ecological and economic systems and demonstrated possibilities for positive restoration and disaster recovery experiences (Hernández et al, 2004; Montes & Borja, 2006).

The inclusion of risk preparedness in World Heritage strategies and management plans is essential given the high priority of the conservation of World Heritage properties for present and future generations. In those parts of the world that are most prone to natural disasters, the need for risk preparedness is perhaps best recognized. In these countries, it is not a question of 'if' it happens but 'when' it happens again, and reducing risks before disasters occur and planning for the likelihood of their re-occurrence hence becomes a more naturally recognized component of managing heritage sites. For all World Heritage sites, regardless of location, climate change and environmental degradation have become significant factors in increasing the risk of human-generated and natural hazards.

Endangered heritage: a threat to sustainability

In what may be considered an era of sustainability, where the concept of sustainable development is widely recognized at all levels, from international organizations and world leaders to national governments and the world's citizens, the evidence seems to indicate that human activities continue to become less sustainable not more. This is reflected in the growing rate at which World Heritage sites have become endangered. While strategies for implementing the convention have become refined and conservation objectives are increasingly integrated with policies on sustainability, lack of political will and resources, as well as political decisions that favour short-term economic interest over long-term conservation, remain a challenge. However, successful implementation of the convention illustrates the capacity of World Heritage sites to serve as platforms to accelerate progress towards sustainable development and the feasibility of achieving sustainability goals. Because of the scale of human-induced modification of the planet, protected areas such as World Heritage sites are crucial for sustaining a large proportion of the world's poorest people by providing them with essential services such as food, water, shelter and medicine. Furthermore, well-managed World Heritage sites offer a safe operating space for creating resilience and mitigating global change.

Poverty alleviation and security

Sustainable management of World Heritage sites can contribute to poverty alleviation and security. The harmful effects of the degradation of ecosystem services (services including air and water purification, the regulation of regional and local climate, natural hazards and pests) 'are being borne disproportionately by the poor, are contributing to growing inequities and disparities across groups of people, and are sometimes the principal factor causing poverty and social conflict' (MEA, 2005, p1). For example, there is evidence that a drought in Syria, considered the worst drought on record, contributed to the recent Syrian conflict, and was more than likely caused by climate change (Kelley et al., 2015; Wendle, 2016). Inadequate governance regimes and policies which encouraged unsustainable agricultural and environmental practices aggravated the devastating impact of the drought which caused widespread crop failure, political unrest and the forced mass migration of rural families (Kelley et al., 2015).

Linking the conservation of World Heritage properties to improving local lives and livelihoods through education and economic well-being as well as resolving broader regional resource use and spatial planning is an essential part of sustainable development. Each World Heritage site is unique and with appropriate governance, management and public engagement has the potential to offer diverse benefits to local and national economies. Depending on the property type, cultural and natural sites can be used to address issues related to poverty through providing opportunities for people to acquire new skills and to access resources for subsistence and alternative livelihoods. Furthermore, through appropriate governance mechanisms and public participation, heritage sites can encourage a rights-based approach to management and support the empowerment of residents and traditional owners. Finally, the conservation of heritage sites may contribute to improved security by helping to maintain natural ecosystem services and to maintain social cohesion and cultural values as well as improve resilience to natural and human-made disasters (UNESCO et al., 2012; Osipova et al., 2014b). However, in the case of endangered sites, there are often complex external threats as well as insufficient management resources (financial, human and otherwise) which can severely reduce their capacity to deliver on these services. Such situations, where human actions render eco-cultural systems unable to provide services important for well-being and security, represent a loss of resilience (Folke et al., 2002, p437).

The following example highlights how poor planning and management of World Heritage can exacerbate issues of poverty and inequality. Following the emergence of Cambodia from a violent and turbulent period in its history, Angkor was simultaneously inscribed on the World Heritage List and the LWHD in 1992. In the early years of inscription, the focus was on the restoration of the monuments of the site with little consideration of the wider environment and the need for socio-economic development. The ensuing rapid growth in tourism was perceived simply as a threat to the site rather than evaluating the impact it would have on the local people and the possibilities it offered. The lack of local services, infrastructure and human resources were rarely considered by the managerial framework put in place by UNESCO (Winter, 2008). The surrounding area was plagued by extreme poverty and the tourism boom resulted in major economic and social inequalities, particularly in the adjacent town of Siem Reap. In 2003, the site was removed from the LWHD and the managerial focus shifted from simply conserving the monuments to considering sustainable development and the role of ethical tourism in the fight against poverty (UNESCO, 2003b). Projects were put in place to promote community-oriented policies in order to improve the equitable distribution of tourism-related benefits. Furthermore, efforts were made to employ a more holistic approach to management which recognized the integral connections between the area's cultural and natural values. Approximately 130,000 people across 112 villages occupied the wider Angkor landscape, which is located in a wetland area north of the freshwater lake of Tonle Sap and surrounded by forests (Figure 8.6).[11] The Angkor Participatory Natural Resource Management and Livelihoods programme aimed to improve the inhabitants' livelihoods by restoring access to natural resources provided by the environment. For example, people traditionally relied on the forest for wood, bamboo and medicines, and on the lake and irrigation system developed by the historical Angkor kingdoms for agriculture. Deforestation, overexploitation and water extraction for urban development and tourism threatened these services (Bowden, 1995). The drop in the water table caused by the unsustainable use of the hydrological system was also threatening the ancient monuments of Angkor through subsidence and collapse. A continued holistic, participatory and coordinated approach to the management of the area must be carefully implemented to address poverty and inequality which persist as major issues.

Challenges to OUV

The primary aim of the convention is the conservation of the OUV of World Heritage sites. However, states parties continue to nominate sites primarily as a means to increase tourism and associated economic development. This is

FIGURE 8.6   Traditional houses on the shore of Tonle Sap Lake, Angkor, Cambodia (credit: Alan Sung)

despite the fact that many countries do not have sufficient resources required for adequate conservation and site management. The World Heritage Committee has come under severe criticism for supporting nominations of sites despite recommendations by the advisory bodies that they do not fulfil the conditions necessary for World Heritage designation. Such is the concern that the Director-General of UNESCO, Irina Bokova, made the following plea on the occasion of the opening of the 36th session of the World Heritage Committee: 'I believe we stand at the crossroads, with a clear choice before us. We can continue to gather, year after year, as accountants of the World Heritage label, adding more sites to the List, adhering less and less strictly to its criteria. Or we can choose another path. We can decide to act and think as visionaries, to rejuvenate the World Heritage Convention and confront the challenges of the 21st century. The World Heritage is not a beauty contest. It is not a race for the greatest number of sites' (personal observation, 24 June 2012).[12]

The following example highlights the challenges to maintaining World Heritage designation as a gold standard for conservation when states parties are motivated to nominate sites for economic gain rather than the conservation of OUV. The Iwami Ginzan Silver Mine and its Cultural Landscape, Japan, was inscribed on the World Heritage List in 2007 despite ICOMOS concerns that neither the OUV nor the nominated criteria had been justified (ICOMOS, 2007). Following its inscription, the site immediately attracted a huge influx of tourists. In the small town of Omori, 88,000 tourists were recorded within an 11-day period in 2008, putting great pressure on the local population of approximately

400 people (Morita, 2010). The number of tourists forced the local authorities to develop a management strategy to ensure that tourism was managed in a culturally and environmentally sustainable manner. The inhabitants of the town developed a 'Charter of Omori-cho Inhabitants' based on the principles of preserving the local 'history, remains and nature' and ensuring the 'inhabitants feel safe, relieved and comfortable' (Morita, 2010, p129). Despite the conflict between the state party's goal to stimulate economic gain through tourism and the advisory bodies' principled approach to impartially evaluating the OUV, the World Heritage designation mobilized the local residents to ensure that the values of those who lived at the heart of the site were realized and the landscape was protected. However, this is not always the case and the fact that OUV is treated as secondary to politics and big business threatens the sustainability of the World Heritage List and the cultural diversity it supports. Furthermore, simply considering the benefits of designation in terms of the tourism potential of sites is ill-conceived in a world where the tourism industry may be devastated overnight by unpredictable and dangerous events such as violent conflict, terrorist activity, disease outbreaks and natural hazards.

While the emphasis by some states parties appears to be on the nomination of sites for purposes of economic development rather than the conservation of OUV, it is not always clear that a focus on preserving OUV provides adequate scope for the promotion of sustainable development. OUV is arguably based on a static notion of heritage and is often evaluated from a technical and site-based approach which does not consider the wider social, economic and environmental contexts, as evidenced in the previous example at Angkor (Torggler et al., 2015, p24). In order to increase the emphasis on the relationship between World Heritage and sustainable development, it is important that much work is done 'to move [...] OUV towards a more holistic, dynamic, and multi-dimensional understanding of heritage's value for society, which may be able to encompass cultural, environmental, social, economic and peace and security elements, and to translate this into guidelines, procedures and actual implementation practice' (ibid., p29).

Environmental degradation

The Millennium Ecosystem Assessment report of 2005 found that 60 per cent of the ecosystem services examined were being degraded or used unsustainably (MEA, 2005, p1). As ecosystems continue to lose their resilience and ability to respond to changing climate, external threats and stochastic events such as droughts and fires, World Heritage properties have an important role to play in setting international standards for conservation and sustainable development. By meeting the conditions of integrity, natural sites are going some way towards fostering resilience of ecosystems, particularly properties inscribed under biodiversity-related criteria (i.e. criterion (ix), significant ongoing ecological and biological processes; and criterion (x), most significant natural habitats for in-situ conservation of biodiversity). Analysis of the contribution of the World Heritage Convention to the global network of protected areas found that the total area of natural World Heritage sites amounted to just over 10% of the total area of all protected areas listed in the World Database on Protected Areas (WDPA). This is a significant contribution as natural World Heritage sites represented only 191 sites at the time of the analysis compared to a total of more than 130,000 protected areas listed in the WDPA, i.e. 0.15 per cent of total number of protected areas (Badman & Bomhard, 2008). The proportion of protected areas represented by World Heritage sites has since increased with the designation of vast sites such as the Lut Desert, Iran, in 2016 (22,780 km^2), Phoenix islands Protected Area, Kiribati, in 2010 (408,250 km^2); and Papahānaumokuākea, USA, in 2010 (362, 075 km^2).

Evidence has shown that well-managed protected areas are an effective conservation strategy in tackling environmental degradation by preventing habitat loss and maintaining species population levels (Watson et al., 2014). The Convention on Biological Diversity has set a target to conserve at least 17 per cent of terrestrial and inland water areas and 10 per cent of coastal and marine areas through a network of protected areas by 2020 (CBD Secretariat, 2010). However management effectiveness is the key to conservation success; and protected areas, including World Heritage sites, have suffered severe ecological degradation as a result, in part, of poor management. The primary reasons for ineffective management are inadequate funding and resources as well as poor governance and conflict. However, the lack of funding is not necessarily associated with struggling economies; some of the richest countries in the world are reneging on their commitments to protect designated areas, including World Heritage sites, by disproportionately cutting budgets for their management (Watson et al., 2014). More problematic is the prevalence of changing policies which aim to open up sites for resource extraction through 'protected area downgrading, downsizing and degazettement (PADDD)' (ibid., p70).[13] Downgrading refers to authorized increases in human activities within a protected area; downsizing refers to boundary changes to accommodate resource extraction; and degazettement is the removal of protected area status from the designated site altogether. In the case of World Heritage sites, PADDD is most likely to occur to facilitate mining and oil and gas exploration. It is critical that states parties realize the value of conserving natural heritage, such as the maintenance of ecosystem services and improvement of social and economic well-being, so that designations such as natural World Heritage sites are recognized, not as a drain on resources, but as a return on investment. According to Crutzen & Stoermer (2000, p18), 'to develop a world-wide accepted strategy leading to sustainability of ecosystems against human induced stresses will be one of the great future tasks of mankind, requiring intensive research efforts and wise application of the knowledge thus acquired in the [...] knowledge or information society'.

Building resilience

The costs to human well-being are difficult to measure, but the available evidence demonstrates that the degradation of ecosystem services is a significant barrier to achieving the UN Sustainable Development Goals as stipulated in the 2030 Agenda for Sustainable Development adopted in 2015. However, well-protected World Heritage sites can support healthy ecosystems. Furthermore, the convention's international perspective can contribute to shared experience and improve the connectivity of the protected ecosystems to the wider landscape and/or seascape. For example, the Third Marine World Heritage Managers Conference, held on the Galápagos Islands in 2016, resulted in an agreement between the managers of the seven marine properties in the Eastern Tropical Pacific region (stretching from the west coast of Mexico to the northern tip of Peru) aimed at developing regional collaboration. This collaboration includes goals to tackle common management problems, share scientific and technical information and seek funding to support conservation (UNESCO, 2016k). The global recognition that accompanies the World Heritage designation has also demonstrated its potential to influence the development industries that might otherwise negatively impact on heritage sites. For example, UNESCO and IUCN have been successful in encouraging leading oil-and-gas firms Tullow Oil, Shell and Total, as well as the International Council on Mining and Metals (ICMM) to commit to not operating within World Heritage properties. This 'no-go' principle has also been endorsed by financial companies, including Paribas, HSBC and JP Morgan, which have committed to not support activities affecting World Heritage sites (WHC, 2015b).

In 2015, the landmark Paris Agreement on climate change was adopted by 195 states parties to the UN Framework Convention on Climate Change (UNFCCC, 2015). The Agreement emphasizes the importance of forest conservation in carbon sequestration as well as the need for disaster risk reduction, strengthening resilience and the importance of capacity building, public awareness and public participation in climate mitigation and adaptation. Each of these measures reflects the potential role of World Heritage sites as useful tools in mitigating climate change. Furthermore, World Heritage forests have the potential to benefit from payment schemes for carbon sequestration such as the Reducing Emissions from Deforestation and Forest Degradation in Developing Countries (REDD+) programme under the UNFCCC.

Cultural and natural heritage should not be considered as a passive victim of natural and human-induced disasters but rather as a tool that can be used proactively to develop and foster the resilience of eco-cultural systems. Well-protected sites support resilient ecosystems which have the capacity to recover from a disturbance and withstand ongoing pressures and stressors. Similarly, thriving and dynamic traditional knowledge systems can contribute to post-disaster recovery through use of traditional skills, practices and local knowledge in rebuilding shelters and site restoration. Often, traditional knowledge, accumulated over generations of experience, can play an effective role in preventing and mitigating disasters (Jigyasu, 2014). Resilience is typically associated with diversity, from species and habitats to economic opportunity and livelihood options (Folke et al., 2002). In gentrified historic towns, for example, resilience may mean coming to terms with economic processes that threaten the diverse social fabric of cities. Gentrification not only displaces lower-income people but also local indigenous culture and heritage. Local businesses may also become gentrified in that they are replaced by chain retailers and big companies increasing homogenization and reducing unique sense of place.

In line with the proposed new epoch, the Anthropocene, scientists have proposed planetary boundaries as a new approach to global sustainability. Planetary boundaries refer to thresholds for nine key biophysical processes, including climate change, global freshwater use, land-system change and rate of biodiversity loss. Crossing the thresholds could possibly trigger non-linear and unpredictable responses which could destabilize the biophysical systems and cause irreversible environmental change (Rockström et al., 2009b). While a lot of work is required to develop the planetary boundaries concept and planetary resilience research, the idea of a 'safe operating space' for human development within those boundaries aims to shift our approach to governance and management towards sustainability (ibid.). However, this is a profound task because the 'predominant paradigm of social and economic development remains largely oblivious to the risk of human-induced environmental disasters at continental to planetary scales' (Stern, 2007, cited in Rockström et al., 2009b). World Heritage Conservation can contribute to our understanding of the critical factors required for ecosystem and cultural resilience. Research and monitoring can help identify the synergies between local pressures and ecosystem stressors, and global processes such as climate change. Efforts to create resilience at the scale of iconic World Heritage sites can lead to substantial global mitigation; for example, reduced deforestation rates in the Amazon propelled Brazil forward in climate change mitigation (Scheffer et al., 2015).

Notes

1 As of 2017 the Anthropocene is not yet a formally defined geological epoch but it is being developed by the Anthropocene Working Group for consideration by the International Commission on Stratigraphy, see: http://quaternary.stratigraphy.org/workinggroups/anthropocene/.
2 The outbreaks of the predatory crown-of-thorn starfish populations are associated with increased terrestrial runoff and flood events. The resulting increase in sediments and nutrients generates denser phytoplankton blooms and increased survival of star fish larvae and consequently increased starfish populations.
3 Bleaching refers to incidents where corals bleach or turn pale in colour, because of the loss of symbiotic algae, which are essential to the corals as nutrient providers.
4 Increasing dissolution of atmospheric carbon dioxide in the oceans acidifies the water, leading to a decrease of calcium carbonate, which is used by some marine organisms to build shells, e.g. corals, lobsters, urchins and oysters.

5 Note that there are no inscribed natural World Heritage sites in Syria.
6 The description under criterion (vi) states that 'the Bamiyan Valley is the most monumental expression of the western Buddhism. It was an important centre of pilgrimage over many centuries. Due to their symbolic values, the monuments have suffered at different times of their existence, including the deliberate destruction in 2001, which shook the whole world'.
7 Nimrud is on Iraq's Tentative List since 2000.
8 Brazil was a member of the World Heritage Committee from the 32nd to the 35th Session (2008–2011).
9 The Arusha Summit on Combating Illegal Wildlife Trade and Promoting Conservation held in Tanzania in November 2014 resulted in the Arusha Declaration on ways to fight against wildlife/environmental crime by strengthening cross-border collaboration between the participating countries as well as bilateral agreements between Tanzania and its neighbouring countries of Mozambique, Zambia and Kenya.
10 IUCN is also a member of a global alliance of UN agencies, NGOs and specialist institutes known as the Partnership for Environment and Disaster Risk Reduction (PEDRR) which was formally established in 2008.
11 Tonle Sap was designated a UNESCO Biosphere Reserve in 1997 in recognition of the unique freshwater lake and wetland ecosystem and rich biodiversity.
12 Full text of the Director-General's opening address to the 36th Session of the World Heritage Committee is available at: http://unesdoc.unesco.org/images/0021/002167/216700e.pdf
13 World Wildlife Fund has launched a website, PADDDTracker.org, which tracks PADDD trends.

9
TOWARDS A HOLISTIC APPROACH

The success of the World Heritage Convention in inviting all the nations of the world to collaborate on the conservation of a global heritage has been conducive to understanding links between culture and the natural world. As ideas about what constitutes the 'common heritage of humanity' evolve, the processes of international conservation continue to shape conservation practice and heritage management, not least in regard to the questions of 'whose heritage', 'who decides' and 'for what purpose'. However, the noble aims of international conservation through global-led local custodianship, set against the backdrop of peace building, have also been challenged. The question is whether World Heritage Conservation can offer the holistic approach that is needed to safeguard natural and man-made heritage within the broader remit of sustainable development. The Istanbul Declaration on the Protection of World Heritage, adopted by the World Heritage Committee in 2016, raised several of the concerns of this book. It welcomed the reference to culture in the 2030 Agenda for Sustainable Development, which reinforced the role of culture and cultural diversity in sustainable development. Furthermore, it asked the states parties to the convention to reflect on how to create synergies between the conventions dealing with culture and biodiversity respectively. It also expressed concern about the deliberate destruction of heritage sites, illegal excavations, looting and trafficking of artefacts, as well as the negative impacts of climate change, environmental hazards and the increasing social and economic pressures on heritage sites (UNESCO, 2016l).

The shift in focus on sustainable development and community-based approaches has proved that the convention has the potential to manifest World Heritage sites as powerful platforms for conservation and sound use of cultural and natural resources. Interdisciplinary approaches and collaboration can help overcome epistemological and organizational divisions to sustain the heritage of humanity for future generations. In a period of unprecedented global change and threats to the environmental, economic, societal and cultural values of humanity, World Heritage Conservation has put endangered heritage to the fore in the broader sustainability debate. However, the future is uncertain as resources continue to decline and protected heritage sites become isolated and encroached upon as a result of urban growth and intensified land development. Mass movements and displacement due to climate change, economic collapse and war have exacerbated the growing disassociation of people from their local heritage leading to a local/global disconnect. Furthermore, the World Heritage Committee has become increasingly politicized in its decisions putting the credibility of the World Heritage process at risk. Conservation is also coming into conflict at the local level with the need to engage and identify with diverse groups of stakeholders and competing interests. The challenge is to encourage stakeholder participation and legitimacy, and to find common ground between the diverse values and interests recognized by the stakeholders, and the outstanding universal value identified by expert evaluation.

International conservation: successes and failures

World Heritage as something that relates to all of humanity has proved a major success in that it seeks to unite rather than separate groups along national and ethnic lines. A global heritage without borders is perhaps best exemplified in serial and transboundary sites such as the Silk Roads and the Prehistoric Pile Dwellings around the Alps. Although these sites require complex management plans, often spread over several countries, they play an important role in cross-border alignment of conservation strategies. Another important contribution of international conservation is the mobilization of financial support and assistance for heritage sites. The World Heritage Fund followed the pioneering footsteps of the World Wildlife Fund and the World Monuments Fund and created momentum in developing sponsorship and bilateral assistance to support conservation.

In spite of the opportunities of international mobilization to conserve World Heritage sites, these are still vulnerable to the impacts of gradual deterioration, sudden natural disasters, deliberate attacks and the outbreak of war. The Hague Convention, or the Convention for the Protection of Cultural Property in the Event of Armed Conflict of 1954, obliges 'occupying powers' who have ratified the convention to protect cultural heritage in times of war and to prevent the exportation of cultural property. The passing of the UN Security Council Resolution 2199 condemning the destruction of cultural heritage in Iraq and Syria was also an attempt to tackle the illicit trade of cultural objects. This echoes the situation in 2012 when concern over the deliberate destruction of sacred tombs at Timbuktu raised the need for Security Council intervention to protect World Heritage.

Although international conservation doctrine has been subject to critique due to a strong influence of Western thought and culture rooted in the

Enlightenment, the global orientation of the World Heritage Convention has opened up new avenues for a broad range of conservation perspectives. This was clearly demonstrated by the international debates on both authenticity and cultural landscapes. Due to its position within the UN system the convention has encouraged dialogue on heritage perspectives in relation to human rights and highlighted the need for rights-based approaches to conservation and recognition of diversity, both to reflect the mosaic of cultural expressions and the diversity of nature. Shifts from modern universalism to post-modern relativism have shed new light on the implementation of the convention, shaping heritage narratives as well as governance models. The rejection of the perception of natural landscapes as 'pristine', without any cultural impact has promoted awareness of traditional knowledge systems in ecosystem stewardship.

Acknowledgement of the need for inclusive approaches has provided opportunity for the recognition of indigenous peoples in conservation. The 'Laponia process' in Sweden demonstrated the linking of traditional management practices with a modern heritage management system. Nonetheless, the right to cultural practices of indigenous peoples is still challenged within the structure of modern nation states. In 2016, the Swedish state lost a court case that granted the exclusive rights to control over hunting and fishing to the Sami people. Similarly, a proposal for the formation of an advisory body of indigenous experts to advise the World Heritage Committee on cultural landscape nominations has not been achieved in spite of good intentions. This reflects the difficulty of reaching a majority agreement on contentious issues within intergovernmental bodies within the UN system. Conversely, at the Meeting of the World Heritage Committee in 2015, for the first time, observers such as NGOs and indigenous representatives were invited to make submissions to the Committee in advance of the final decisions.

The UN sustainable development goals and the recognition of the need to mainstream conservation and sustainability as a matter of national priority have stimulated a synergistic approach to the different UN programmes and conventions. ICOMOS increasingly works with UN Habitat, the United Nations Human Settlements Programme, on issues relating to urban sustainability. Furthermore, the World Heritage Convention is a member of the Biodiversity Liaison Group, which aims to identify areas of collaboration in the implementation of the seven biodiversity-related conventions.[1] This is an important development as the methods promoted by the conventions to protect and monitor species and/or ecosystems are often complementary and there is much room for cooperation.

The harmonization of activities is also relevant at the level of the states parties where the obligations for periodic reporting under the different conventions have become a costly and time consuming administrative burden, sometimes to the detriment of conservation activities and even as a deterrent to further designations. There is often lack of awareness and understanding amongst the general public over the meaning and relevance of the different designations, particularly where a site has multiple titles. Also, application of the conventions does not always reflect integrated conservation. The List of Intangible Cultural Heritage is quite distinct from the World Heritage List and both operate separately, in spite of the close interdependency between tangible and intangible heritage. Therefore, collaborative efforts across conventions to reduce administration, integrate conservation activities and improve public appreciation are timely. Despite the paper work, a major success regarding the implementation of the World Heritage Convention has been the systematic monitoring of sites. The regular submission of state of conservation reports provides for an effective method of reviewing the conservation status of World Heritage sites. In addition, the continued conservation of sites is supported by the advisory bodies which undertake missions to evaluate sites at the request of the World Heritage Committee.

The visitor economy has the potential to have both positive and negative effects on World Heritage properties and their conservation. While tourism has become a driver and motivation for the inscription of sites on the World Heritage List, the original intent of the convention was primarily conservation. Overemphasis on catering for visitors not only creates risks of depriving sites of their physical heritage values but also their vibrancy and relevance to local communities and sustainability thereof. In Venice, both a World Heritage site and a Ramsar site, the ecocultural system is subject to both natural and man-made threats. The 'Venice syndrome' depicts a situation in which a city's cultural and natural resources are exploited to the extent of self-destruction.[2] In March 2016, Europa Nostra announced its ranking of the Venice Lagoon as the most endangered site in Europe. Compared to the flooding of 1966, the scenario is more complex this time, including factors such as sea level rise; erosion of natural and cultural assets due to intensified commerce; increased traffic flows of large-scale container and cruise ships; erosion of the seabed and salt marshes; and pollution and industrial fishing. This has been exacerbated by short-term economic goals, depopulation of the city and a complex governance structure (Europa Nostra, 2016). Unless there is political will to readjust, even the most exemplary site management plan will not solve the problems.

The Venice syndrome captures the trajectory of many historic towns globally where the processes of gentrification and market-led activities have pushed out residents from their own localities. The curious visitor who wants to discover something of Venetian life has to move beyond the central districts in the search for authenticity. Changed social organization at World Heritage sites due to unsustainable touristification is to some extent the effect of local community interests themselves. Some groups are better able to reap financial benefits from the economic gains that tourism brings. In addition, heritage commodification under the influence of neo-liberal economies threatens conservation and authentic experiences due to spectacularization and packaging of idealized versions of heritage for profit rather than for the health of the world's biocultural diversity.

Increased tourism pressure at sites also results in infrastructure development that may not be consistent with the character of the place. The life of historic towns such as Venice and Dubrovnik is threatened by their conversion into centres for hotels and seasonal accommodation to cater for the visitors. Similarly, the cultural and natural significance of Machu Picchu in Peru has been threatened by uncontrolled urban development as well as lobbying by international hotel companies for cable car access. The existing tourist traffic generates waste disposal problems, pollution, erosion and overcrowding, which jeopardizes the integrity of the site and increases risks of landslides. The need for implementing sustainable heritage principles is more urgent than ever if places are to recover from the negative side effects of tourism.

Tool for sustainable development

The developmental role of World Heritage sites became increasingly evident as heritage conservation was integrated with strategies for international development. The World Heritage portfolio was linked to the broader concerns of the World Bank and United Nations Environmental Programme and eventually considered in the review process of the Millennium Development Goals, where formerly links to heritage conservation and poverty alleviation had been unacknowledged. The Sustainable Development Goals, stipulated in the 2030 Development Agenda for Sustainable Development, still consider this link only indirectly. However, the use of World Heritage sites in international development work spearheaded or at least contributed to shifting policy towards promoting heritage as a tool for sustainable development.

This best practice impetus of World Heritage Conservation is critically needed as the original intent of the convention, namely conserving heritage as a means to foster peace, is at risk of being diluted. World Heritage is now at a crossroads. The question is whether to simply carry on with business as usual or to make deliberate shifts towards comprehensive efforts to place conservation strategies at the centre of the sustainability debate. This is pertinent considering global developments. Many countries are torn by failing electoral systems, political polarization and rejection of modern democracies in response to global, technological, economic, social and environmental change.

World Heritage designation has in recent times tended to be driven by economic motives and aspirations of using the status as a means to generate tourism income. As demonstrated by the 'Venice syndrome', the argument of a tension existing between the uses of heritage as economic versus cultural capital is highly relevant (Graham et al., 2000). On a more positive note, there is a strong potential for World Heritage sites to be used as platforms for sustainable development. The variety of protected cultural and natural resources represented by World Heritage can contribute directly to alleviating poverty and inequality by providing access to ecosystem services, creating locally based employment built around the protection, conservation and management of resources, as well as creating a sense of place and well-being through the process of maintaining local heritage of global significance. By its very nature, World

Heritage encourages a sustainable approach to its stewardship and is often the product of an age-old interaction between humans and their environment and/ or exists today because of its local value and a comparatively balanced approach to its use and exploitation.

This is epitomized by the cultural landscape concept which has signalled the emergence of the international recognition of intrinsic links between communities, their heritage and their natural environment. From a sustainability perspective it is becoming widely accepted within governance models and heritage discourse that the separation of people from nature makes little sense. The separation of natural and cultural worlds in policy and decision-making processes makes it difficult to find sustainable solutions to complex problems. Furthermore, it has helped to improve recognition of the humanized lived-in landscape and there is potential for the same recognition of the cultural aspects of natural environments beyond this category. World Heritage recognition is an important incentive as the conservation of cultural landscapes requires extensive knowledge of the human–environment interactions and values. Such an understanding and the facility to collect this knowledge are often lacking in many official agencies and conventional conservation authorities. The conservation of lived-in landscapes demands an innovative approach in governance and management systems that separate cultural and natural activities and where consultation with local populations is limited or even non-existent. The World Heritage Convention provides an opportunity to encourage nominations that epitomize such an approach and to support states parties in the identification and nomination process.

Sustainable development is a broad concept and is associated with a wide range of perceptions and perspectives relating to the planetary boundaries of the Earth system. Successful management of sites requires cross-sectoral and cross-disciplinary approaches and a clear vision for how sites are to be conserved and developed. World Heritage can contribute substantially to the practice of sustainable development across its dimensions: ecology, economy, equity and culture. It is this opportunity to demonstrate an understanding of sustainability across these four dimensions that is particularly exciting about the convention. Sustainability is far too often considered simply from the perspective of economics and/or the environment. It is necessary to develop indicators, concepts and tools such as carrying capacity to determine sustainability in the broadest sense of the word and set limits for acceptable change. For example, the achievement of sustainable tourism requires policies that balance goals of generating economic revenue with safeguarding measures that protect heritage resources and sustain local communities. It is essential to place humans and biodiversity at the centre of conservation strategies.

The shift in thinking with regard to the links between best practices in World Heritage management and human rights is an important step in promoting the cause of social equity. The fifth 'C' of the World Heritage Committee's strategic objectives, i.e. to enhance the role of communities in the implementation of the convention, promotes the rights of local custodians, indigenous peoples and marginalized groups to have a meaningful role in the identification and management of their heritage. This is a difficult issue to address across the diversity of national governance structures represented by the states parties to the convention. However, the level of stakeholder participation in nominations and management planning is critically reviewed as part of the evaluations of nomination documents and is increasingly referred to in committee decisions. The World Heritage Centre and the advisory bodies put considerable effort into emphasizing the importance of participatory approaches through their respective capacity building programmes. The fact that the World Heritage Committee adopted a strategic objective linked to equitable and integrated management indicates the potential to progress a rights-based approach in World Heritage policies. The focus on local communities in World Heritage can instigate a shift away from exclusive focus on tourism. For example, in Norway, strategic planning for establishing 'World Heritage centres' over 'visitor centres' at World Heritage sites signals a shift away from focus on tourism to a community-based approach. Communication about World Heritage can potentially develop into powerful narratives of sustainable development, including peace building, which is imperative to achieve resilient societies that place the local community engagement at the centre of conservation strategies.

Recognition of culture as the 'fourth pillar' in sustainable development theory makes it a more distinctive factor in sustainability thinking since cultural heritage is then considered more explicitly as a finite resource. Arguably, culture may be integrated with the economic, environmental and social dimensions of sustainable development. However, its recognition as a standalone entity stresses the intrinsic value of culture instead of its being simply attached with economic, social and environmental meanings.

The World Heritage label creates opportunities for economic development by attracting people and investment, not only linked to tourism, since well-preserved environments are usually a quality assurance of attractive and distinctive places. Strategies for economic development need to be linked to goals of conservation and sustainable use of heritage resources. In the case of World Heritage cities, designation can be used as a place-making catalyst by conserving a city's OUV and promoting heritage-led development. This creates an environment which is better able to withstand external threats and more conducive to address risks from natural and manmade disasters compared to those areas where there is lack of planning, regulation, consensus and local involvement. Furthermore, it creates resilience to resist the negative impacts of development, such as gentrification and land-use change, that exclude and marginalize local residents.

The mandatory management plan process constitutes an opportunity for negotiation and alignment of various interests and perspectives to achieve sustainable development. The management plan needs to identify objectives and a long-term vision for the World Heritage site based on broad stakeholder participation and interdisciplinary collaboration. It needs to strike a balance between conservation, access, local community interests and sustainable economic use, while ensuring conservation of a site's OUV, of which authenticity and integrity are vital parts, as the primary objective (Negussie, 2012). An integrated site management plan is by nature interdisciplinary in approach and includes both framework and action planning. It has the potential to form a platform of engagement, research and decision-making for well-informed strategies to address issues such as education, tourism, energy efficiency and risk preparedness for long-term conservation and sustainable development.

Challenges and need for credibility

A cause for concern in recent years is the number of decisions that the World Heritage Committee has made contrary to the advice of the advisory bodies. They represent one of the principal checks on the autonomy of the Committee in approving sites for inclusion on the World Heritage List and the List of World Heritage in Danger. New nominations have been accepted despite recommendations that they do not meet the standards of OUV. Similarly, recommendations for placing threatened sites on the LWHD have been resisted by the Committee. Such decisions challenge the credibility of the convention and diminish its original intent. The extensive lobbying that goes on between delegations at Committee meetings is also troublesome. There is a need to guard against such politicization.

To some extent the discrepancy between the advice of the advisory bodies and the Committee decisions also relates to more fundamental biases and perceptions of the convention as Eurocentric and authority driven. The composition of the advisory bodies in the use of regional expertise has been questioned by sections within the Committee. The critiques have referred to concerns that the assessors of World Heritage nominations were drawn from a limited pool of European and North American professionals at the cost of other regional and local expertise. This has resulted in a review of the evaluation methods used by the advisory bodies and greater transparency in the evaluation process. The advisory bodies work to include consultation at international, regional and local levels. However, there is still space for improvement. ICOMOS, for example, is under-represented in Africa. Furthermore, there are diverging opinions on the importance of management frameworks being in place before site inscription. Committee members representing less economically developed nations argue that inscriptions should be prioritized to support the protection of sites.

Eurocentrism has extended to imbalances in the World Heritage List in terms of heritage representation, although attempts have been made to rectify this through the Global Strategy for a Representative, Balanced and Credible World Heritage List. The strategy has been positive in widening the scope of sites, both regionally and typologically, but its strategic approach to addressing imbalances in the List is both its strength and weakness. It can be seen as an artificial widening of heritage sites which results in a risk of overemphasizing the balancing act itself and perhaps even manipulation. Furthermore, the Global

Strategy is largely targeted at the less economically developed countries which have fewer resources for implementing the convention.

The need for credibility extends to the activities of the states parties. The conservation of global heritage faces considerable challenges from illegal trade in cultural and natural resources, armed conflict, resource extraction and unsound development. The threats are exacerbated by the lack of application of other conventions such as the Convention on International Trade in Endangered Species (CITES) and the UNESCO Convention for the Protection of Cultural Heritage in the Event of Armed Conflict, as well as a failure to implement complementary policies at both national and international level. In order to avoid a hypocritical approach to conservation, states parties must attempt to outline a cohesive policy approach that incorporates guidelines and principles on conservation and sustainable development across the different government sectors. Madagascar, for example, called on other states parties to tackle the illegal trade and smuggling of valuable wood products across their borders in order to help stifle the illegal logging that was threatening the OUV of the Rainforests of the Atsinanana. From this perspective World Heritage has the potential to integrate conservation agendas with broader policies nationally and internationally.

The concept of OUV is limited when it overrides other heritage values in importance. It then becomes a dominant or authorized heritage discourse (Smith, 2006). While the Operational Guidelines allow for adjustments, the designation of OUV can work against the evolving nature of heritage understanding. It is not always consistent with social and societal interest as a whole as demonstrated by the delisting of Dresden and the resistance of World Heritage inscription in some parts of the world. The delisting of Dresden Elbe Valley, Germany, in 2009 and the Arabian Oryx Sanctuary, Oman, in 2007 discredits the concept of World Heritage as a superior motive for conservation. In Ireland, people living in the area adjacent to a tentative World Heritage property, the Céide Fields, signed a petition asking that the site not be put forward for nomination for fear of restrictions on planning and development in the area. Delisting of sites raises questions about the credibility of the convention from two perspectives. Firstly, the fact that the relevant states parties recognized that their actions would result in the de-listing of their sites and went ahead anyway, places a priority on development over the loss of World Heritage designation. Secondly, its lack of implementation, even when the OUV of a site is severely threatened, raises the issue of the level of transgressions that the Committee is willing to tolerate from states parties before they are penalized for damaging World Heritage properties.

Attempts have been made to introduce 'bottom-up' approaches to World Heritage governance alongside what has been mainly 'top-down' in the past. The integration of a myriad of stakeholders at different levels is both an opportunity and a challenge. The authority of experts' knowledge becomes challenged in bottom-up governance regimes. Furthermore, many countries still lack a culture of democracy and suspicion of state authorities, and perceptions of UNESCO as an outside actor remains an obstacle to overcome. There are perceptions of international rule-making overriding local decision-making and thereby the principle of local democracy. There is the additional complication that the term 'local communities' is undefined and vague. Local communities consist of heterogeneous groupings representing different and often clashing interests and with varying levels of ability to exercise influence. The question here is what measures need to be taken to buffer against political decisions and to ensure alignment with a rights-based approach to heritage.

Private funding and increased usage of sites for economic purposes exposes the World Heritage brand to exploitation for commercial purpose. In Morelia, a historic town in Mexico, the World Heritage label was presented together with the Coca-Cola logo. While this could be seen as contradictory to UNESCO guidelines on use of its logos, Coca-Cola had sponsored the site. If UNESCO continues to rely on private donations to secure its work in the future, sites will henceforth require a clear communication policy to guard against inappropriate commercialization of the World Heritage label.

The destruction of the Bamiyan Buddhas of Afghanistan highlighted the role of World Heritage sites as powerful international symbols, also vulnerable to attack. The fact that the statues were part of the common heritage of humanity, despite that they were not inscribed on the World Heritage List at the time, played a major role in how the Western media and international community responded to their destruction by the Taliban. The act of destruction was used by the Taliban to reach an international audience to highlight their professed oppression, political exclusion and religious beliefs (Harrison, 2010). The international symbolism of World Heritage sites could create a precarious situation where the List is reduced to a check list for tourists or a target list for terrorists.

The goal of ensuring international cooperation and assistance to safeguard World Heritage sites is imperative to maintaining the credibility of the convention. The Budapest Declaration on World Heritage reinforced this goal and the Committee's commitment to building effective capacity building within states parties for the implementation of the convention. However, with an expanding number of sites all facing a diversity of threats it is a major challenge to secure the necessary resources. UNESCO has itself been faced with reduced means to carry out its duties in the field of World Heritage. This became particularly problematic in 2011 when the USA withheld its membership dues due to Palestine's acceptance as a member state of UNESCO and state party to the convention. The World Heritage Centre is now facing a financial crisis. At the Committee meeting in 2015 it was confirmed that less than half of its staff was supported by regular funding. Similarly, funding for the advisory bodies has significantly reduced and they are faced with a growing body of work that largely depends on voluntary effort.

Holistic conservation

Interdisciplinary approaches and collaboration, both in practice and in scholarly research, are indispensable to overcoming divisions both within and between cultural and natural heritage conservation and to sustaining the heritage of humanity for future generations. A holistic approach to heritage conservation recognizes that humans and the environment are part of a single system. It is an uphill and challenging battle to protect areas of natural wilderness or monuments and historic centres in a so-called sea of developed and transformed landscapes. The 'fortress approach', which constantly fights against human incursion and encroachment on the pristine heritage area, is an exhausting, exclusive and resource-poor battle.

Holistic conservation requires a re-evaluation of the uses of heritage together with the broader landscape so that, in managing the whole, the altered landscape also plays a vital role in nurturing heritage conservation. It is increasingly recognized that sustainably managed farms, for example, can contribute successfully to biodiversity conservation. The Mediterranean, a biodiversity hotspot, has been farmed by humans for thousands of years and is one of the most biodiverse regions on the terrestrial landscape. The point here is to learn the value of the human-altered landscape, the interconnectedness of culture and nature and to foster heritage sites as places of living heritage. The way forward is to integrate conservation and sustainable development to encourage landscapes that are more hospitable to heritage conservation strategies and to reduce the stark borders or blur the line between heritage properties and the surrounding environment ('them and us'). Heritage sites can be reconnected to the surrounding landscape through corridors that create a regional network of important areas for conservation. Ecosystems, for example, can be linked through a variety of conservation strategies including restored habitats, urban parks and linear features such as hedgerows, rivers and canals.

Holistic conservation is not limited to the terrestrial environment. It is equally important to apply the landscape or seascape concept to the marine environment to recognize the intimate links between people and the marine ecosystems. Marine World Heritage sites make up 20 per cent of all marine protected areas on the planet and can play a lead role in innovative approaches to tackling ecological, cultural and socio-economic questions particular to this environment. Marine spatial planning and management techniques encourage the application of multiple-use zonation which can accommodate different stakeholders with different objectives and allow for future-oriented, sustainable long-term conservation objectives.

World Heritage Conservation is proposed as an interdisciplinary field of study and practice emanating from international conservation with its ambitions to deal with culture and nature within a single framework. It is concerned with linking culture and nature conservation, both in theory and practice, through shared global experiences. The knowledge gained may be translated into broader heritage and environmental research, policy and practice beyond the interest of World Heritage sites. International cooperation, innovation and the sharing of ideas and information are needed to strengthen the holistic perspective which brings together diverse methods and tools in tackling global environmental change and crises of humanity.

Holistic conservation raises the question of how much should humans interfere in the protection of cultural and natural heritage. In the Anthropocene the importance of understanding the relationship of man and nature – and 'mankind as a major environmental force' – will grow in importance (Crutzen, 2002, p23). The Millennium Ecosystem Assessment identified that approximately 60 per cent of ecosystem services are being degraded or used unsustainably. Approximately 55 per cent of the planet's ecosystems have been altered by humans and converted to so-called anthropogenic biomes, e.g. human settlements, croplands and rangelands (MEA, 2005). To halt the current rate of cultural and biodiversity loss, extensive intervention and strategic management is required. However, the level of intrusiveness of the interventions requires careful consideration. The natural state that we try to restore is often unclear. Consequently, extensive resources may be applied to the removal of invasive species and restoration of the natural landscape to some point in the past, some pre-modern ideal that may not have the capacity to continue in the current altered environment.

In the case of cities, the historic urban landscape approach emerged from the search for a holistic approach to conserving cities, drawing on the link between cultural and natural factors in the conservation of built environments, the challenges created by rapid economic and social changes and the role of cities as centres of creativity (Banderin & Van Oers, 2012; UNESCO, 2011). It seeks to reconcile conservation and development through culture-led development and sound management of change. New tools are needed to help determine acceptable limits of change since change is necessary to meet the demands of contemporary society and for the survival of cities.

There are significant challenges to fostering interdisciplinarity including developing a common language and knowledge base, identifying realistic expectations and dealing proactively with misunderstandings. Also, the greater establishment may create obstacles such as institutional resistance to relinquish ownership of projects, or lack of resources for collaboration and organization of interdisciplinary efforts. World Heritage Conservation can play a significant role in developing interdisciplinary approaches and sharing knowledge between societies. In line with the UNESCO mission for education and capacity building, World Heritage properties can act as sites of educational exchange and research – as laboratories – enabling visitors, the public and academia, to learn about other cultures, their strategies for sustainable livelihoods and their traditional practices and interactions with the environment.

In addressing the commonalities between culture and nature conservation, Harmon (2007, p384) critically asked: 'Is there really any evidence that a truly interdisciplinary approach to the conservation of natural and cultural heritage, one that takes both into account consistently and systematically, will actually produce synergistic, and therefore presumably more effective, results?' While this question has yet to be fully answered and addressed with further empirical evidence, Harmon noted that it is at least worth a try considering the dire environmental circumstances in which we find ourselves. The concepts used in international conservation have increasingly become applicable to both culture and nature, e.g. authenticity, integrity, diversity, reconstruction, adaptation, restoration, rehabilitation and resilience. In addition, new cross-cultural-natural terminology has emerged in relation to diversity, such as biocultural diversity and ecocultural resilience. Disciplines dealing with cultural and natural heritage respectively can learn from each other about the meaning of intrinsic and extrinsic values. The intrinsic-value argument in cultural heritage conservation is comparable with that of environmental conservation, in which nature is considered as having an inherent value apart from its utilitarian value. Hence, culture should be afforded greater recognition and a more distinctive role in sustainable development theory.

Integrated conservation is still challenged by and has to overcome a conflict between modern ideals based on Enlightenment in Western secular tradition and pre-modern and traditional perspectives. This is particularly relevant in post-colonial countries where, historically, there has been limited understanding of 'indigenous' cultures. Efforts to incorporate a holistic approach to protecting cultural and natural heritage are also challenged by the interpretation of the cultural and natural criteria in the Operational Guidelines. The natural criteria exclude the notion of natural environments created by human endeavours and may be considered to be out of step with the idea of cultural landscapes. However, in light of the fact that development is frequently prioritized over conservation by states parties, it may represent a viable fear on behalf of the conservation community that incorporation of human activities into the natural criteria opens up scope for states parties to retrospectively introduce activities incompatible with the protection of endangered species and ecosystems. Fundamentally, however, the concept of World Heritage cultural landscapes has increased international recognition of the intrinsic linking of people, their heritage and natural environment with greater emphasis on the intangible values of places. A continued emphasis on community involvement and participation should move significantly towards recognizing the interconnectedness of cultural and natural values and creating a common sense of heritage.

Finally, holistic conservation places human rights at the centre of strategies to conserve landscapes and seascapes stretching beyond national borders. This ultimate goal of bridging people and living creatures across the globe into a single interconnected ecocultural system (Pilgrim & Pretty, 2010) is very important to resist narrowly framed understandings of heritage. Holistic conservation and resilience strategies to conserve and maintain global heritage do not ensure eternal survival of culture and nature, but they do remind us that the battle for heritage belongs to humanity as a whole and still requires the mobilization of international support and cooperation for building peace in the minds of humankind.

Notes

1 The seven biodiversity-related conventions are: the Convention on Biological Diversity, 1992; the Convention on Conservation of Migratory Species, 1979; the Convention on International Trade in Endangered Species of Wild Fauna and Flora, 1975; the International Treaty on Plant Genetic Resources for Food and Agriculture, 2004; the Convention on Wetlands of International Importance, 1971; the Convention concerning the Protection of the World Cultural and Natural Heritage, 1972; and the International Plant Protection Convention, 1952.
2 The Venice Syndrome was captured in a documentary film with the same name.

REFERENCES

Abdulla, A., Obura, D., Bertzky, B. and Shi, Y. (2013) *Marine Natural Heritage and the World Heritage List: Interpretation of World Heritage Criteria in Marine Systems, Analysis of Biogeographic Representation of Sites, and a Roadmap for Addressing Gaps*, Gland, Switzerland: IUCN,

AFP, Agence France-Presse (2012) 'Ancient Greek sites could soon be available for rent', www.rawstory.com/rs/2012/01/17/ancient-greek-sites-could-soon-be-available-for-rent/, accessed 21 April 2014.

AFP (2015) 'Historical sites in Syria are being looted on an industrial scale', *The Guardian*, 16 September.

Albert, M.T. and Ringbeck, B. (2015) *40 Years World Heritage Convention: Popularizing the Protection of Cultural and Natural Heritage*, Berlin: De Gruyter.

Alexander, M. (2010) *A Management Planning Guide*, Talgarth, Wales: CMS Consortium.

Ali, C. (2013) 'Syrian heritage under threat', *Journal of Eastern Mediterranean Archaeology & Heritage Studies*, vol. 1, no. 4, pp. 351–366.

Alpine Working Group (2014) 'Activity Report: Working Group UNESCO World Heritage, Alpine Convention', www.alpconv.org/en/organization/groups/past/WGUNESCO/Documents/ActivityReportUNESCO.pdf, accessed 26 February 2016.

Anderson, K. and Gale, F. (1992) *Inventing Places: Studies in Cultural Geography*, Melbourne: Longman Cheshire.

Antrop, M. (2006) 'Sustainable landscapes: contradictions, fiction or utopia?' *Landscape and Urban Planning*, vol. 75, nos 3–4, pp. 187–197.

Araoz, G. (2011) Email correspondence from the President of ICOMOS informing the National Committees of ICOMOS of his observations from the World Heritage Committee meeting, 6 July 2011.

ARCCH, Authority for Research and Conservation of Cultural Heritage (2013) *A Management Plan for the Rock-Hewn Churches of Lalibela World Heritage Site Ethiopia*, Addis Ababa: ARCCH.

Ashworth, G.J. and van der Aa, B.J.M. (2006) 'Strategy and policy for the World Heritage Convention: goals, practices and future solutions', in A. Leask and A. Fyall (eds) *Managing World Heritage Sites*, Oxford: Butterworth-Heinemann.

Askew, M. (2010) 'The magic list of global status: UNESCO, World Heritage and the agendas of states', in S. Labadi and C. Long (eds) *Heritage and Globalization*, Abingdon: Routledge.

Assefa-Wondimu, G. (2007) 'Managing Tourism at the World Heritage Site of Lalibela, Ethiopia', MSc thesis, World Heritage Management Programme, University College Dublin, Dublin.

Atlantic Charter (1941) 'Declaration of Principles Issues by the President of the United States and the Prime Minister of the United Kingdom', North Atlantic Treaty Organization, www.nato.int/cps/en/natolive/official_texts_16912.htm, accessed 3 November 2013.

Australia ICOMOS (1999) *Charter for the Conservation of Places of Cultural Significance, (Burra Charter),* Burwood, VIC: Australia ICOMOS.

Australia ICOMOS (2013a) *Practice Note: Understanding and Assessing Cultural Significance,* Burwood, VIC: Australia ICOMOS Inc.

Australia ICOMOS (2013b) *The Burra Charter: The Australia ICOMOS Charter for Places of Cultural Significance,* Burwood, VIC: Australia ICOMOS Inc.

AWHF, African World Heritage Fund (2016) 'African World Heritage Fund', www.awhf.net, accessed 10 December 2016.

Ayad, C. (1999) 'Petra's new invaders', *UNESCO The Courier,* July/August, pp. 40–42.

Badman, T. (2012) 'Over and out from an eternal optimist', Blog: the inside track on global conservation, https://portals.iucn.org/blog/2012/07/06/over-and-out-from-an-eternal-optimist/, accessed 16 January 2014.

Badman, T. and Bomhard, B., (2008) *World Heritage and Protected Areas,* Gland, Switzerland: IUCN.

Ban, K. (2013) *Mainstreaming of the Three Dimensions of Sustainable Development throughout the United Nations System,* Report of the Secretary-General, UN General Assembly, A/68/79–E/2013/69, New York: UN.

Banderin, F. and van Oers, R. (2012) *The Historic Urban Landscape: Managing Heritage in an Urban Century,* Chichester: Wiley-Blackwell.

Bangkok Post (2011) 'Govt reverses WHC pull out', www.bangkokpost.com/news/local/261235/govt-reverses-whc-pull-out, accessed 11 March 2014.

Barbato, G. and Turner, M. (2015) *Report of the Joint World Heritage Centre/ICOMOS Mission,* Paris: UNESCO.

Barry, G. (2014) 'Terrestrial ecosystem loss and biosphere collapse', *Management of Environmental Quality,* vol. 25, no. 5, pp. 542–563.

Bartolomé, J. and Vega, I. (2002) *Mining in Doñana: Learned Lessons,* Madrid: WWF Spain.

Batisse, M. and Bolla, G. (2005) *The Invention of World Heritage,* History Papers 2, Paris: Association of Former UNESCO Staff Members, AFUS.

BBC (2015) 'Looted Iraqi museum in Baghdad reopens 12 years on', BBC News www.bbc.com/news/world-middle-east-31672857 accessed 20 June 2016.

Berg, L. (1978) 'The salvage of the Abu Simbel temple', *Monumentum,* vol. 17, pp. 25–56.

Bertzky, B., Shi, Y., Hughes, A., Engels, B., Ali, M.K. and Badman, T. (2013) *Terrestrial Biodiversity and the World Heritage List: Identifying Broad Gaps and Potential Candidate Sites for Inclusion in the Natural World Heritage Network,* Gland, Switzerland: IUCN and Cambridge: UNEP-WCMC.

Bevir, M. (2013) *Governance: A Very Short Introduction,* Oxford: Oxford University Press.

Billgren, C. and Holmén, H. (2008) 'Approaching reality: comparing stakeholder analysis and cultural theory in the context of natural resource management', *Land Use Policy,* vol. 24, no. 4, pp. 550–562.

Bird, E.A.R. (1987) 'The social construction of nature: theoretical approaches to the history of environmental problems', *Environmental Review*, vol. 11, no. 4, pp. 255–264.

Blaenavon World Heritage Site Partnership (2011) *Blaenavon Industrial Landscape World Heritage Site Management Plan 2011–2016*, Torfaen: Torfaen County Borough Council.

Bokova, I. (2013) 'Introduction by the Director-General', in *C/5 Resolutions 2014–2017 Volume 1*, Document 37, Paris: UNESCO.

Borgwardt, E. (2006) 'When you state a moral principle, you are stuck with it; The 1941 Atlantic Charter as a human rights instrument', *Virginia Journal of International Law*, vol. 46, no. 1, pp. 501–562.

Borrini-Feyerabend, G., Johnston, J. and Pansky, D. (2006) 'Governance of protected areas', in M. Lockwood, G.L. Worboys and A. Kothari (eds), *Managing Protected Areas: A Global Guide*, London: Earthscan.

Borrini-Feyerabend, G., Farvar, M.T., Nguinguiri, J.C. and Ndangang, V.A. (2007) *Co-management of Natural Resources: Organizing, Negotiating and Learning-by-Doing*, 2nd Edition, GTZ and IUCN, Heidelberg: Kasparek Verlag.

Bott, A.L., Grabowski, S. and Wearing, S. (2011) 'Stakeholder collaboration in a prospective World Heritage area: the case of Kokoda and the Owen Stanley Ranges', *Cosmopolitan Civil Societies Journal*, vol. 3, no. 2, pp. 35–54.

Bouchenaki, M. (2003) 'The interdependency of the tangible and intangible cultural heritage', ICOMOS 14th General Assembly and Scientific Symposium, www.icomos.org/victoriafalls2003/papers/2%20-%20Allocution%20Bouchenaki.pdf, accessed 3 March 2013.

Bowcott, O. (2016) 'ICC's first cultural destruction trial to open in The Hague', *The Guardian*, 28 February 2016.

Bowden, D. (1995) 'Angkor: planning for sustainable tourism', *Expedition*, vol. 37, no. 3, pp. 31–42.

Brashares, J.S., Arcese, P., Sam, M.K., Coppolillo, P.B., Sinclair, A.R. and Balmford, A. (2004) 'Bushmeat hunting, wildlife declines, and fish supply in West Africa', *Science*, vol. 306, no. 5699, pp. 1180–1183.

Breeze, D.J. and Jilek, S. (2008) *Frontiers of the Roman Empire: The European Dimension of a World Heritage Site*, Edinburgh: Historic Scotland.

Briggs, J. (2005) 'The use of indigenous knowledge in development: problems and challenges', *Progress in Development Studies*, vol. 5, no. 2, pp. 99–114.

Brundtland, G.H., Ehrlich, P., Goldemberg, J., Hansen, J., Lovins, A., Likens, G., Lovelock, J., Manabe, S., May, B., Mooney, H., Robert, K., Salim, E., Sato, G., Solomon, S., Stern, N., Swaminathan, M.S. and Watson, B. (2012) *Environment and Development Challenges: The Imperative to Act*, Blue Planet Synthesis paper for UNEP, London: UNEP.

Bullock, J.M., Aronson, J., Newton, A.C., Pywell, R.F. and Rey-Benayas, J.M. (2011) 'Restoration of ecosystem services and biodiversity: conflicts and opportunities', *Trends in Ecology & Evolution*, vol. 26, no. 10, pp. 541–549.

Cameron, C. and Rössler, M. (2013) *Many Voices, One Vision: The Early Years of the World Heritage Convention*, Farnham: Ashgate.

Campbell, P.B. (2013) 'The illicit antiquities trade as a transnational criminal network: characterizing and anticipating trafficking of cultural heritage', *International Journal of Cultural Property*, vol. 20, pp.113–153.

Campese, J., Sunderland, T., Greiber, T. and Oviedo, G. (eds) (2009) *Rights-Based Approaches: Exploring Issues and Opportunities for Conservation*, Bogor, Indonesia: CIFOR and IUCN.

Carrington, D. (2013) 'Stop ivory poaching or face sanctions, nations warned at CITES', *The Guardian*, Wednesday 6 March 2013.

CBD Secretariat (2004a) *Addis Ababa Principles and Guidelines for the Sustainable Use of Biodiversity*, Montreal: Secretariat of the Convention on Biological Diversity.

CBD Secretariat (2004b) *The Ecosystem Approach: CBD Guidelines*, Montreal: Secretariat of the Convention on Biological Diversity.

CBD Secretariat (2009) 'What are invasive alien species?' www.cbd.int/idb/2009/ about/what/, accessed 4 August 2015.

CBD Secretariat (2010) *Global Biodiversity Outlook 3*, Montreal: Secretariat of the Convention on Biological Diversity.

CBD Secretariat (2011) *Strategic Plan for Biodiversity 2011–2020 and the Aichi Targets: Living in Harmony with Nature*, Montreal: Secretariat of the Convention on Biological Diversity.

Ceballos, G., Ehrlich, P.R., Barnosky, A.D., Garcia, A., Pringle, R.M. and Palmer, T.M. (2015) 'Accelerated modern human-induced species losses: entering the sixth mass extinction', *Science Advances*, vol. 1, no. 5, e1400253.

CEPF, Critical Ecosystem Partnership Fund (2013) 'Mediterranean Basin', www.cepf.net/resources/hotspots/Europe-and-Central-Asia/Pages/Mediterranean-Basin.aspx, accessed 13 July 2016.

Chirikure, S., Manyanga, M., Webber, N. and Pwiti, G. (2010) 'Unfulfilled promises? Heritage management and community participation at some of Africa's cultural heritage sites', *International Journal of Heritage Studies*, vol. 16, no. 1–2, pp. 30–44.

Chung, S.J. (2005) 'East Asian values in historic conservation', *Journal of Architectural Conservation*, vol. 11, no. 1, pp. 55–70.

CHwB, Cultural Heritage without Borders (2016) 'History', http://chwb.org/who-we-are/history/, accessed 26 December 2016.

Clavero, M. and García-Berthou, E. (2005) 'Invasive species are a leading cause of animal extinctions', *Trends in Ecology and Evolution*, vol. 20, no. 3, p. 110.

Cleere, H. (1989) *Archaeological Heritage Management in the Modern World*, London: Unwin Hyman.

Clottes, J. (2011) *Rock Art in Central Asia: A Thematic Study*, Paris: ICOMOS.

Colette, A. (2007) *Case Studies on Climate Change and World Heritage*, Paris: UNESCO World Heritage Centre.

Commission on Global Governance (1995) *Our Global Neighbourhood: The Report of the Commission on Global Governance*, Oxford: Oxford University Press.

COST (2011) Cost (European Cooperation in the field of scientific and technical research) 'Action IS1007 – Investigating cultural sustainability', www.culturalsustainability.eu/ accessed January 2013.

Cotula, L., Vermeulen, S., Leonard, R. and Keeley, J. (2009) *Land Grab or Development Opportunity? Agricultural Investment and International Land Deals in Africa*, London and Rome: IIED/FAO/IFAD.

Crutzen, P.J. (2002) 'Geology of mankind', *Nature*, vol. 415, p. 23.

Crutzen, P.J. and Stoermer, E.F. (2000) 'The Anthropocene', *Global Change Newsletter*, no. 41, pp. 17–18.

Cullen, C. (2012) 'Presentation' in J. Pascual (ed) *Rio+20 and Culture: Advocating for Culture as a Pillar of Sustainability*, Barcelona: UCLG.

Cunliffe, E. (2014) 'The impact of the civil war on the cultural heritage', in C. Machat, M. Petzet and J. Ziesemer (eds) *Heritage at Risk: World Report 2011–2013 on Monuments and Sites in Danger*, Berlin: Hendrik Bäßler Verlag.

Dallen, T. (1999) 'Cross-border partnership in tourism resource management: international parks along the US-Canada border', *Journal of Sustainable Tourism*, vol. 7, no. 3–4, pp. 182–205.

Daly, H.E. and Farley, J. (2011) *Ecological Economics: Principles and Applications*, Washington, DC: Island Press.

Day, J. (2008) 'The need and practice of monitoring, evaluating and adapting marine planning and management: lessons from the Great Barrier Reef', *Marine Policy*, vol. 32, no. 5, pp. 823–831.

Delmonaco, G., Margottini, C. and Spizzichino, D. (2010) 'Weathering processes, structural degradation and slope-structure stability of rock-hewn churches of Lalibela, Ethiopia', *Engineering Geology Special Publications*, vol. 23, pp. 131–147.

Demeritt, D. (2002) 'What is the "social construction of nature"? A typology and sympathetic critique', *Progress in Human Geography*, vol. 26, no. 6, pp. 767–790.

Demetriou, D. (2012) 'Japan suffers biggest decline in tourism since 1950', *The Telegraph*, 19 January, http://www.telegraph.co.uk/news/worldnews/asia/japan/9024997/Japan-suffers-biggest-decline-in-tourism-since-1950.html, accessed 21 April 2014.

Dessein, J., Soini, K., Fairclough, G. and Horlings, L. (2015) *Culture In, For and As Sustainable Development: Conclusions from the COST Action IS1007 Investigating Cultural Sustainability*, Jyväskylä, Finland: University of Jyväskylä.

Di Giovine, M.A. (2008) *The Heritage-scape: UNESCO, World Heritage and Tourism*, Plymouth: Lexington Books.

Dilley, M., Chen, R.S., Deichmann, U., Lerner-Lam, A.L., Arnold, M., Agwe, J., Buys, P., Kjekstad, O., Lyon, B. and Yetman, G. (2005) *Natural Disaster Hotspots: A Global Risk Analysis*, Washington, DC: The World Bank Hazard Management Unit.

Dixit, A.M., Yatabe, R., Dahal, R.K. and Bhandary, N.P. (2013) 'Initiatives for earthquake disaster management in the Kathmandu valley', *Natural Hazards*, vol. 69, pp. 631–654.

Djoghlaf, A. and Dodds, F. (2011) *Biodiversity and Ecosystem Insecurity: A Planet in Peril*, London: Earthscan.

Douvere, F. (2015) *World Heritage Marine Sites: Managing Effectively the World's Most Iconic Marine Protected Areas*, Paris: UNESCO.

Douvere, F. and Badman, T. (2012) *Reactive Monitoring Mission to Great Barrier Reef, Australia: 6th–14th March 2012*, Paris: UNESCO World Heritage Centre.

Dudley, N. (2011) *Authenticity in Nature: Making Choices About the Naturalness of Ecosystems*, London: Earthscan.

Dunne, B. (2012) 'St. Katherine's World Heritage Site, South Sinai: the conservation of the Bedouin high mountain orchard gardens and the roles of tourism and tradition', unpublished MSc, University College Dublin, Dublin.

Durán, A.P., Rauch, J. and Gaston, K.J, (2013) 'Global spatial coincidence between protected areas and metal mining activities', *Biological Conservation*, vol. 160, pp. 272–278.

Dyczek, P., Jilek, S. and Lemke, M. (2011) *In the Footsteps of the Romans: Guidelines to Nominate New Danube Limes Sections in other Danube Countries*, Warsaw: Centre for Research on the Antiquity of South-eastern Europe, University of Warsaw.

Edinburgh World Heritage, Historic Scotland and City of Edinburgh Council (2011) *The Old and New Towns of Edinburgh World Heritage Site Management Plan 2011–2016*, Edinburgh: Edinburgh World Heritage.

Egyptian Supreme Council of Antiquities (2000) *Periodic Report on the Nubian Monuments from Abu-Simbel to Philae World Heritage Property*, Paris: UNESCO World Heritage Centre.

Elliott, J.A. (2013) *An Introduction to Sustainable Development*, London: Routledge.

Eloundou, L. and Avango, D. (2012) *Reactive Monitoring Mission to Mapungubwe Cultural Landscape World Heritage Property, South Africa, 15–20 January 2012*, Paris: UNESCO World Heritage Centre.

Engels, B., Ohnesorge, B. and Burmester, A. (2009) *Nominations and Management of Serial Natural World Heritage Properties: Present Situation, Challenges and Opportunities*, Proceedings of a workshop organized by the German Federal Agency for Nature Conservation (BfN) in cooperation with the UNESCO World Heritage Centre and IUCN November 26th–30th, 2008, Bonn: Bundesamt für Naturschutz (BfN).

English Heritage (2005) *Traditional Buildings Craft Skills*, Swindon: National Heritage Training Group, English Heritage.

Ens, E.J., Pert, P., Clarke, P.A., Budden, M., Clubb, L., Doran, B., Douras, C., Gaikwad, J., Gott, B., Leonard, S., Locke, J., Packer, J., Turpin, G. and Wason, S. (2015) 'Indigenous biocultural knowledge in ecosystem science and management: review and insight from Australia', *Biological Conservation*, vol. 181, pp. 133–149.

Epler, B. (2007) *Tourism, the Economy, Population Growth and Conservation in Galápagos*, Puerto Ayora, Ecuador: Charles Darwin Foundation.

Epler-Wood, M. (2002) *Ecotourism: Principles, Practices and Policies for Sustainability*, Paris: United Nations Environment Programme/Division of Technology, Industry and Economics.

Europa Nostra (2016) 'Venice Lagoon: the most endangered site in Europe', press release, 16 March.

EX.PO AUS (2015) *Assessing and Monitoring the Management Effectiveness of the UNESCO World Heritage Sites on the Adriatic, Extension of Potentiality of Adriatic UNESCO Sites Project*, Kotor, Montenegro: Center for Conservation and Archaeology of Montenegro.

Feilden, B.M. and Jokilehto, J. (1998) *Management Guidelines for World Cultural Heritage Sites*, Rome: ICCROM.

Finke, G. (2013) 'Cultural landscapes and protected areas: unfolding the linkages and synergies', *World Heritage*, no. 70, pp. 16–25.

Folke, C., Carpenter, S., Elmqvist, T., Gunderson, L., Holling, C.S. and Walker, B. (2002) 'Resilience and sustainable development: building adaptive capacity in a world of transformations', *Ambio*, vol. 31, no. 5, pp. 437–440.

Francioni, F. and Lenzerini, F. (2003) 'The destruction of the Buddhas of Bamiyan and international law', *European Journal of International Law*, vol. 14, no. 4, pp. 619–651.

Francioni, F. and Lenzerini, F. (2008) *The 1972 World Heritage Convention: A Commentary*, Oxford: Oxford University Press.

Fukuyama, F. (2013) 'What is governance?', *Governance: An International Journal of Policy, Administration, and Institutions*, vol. 26, no. 3, pp. 347–368.

FZS, Frankfurt Zoological Society (2016) 'History of FZS', https://fzs.org/en/about-us/history/, accessed 11 December 2016.

Galápagos Conservancy (2015) 'Endangered species', www.galapagos.org/conservation/conservation/conservationchallenges/endemic-species/, accessed 14 October 2015.

Galla, A. (2012) *World Heritage: Benefits Beyond Borders*, Cambridge: Cambridge University Press/UNESCO.

Gamboni, D. (2001) 'World Heritage: shield or target?' *The Getty Conservation Institute Newsletter*, vol. 16, no. 2, pp. 5–11.

Garstecki, T. and Amr, Z. (2011) *Biodiversity and Ecosystem Management in the Iraqi Marshlands: Screening Study on Potential World Heritage Nomination*, Amman, Jordan: IUCN,.

Gaston, K.J. and Spicer, J.I. (2004) *Biodiversity: An Introduction*, 2nd edition, Oxford: Blackwell Publishing.

GBRMPA, Great Barrier Reef Marine Park Authority (2014) *Great Barrier Reef Outlook Report 2014*, Townsville, Australia: GBRMPA.

GBRMPA, Great Barrier Reef Marine Park Authority (2015) 'Traditional use of Marine Resources Agreements', available at GBRMPA website: www.gbrmpa.gov.au/

our-partners/traditional-owners/traditional-use-of-marine-resources-agreements, accessed 1 June 2015.

Geo-Naturpark (2015) 'Geo-Naturpark Bergstrasse-Odenwald', www.geo-naturpark. net/en/wir-ueber-uns.php, accessed 15 November 2015.

Gerber, J. (1997) 'Beyond dualism – the social construction of nature and the natural *and* social construction of human beings', *Progress in Human Geography*, vol. 21, no. 1, pp. 1–17.

GFDRR (2014) 'Global Facility for Disaster Reduction and Recovery: what we do', www.gfdrr.org/pillar-1-risk-identification, accessed 24 March 2014.

GHF (2010) *Saving Our Vanishing Heritage: Safeguarding Endangered Cultural Heritage Sites in the Developing World*, San Franciso, CA: Global Heritage Fund.

GHF (2012) 'Global Heritage Fund', www.globalheritagefund.org, accessed 19 August 2012.

GHF (2015) 'Global Heritage Fund Bi-Annual Report 2014–2015', http:// globalheritagefund.org/index.php/news-resources/library/annual-reports/bi-annual-report-2014-2015/, accessed 4 December 2016.

Gillespie, J. (2013) 'World Heritage management: boundary-making at Angkor Archaeological Park, Cambodia', *Journal of Environmental Planning and Management*, vol. 56, no. 2, pp. 286–304.

Girard, L.F. (2012) 'Creativity and the human sustainable city: principles and approaches for nurturing city resilience', in L.F. Girard, T. Baycan and P. Nijkamp (eds) *Sustainable City and Creativity: Promoting Creative Urban Initiatives*, Farnham: Ashgate.

Gori, M. (2013) 'The stones of contention: the role of archaeological heritage in Israeli-Palestinian conflict', in *Journal of the World Archaeological Congress*, vol. 9, no. 1, pp. 213–229.

Goudie, A. and Seely, M. (2011) *World Heritage Desert Landscapes: Potential Priorities for the Recognition of Desert Landscapes and Geomorphological Sites on the World Heritage List*, Gland, Switzerland: IUCN.

Government of Ireland (2012) 'Our Sustainable Future – A Framework for Sustainable Development in Ireland', Department of the Environment, Community and Local Government, http://developmenteducation.ie/resource/our-sustainable-future-a-frame work-for-sustainable-development-in-ireland, accessed 4 January 2014.

Government of Italy (2008) 'Nomination of the Dolomites for inscription on the World Natural Heritage List UNESCO', http://whc.unesco.org/en/list/1237/documents/ accessed October 2014.

Graham, B., Ashworth, G.J. and Tunbridge, J.E. (2000) *A Geography of Heritage: Power, Culture and Economy*, London: Arnold.

Green, C. (2010) 'Traditional knowledge and the Sami struggle in Sweden', in B. Frostell (ed) *Science for Sustainable Development: The Social Challenge with Emphasis on the Conditions for Change*, Proceedings of the 2nd VHU Conference on Science for Sustainable Development, Linköping, Sweden, 6–7 September 2007.

Greider, T. and Garkovich, L. (1994) 'Landscapes: the social construction of nature and the environment', *Rural Sociology*, vol. 59, no. 1, pp. 1–24.

Griggs, D., Stafford-Smith, M., Gaffney, O., Rockström, J., Öhman, M.C., Shyamsundar, P., Steffan, W., Glaser, G., Kanie, N. and Noble, I. (2013) 'Sustainable development goals for people and planet', *Nature*, vol. 495, pp. 305–307.

Gustafsson, C. (2009) 'The Halland Model: a trading zone for building conservation in concert with labour market policy and the construction industry, aiming at regional sustainable development', PhD dissertation, Chalmers University of Technology, Gothenburg, Sweden.

Hale, T., Held, D. and Young, K. (2013) *Gridlock: Why Global Cooperation Is Failing When We Need It Most*, Cambridge: Polity Press, Cambridge.

Hall, M. (2011) *Towards World Heritage: International Origins of the Preservation Movement 1870–1930*, Farnham: Ashgate.

Han, J. (2008) 'Impact of the climate change on the frozen tombs in the Altai Mountains', in M. Petzet and J. Ziesemer (eds) *Heritage at Risk: ICOMOS World Report 2006/2007 on Monuments and Sites in Danger*, Altenburg, Germany: E. Reinhold-Verlag.

Harmon, D. (2007) 'A bridge over the chasm: finding ways to achieve integrated natural and cultural heritage conservation', *International Journal of Heritage Studies*, vol. 13, no. 4–5, pp. 380–392.

Harrison, D. and Hitchcock, M. (2005) *The Politics of World Heritage: Negotiating Tourism and Conservation*, Clevedon: Channel View Publications.

Harrison, R. (2010) 'The politics of heritage', in R. Harrison (ed) *Understanding the Politics of Heritage*, Manchester: Manchester University Press.

Harvey, D. (2001) 'Heritage pasts and heritage presents: temporality, meaning and the scope of heritage studies', *International Journal of Heritage Studies*, vol, 7, no. 4, pp. 319–338.

Hassan, F.A. (2007) 'The Aswan High Dam and the International Rescue Nubia Campaign', *African Archaeological Review*, vol. 24, no. 3–4, pp. 73–94.

Hauser-Schäublin, B. (2011) 'Preah Vihear: from object of colonial desire to a contested World Heritage Site', in B. Hauser-Schäublin (ed) *World Heritage Angkor and Beyond: Circumstances and Implications of UNESCO Listings in Cambodia*, Göttingen: Göttingen University Press.

Hawkes, J. (2001) *The Fourth Pillar of Sustainability: Culture's Essential Role in Public Planning*, Melbourne: Cultural Development Network and Common Ground Publishing.

Hernández, E., Carmona, J. and Schmidt, G. (2004) *Report on the Situation of the Aznalcóllar Mine and the Guadiamar Green Corridor*, Madrid: WWF Spain.

Hill, M., Briggs, J., Minto, P., Bagnall, D., Foley, K. and Williams, A. (2001) *Guide to Best Practices in Seascape Assessment, Maritime (Ireland/Wales) INTERREG Programme (1994–1999)*, Dublin: The Marine Institute.

HMFSC, Heritage Management Framework Steering Committee (2013) *Angkor: Heritage Management Framework*, Paris: UNESCO.

Hockings, M. and Philips, A. (1999) 'How well are we doing? Some thoughts on the effectiveness of protected areas', *Parks*, vol. 9, no. 2, pp. 5–14.

Hockings, M., Leverington, F. and James, R. (2006a) 'Evaluating management effectiveness', in M. Lockwood, G.L. Worboys and A. Kothari (eds) *Managing Protected Areas: A Global Guide*, London: Earthscan.

Hockings, M., Stolton, S., Leverington, F., Dudley, N. and Courrau, J. (2006b) *Evaluating Effectiveness: A Framework for Assessing Management Effectiveness of Protected Areas*. 2nd edition. Gland, Switzerland: IUCN.

Hockings, M, James, R., Stolton, S., Dudley, N., Mathur, V., Makombo, J., Courrau, J. and Parish, J. (2008) *Enhancing our Heritage Toolkit: Assessing Management Effectiveness of Natural World Heritage Sites*, World Heritage Papers 23, Paris: UNESCO, World Heritage Centre.

Holling, C.S. (1978) *Adaptive Environmental Assessment and Management*, Chichester: John Wiley and Sons.

Hopwood, B., Mellor, M. and O'Brien, G. (2005) 'Sustainable development: mapping different approaches', *Sustainable Development*, vol. 13, pp. 38–52.

Howard, A.J. (2013) 'Managing global heritage in the face of future climate change: the importance of understanding geological and geomorphological processes and hazards', *International Journal of Heritage Studies*, vol. 19, no. 7, pp. 632–658.

Howard, P. (2003) *Heritage: Management, Interpretation, Identity*, London: Continuum.

Hughes, J.D. (2016) *What is Environmental History?* Cambridge: Polity, UK.

Hughes, T.P., Gunderson, L.H., Floke, C., Baird, A.H., Bellwood, D., Berkes, F., Crona, B., Helfgott, A., Leslie, H., Norberg, J., Nyström, M., Olsson, P., Österblom, H., Scheffer, M., Schuttenberg, H., Steneck, R.S., Tengö, M., Troell, M., Walker, B., Wilson, J. and Worm, B. (2007) 'Adaptive management of the Great Barrier Reef and the Grand Canyon World Heritage Areas', *Ambio*, vol. 36, no. 7, pp. 586–592.

ICCROM (2013) ICCROM Statutes, as revised and approved by the 28th Session of the General Assembly on 29 November 2013.

ICOMOS (1964) *International Charter for the Conservation and Restoration of Monuments and Sites (Venice Charter)*, Paris: ICOMOS.

ICOMOS (1983) 'Advisory Body Evaluation: Sao Miguel das Missoes', http://whc. unesco.org/en/documents/153092, accessed 13 July 2016.

ICOMOS (1984) 'Advisory Body Evaluation: the Statue of Liberty', http://whc.unesco. org/archive/advisory_body_evaluation/307.pdf, accessed 13 July 2016.

ICOMOS (1987a) 'Advisory Body Evaluation: insular Venice and its Lagoon', http://whc. unesco.org/archive/advisory_body_evaluation/394.pdf, accessed 13 July 2016.

ICOMOS (1987b) *Charter for the Conservation of Historic Towns and Urban Areas (Washington Charter)*, Paris: ICOMOS.

ICOMOS (1993) *Tourism and World Heritage Cultural Sites: The Site Manager's Handbook*, Madrid: World Tourism Organization.

ICOMOS (1994) 'The Nara Document on Authenticity', www.icomos.org/charters/ nara-e.pdf, accessed 13 July 2016.

ICOMOS (1995) 'Advisory Body Evaluation: Sintra', http://whc. unesco.org/archive/ advisory_body_evaluation/723.pdf, accessed 13 July 2016.

ICOMOS (1998) 'Declaration of ICOMOS marking the 50th anniversary of the Universal Declaration of Human Rights', www.icomos.org/charters/Stockholm-e. pdf, accessed 13 July 2016.

ICOMOS (1999a) *International Cultural Tourism Charter: Managing Tourism at Places of Heritage Significance*, Paris: ICOMOS.

ICOMOS (1999b) *The Charter on the Built Vernacular Heritage*, Paris: ICOMOS.

ICOMOS (2000a) 'Advisory Body Evaluation: coffee plantations (Cuba)', http:// whc.unesco.org/archive/advisory_body_evaluation/1008.pdf, accessed 13 July 2016.

ICOMOS (2000b) 'Advisory Body Evaluation: Southern Öland', http://whc.unesco.org/ archive/advisory_body_evaluation/968.pdf, accessed 13 July 2016.

ICOMOS (2004a) 'Evaluation Dresden Elbe Valley (Germany) no. 1156', whc.unesco. org/en/list/1156/documents/, accessed 13 September 2014.

ICOMOS (2004b) *The World Heritage List: Filling the Gaps: An Action Plan for the Future*, Paris: ICOMOS.

ICOMOS (2005) 'Advisory Body Evaluation: Struve Geodetic Arc no. 1187', http://whc. unesco.org/archive/advisory_body_evaluation/1187.pdf, accessed 13 July 2016.

ICOMOS (2006) *The World Heritage List: Filling the Gaps: An Action Plan for the Future*, Paris: ICOMOS.

ICOMOS (2007) 'ICOMOS Evaluation: Iwami Ginza Silver Mine (Japan) no. 1246', whc.unesco.org/en/list/1246/documents/, accessed March 2016.

ICOMOS (2008a) *Québec Declaration on the Preservation of the Spirit of Place*, Québec: ICOMOS General Assembly.

ICOMOS (2008b) 'Advisory Body Evaluation: the Mijikenda Kaya Forests (Kenya), no. 1231 rev'., http://whc.unesco.org/en/list/1231/documents/, accessed September 2012.

ICOMOS (2010a) 'Advisory Body Evaluation: Camino Real de Tierra Adentro (Mexico), no. 1351', http://whc.unesco.org/archive/advisory_body_evaluation /1351. pdf, accessed 13 July 2016.

ICOMOS (2010b) 'International Secretariat e-news, no. 58', 26 August, www.icomos. org/publications/e-news/2010/E-news_58_20100826.pdf, accessed 14 March 2014.

ICOMOS (2011a) *Evaluations of Nominations of Cultural and Mixed Properties to the World Heritage List*, WHC-11/35.COM/INF.8B1, Paris: ICOMOS.

ICOMOS (2011b) 'The Valletta principles for the safeguarding and management of historic cities, towns and urban areas', 17th ICOMOS General Assembly, Paris.

ICOMOS (2011c) *Guidance on Heritage Impact Assessments for Cultural World Heritage Properties*, Paris: ICOMOS.

ICOMOS (2012) 'From the emergence of the concept of World Heritage to the creation of ICOMOS', www.icomos.org/en/about-icomos/mission-and-vision/history, accessed 30 September 2012.

ICOMOS Norway (2008) 'Climate change and the effect on Norwegian World Heritage sites', in M. Petzet and J. Ziesemer (eds) *Heritage at Risk: ICOMOS World Report 2006/2007 on Monuments and Sites in Danger*, Altenburg, Germany: E. Reinhold-Verlag.

ICOMOS and TICCIH (2011) *Dublin Principles: Joint ICOMOS-TICCIH Principles for the Conservation of Industrial Heritage Sites, Structures, Areas and Landscapes*, Paris: ICOMOS.

IFM, International Fund for Monuments (1967) *Lalibela-Phase I: Adventure in Restoration*, New York: International Fund for Monuments.

Ilukol, J. and Cave, C. (2012) 'Protected areas and rural livelihoods: the case of a World Heritage site in Western Uganda', in M.-T. Albert, M. Richon, M.J. Viñals and A. Witcomb (eds) *Community Development through World Heritage*, World Heritage Papers 31, Paris: UNESCO.

International Rhino Foundation (2013) 'Indian rhino vision 2020', www.rhinos.org/ indian-rhino-vision-2020, accessed August 2013.

INTERPOL (2016) *Protecting Cultural Heritage: An Imperative for Humanity*, New York: UN.

IPCC (2001) *Climate Change 2001: The Scientific Basis. Contribution of Working Group I to the Third Assessment Report of the Intergovernmental Panel on Climate Change*, Cambridge: Cambridge University Press.

IUCN (1980) *World Conservation Strategy: Living Resource Conservation for Sustainable Development*, Gland, Switzerland: IUCN-UNEP-WWF.

IUCN (1982) *The World's Greatest Natural Areas; An Indicative Inventory of Natural Sites of World Heritage Quality*, Gland, Switzerland: IUCN.

IUCN (1989) 'Advisory Body Evaluation: Victoria Falls/Mosi-Oa-Tunya', http://whc. unesco.org/archive/advisory_body_evaluation/509.pdf, accessed 13 July 2016.

IUCN (1994) 'World Heritage nomination: IUCN summary 654: Jiddat Al Harasis and adjoining areas (Sultanate of Oman)', whc.unesco.org/en/list/654/documents/, accessed 13 September 2014.

IUCN (1997) *Resolutions and Recommendations, World Conservation Congress, Montreal, Canada, 11–23 October 1996*, Gland, Switzerland: IUCN.

IUCN (2000) IUCN 'Policy statement on sustainable use of wild living resources' (Resolution 2.29), adopted at the IUCN World Conservation Congress, October 2000, Amman, Jordan.

IUCN (2003a) *Recommendations: Vth IUCN World Parks Congress*, Gland, Switzerland: IUCN.

IUCN (2003b) *The Durban Accord: Vth IUCN World Parks Congress, Durban, South Africa*, Gland, Switzerland: IUCN .

IUCN (2004) 'The World Heritage list: future priorities for a credible and complete list of natural and mixed sites', A strategy paper prepared by IUCN, Gland, Switzerland: IUCN.

IUCN (2005a) *Benefits Beyond Boundaries: Proceedings of the Vth IUCN World Parks Congress*, Gland, Switzerland: IUCN.

IUCN (2005b) *IUCN Evaluation of Nominations of Natural and Mixed Properties to the World Heritage List,* WHC-05/29.COM/INF.8B.2, Report to the World Heritage Committee Twenty-ninth session 10–16 July 2005, Durban, South Africa.

IUCN (2006) 'Indicators of sustainable use and biological diversity (Agenda item 23)', position paper, Eighth meeting of the Conference of the Parties to the Convention on Biological Diversity (COP8), Curitiba, Brazil, 20–31 March 2006.

IUCN (2007) 'Ecosystem and relic cultural landscape of Lopé-Okanda (Gabon) – ID No. 1147', Rev, Word Heritage nomination, IUCN technical evaluation, Gland, Switzerland: IUCN.

IUCN (2008) 'About invasive species; what are they?' Invasive Species Specialist Group, www.issg.org/is_what_are_they.htm, accessed 4 August 2015.

IUCN (2010) *50 Years of Working for Protected Areas: A Brief History of IUCN World Commission on Protected Areas*, Gland, Switzerland: IUCN.

IUCN (2012) *Statutes, Including Rules of Procedure of the World Conservation Congress, and Regulations*, Gland, Switzerland: IUCN.

IUCN (2013a) 'IUCN World Heritage advice note: mining and oil/gas projects', http://cmsdata.iucn.org/downloads/iucn_advice_note_on_mining_in_wh_sites_final_060512__2_.pdf, accessed October 2014.

IUCN (2013b) 'IUCN Evaluations of Nominations of Natural and Mixed Properties on the World Heritage List', WHC-13/37.COM/INF.8B2, 37th Session Phnom Penh, Cambodia, 16–27 June 2013.

IUCN (2013c) 'Ecosystem management', www.iucn.org/theme/ecosystem-management, accessed 5 August 2013.

IUCN (2016) 'Environmental governance', www.iucn.org/es/node/25470, accessed 14 December 2016.

IUCN and ICOMOS (2015) *Connecting Practice Project: Final Report*, http://cmsdata.iucn.org/downloads/connecting_practice_report_iucn_icomos_pdf, accessed 20 October 2015.

IUCN SUSG (Sustainable Use Specialist Group) Technical Advisory Committee of the IUCN Species Survival Commission (2001) *Analytic Framework for Assessing Factors that Influence Sustainability of Uses of Wild Living Natural Resource*, Gland, Switzerland: IUCN.

Jahn, T., Becker, E., Florian, K. and Schramm, E. (2011) 'Understanding social-ecological systems: frontier research for sustainable development. Implications for European research policy', www.researchgate.net/publication/237402615, accessed 20 October 2015.

Jeffries, M.J. (2006) *Biodiversity and Conservation*, 2nd edition, London: Routledge.

Jigyasu, R. (2014) 'Fostering resilience: towards reducing disaster risks to World Heritage', *World Heritage*, no. 74, pp. 4–15.

Jing, F. and Nanda, R. (2011) *Report on the Joint World Heritage Centre/ICOMOS Reactive Monitoring Mission to Kathmandu Vally, Nepal*, C 1121bis, Paris: UNESCO.

Johnston, C. (1992) *What is Social Value? A Discussion Paper*. Canberra: Australian Heritage Commission, Australian Government Publishing Service.

Jokilehto, J. (2006) 'Considerations on authenticity and integrity in World Heritage context', *City & Time*, vol. 2, no. 1, pp. 1–16.

Jones, B.T.B., Makonjio Okello, M. and Wishitemi, B.E.L. (2005b) 'Pastoralists, conservation and livelihoods in East and Southern Africa: reconciling continuity and change through the protected landscape approach', in J. Brown, N. Mitchell and M. Beresford (eds) *The Protected Landscape Approach: Linking Nature, Culture and Community*, Gland, Switzerland: IUCN.

Jones, B.T.B., Stolton, S. and Dudley, N. (2005a) 'Private protected areas in East and Southern Africa: contributing to biodiversity conservation and rural development', *Parks*, vol. 15, no. 2, pp. 67–77.

Jonsson, Å. (2013) 'Laponia World Heritage: a new management of protected areas where Sami traditional knowledge is of high significance', Presentation at World Indigenous Network Conference, 28 May 2013.

Kates, R.W., Parris, T.M. and Leiserowitz, A.A. (2005) 'What is sustainable development?', *Environment*, vol. 47, no. 3, pp. 8–21.

Kellert, S.R., Mehta, J.N., Ebbin, S.A. and Lichtenfeld, L.L. (2000) 'Community natural resource management: promise, rhetoric and reality', *Society and Natural Resources*, vol. 13, pp. 705–715.

Kelley, C.P., Mohtadi, S., Cane, M.A, Seager, R. and Kushnir, Y. (2015) 'Climate change in the Fertile Crescent and implications of the recent Syrian drought', *Proceedings of the National Academy of Sciences of the USA*, vol. 112, no. 11, pp. 3241–3246.

Keough, E.B. (2011) 'Heritage in peril: a critique of UNESCO's World Heritage Program', *Washington University Global Studies Law Review*, vol. 10, no. 3, pp. 593–615.

Kideghesho, J.R. (2016) 'The elephant poaching crisis in Tanzania: a need to reverse the trend and the way forward', *Tropical Conservation Science*, vol. 9, no. 1, pp. 369–388.

Koch, P. (2013) 'Overestimating the shift from government to governance: evidence from Swiss metropolitan areas', *Governance: An International Journal of Policy, Administration, and Institutions*, vol. 26, no. 3, pp. 397–423.

Labadi, S. (2007) *World Heritage Challenges for the Millennium*, Paris: UNESCO World Heritage Centre.

Lamb, D. and Gilmour, D. (2003) *Rehabilitation and Restoration of Degraded Forests*, Gland, Switzerland: IUCN.

Laponia (2013) 'Laponiaprocessen', www.laponia.nu/laponiatjuottjudus-2/laponiaprocessen/, accessed 25 October 2013.

Larsen, P.B. and Wijesuriya, G. (2015) 'Nature-culture interlinkages in World Heritage: bridging the gap', *World Heritage*, no. 75, pp. 4–15.

League of Nations (1919) The Covenant of the League of Nations.

Leask, A. and Fyall, A. (2006) *Managing World Heritage Sites*, London: Routledge.

Lennon, J. (2006) 'Cultural heritage management', in M. Lockwood, G.L. Worboys and A. Kothari (eds) *Managing Protected Areas: A Global Guide*, London: Earthscan.

Lisitzin, K. (2012) Workshop report for the World Heritage national focal points from Central, Eastern and South-Eastern Europe within the framework of the second cycle of the periodic reporting exercise on the implementation of the World Heritage Convention. Tbilisi, Georgia, 14–16 November 2012.

Lockwood, M. (2006) 'Management planning', in M. Lockwood, G. Worboys and A. Kothari (eds) *Managing Protected Areas: A Global Study*, London: Earthscan.

Logan, W. (2012) 'Cultural diversity, cultural heritage and human rights: towards heritage management as human rights-based cultural practice', *International Journal of Heritage Studies*, vol. 18, no. 3, pp. 231–244.

Lorenzi, S. and Borrini-Feyerabend, G. (2009) 'Community conserved areas: legal framework for the natural park of the Ampezzo Dolomites (Italy)', IUCN-Environmental Policy and Law Paper No. 81, Gland, Switzerland: IUCN.

LWC, Lewa Wildlife Conservancy (2011) 'Lewa standards', www.lewa.org /fileadmin/ user/pdf/THE_LEWA_STANDARD_Feb_2011.pdf, accessed August 2013.

Mackay, R. and Sullivan, S. (2008) 'Living with Heritage at Angkor', ICOMOS 16th General Assembly and International Scientific Symposium, Quebec, Canada. http:// openarchive.icomos.org/74/1/77-JUT6-142.pdf, accessed August 2014.

MacKenzie, D. (2013) 'Lasting costs of Syrian war', *New Scientist*, vol. 219, issue 2934, pp. 8–9.

Mackin, D. and Davidson, A. (2012) *Study of the Economic Value of Northern Ireland's Historic Environment – Technical Report* submitted to the Department of the Environment, London: EFTEC.

Maclaurin, J. and Sterelny, K. (2008) *What is Biodiversity?*, Chicago, IL: The University of Chicago Press.

Maffi, L. (2010) 'Biocultural diversity and the future of sustainability', in L. Maffi and E. Woodley (eds) *Biocultural Diversity Conservation: A Global Source Book*, London: Earthscan.

Magin, C. and Chape, S. (2004) *Review of the World Heritage Network: Biogeography, Habitats and Biodiversity*, Gland, Switzerland: UNEP-WCMC, IUCN.

Makino, M., Matsuda, H. and Sakurai, Y. (2009) 'Expanding fisheries co-management to ecosystem-based management: a case in the Shiretoko World Natural Heritage area, Japan', *Marine Policy*, vol. 33, no. 2, pp. 207–214.

Makuvaza, S. (2012) 'Who owns the special area at Victoria Falls World Heritage site? Political organizational and governmental interests', *The Historic Environment*, vol. 3, no. 1, pp. 42–63.

Manacorda, S. and Chappell, D. (2011) *Crime in the Art and Antiquities World; Illegal Trafficking in Cultural Property*, New York: Springer.

Margules, C.R. and Pressey, R.L. (2000) 'Systematic conservation planning', *Nature*, vol. 405, pp. 243–253.

Mason, R. (2002) 'Assessing values in conservation planning: methodological issues and choices', in M. de la Torre (ed) *Assessing the Values of Cultural Heritage*, Los Angeles, CA: The Getty Conservation Institute.

Mayer, W. (2014) 'Historic Cairo', in C. Machat, M. Petzet and J. Ziesemer (eds) *Heritage at Risk: World Report 2011–2013 on Monuments and Sites in Danger*, Berlin: Hendrik Bäßler Verlag.

McClanahan, T. (2004) 'The limits to Beyond Boundaries,' *Parks*, vol. 14, no. 2, pp. 30–33.

MEA, Millennium Ecosystem Assessment (2005) *Ecosystems and Human Well-being: Biodiversity Synthesis*, Washington, DC: World Resources Institute.

Meskell, L. (2014) 'State of conservation: protection, politics, and pacting within UNESCO's World Heritage Committee', *Anthropological Quarterly*, vol. 87, no. 1, pp. 217–243.

Meskell, L. (2015) 'Transacting UNESCO World Heritage gifts and exchanges on a global stage', *Social Anthropology*, vol. 23, no. 1, pp. 3–21.

Millar, S. (2006) 'Stakeholders and community participation', in A. Leask and A. Fyall (eds) *Managing World Heritage Sites*, Oxford: Butterworth-Heinemann.

Mirindi, J.P.J. (2004) 'Conserving biodiversity in times of conflict', in Y. Kaboza and G. Debonnet (eds) *Promoting and Preserving Congolese Heritage, Linking Biological and Cultural Diversity*, World Heritage Papers 17, Paris: UNESCO World Heritage Centre.

Miura, K. (2011) 'World Heritage making in Angkor: global, regional, national and local actors, interplays and implications', in B. Hauser-Schäublin (ed) *World Heritage*

Angkor and Beyond: Circumstances and Implications of UNESCO Listings in Cambodia, Göttingen Studies in Cultural Property, Göttingen, Germany: University of Göttingen.

Mohamed, S.A. (1980) 'Victory in Nubia: Egypt, UNESCO and the world community in the greatest archaeological rescue campaign of all time', *The UNESCO Courier*, no. 2, pp. 5–12.

Monteil, K. and Kinahan, J. (2015) *Report on the Joint UNESCO-ICOMOS Reactive Monitoring Mission to Lower Valley of the Omo World Heritage Property, Federal Democratic Republic of Ethiopia*, Paris: UNESCO.

Montes, C. and Borja, F. (2006) 'The Guadiamar green corridor: a research programme, example of science's social responsibility', in F.G. Novo and C.M. Cabrera (eds) *Doñana Water and Biosphere*, Doñana 2005 Project, Madrid: Ministry of the Environment.

Moran, E.F. (2008) *Human Adaptability: An Introduction to Ecological Anthropology*, Boulder, CO: Westview Press.

Morita, M. (2010) 'Reconciliation between preservation and tourism promotion: a case study of the Iwami Ginzan World Heritage Site in Japan', *[Journal of the Faculty of Humanities of Okazaki Gakuen University]*, vol. 12, pp. 123–132.

Mowforth, M. and Munt, I. (2009) *Tourism and Sustainability: Development, Globalisation and New Tourism in the Third World*, London: Routledge.

Muller, E. and Patry, M. (2011) 'World Heritage sites, Biosphere reserves and model forests: connecting Mesoamerica', in *Adapting to Change The State of Conservation of World Heritage Forests in 2011*, World Heritage Papers 30, Paris: UNESCO, World Heritage Centre.

Muller, E., Appleton, M.R., Ricci, G., Valverde, A. and Reynolds, D.W. (2015) 'Capacity development', in G.L. Worboys, M. Lockwood, A. Kothari, S. Feary and I. Pulsford (eds) *Protected Area Governance and Management*, Canberra: ANU Press.

Mumma, A. (2003) 'Community-based legal systems and the management of World Heritage sites', in E. Merode, R. Smeets and C. Westrik (eds) *Linking Universal and Local Values: Managing a Sustainable Future for World Heritage,* World Heritage Papers, no. 13, Paris: UNESCO, World Heritage Centre.

Mundy, K. (1999) 'Educational multilateralism in changing world order: UNESCO and the limits of the possible', *International Journal of Educational Development*, vol. 19, no. 1, pp. 27–52.

Myers, N., Mittermeier, R.A., Mittermeier, C.G., da Fonseca, G.A.B. and Kent, J. (2001) 'Biodiversity hotspots for conservation priorities', *Nature*, vol. 403, pp. 853–858.

Negussie, E. (2004) 'What is worth conserving in the urban environment? Temporal shifts in cultural attitudes towards the built heritage in Ireland', *Irish Geography*, vol. 37, no. 2, pp. 202–222.

Negussie, E. (2006a) 'Documentation, representation and World Heritage sites: comparative reflections on Sweden and Ireland', Documentation for conservation and development – New heritage strategy for the future, Forum UNESCO/University and Heritage, 11th International Seminar, Florence 11–15 September 2006.

Negussie, E. (2006b) 'Implications of neo-liberalism on built heritage management in Sweden and Ireland: institutional and ownership structures', *Urban Studies*, vol. 43, no. 10, pp. 1803–1824.

Negussie, E. (2012) 'Conserving the rock-hewn churches of Lalibela as a World Heritage site: a case for international support and local participation', in ICOMOS (ed) *Changing World, Changing Views of Heritage: Heritage and Social Change*, Proceedings of the ICOMOS Scientific Symposium, Dublin Castle, 30 October 2010, Paris: ICOMOS.

Negussie, E. (2015a) 'Ett stadslandskap värt att bevara', in C. Emdén (ed) *Visby världsarvsstad*, Visby, Sweden: Gotlands Museum Fornsalens Förlag.

Negussie, E. (2015b) 'Managing Dublin City as a historic urban landscape in the prospect of World Heritage nomination, project report', unpublished report, commissioned by Dublin City Council, Dublin.

Negussie, E. and Assefa-Wondimu, G. (2012) 'Managing World Heritage sites as a tool for development in Ethiopia: the need for sustainable tourism', in M.-T. Albert, M. Richon, M.J. Viñals and A. Witcomb (eds) *Community Development through World Heritage*, World Heritage Papers 31, Paris: UNESCO.

Negussie, E. and Fernández-Salinas, V. (2013) 'Impact of the Cajasol (Pelli) Tower on the skyline of Seville', *CIVVIH Newsletter*, no. 20, pp. 15–16.

Negussie, E. and Westerlund-Bjurström, K. (2014) 'Using HUL to introduce a new heritage driven concept for city development: the Stockholm experience', 18th ICOMOS General Assembly and Scientific Symposium on Heritage and Landscape as Human Values, 9–14 November 2014, Florence, Italy.

Nellemann, C., Henriksen, R., Raxter, P., Ash, N. and Mrema, E. (2014) *The Environmental Crime Crisis: Threats to Sustainable Development from Illegal Exploitation and Trade in Wildlife and Forest Resources: A UNEP Rapid Response Assessment*, Nairobi: United Nations Environment Programme and Arendal: GRID-Arendal.

Nixon, R.M. (1971) 'Special message to the Congress proposing the 1971 Environmental Program, February 8, 1971', in *Public Papers of the President of the United States*, Washington, DC: US Government Printing Office.

Nunes, P.A.L.D. and van den Bergh, J.C.J.M. (2001) 'Economic valuation of biodiversity: sense or nonsense?', *Ecological Economics*, vol. 39, pp. 203–222.

Nursey-Bray, M. and Rist, P. (2009) 'Co-management and protected area management: achieving effective management of a contested site, lessons from the Great Barrier Reef World Heritage Area (GBRWHA)', *Marine Policy*, vol. 33, no. 1, pp. 118–127.

Obura D.O., Church, J.E. and Gabrié, C. (2012) *Assessing Marine World Heritage from an Ecosystem Perspective: The Western Indian Ocean*, World Heritage Papers 32, Paris: UNESCO World Heritage Centre.

Offenhäußer, D., Zimmerli, W.C. and Albert, M-T. (2010) *World Heritage and Cultural Diversity*, Bonn: German Commission for UNESCO.

OHCHR and UNEP (2012) *Human Rights and the Environment – Rio+20: Joint Report OHCHR and UNEP, Office of the High Commissioner for Human Rights and United Nations Environment Programme*, Nairobi: UNEP.

Orbasli, A. (2000) *Tourists in Historic Towns*, London: E&FN Spon.

Osipova, E., Wilson, L., Blaney, R., Shi, Y., Fancourt, M., Strubel, M., Salvaterra, T., Brown, C. and Verschuuren, B. (2014a) *The Benefits of Natural World Heritage: Identifying and Assessing Ecosystem Services and Benefits Provided by the World's Most Iconic Places*, Gland, Switzerland: IUCN.

Osipova, E., Shi, Y., Kormos, C., Shadie, P., Zwahlen, P. and Badman, T. (2014b) *IUCN World Heritage Outlook 2014: A Conservation Assessment of all Natural World Heritage Sites*, Gland, Switzerland: IUCN.

Osti, M., Coad, L., Fisher, J.B., Bomhard, B. and Hutton, J.M. (2011) 'Oil and gas development in the World Heritage and wider protected area network in sub-Saharan Africa', *Biodiversity Conservation*, vol. 20, pp. 1863–1877.

Oxford English Dictionary (2015) 'Interdisciplinary', www.oed.com/view/Entry/97720?r edirectedFrom=interdisciplinary#eid, accessed 28 October 2015.

Oxford English Dictionary (2016) 'Community', https://en.oxforddictionaries. com/ definition/community, accessed 16 July 2016.

Parks and Wildlife Service (1999) *Tasmanian Wilderness World Heritage Area Management Plan*, Hobart, Australia: Parks and Wildlife Service, Tasmania.

Parks and Wildlife Service (2004) *State of the Tasmanian Wilderness World Heritage Area: An Evaluation of Management Effectiveness*, Report No. 1, Hobart, Australia: Department of Tourism Parks Heritage and the Arts.

Paroff, S.P. (2004) 'Another victim of the war in Iraq: the looting of the national museum in Baghdad and the inadequacies of international protection of cultural property', *Emory Law Journal*, vol. 53, pp. 2021–2054.

Partow, H. (2008) 'Environmental impact of wars and conflicts', in M.K. Tolba and N.W. Saab (eds) *Arab Environment: Future Challenges,* Beirut: Arab Forum for Environment and Development.

Pedersen, A. (2002) *Managing Tourism at World Heritage Sites: A Practical Manual for World Heritage Site Managers*, Paris: UNESCO World Heritage Centre.

Pejchar, L. and Mooney, H.A. (2009) 'Invasive species, ecosystem services and human wellbeing', *Trends in Ecology and Evolution*, vol. 24, no. 9, pp. 497–504.

Perdan, S (2004) 'Introduction to sustainable development', in A. Azapagic, S. Perdan and R. Clift, (eds) *Sustainable Development in Practice: Case Studies for Engineers and Scientists*, Chichester: John Wiley & Sons.

Petzet, M. (2008) 'Introduction', in M. Petzet and J. Ziesemer (eds) *Heritage at Risk: ICOMOS World Report 2006/2007 on Monuments and Sites in Danger*, Altenburg, Germany: E. Reinhold-Verlag.

Phillips, A. (1995) 'Cultural landscapes: an IUCN perspective', in B. von Droste, H. Plachter, and M. Rössler (eds) *Cultural Landscapes of Universal Value: Components of a Global Strategy*, Jena, Germany: Gustav Fischer Verlag.

Phillips, A. (1998) 'The nature of cultural landscapes: a nature conservation perspective', *Landscape Research,* vol. 23, no. 1, pp. 21–38.

Philips, A. (2003) 'Turning ideas on their head: The new paradigm for protected areas', in H. Jaireth and D. Smyth (eds) *Innovative Governance: Indigenous Peoples, Local Communities and Protected Areas*, New Delhi: Ane Books,.

Philips, A. (2005) 'Landscape as a meeting ground: Category V Protected Landscapes/Seascapes and World Heritage Cultural Landscapes', in J. Brown, N. Mitchell and M. Beresford (eds) *The Protected Landscape Approach: Linking Nature, Culture and Community*, Gland, Switzerland: IUCN.

Pilgrim, S. and Pretty, J. (2010) *Nature and Culture: Re-building Lost Connections*, London: Earthscan.

Pocock, D. (1997) 'Some reflections on World Heritage', *Area*, vol. 29, no. 3, pp. 260–68.

Polet, G. and Ling, S. (2004) 'Protecting mammal diversity: opportunities and constraints for pragmatic conservation management in Cat Tien National Park, Vietnam', *Oryx*, vol. 38, no. 2, pp. 186–196.

Posey, D.A. (2000) *Cultural and Spiritual Values of Biodiversity*, London: Intermediate Technology Publications.

Pressouyre, L. (1996) *The World Heritage Convention 20 Years Later*, Paris: UNESCO.

Pretty, J. (2008) 'How do biodiversity and culture intersect?', Conference Paper, Sustaining Cultural and Biological Diversity in a Rapidly Changing World: Lessons for Global Policy, American Museum of Natural History's Center for Biodiversity and Conservation, IUCN, April 2–5, 2008.

Pretty, J. (2011) 'Interdisciplinary progress in approaches to address social-ecological and ecocultural systems', *Environmental Conservation*, vol. 38, no. 2, pp. 127–139.

Proctor, J.D. (1998) 'The social construction of nature: relativist accusations, pragmatist and critical realist responses', *Annals of the Association of American Geographers*, vol. 88, no. 3, pp. 352–376.

Proctor, J.D. and Pincetl, S. (1996) 'Nature and the reproduction of endangered space: the spotted owl in the Pacific Northwest and southern California', *Environment and Planning D: Society and Space*, vol. 14, pp. 683–708.

Randolph, S. and Stiles, D. (2011) *Elephant Meat Trade in Central Africa; Cameroon Case Study*, Gland, Switzerland: IUCN.

Rao, K. (2010) 'A new paradigm for the identification, nomination and inscription of properties on the World Heritage List', *International Journal of Heritage Studies*, vol. 16, no. 3, pp. 161–172.

Rashkow, E.D. (2014) 'Idealizing inhabited wilderness: a revision to the history of indigenous peoples and national parks', *History Compass* vol. 12, no. 10, pp. 818–832.

Rebanks, J. (2009) *World Heritage Status: Is There Opportunity for Economic Gain?*, Kendal: Rebanks Consulting Ltd and Trend Business Research Ltd on behalf of the Lake District World Heritage Project.

Redclift, M. (2005) 'Sustainable development (1987–2005): an oxymoron comes of age', *Sustainable Development*, vol. 13, pp. 212–227.

Resilience Alliance (2010) 'Assessing resilience in social-ecological systems: workbook for practitioners (version 2)', www.resalliance.org/files/ResilienceAssessmentV2_2. pdf, accessed 20 October 2015.

Richon, M. (2007) 'Borrowing someone else's toolbox could be the solution', in M.T. Albert, R. Bernecker, D.G. Perez, N. Thakur and Z. Nairen (eds) *Training Strategies for World Heritage Management*, Cottbus, Germany: Deutsche UNESCO-Kommission e. V.

Robinson, M. (1999) 'Is cultural tourism on the right track?', *UNESCO the Courier*, July/August, pp. 22–23.

Rockström, J., Steffen, W., Noone, K., Persson, Å., Chapin, III, F.S., Lambin, E.F., Lenton, T.M., Scheffer, M., Folke, C., Schellnhuber, H.J., Nykvist, B., de Wit, C.A., Hughes, T., van der Leeuw, S., Rodhe, H., Sörlin, S., Snyder, P.K., Costanza, R., Svedin, U., Falkenmark, M., Karlberg, L., Corell, R.W., Fabry, V.J., Hansen, J., Walker, B., Liverman, D., Richardson, K., Crutzen, P. and Foley, J.A. (2009a) 'A safe operating space for humanity', *Nature*, vol. 461, pp. 472–475.

Rockström, J., Steffen, W., Noone, K., Persson, Å., Chapin, III, F.S., Lambin, E.F., Lenton, T.M., Scheffer, M., Folke, C., Schellnhuber, H.J., Nykvist, B., de Wit, C.A., Hughes, T., van der Leeuw, S., Rodhe, H., Sörlin, S., Snyder, P.K., Costanza, R., Svedin, U., Falkenmark, M., Karlberg, L., Corell, R.W., Fabry, V.J., Hansen, J., Walker, B., Liverman, D., Richardson, K., Crutzen, P. and Foley, J.A. (2009b) 'Planetary boundaries: exploring the safe operating space for humanity', *Ecology and Society*, vol. 14, no. 2, pp. 32.

Rosen, E. and Smith, K. (2010) 'Summarizing the evidence on the international trade in illegal wildlife', *EcoHealth*, vol. 7, no. 1, pp. 24–32.

Rössler, M. (2003) 'Linking nature and culture: World Heritage cultural landscapes', in *Cultural Landscapes: The Challenges of Conservation*, World Heritage Papers 7, Paris: UNESCO.

Rössler, M. (2005) 'World Heritage cultural landscapes: a global perspective', in J. Brown, N. Mitchell and M. Beresford (eds) *The Protected Landscape Approach: Linking Nature, Culture and Community*, Gland, Switzerland: IUCN.

Rössler, M. (2012) 'Partners in site management. A shift in focus: heritage and community involvement', in M. Albert, M. Richon, M. José Viñals and A. Witcomb (eds) *Community Development through World Heritage*, World Heritage Papers 31, Paris: UNESCO.

RRF, Rapid Response Facility (2016) 'Rapid Response Facility', www.rapid-response. org, accessed 10 December 2016.

Russo, A.P. (1999) 'Venice: coping with culture vultures', *UNESCO the Courier*, July/August, pp. 42–43.

RWTH-Aachen University (2015) 'Master Plan Castra Bonnensia: Master Plan Römerlager Bonn as part of the UNESCO application "Lower Germanic Limes" (Extension of transnational World Heritage Site Frontiers of the Roman Empire), UNESCO Chair projects', www.isl.rwth-aachen.de/cms/ISL/Der-Lehrstuhl/UNESCO-Chair/Team/Planung-Management/~gued/Masterplan-Bonner-Roemerlager/lidx/1/, accessed 4 June 2016.

Salafsky, N., Salzer, D., Stattersfield, A.J., Hilton-Taylor, C., Neugarten, R., Butchart, S.H., Collen, B., Cox, N., Master, L.L., O'Connor, S. and Wilkie, D. (2007) 'A standard lexicon for biodiversity conservation: unified classifications of threats and actions', *Conservation Biology*, vol. 22, no. 4, pp. 897–911.

Sandwith, T., Shine, C., Hamilton, L. and Sheppard, D. (2001) 'Transboundary protected areas for peace and cooperation', in A. Phillips (ed) *Best Practice Protected Area Guidelines Series*, no. 7, Gland, Switzerland: IUCN.

Savio, I. (2004) *Report on the ICOMOS Reactive Monitoring Mission to World Heritage Site Antigua Guatemala, 9–13 February 2004*, Paris: ICOMOS.

Scheffer, M., Barrett, S., Carpenter, S.R., Folke, C., Green, A.J., Holmgreen, M., Hughes, T.P., Kosten, S., van de Leemput, I.A., Nepstad, D.C., van Nes, E.H., Peeters, E.T.H.M. and Walker, B. (2015) 'Creating a safe operating space for iconic ecosystems: manage local stressors to promote resilience to global change', *Science*, vol. 347, pp. 1317–1319.

Schelhas, J. (2001) 'The USA national parks in international perspective: have we learned the wrong lesson?' *Environmental Conservation*, vol. 28, no. 4, pp. 300–304.

Schoch, D. (2014) 'Whose World Heritage? Dresden's Waldschlösschen bridge and UNESCO's delisting of the Dresden Elbe Valley', *International Journal of Cultural Property*, vol. 21, pp.199–223.

Shackley, M. (1998) *Visitor Management: Case Studies from World Heritage Sites*, Oxford: Butterworth-Heinemann.

Sharpe, E. (2014) 'Farmers bulldoze ancient tombs at Cyrene to sell plot to developers, (*The Art Newspaper,* September 4, 2013)', in C. Machat, M. Petzet and J. Ziesemer (eds) *Heritage at Risk: World Report 2011–2013 on Monuments and Sites in Danger*, Berlin: Hendrik Bäßler Verlag.

SICE (2015) 'Trade agreements and related sections, Foreign Trade Information System', www.sice.oas.org/, accessed 1 October 2015.

Silverman, H. (2010) 'Border wars: the ongoing temple dispute between Thailand and Cambodia and UNESCO's World Heritage List', *International Journal of Heritage Studies*, vol. 17, no. 1, pp. 1–21.

Singh, S. (1985) 'India's action plan for wildlife conservation and role of voluntary bodies', *Environmentalist*, vol. 5, no. 1, pp. 31–37.

Smith, L. (2006) *Uses of Heritage*, London: Routledge.

Snyder, G. (1998) 'Nature as seen from Kitkitdizzie is no social construction', *Whole Earth*, Winter, www.wholeearth.com/issue/1340/article/55/nature.as.seen.from.kitkitdizze.is.no.social.construction, accessed 14 April 2014.

Sørensen, M.S. and Evans, C. (2011) 'The challenges and potentials of archaeological heritage in Africa: Cape Verdean reflections', *African Archaeological Review*, vol. 28, no. 1, pp. 39–54.

Soulé, M.E. (1995) 'The social siege of nature', in M.E. Soulé and G. Lease (eds) *Reinventing Nature?: Responses to Postmodern Deconstruction*, Washington, DC: Island Press.

Spennemann, D.H.R. (2005) 'Risk assessments in heritage planning in Victoria and New South Wales: a survey of conservation plans and heritage studies', *Australasian Journal of Environmental Management*, vol. 12, no. 2, pp. 89–96.

Spoelder, P., Lockwood, M., Cowell, S., Gregerson, P. and Henchman, A. (2015) 'Planning', in G.L. Worboys, M. Lockwood, A. Kothari, S. Feary and I. Pulsford (eds) *Protected Area Governance and Management*, Canberra: ANU Press.

Stanley-Price, N. (2004) 'Introduction', in *Monitoring World Heritage*, World Heritage Papers 10, Paris: UNESCO, World Heritage Centre.

Steinberg, P.F. and VanDeveer, S.D. (2012) *Comparative Environmental Politics: Theory, Practice and Prospects*, Cambridge, MA: Massachusetts Institute of Technology Press.

Stephenson, J. (2008) 'The cultural values model: an integrated approach to values in landscapes', *Landscape and Urban Planning*, vol. 84, pp. 127–139.

Stern, N. (2007) *The Economics of Climate Change: The Stern Review*, Cambridge: Cambridge University Press.

Stirton, B. (2010) 'Brent Stirton's best photograph – Congo wildlife rangers carry a dead silverback', *The Guardian*, 22 October 2015, https://www.theguardian.com/artanddesign/2015/oct/22/brent-stirton-best-photograph-dead-silverback-gorilla-congo-virunga, accessed 10 August 2017.

Stockholm Resilience Centre (2016) 'What is resilience: an introduction to a popular concept', http://stockholmresilience.org/research/research-news/2015-02-19-what-is-resilience.html, accessed 13 June 2017.

Stolton, S. and Dudley, N. (1999) 'A preliminary survey of management status and threats in forest protected areas', *Parks*, vol. 9, no. 2, pp. 27–33.

Stovel, H. (1998) *Risk Preparedness: A Management Manual for World Cultural Heritage*, Rome: ICCROM.

Tanner, R., Freimund, W., Hayden, B. and Dolan, B. (2007) 'The Waterton Glacier International Peace Park: conservation and border security', in H.A. Saleem (ed) *Peace Parks: Conservation and Conflict Resolution*, Cambridge, MA: Massachusetts Institute of Technology Press.

TEEB, The Economics of Ecosystems & Biodiversity (2016) 'The initiative', www.teebweb.org/about/the-initiative/, accessed 22 July 2016.

The Heritage Council (2009) *Brú na Bóinne World Heritage Site Research Framework*, Kilkenney: The Heritage Council.

The Market Research Group (2007) *The Purbeck Section of the Dorset & East Devon World Heritage Site Carrying Capacity Evaluation Report*, Bournemouth: The Market Research Group on behalf of the World Heritage Steering Group, The Purbeck Heritage Committee and the Dorset AONB.

The Telegraph (1984) 'Singapore to withdraw from UNESCO', 28 December 1984.

Thomas, C. (2012) 'World Heritage site status – a catalyst for heritage-led sustainable regeneration: Blaenavon Industrial Landscape, UK', in A. Galla (ed) *World Heritage: Benefits Beyond Borders*, Cambridge: Cambridge University Press.

Throsby, D. (2002) 'Cultural capital and sustainability concepts in the economics of cultural heritage', in M. de la Torre (ed) *Assessing the Values of Cultural Heritage*, Los Angeles, CA: The Getty Conservation Institute.

Throsby, D. (2011) 'The political economy of art: Ruskin and contemporary cultural economics', *History of Political Economy*, vol. 43, no. 2, pp. 275–294.

TIES, The International Ecotourism Society (2016) 'What is ecotourism', www.ecotourism.org/what-is-ecotourism, accessed 29 August 2016.

Timothy, D.J. and Boyd, S.W. (2003) *Heritage Tourism*, London: Pearson Education.

Torggler, B., Murphy, R., France, C. and Portolés, J.B. (2015) 'UNESCO's work on culture and sustainable development: evaluation of a policy theme', Internal Oversight Service, Paris: UNESCO.

Train, R.E. (2003) 'World heritage: a vision for the future', in *World Heritage 2002: Shared Legacy, Common Responsibility*, Paris: UNESCO World Heritage Centre.

Transboundary Consulting Africa (2012) 'Situational analysis: World Heritage and impacts of development in Africa', Final Draft Report, African World Heritage Fund, www.awhf.net/, accessed 12 October 2013.

Tunbridge, J.E. (1994) 'Whose heritage? Global problem, European nightmare', in G.J. Ashworth and P.J. Larkham (eds) *Building a New Heritage: Tourism, Culture and Identity in the New Europe*, London: Routledge.

Turner, S.D. (2012) *World Heritage Sites and Extractive Industries*, working report, Gland, Switzerland: IUCN.

UN (undated) 'Who are indigenous peoples?', United Nations Permanent Forum on Indigenous Issues, www.un.org/esa/socdev/unpfii/documents/5session _factsheet1. pdf, accessed 13 July 2016.

UN (1972) 'Declaration of the United Nations Conference on the Human Environment', United Nations Conference on the Human Environment, www. unep.org/documents.multilingual/default.asp?documentid=97&articleid=1503, accessed 19 November 2013.

UN (1992) *Convention on Biological Diversity,* New York: United Nations.

UN (2000) *United Nations Millennium Declaration*, New York: United Nations.

UN (2001) *Road Map Towards the Implementation of the United Nations Millennium Declaration*, Report of the Secretary-General, United Nations General Assembly, A/56/326, New York: United Nations.

UN (2002) 'Johannesburg declaration on sustainable development', A/CONF.199/20. World Summit on Sustainable Development, 4 September 2002.

UN (2008) 'Declaration on the rights of Indigenous Peoples', Resolution adopted by the General Assembly, A/61/L.67, New York: United Nations.

UN (2012) *Report of the United Nations Conference on Sustainable Development*, New York: United Nations.

UN (2013) Draft resolution submitted by the Vice-Chair of the Committee, Waruna Sri Dhanapala (Sri Lanka), on the basis of informal consultations on draft resolution A/C.2/68/L.34, A/C.2/68/L.69.

UN (2014a) 'General Assembly of the United Nations', www.un.org/en/ga/, accessed 15 February 2014.

UN (2014b) 'Promotion of sustainable tourism, including ecotourism, for poverty eradication and environment protection', A/RES/69/233, Resolution adopted by the General Assembly on 19 December 2014.

UN (2015a) 'We are the first generation that can end poverty, the last that can end climate change: secretary stresses at university ceremony', press release 28 May 2015, SG/SM/16800.

UN (2015b) 'Transforming our world: the 2030 Agenda for Sustainable Development', Resolution adopted by the General Assembly on 25 September 2015, A/RES/70/1, New York: United Nations.

UN (2015c) 'COP21: UN chief calls on civil society to keep governments accountable on climate commitments', News Centre www.un.org/apps/ news/story. asp?NewsID=52781#.V0cOTkZhRCA, accessed 20 January 2016.

UN (2015d) *Promotion and Protection of the Rights of Indigenous Peoples with Respect to their Cultural Heritage*: Study by the Expert Mechanism on the Rights of Indigenous Peoples, Human Rights Council, Document: A/HRC/30/53, New York: United Nations.

UN (2016) 'ICC finds Malian extremist guilty of war crimes in destroying historic sites in Timbuktu', UN News Centre, www.un.org/apps/news/story.asp?NewsID=55137#. WVUk84Tyvcs, accessed 30 September 2016.

UN General Assembly (2012) 'The future we want', Resolution: A/RES/66/288, New York: United Nations.

UN General Assembly (2013) *Mainstreaming of the Three Dimensions of Sustainable Development throughout the United Nations System*, Report of the Secretary-General, A/68/79–E/2013/69, New York: United Nations.

UN-NGLS (2007) *Intergovernmental Negotiations and Decision Making at the United Nations: A Guide*, New York and Geneva: UN Non-Governmental Liaison Service.

UN Secretariat (2010) 'Use of the UN Convention against Transnational Organized Crime for protection against trafficking in cultural property', Conference of the Parties to the UN Convention against Transnational Organized Crime, 5th Session, Document CTOC/COP/2010/12, Vienna: United Nations.

UN Secretariat (2015) 'Workshop 3: strengthening crime prevention and criminal justice responses to evolving forms of crime, such as cybercrime and trafficking in cultural property, including lessons learned and international cooperation', Thirteenth UN Congress on Crime Prevention and Criminal Justice, Document A/CONF.222/12, Doha, Qatar: United Nations.

UN Security Council (2013) 'Resolution 2100, the situation in Mali', adopted by the Security Council at its 6952nd meeting, on 25 April 2013, S/RES/2100, New York: United Nations.

UN System Task Team (2012) 'Culture: a driver and an enabler of sustainable development, thematic think piece, UN System Task Team on the post-2015 UN Development Agenda', Paris: UNESCO.

UNDP, United Nations Development Programme (1997) *Governance for Sustainable Human Development: A UNDP Policy Document*, New York: United Nations Development Programme.

UNDP (2008) *Capacity Development Practice Note*, New York: United Nations Development Programme.

UNECE, United Nations Economic Commission for Europe (2013) 'Aarhus Convention', www.unece.org/env/pp/introduction.html, accessed August 2013.

UNEP, United Nations Environment Programme (1972) 'Declaration of the United Nations Conference on the Human Environment', www.unep.org/documents. multilingual/default.asp?documentid=97&articleid=1503, accessed 13 July 2016.

UNEP (1992) 'Rio Declaration on environment and development', United Nations Conference on Environment and Development, Rio de Janeiro, 3–14 June 1992, www.unep.org/documents.multilingual/default.asp?documentid=78&article id=1163, accessed 13 July 2016.

UNEP (2011) *Outcomes of the Joint Meeting of the CBD Liaison Group on Bushmeat and the CITES Central Africa Bushmeat Working Group, Nairobi*, Document: UNEP/CBD/LG-Bushmeat/2/4, Montreal: CBD Secretariat.

UNEP (2012) *Global Environment Outlook 5: Summary for Policy Makers,* Nairobi: United Nations Environment Programme.

UNEP (2014) 'Agenda item 14, XII/3 Resource mobilization, decision adopted by the Conference of the Parties to the Convention on Biological Diversity', UNEP/CBD/COP/DEC/XII/3, Montreal: CBD Secretariat.

UNESCO (1945) *Constitution of the United Nations Educational, Scientific, and Cultural Organization*, Paris: UNESCO.

UNESCO (1954) *Convention for the Protection of Cultural Property in the Event of Armed Conflict with Regulations for the Execution of the Convention*, Paris: UNESCO.

UNESCO (1962) 'Information about the international campaign to save the monuments of Nubia; progress of the campaign from 4 August to 31 December 1961', UNESCO/ CUA/113, Paris, 23 February 1962.

UNESCO (1970) *Convention on the Means of Prohibiting and Preventing the Illicit Import, Export and Transfer of Ownership of Cultural Property*, Paris: UNESCO.

UNESCO (1972) *Convention Concerning the Protection of the World Cultural and Natural Heritage*, Paris: UNESCO.

UNESCO (1976) 'Informal consultation of intergovernmental and non-governmental organisations on the implementation of the Convention Concerning the Protection of the World Cultural and Natural Heritage', Morges, 19–20 May 1976. Final Report, http:// unesdoc.unesco.org/images/0002/000213/021374Eb.pdf, accessed 26 January 2014.

UNESCO (1977a) 'Opening of the session, UNESCO World Heritage Committee Decisions', 01COM11.4, UNESCO World Heritage Centre, Paris.

UNESCO (1977b) *Intergovernmental Committee for the Protection of the World Cultural and Natural Heritage: First Session*, Final Report, World Heritage Committee Document CC-77/CONF.001/9, Paris: UNESCO.

UNESCO (1978) *Operational Guidelines for the Implementation of the World Heritage Convention*, Paris: UNESCO World Heritage Centre.

UNESCO (1980a) *Operational Guidelines for the Implementation of the World Heritage Convention*, Paris: UNESCO World Heritage Centre.

UNESCO (1980b) *Report of the Rapporteur on the Fourth Session of the World Heritage Committee*, Document CC-80/CONF.016/10, Paris: UNESCO.

UNESCO (1983) *Operational Guidelines for the Implementation of the World Heritage Convention*, Paris: UNESCO World Heritage Centre.

UNESCO (1984) 'World Heritage Committee Eighth Ordinary Session', SC/84/ CONF.004/9, Buenos Aires, Argentina, 29 October–2 November 1984.

UNESCO (1988) *Operational Guidelines for the Implementation of the World Heritage Convention*, UNESCO World Heritage Centre, Paris.

UNESCO (1989) *Report of the World Heritage Committee, Thirteenth Session, Paris 11–15 December 1989*, SC-89/CONF.004/12, Paris: UNESCO.

UNESCO (1992a) 'Item 6 of the provisional agenda: evaluation report on the implementation of the Convention, World Heritage Committee', Document WHC-92/CONF.002/3, Paris: UNESCO.

UNESCO (1992b) *Operational Guidelines for the Implementation of the World Heritage Convention*, Paris: UNESCO.

UNESCO (1992c) 'Properties inscribed on the World Heritage List. Decision: 667, Angkor Cambodia', World Heritage Committee, Sixteenth Session, Santa Fe, USA, 7–14 December, Document WHC-92/CONF.002/12, World Heritage Committee, Paris: UNESCO.

UNESCO (1994a) *Operational Guidelines for the Implementation of the World Heritage Convention*, Paris: UNESCO.

UNESCO (1994b) 'Inscription: Arabian Oryx Sanctuary (Oman)', World Heritage Committee Decision: CONF 003XI, Paris: UNESCO.

UNESCO (1994c) 'Report of the Expert Meeting on the "Global Strategy" and thematic studies for a representative World Heritage List, 20–22 June', World Heritage Committee Document WHC-94/CONF.003/INF.6, Paris: UNESCO.

UNESCO (1995a) 'Inscription: Sintra Cultural Landscape (Portugal)', CONF 203 VIII.C.1, http://whc.unesco.org/en/decisions/3095, accessed 13 July 2016.

UNESCO (1995b) *Operational Guidelines for the Implementation of the World Heritage Convention*, Paris: UNESCO.

UNESCO (1996a) *Operational Guidelines for the Implementation of the World Heritage Convention*, Paris: UNESCO.

UNESCO (1996b) 'Report of the expert meeting on evaluation of general principles and criteria for nominations of natural World Heritage sites', Parc national de la Vanoise, Document WHC-96/CONF.202/INF.9, Paris: UNESCO.

UNESCO (1998) SOC: 'World Heritage Sites in Central America', World Heritage Committee Decision: WHC-98/CONF 203 VII.42, Paris: UNESCO.

UNESCO (1999a) *Second Protocol to The Hague Convention of 1954 for the Protection of Cultural Property in the Event of Armed Conflict 1999*, Paris: UNESCO.

UNESCO (1999b) 'Declaration on science and the use of scientific knowledge', Science for the twenty-first Century, A new commitment, World Conference on Science, Budapest Hungary, Paris: UNESCO.

UNESCO (1999c) 'Science agenda: framework for action', Science for the twenty-first Century, A new commitment, World Conference on Science, Budapest Hungary, Paris: UNESCO.

UNESCO (1999d) 'Introductory note to the Science Agenda-Framework for Action', Science for the twenty-first Century, A new commitment, World Conference on Science, Budapest Hungary, Paris: UNESCO.

UNESCO (2001a) *Universal Declaration on Cultural Diversity*, Paris: UNESCO.

UNESCO (2001b) 'Item 11 of the provisional agenda: Progress Report on Global Training Strategy', WHC-01/CONF.208/14, Twenty-fifth session of the World Heritage Committee, Helsinki, Finland 11–16 December 2001.

UNESCO (2002) *The Budapest Declaration on World Heritage*, World Heritage Committee Document WHC-02/CONF.202/5, Paris: UNESCO.

UNESCO (2003a) *Convention for the Safeguarding of the Intangible Cultural Heritage*, Paris: UNESCO.

UNESCO (2003b) 'Paris Declaration: safeguarding and development of Angkor', http://unesdoc.unesco.org/images/0015/001588/158898E.pdf, accessed 29 March 2015.

UNESCO (2004) 'Dresden Elbe Valley, World Heritage List', http://whc.unesco.org/en/list/1156, accessed 26 August 2014.

UNESCO (2005a) *Convention on the Protection and Promotion of the Diversity of Cultural Expressions*, Paris: UNESCO.

UNESCO (2005b) *Operational Guidelines for the Implementation of the World Heritage Convention*, Paris: UNESCO.

UNESCO (2006a) 'State of conservation (Dresden Elbe Valley)', World Heritage Committee Decision 30 COM 7B.77, Paris: UNESCO.

UNESCO (2006b) 'Greece: Acropolis, Athens, State of Conservation of World Heritage Properties in Europe', http://whc.unesco.org/archive/periodicreporting/EUR/cycle01/section2/404-summary.pdf.

UNESCO (2006c) *Predicting and Managing the Effects of Climate Change on World Heritage*, Paris: UNESCO.

UNESCO (2007a) 'Periodic reporting', World Heritage Committee Decision 31 COM 11D.1, http://whc.unesco.org/en/decisions/2226, accessed 13 July 2016.

UNESCO (2007b) 'Item 7B of the provisional agenda: state of conservation of World Heritage properties inscribed on the World Heritage List, Arabian Oryx Sanctuary

(Oman) (N 654)', World Heritage Committee Document WHC-07/31.COM/7B, Paris: UNESCO.

UNESCO (2007c) *World Heritage: Challenges for the Millennium*, Paris: UNESCO World Heritage Centre.

UNESCO (2007d) 'Decisions adopted at Thirty-first Session of the World Heritage Committee', WHC-07/31.COM/24, Christchurch, New Zealand, 23 June–2 July 2007.

UNESCO (2007e) 'Item 18 of the provisional agenda: International Assistance, Decision 31 COM 18B', World Heritage Committee, Thirty-first Session, Christchurch, New Zealand, 23 June–2 July 2007.

UNESCO (2007f) 'Galápagos Islands, Ecuador', World Heritage Committee Decision: 31 COM 7B.35, Paris: UNESCO.

UNESCO (2007g) 'Item 7.2 of the provisional agenda: issues related to the state of conservation of World Heritage properties: strategy for reducing risks from disasters at World Heritage properties', World Heritage Committee Decision: WHC-07/31. COM/7.2, Paris: UNESCO.

UNESCO (2008a) *Enhancing Our Heritage Toolkit Assessing Management Effectiveness of Natural World Heritage Sites*, World Heritage Papers, no. 33, Paris: UNESCO.

UNESCO (2008b) 'Frontiers of the Roman Empire', World Heritage List, whc.unesco. org/en/list/430, accessed 14 November 2014.

UNESCO (2008c) *Business Planning for Natural World Heritage Sites: A Toolkit*, Paris: UNESCO.

UNESCO (2008d) 'Archaeological site of Panamá Viejo and historic district of Panamá (Panama) (C 790 bis)', Item 7B of the provisional agenda: State of conservation of World Heritage properties inscribed on the World Heritage List, World Heritage Committee Document WHC-08/32.COM/7B, Paris: UNESCO.

UNESCO (2009a) *World Heritage and Buffer Zones*, World Heritage Papers 25, Paris: UNESCO.

UNESCO (2009b) 'Examination of nominations – Sacred site of the Temple of Preah Vihear (Cambodia)', Decision: 32 COM 8B.102 http://whc.unesco.org/en/decisions /1548, accessed 13 July 2016.

UNESCO (2009c) 'Dresden Elbe Valley (Germany)', (C1156) World Heritage Committee Decision: 33 COM 7A.26, Paris: UNESCO.

UNESCO (2009d) 'Guidelines and procedures for the UNITWIN/UNESCO Chairs Programme', ED/UNITWIN/2006/PI/1 rev.4, http://unesdoc.unesco.org/images/ 0014/001439/143918e.pdf, accessed 26 January 2016.

UNESCO (2009e) 'Progress report on the African World Heritage Fund', WHC-09/33. COM/6A, Thirty-third session, Seville, Spain 20–30 June 2009.

UNESCO (2010a) 'Papahānaumokuākea', World Heritage List, whc.unesco.org/en/ list/1326, accessed 14 November 2014.

UNESCO (2010b) 'Report of the decisions adopted by the World Heritage Committee at its 34th Session', WHC-10/34.COM/20, Brasilia, Brazil 25 July–3 August 2010.

UNESCO (2010c) 'Archaeological site of Panamá Viejo and historic district of Panamá (Panama) (C 790 bis)', Item 7B of the provisional agenda: State of conservation of World Heritage properties inscribed on the World Heritage List, World Heritage Committee Document WHC-10/34.COM/7B.Add, Paris: UNESCO.

UNESCO (2011a) *Recommendation on the Historic Urban Landscape*, Paris: UNESCO.

UNESCO (2011b) 'Item 11 of the provisional agenda: future of the World Heritage Convention', Document: WHC-11/18.GA/11, Paris: UNESCO.

UNESCO (2011c) 'Temple of Preah Vihear (Cambodia) (C 1224rev)', COM 35 7B62, http://whc.unesco.org/en/decisions/4470/, accessed 13 July 2016.

UNESCO (2011d) 'Item 7B of the provisional agenda: state of conservation of World Heritage properties inscribed on the World Heritage List', WHC-11/35.COM/7B, Paris: UNESCO.

UNESCO (2011e) *Evaluation of the Global Strategy and the PACT Initiative*, World Heritage Committee Document: WHC-11/35.COM/9A, Paris: UNESCO.

UNESCO (2011f) 9B 'Presentation and adoption of the World Heritage strategy for capacity building', Document WHC-11/35.COM/9B, World Heritage Committee, Paris: UNESCO.

UNESCO (2011g) 'Item 9 of the provisional agenda: global strategy for a representative, balanced and credible World Heritage List', WHC-11/35.COM/9B, World Heritage Committee, Thirty-fifth session, Paris, Spain 19–29 June 2011.

UNESCO (2012a) 'UNESCO: the organization's history', www.unesco.org/new/en/unesco/about-us/who-we-are/history/, accessed 19 July 2012.

UNESCO (2012b) 'Future of the World Heritage Convention: progress report on implementation', UNESCO World Heritage Committee Decisions WHC-12/36.COM/12A, UNESCO World Heritage Centre, Paris.

UNESCO (2012c) 'Item 5 of the provisional agenda: Reports of the World Heritage Centre and the advisory bodies', 36th Session of the World Heritage Committee, WHC-12/36.COM/5B, Paris: UNESCO.

UNESCO (2012d) 9B: 'Follow-up to the capacity-building strategy', World Heritage Committee WHC-12/36.COM/9B, Paris: UNESCO.

UNESCO (2012e) *Managing Natural World Heritage: World Heritage Resource Manual*, Paris: UNESCO.

UNESCO (2012f) 'Item 7C of the provisional agenda: reflection on the trends of the state of conservation', World Heritage Committee Document WHC-12/36.COM/7C, Paris: UNESCO.

UNESCO (2012g) *Operational Guidelines for the Implementation of the World Heritage Convention*, Paris: UNESCO.

UNESCO (2012h) 'Item 7B of the provisional agenda: state of conservation of World Heritage properties inscribed on the World Heritage List', Document WHC-12/36.COM/7B.Add, World Heritage Committee, Paris: UNESCO.

UNESCO (2012i) 'Decisions 36COM 7B.55 Rock-Art Sites of Tadrart Acacus (Libya) (C 287)', World Heritage Committee, Thirty-sixth session, Saint Petersburg, Russian Federation 24 June–6 July 2012.

UNESCO (2012j) 'Statement of compulsory and voluntary contributions 31 December 2015', http://whc.unesco.org/en/funding, accessed 26 December 2016.

UNESCO (2012k) 'Funding', http://whc.unesco.org/en/funding, accessed 27 December 2016.

UNESCO (2012l) 'Examination of international assistance requests', Decision 34COM 15.2, Brasilia, http://whc.unesco.org/en/decisions/3393, accessed 19 August 2012.

UNESCO (2012m) 'Director-General deeply concerned by wildfires in Southern Europe', www.unesco.org/new/en/natural-sciences/about-us/single-view/news/director_general_deeply_concerned_by_wildfires_in_southern/, accessed 10 October 2014.

UNESCO (2012n) 'Fortifications on the Caribbean side of Panama: Portobelo-San Lorenzo', World Heritage List, whc.unesco.org/en/list/135, accessed 14 August 2012.

UNESCO (2012o) 'Archaeological site of Panamá Viejo and historic district of Panamá (Panamá) (C 790bis)', Item 7B of the provisional agenda: State of conservation of World Heritage properties inscribed on the World Heritage List, World Heritage Committee Document WHC-12/36.COM/7B.Add, Paris: UNESCO.

UNESCO (2013a) 'The rescue of Nubian monuments and sites', UNESCO World Heritage Centre, whc.unesco.org/en/activities/173/, accessed 19 November 2013.

UNESCO (2013b) 'Nubia Museum, Aswan', UNESCO www.unesco.org/new/en/culture/themes/museums/museum-projects/nubia-museum-aswan/, accessed 19 November 2013.

UNESCO (2013c) 'The Hangzhou declaration: placing culture at the heart of sustainable development policies, International congress culture: key to sustainable development', www.unesco.org/new/en/culture/themes/culture-and-development/hangzhou-congress/, accessed 26 May 2014.

UNESCO (2013d) 'Summary records, 19th Session of the General Assembly of States Parties to the Convention Concerning the Protection of the World Cultural and Natural Heritage', WHC-13/19.GA/INF.12, Paris: UNESCO.

UNESCO (2013e) 'Extensions of properties already inscribed on the World Heritage List: Mount Kenya National Park/Natural Forest', World Heritage Committee Decision: 37 COM 8B.9, http://whc.unesco.org/en/decisions/5125, accessed 15 June 2014.

UNESCO (2013f) 'Item 7B of the provisional agenda: state of conservation of World Heritage properties inscribed on the World Heritage List', Document: WHC-13/37. COM/7B, World Heritage Committee, Paris: UNESCO.

UNESCO (2013g) 'Integrated comprehensive strategy for category 2 institutes and centres under the auspices of UNESCO', 37C/Resolution 93 (November 2013), Paris: UNESCO.

UNESCO (2013h) 'Archaeological site of Panamá Viejo and historic district of Panamá (Panamá) (C 790bis)', Item 7B of the provisional agenda: State of conservation of World Heritage properties inscribed on the World Heritage List, World Heritage Committee Document WHC-13/37.COM/7B.Add, Paris: UNESCO.

UNESCO (2013i) 'Selous Game Reserve (United Republic of Tanzania) (N 199bis)', Item 7B of the provisional agenda: State of conservation of the properties inscribed on the World Heritage List, World Heritage Committee Document WHC-13/37. COM/7B, Paris: UNESCO.

UNESCO (2014a) 'Medium-term strategy 2014-2021', UNESCO General Conference Resolution: 37 C/Res.1, Paris: UNESCO.

UNESCO (2014b) *Report on the World Heritage Thematic Programmes*, World Heritage Committee Document WHC-14/38.COM/5E, Paris: UNESCO.

UNESCO (2014c) 'Acropolis, Athens', http://whc.unesco.org/en/list/404, accessed 21 December 2016.

UNESCO (2014d) 'Blaenavon industrial landscape', http://whc.unesco.org/en /list/984, accessed 14 February 2014.

UNESCO (2014e) 'Old Bridge area of the old City of Mostar', World Heritage List whc.unesco.org/en/list/946, accessed 1 February 2014.

UNESCO (2014f) 'Cultural landscape and archaeological remains of the Bamiyan Valley', World Heritage List, whc.unesco.org/en/list/208, accessed 1 February 2014.

UNESCO (2014g) 'Timbuktu', World Heritage List, whc.unesco.org/en/list/119/, accessed 22 March 2014.

UNESCO (2015a) 'Policy for the integration of a sustainable development perspective into the processes of the World Heritage Convention', Resolution 20 GA 13, General Assembly of the States Parties to the Convention, Paris: UNESCO.

UNESCO (2015b) *Operational Guidelines for the Implementation of the World Heritage Convention*, Paris: UNESCO.

UNESCO (2015c) 'Messel Pit Fossil Site', UNESCO World Heritage List, whc.unesco.org/en/list/720, accessed 15 November 2015.

UNESCO (2015d) 'State of conservation of World Heritage properties; emerging and recurring conservation issues', UNESCO World Heritage Committee Decisions WHC-15/39.COM/7, UNESCO World Heritage Centre, Paris.

UNESCO (2015e) 'Rules of procedure, UNESCO Intergovernmental Committee for the Protection of the World Cultural and Natural Heritage', WHC-2015/5, UNESCO World Heritage Centre, Paris.

UNESCO (2015f) 'Resolutions adopted by the General Assembly of States Parties to the World Heritage Convention at its 20th session', WHC-15/20.GA/15, Paris: UNESCO.

UNESCO (2015g) 'Item 9 of the provisional agenda: Global strategy for a representative, balanced and credible World Heritage List: Report on the Follow-up to Resolution 19 GA 9, Twentieth Session of the General Assembly of States Parties to the Convention Concerning the Protection of the World Cultural and Natural Heritage', WHC-15/20.GA/9, Paris: UNESCO.

UNESCO (2015h) 'Cape Floral region protected areas, South Africa', World Heritage Committee Decision 39 COM 8B.2, http://whc.unesco.org/en/decisions/6352, accessed 15 May 2016.

UNESCO (2015i) 'General decision on the World Heritage properties of the Syrian Arab Republic', World Heritage Committee Decision: 39 COM 7A.36, Paris: UNESCO.

UNESCO (2015j) 'Selous Game Reserve (United Republic of Tanzania) (N 199bis)', Item 7A of the provisional agenda: State of conservation of the properties inscribed on the List of World Heritage in Danger, World Heritage Committee Document WHC-15/39.COM/7A, Paris: UNESCO

UNESCO (2016a) 'The Ahwar of southern Iraq: Refuge of biodiversity and the relict landscape of the Mesopotamian cities', UNESCO World Heritage List, whc.unesco.org/en/list/1481, accessed 22 August 2016.

UNESCO (2016b) 'UNESCO global geoparks', Earth Sciences, www.unesco.org/new/en/natural-sciences/environment/earth-sciences/unesco-global-geoparks/, accessed 5 January 2016.

UNESCO (2016c) 'Committee takes decisions for the protection of cultural property in armed conflicts', www.unesco.org/new/en/culture/themes/single-view/news/committee_takes_decisions_for_the_protection_of_cultural_pro/, accessed 14 December 2016.

UNESCO (2016d) 'Item 7B of the provisional agenda: state of conservation of properties inscribed on the World Heritage List', WHC/16/40.COM/7B.Add, World Heritage Committee, Fortieth session, Istanbul, Turkey, 10–20 July 2016.

UNESCO (2016e) 'Category 2 centres under the auspices of UNESCO related to World Heritage', http://whc.unesco.org/en/category2centres/, accessed 26 December 2016.

UNESCO (2016f) 'Item 6 of the provisional agenda: follow-up to the World Heritage Capacity-Building strategy and Progress report on the World Heritage-related category 2 centres', WHC/16/40.COM/6, World Heritage Committee: Fortieth Session Istanbul, Turkey 10–20 July 2016.

UNESCO (2016g) *Cultural, Urban, Future: Global Report on Culture for Sustainable Urban Development*, Paris: UNESCO.

UNESCO (2016h) 'Private sector partners for World Heritage meet in Bonn during 39th Committee session', http://whc.unesco.org/en/news/1319/, accessed 11 December 2016.

UNESCO (2016i) 'Bam and its cultural landscape', World Heritage List, whc.unesco.org/en/list/1208/, accessed 1 May 2016.

UNESCO (2016j) 'Selous Game Reserve (United Republic of Tanzania) (N 199bis)', Item 7A of the provisional agenda: State of conservation of the properties inscribed on the List of World Heritage in Danger, World Heritage Committee Document WHC/16/40.COM/7A.Add, UNESCO Paris.

UNESCO (2016k) 'Seven marine sites sign historic agreement', World Heritage Centre, whc.unesco.org/en/news/1575/, accessed November 2016.

UNESCO (2016l) 'Istanbul declaration on the protection of World Heritage', 40th Session of the World Heritage Committee, Istanbul, 11 July 2016.

UNESCO (2017) 'Welcome to the UNESCO Sustainable Tourism Toolkit', http://whc. unesco.org/sustainabletourismtoolkit/welcome-unesco-world-heritage-sustainable-tourism-toolkit, accessed 1 August 2017.

UNESCO and UNEP (2003) 'Cultural diversity and biodiversity for sustainable development'. A jointly convened UNESCO and UNEP high-level roundtable held on 3 September 2002 in Johannesburg during the World Summit on Sustainable Development, Nairobi: UNEP.

UNESCO General Conference (2012) 'General Conference resolution 36 C/Res.37 for Major Programme IV. Culture Sector, Major Programme 2012–2013', 36 C/5, Paris: UNESCO.

UNESCO, ICCROM, ICOMOS and IUCN (2010) *Managing Disaster Risks for World Heritage Resource Manual*, Paris: UNESCO.

UNESCO, ICCROM, ICOMOS and IUCN (2012) *Managing Natural World Heritage, World Heritage Resource Manual*, Paris: UNESCO.

UNESCO, ICCROM, ICOMOS and IUCN (2013) *Managing Cultural World Heritage, World Heritage Resource Manual*, Paris: UNESCO.

UNFCCC (2015) 'Adoption of the Paris Agreement', United Nations Framework Convention on Climate Change, Bonn, Germany, https://unfccc.int/resource/docs/2015/cop21/eng/l09r01.pdf, accessed 4 November 2016.

UNISDR (2004) *Terminology: Basic Terms of Disaster Risk Reduction*, Geneva: UNISDR.

UNISDR (2014) 'What is disaster risk reduction?', www.unisdr.org/who-we-are/what-is-drr, accessed 20 July 2014.

UNISDR (2015) *PreventionWeb: 25 April 2015 Nepal Earthquake Disaster Risk Reduction Situation Report*, DRR sitrep 2015-001-May 4 2015, UNISDR, Geneva.

UNOCHA (2016) 'Syrian Arab Republic', www.unocha.org/syria, accessed June 2016.

UNWTO, UN World Tourism Organization (1999) 'Global code of ethics for tourism', adopted by resolution A/RES/406(XIII) at the thirteenth WTO General Assembly, Santiago, Chile, 27 September–1 October 1999.

UNWTO (2015) 'UNWTO tourism highlights', www.e-unwto.org/doi/pdf/10.18111/9789284416899, accessed 19 May 2016.

URBACT (2010) 'URBACT II: Analytical case study, Visitor Centre World Heritage Regensburg, Hero project, European Programme for Sustainable Urban Development', www.regensburg.de/sixcms/media.php/280/Regensburg_case_study.pdf, accessed 21 December 2016.

US Congress, (1964) The Wilderness Act, Public Law 88-577 (16 U.S. C. 1131-1136) 88th Congress, Second Session September 3, 1964, www.wilderness.net/NWPS/legisAct#2, accessed 24 April 2014.

van der Auwera, S. (2013) 'UNESCO and the protection of cultural property during armed conflict', *International Journal of Cultural Policy*, vol. 19, no. 1, pp.1–19.

Vatandoust, R. and Zargar, A. (2003) 'Iran', in S. Burke, D. Bumbaru and M. Petzet (eds) *ICOMOS World Report 2001–2002 on Monuments and Sites in Danger*, Paris: ICOMOS.

Vaz, E., Cabral, P., Caetano, M., Nijkamp, P. and Painho, M. (2012) 'Urban heritage endangerment at the interface of future cities and past heritage: a spatial vulnerability assessment', *Habitat International*, vol. 36, pp. 287–294.

Veillon, R. (2014) *State of Conservation of World Heritage Properties; A Statistical Analysis (1979–2013)*, Paris: UNESCO World Heritage Centre.

Waas, T., Hugé, J., Verbruggen, A. and Wright, T. (2011) 'Sustainable development: a bird's eye view', *Sustainability*, vol. 3, pp.1637–1661.

Walasek, H. (2016) 'Domains of restoration: actors and agendas in post-conflict Bosnia-Herzegovina', in H. Walasek (ed) *Bosnia and the Destruction of Cultural Heritage*, London: Routledge.

Walker, B., Holling, C.S., Carpenter, S.R. and Kinzig, A. (2004) 'Resilience, adaptability and transformability in social-ecological systems', *Ecology and Society*, vol. 9, no. 2, www.ecologyandsociety.org/vol9/iss2/art5/, accessed 20 October 2015.

Walters, C.J. (1986) *Adaptive Management of Renewable Resources*, New York: Macmillan.

Waterton, E. and Smith, L. (2010) 'The recognition and misrecognition of community heritage', *International Journal of Heritage Studies*, vol. 16, no. 1–2, pp. 4–15.

Watkins, G. and Cruz, F. (2007) *Galápagos at Risk: A Socioeconomic Analysis of the Situation in the Archipelago*, Puerto Ayora, Ecuador: Charles Darwin Foundation.

Watson, J.E.M., Dudley, N., Segan, D.B. and Hockings, M. (2014) 'The performance and potential of protected areas', *Nature*, vol. 515, pp. 67–73.

WCED (1987) *Report of the World Commission on Environment and Development: Our Common Future*, Oxford: Oxford University Press.

Wells, J. (2007) 'The plurality of truth in culture, context, and heritage: a (mostly) post-structuralist analysis of urban conservation charters', *City & Time*, vol. 3, no. 2, pp. 1–14.

Wendle, J. (2016) 'Syria's climate refugees', *Scientific American*, vol. 314, no. 3, pp. 42–47.

West, J.M. and Salm, R.V. (2003) 'Resistance and resilience to coral bleaching: implications for coral reef conservation and management', *Conservation Biology*, vol. 17, pp. 956–967.

West, P. and Brockington, D. (2006) 'An anthropological perspective on some unexpected consequences of protected areas', *Conservation Biology*, vol. 20, no. 3, pp. 609–616.

WHC, World Heritage Centre (2004) *Periodic Report and Regional Programme, Arab States 2000–2003*, World Heritage Reports 11, Paris: UNESCO.

WHC (2006) *The UNESCO World Heritage Centre's Natural Heritage Strategy*, Paris: UNESCO World Heritage Centre.

WHC (2013) 'Heritage and resilience: issues and opportunities for reducing disaster risks', http://whc.unesco.org/en/events/1048/, accessed 20 October 2015.

WHC (2015a) 'State of Conservation Information System SOC', http://whc.unesco.org/en/soc/, accessed 4 March 2016.

WHC (2015b) 'UNESCO and IUCN welcome new no-go pledge for World Heritage sites by Tullow Oil', http://whc.unesco.org/en/news/1379/, accessed 20 November 2015.

WHC and IUCN (2006) *Mission Report: Mosi-oa-Tunya, Victoria Falls (Zambia/ Zimbabwe) 20–25 November 2006,* Paris: World Heritage Centre.

WHC and IUCN (2007) *Galápagos Islands (Ecuador) Report of the Reactive Monitoring Mission, 8–13 April 2007*, Paris: World Heritage Centre.

WHC and IUCN (2012) *Mission Report: Mission Report: Great Barrier Reef, Australia.* WHC-12/36.COM. 7B.Add, Paris: World Heritage Centre.

Wild, R. and McLeod, C. (2008) *Sacred Natural Sites: Guidelines for Protected Areas Managers*, Gland, Switzerland: IUCN.

Wilkie, D.S. and Carpenter, J.F. (1999) 'Bushmeat hunting in the Congo Basin: an assessment of impacts and options for mitigation', *Biodiversity & Conservation*, vol. 8, no. 7, pp. 927–955.

Wilshusen, P.R., Brechin, S.R., Fortwangler, C.L. and West, P.C. (2002) 'Reinventing a square wheel: critique of a resurgent "protection paradigm" in international biodiversity conservation', *Society and Natural Resources*, vol. 15, pp 17–40.

Winter, T. (2008) 'Post-conflict heritage and tourism in Cambodia: the burden of Angkor', *International Journal of Heritage Studies*, vol. 14, no. 6, pp. 524–539.

Witcomb, A. (2012) 'Tensions between World heritage and local values; the case of Freemantle Prison (Australia)', in M. Albert, M. Richon, M. José Viñals and A. Witcomb (eds) *Community Development through World Heritage*, World Heritage Papers 31, Paris: UNESCO.

WMF, World Monuments Fund (2005) *WMF at 40: Changing the Face of Preservation*, New York: World Monuments Fund.

WMF (2015) *Fund Annual Report 2014*, New York: World Monuments Fund.

Worboys, G. (2008) 'Large scale connectivity conservation in mountains: a critical response to climate change', A paper presented to the international workshop on protected area management and biodiversity conservation, East Asia, Taipei, Taiwan, 2–3 September 2008.

Worboys, G., Francis, W.L. and Lockwood, M. (2010) *Connectivity Conservation Management: A Global Guide*, London: Routledge.

World Indigenous Network (2014) 'World Indigenous Network: Connecting Indigenous and local community land and sea managers', www.winlsm.net/, accessed 12 October 2014.

WWF, World Wildlife Fund (1961) 'We must save the world's wild life: an international declaration', 29 April, Morges, Switzerland.

WWF (2008) *A Roadmap for a Living Planet*, Gland, Switzerland: World Wide Fund for Nature.

WWF (2011a) *WWF: 50 Years of Conservation*, Gland, Switzerland: World Wide Fund for Nature.

WWF (2011b) *Annual Report 2011: World Wildlife Fund's 50th Anniversary Year*, Washington, DC: World Wide Fund for Nature.

WWF (2012) 'World Wildlife Fund', http://worldwildlife.org, accessed 19 August 2012.

Yashina, T. (2009) *Global Change in Mountain Sites (GLOCHAMOST): Coping Strategies for Mountain Biosphere Reserves, Assessment Report on the Katunskiy State Nature Biosphere Reserve*, Ust-Koska, Russia: Ministry of the Natural Resources and Ecology of the Russian Federation.

INDEX